The Hybrid Practition
Building, Teaching, Researching

The Hybrid Practitioner

Building, Teaching, Researching Architecture

Edited by
Caroline Voet,
Eireen Schreurs and
Helen Thomas

Leuven University Press

The publication of this work was supported by the KU Leuven Fund for Fair Open Access and KU Leuven, Faculty/Department of Architecture

Published in 2022 by Leuven University Press / Presses Universitaires de Louvain / Universitaire Pers Leuven. Minderbroedersstraat 4, B-3000 Leuven (Belgium).

ISBN 978 94 6270 332 2 (Paperback)
ISBN 978 94 6166 455 6 (ePDF)
ISBN 978 94 6166 474 7 (ePUB)
https://doi.org/10.11116/9789461664556
D/2022/1869/40
NUR: 648

Layout: Theo van Beurden
Cover design: Anton Lecock
Cover illustration: MDF and veneer model of a passage in the Museum Boijmans van Beuningen in Rotterdam, scale 1:5, by Shamila Gostelow and Silja Siikki. Photograph: Shamila Gostelow and Silja Siikki

Table of Contents

.

Introduction

Helen Thomas, Caroline Voet, Eireen Schreurs

Positioning Architects in Academia

"Are architects who write a dying race?"[1] asked Belgian architectural theorist and historian Hilde Heynen in 2017, reflecting on the position of the practising architect as a writing scholar in the academic field. In her article, Heynen compares Joan Ockman's *Architecture Culture 1943–1968: A Documentary Anthology* with Michael Hays's selection in *Architecture Theory since 1968*. She observes that Ockman's book includes seventy-four texts, forty-six of which were written by (practising) architects, while in Hays's collection, only fifteen of the forty-eight authors are architects.[2] The change in the 1970s that Heynen points out marked what has turned out to be a caesura in the involvement of practising architects in the construction of architectural history and theory. This coincided with the publication of Manfredo Tafuri's *Design and Utopia*, 1973, whose neo-Marxist argument took a critical stance to the utopian claims of modern architecture as a mechanism for societal reform.[3] Tafuri's position is indicative of the distancing of architectural history and theory from the sphere of production and the world of action as it became enclosed within an increasingly self-referential intellectual realm.

Almost half a century has passed since then, and during that time, there have been various countermovements to this isolating tendency. One of these emerges from transformations in academic funding structures during the 1990s, when design and architectural practice as manifest in academia became a necessary subject of discussion, as they were redefined for the purposes of research audits. This involved the reframing of the material, intellectual, and practical research carried out in a professional context by practising architects leading design studios as an academic activity. One outcome of this was the phenomenon of the design-led doctoral programme in schools of architecture, and in the process, pursuits such as drawing, user consultation, and model making, for example, took on new abstract dimensions. Methodological frameworks for the academisation of design as a process coalesced under the name of artistic research,[4] in which architectural practice became a theorised creative process that sought to define itself in relation to academic research.[5]

In October 2020, KU Leuven hosted a (remote) symposium, The Practice of Architectural Research: Perspectives on Design and Its Relation to History and Theory, to examine the implications of this now long-standing relationship between academia and design practice. The papers and debates of the symposium were developed through a rigorous, selective editorial process informed by consultation, conversation, disagreement, revision, and deep reflection on the reciprocal relationships between the creative production of design and the reflective outcomes of history and theory. While the discussions of the editorial team focused on the myriad ways in which academia and practice could dovetail, the team also recognised a mostly implicit, but sometimes explicit, tendency in the essays to envision the space between practice and academia. As reflections, they return to the core of architecture through a reconstitution of the relationship between architectural practice, history, and theory, moving away from design-driven research. A substantial proportion of the contributions start from the idea that the connection between the architect and the built form is not, as Tafuri argued, purely utopian, subjective, or self-referential and therefore unscholarly, partial, and irrelevant. By foregrounding this idea, the editors counter Tafuri in acknowledging the architect's relationship with the architectural object – the building, but also drawings and other artefacts from the process of its making.

It was during this editorial process that the figure of the hybrid practitioner became clear. Within the open dialogue fostered by the different backgrounds of the editors – practising architect, academic, architectural historian, writer, publisher, editor – the selected authors were asked to address this hybrid condition, each from their own perspective. By assembling these interpretations of the hybrid viewpoint, this volume embraces alternative processes that sometimes eschew logical, rational and linear progression, and existing structures of academic knowledge to open up possibilities for fruitful new academic knowledge. As a reflection on the symposium, editor Eireen Schreurs, together with Eva Storgard and Marjan Michels, collected echoes of its assertions and debates into a critical dialogue. Their essay "Roles and Challenges of the Hybrid Practitioner" elaborates the editors' definition by analysing the different roles and positions presented and discussed at the event.

The Hybrid Practitioner

A question arises in this context about what it is that the professional, practising "architect who writes" (in the sense of Heynen's question) brings to the academic discipline of architectural studies. The reality of contemporary architectural practice reveals that "writing" for architects is a euphemism for a much wider set of activities – teaching, consultation, drawing, and social media, for example – with a myriad of creative, theoretical, and reflective uses. This is shown in the biographies of the twenty-four contributors to this volume: all but one has architectural training, and of these, eighteen have spent at least two years in professional practice, although just eight run a traditional architectural office. Currently, a third of the authors work exclusively in academia, another third combine running an architectural practice with teaching, and the remainder combine academia with other occupations, which include publishing, editing, curating, and consultation.

Architects producing buildings, engaged in professional practice that is, inhabit a reality that is unlike that of academia; this difference provides the ground for alternative approaches, interpretations, and frameworks of knowledge to come into play. Shelley McNamara's response to the opening paper of the Leuven symposium reveals the tension this creates and the creative potential that it embodies:

> what do you mean by reality? For you – is it clarity? Or is it the physical ... what is it?[6]

For architects like McNamara and others listening in and participating in the symposium who were and are embedded in the complexities of professional practice, which requires the assumption of fiscal and legislative responsibilities – the taking of risks and making of liabilities that they might have to pay for, literally, with money, reputation, or dignity – reality is exacting. Its place is out there in the open; architects perform in an unpredictable arena swirling with commercial, social, and ethical concerns. Their work is a constant negotiation with many different requirements and the characters that represent them – beyond the clients who commission projects, there are planners and safety officers, contractors, suppliers, and project managers, employees, fellow design team members. A crowd of collaborating adversaries is involved. All this before the product of this myriad communicating and compromising – the building, that is – can become itself, a subject for architectural critics, historians, bloggers, and other commentators. The conceptual journey that the building as physical and cultural object makes, helped along by these interpreters into becoming part of the constellation of exemplary artefacts that constitutes the architectural canon, is intense and precarious.

The chances of a successful transition from a building to a work of architecture depends upon a process requiring skills beyond the ability to juggle the complex demands of architectural production, many of which are invisible. Entry into the cultural and academic arena, the canon, involves engagement with one or more intellectual milieux. Unlike that of the workforce that brings the building into being, this cerebral labour is carried out by a protagonist – a named architect or perhaps a partnership – to whom the architectural object is attributed. At this point, the work comes closer to resembling that carried out in academia, where the field of action, the reality, is more clearly defined and predictable. Reconciling the experience of producing a building with that of defining it as a cultural object requires the suppression of many aspects of architectural production for various reasons – professional integrity on the part of the architect, for example, or the banality of technical or legislative complexity explained in layman's terms. The narrative produced is partial, and it could be argued that (hybrid) practitioners write best when they are not the apologists of their own work; their knowledge, perspective, and intuition applied to something external but in relation to their work, or even outside it, is re-embodied in their practice. Following the same reasoning, the work of the academic and the scholar is valuable to the practitioner because theoretical thinking reveals alternative explanations and interpretations, and through these, insight, for example, into the structures of power and economy in which the professional architect operates. The academic functions outside the professional arena. One of the roles of academic work in the school of architecture is to provide the perspective that is essential for self-conscious practice, in that it provides the means to step back and see the wider picture within which to define and choose a place and develop a modus operandi that in itself contributes to transformative intellectual debates.

A number of contributors to this volume are looking for a relationship to history, not as a timeline, but as a layered landscape that can be excavated to find things hidden beneath the assumptions of conventions. Their distinguishing feature is that they work from intuition and a quest for inspiration, and they do not always and exclusively search for an underlying logic. This involves looking at drawings, reading, being in the archives and, as Rebecca Solnit points out,

> finding things that are written out of history or never written into it, odd trends and faded heroes, movements that had lost their sheen, detours from the official road of art history, a windowless room of orphans and exiles [...] The process can be incandescent with excitement, whether from finding some unexpected scrap of information or from recognizing patterns that begin to arise as the fragments begin to assemble.[7]

Architects and Historians

This version of a hybrid practitioner – one who understands what it means to oversee the design and construction of buildings in their name, often running the business that sustains this activity, while at the same time contributing to the discourse of architectural culture through intellectual work – has a different approach from those who produce solely within an academic environment. Authenticity of knowledge and subsequent authority of interpretation are qualities that perpetuate in discussions about the production and, increasingly, the role of the architectural canon. A principal location of this discourse is the school of architecture, with its particular environment, where the academic meets the practical in an unusual juxtaposition. The entanglement of practice and academia enriches the toolbox of research methods and the usefulness of the object as a starting point, and creative thinking adds to the existing discourse – processes of storytelling, for example, emerge from the designer's imagination. The vocational nature of the curriculum for architects in training also complicates the role of history and theory as elements within it. The question of how the abstract intellectual methodologies and forms of knowledge that these subjects embody can contribute to the practical purposes of design education is constantly recurring.

At the Leuven symposium, these concerns about the role of history, theory, and research as useful to practising architects in a reciprocal relationship remained pertinent but set within a very different context. The now common acknowledgement that history is an ideological construct originating from many directions, which has been propelled through processes of postmodern "unpacking," feminism, and decolonisation, for example, and the recognition that works of architecture do not simply emerge from the zeitgeist-reading mind of the hero architect, meant that the participants of the symposium no longer inhabited one of two camps. Each embodied a hybrid practice that combined one or more professional, academic, or creative roles or activities.

The Question of Operative Criticism

From the moment that architecture was named as an artistic practice, its defining canon has had an associated rhetoric that has embraced a multitude of voices: from the classical treatises of Vitruvius and Alberti, to the manifestos of Filippo Marinetti and Le Corbusier, the theoretical writing of Sigfried Giedion, Diane Ghirardo, and Beatriz Colomina, and the historical readings of Kenneth Frampton, Harry Mallgrave, and Yasmeen Lari. Many of these bridged the gap between architectural production and theoretical construction by developing a tradition of architectural thinking that proposed an exemplary building practice that was represented, interpreted, and promoted through drawing and writing. In this sense, the production of architecture itself provided the primary source material – on one hand the records pertaining to its production such as drawings and other documents as briefs, notes, letters and diaries, or testimonies retrieved through oral history, and on the other hand the material, formal, and morphological reality of the finished building on its site. This ontological study, for which the built object was the subject, superimposed architectural practice and its creative processes on its motivations, intentions, and interpretations.

This was problematic for Tafuri, who characterised those who both theorise and practice professionally as split personality.[8] He was critical of the mix of "mystifications and brilliant eversions, historical and ahistorical attitudes, bitter intellectualisations and mild mythologies" that this produced.[9] He proposed for the architectural historian and theorist the role of "critic," whose foremost task was to

> diagnose exactly, and to avoid moralizing in order to see. The critic is courageous and exempts an honest scrutiny, questioning the legitimacy of a modern movement as a monolithic corpus of ideas, poetics, and linguistic traditions.[10]

From this perspective, the theoretical positioning and historical teleology of a designer is merely subjective, because the architect's motives cloud judgement and disable the ability to diagnose precisely and scrutinise honestly. [11] Their ensuing position cannot be critical, which renders it useless within the scholarly field. Tafuri developed an argument against what he called the "operative criticism" of the designer, that is

> an analysis of architecture (or of the arts in general) that, instead of an abstract survey, has as its objective the planning of a precise poetical tendency, anticipated in its structures and derived from historical analyses programmatically distorted and finalised.[12]

Tafuri's critique was embedded in a time and place of rejection of the commercial environment in which professional architects have to operate. This provoked a retreat into an imaginary practice, or paper architecture, that critiqued through design – through drawing, narrative, theory – the products and practices generated by the market. The intellectual culture of architecture, seeking to define itself, began to engage in interdisciplinary exchanges – with social studies, geography, and philosophy, for example. Architects who call their work on paper – drawing, model making, teaching, or even writing – *practice* became more concerned with the deployment and elaboration of metaphorical and metonymic constructions than with the analysis of the ontological underpinnings of architectural practice. Architectural commentators such as Paulo Portoghesi[13] and Bernard Tschumi lamented the loss of this tradition that deals with architectural form and intentions. According to Tschumi in 1993,

> Current writing in architectural theory, participating in an exchange of ideas between disciplines – the arts, philosophy, literary criticism – differs significantly from the texts produced up to 1968. Most post-war written work yearned towards responsible ways and means to correct the ills of society.[14]

The utopian approach of modern architecture, so criticised by Tafuri, blends ethics with aesthetics and the belief that architectural form can cure. This volume responds to this call to interweave the practical and the academic by incorporating architectural history and theory into the process of design and by investigating the mediating role that the hybrid practitioner can play in the making of architectural culture. This perspective includes rather than discredits the intentions of the architect in the discussion, therefore unlocking alternative paths for operative critique. One such position is the acknowledgement that built form is the materialisation of the rules and structures that are at the core of the discipline. Now that the self-evident morality of modernism's grand narrative has been replaced through multiple engagements and alternative oeuvres, the intentions and formal translations of their protagonists can be compared. Within this approach, architecture is understood as a fundamentally transformative act that incorporates its process of invention and production and its various experiences. The precise description and notation of this inclusive process of design demystifies design knowledge and creates alternative historiographies. In explicitly addressing the relation between architectural intent, form, and space, architects are given tools to reflect upon their work in practice, but also to inspire and take action.

The Hybrid Practitioner: Five Frameworks

Not all the authors contributing to this book are employed in architectural practice, but instead represent a variety of hybrid forms of architectural production. This reflects an intent to identify and examine the kinds of writing and other forms of reflective work that architects do to step back from the reality of practice and the hybrid characters that they become in order to do this. The reciprocal nature of the relationship between research and production, between theoretical and historical investigation and architectural practice, between teaching and the development of intellectual structures lies at the heart of each of the five sections that organise the book. Seeking the characteristics of the hybrid practitioner in the identities of the participants of the symposium, the following qualities emerge: a research relationship to the object that is operative, in the sense that the architect is using history and theory, reference and source, to reflect on and develop their own creative practice. This may directly affect creative work or function as a parallel narrative, but either way, it is embraced as a subjective teleology. The architect with a background in practice has an empirical understanding of how things are made. This means that for them, architectural objects are more readily perceived in their spatial and geographical context than their historical and temporal one. This empirical knowledge extends to the collaborative nature of creative work and the constellation of different perspectives and expertise that contribute to the architectural object. The hybrid practitioner takes on roles other than professional practice in order to write – and these enhance and expand existing and new qualities and proficiencies. To cultivate them, the architectural prac-titioner draws from and interprets the skills of the academic, which include an awareness of a wider, deeper context and debate, a methodological approach to evidence and interpretation, the importance of the distant perspective, and an ambition to be scholarly.

Each of the five parts proposes an arena for the hybrid practitioner.

The first, titled "The Practice Perspective and Its Framework," provides an agenda for exchange and reflection between architectural theory, writing, design, and making. Where the relation between design practice and research has been extensively examined, what is on the table here is the relation between architectural practice and the formation of theory or history.

Part 2, "Reciprocal Negotiations: Teaching Architecture," is concerned with the negotiations that take place in the school of architecture. The essays explore the potential of reciprocal communication, or negotiation between people, but also between approaches, methodologies, and ways of thinking, to suggest new subjects of investigation. In addition, new tools with which to examine and instrumentalise the process and outcomes of research are created in this col-laborative work.

Part 3, "Different Worlds and Other Places," questions the paradigm of a sin-gle reality. Postcolonial, new materialist, literary, and feminist theories provide a podium for other agents and other viewpoints, while testing and developing other methods such as storytelling and "utopian drawings." Translated into architecture terms, these theories allow for a revisiting of long finished projects, and they are able to reconstruct established views on them.

The four essays in Part 4, "Stepping Back from the Object," engage with another strategy for stepping outside the creative practice of designing and away from the designed object itself. The authors make a space in which they can define and develop their own historical, creative, and theoretical approaches through mechanisms of reflection, assimilation, and dissemination.

Part 5, "The Values of the Object," takes architectural objects as the subject of research – not only their physical presence but also the processes of invention and construction. The return to the architectural object as a research field has become relevant with the acknowledgement of alternative world views and the redefinition since the 1980s of seemingly immutable terms (as diverse as gender, form, and style, for example). As a result, research questions and subjects can no longer automatically rely on a previously established research canon. Only by revisiting the reality of the object rather than focusing on its iconic value can one see them as sites where architectural practices ultimately influence the future of architectural culture.

Notes

1. Hilde Heynen, "Zijn schrijvende architecten een uitstervend ras?," *A+267, Dis-cours* (August–September 2017): 42–43.
2. Joan Ockman, ed., *Architecture Culture 1943–1968. A Documentary Anthology* (New York: Columbia Books of Architecture and Rizzoli, 1993); and Michael Hays, *Architecture Theory since 1968* (Cambridge, MA: MIT Press, 1998).
3. Manfredo Tafuri, *Progetto Et Utopia: Architettura E Sviluppo Capitalistico* (Bari: Laterza, 1973). Manfredo Tafuri, *Architecture and Utopia: Design and Capitalist Development* (Cambridge, MA: MIT Press, 1973).
4. See, for example, Henk Borgdorff, "The Production of Knowledge in Artistic Research," in *The Routledge Companion to Research in the Arts*, ed. M. Biggs and H. Karlsson (London: Routledge, 2011), 44–63. R. Hughes, "Pressures of the Unspeakable: Communicating Practice as Research," in *Communicating (by) Design*, ed. J. Verbeke and A. Jakimowicz (Gothenburg and Brussels: Chalmers University of Technology and Sint-Lucas School of Architecture, 2009), 247–259.
5. The concept of *Wissenschaftliche Forschung* in German-speaking countries does not directly translate into English as scientific research, but as academic research. For example, *Geisteswissenschaften* translates as the humanities, which includes history, archaeology, philosophy, literature, and languages.
6. Shelley McNamara asked this question at the symposium The Practice of Architectural Research, YouTube video, 8 October 2020, https://www.youtube.com/watch?v=odD6w-294TEE&t=3392s (1:05:40).
7. Rebecca Solnit, *Recollections of My Nonexistence* (London: Granta, 2020), 120.
8. Manfredo Tafuri, "Introduction," *Theories and History of Architecture* (London: Granada, 1980).
9. Manfredo Tafuri, "Introduction"
10. Manfredo Tafuri, "Introduction"
11. See Anthony Vidler, "Theories in and of History," https://www.e-flux.com/architecture/history-theory/225183/theories-in-and-of-history/ (accessed 18 January 2021) for the context of Manfredo Tafuri's definition and critique of operative criticism.
12. Manfredo Tafuri, *Theories and History of Architecture* (London: Granada, 1980), 141.
13. Paulo Portoghesi, "Introduction," *Postmodern. The Architecture of the Post-Industrial Society* (New York: Rizzoli, 1983).
14. Bernard Tschumi, "Introduction," in *Architecture Culture 1943–1968. A Documentary Anthology*, ed.O. Joan (New York: Columbia Books of Architecture and Rizzoli, 1993), 11.

Bibliography

Borgdorff, Henk. "The Production of Knowledge in Artistic Research." In *The Routledge Companion to Research in the Arts*, edited by M. Biggs and H. Karlsson, 44–63. London: Routledge, 2011.

Hays, Michael. *Architecture Theory since 1968*. Cambridge, MA: MIT Press, 1998.

Heynen, Hilde. "Zijn schrijvende architecten een uitstervend ras?" *A+267, Dis-cours* (August–September 2017): 42–43.

Hughes, Rolf. "Pressures of the Unspeakable: Communicating Practice as Research." In *Communicating (by) Design*, edited by Johan Verbeke and Adam Jakimowicz, 247–259. Gothenburg and Brussels: Chalmers University of Technology and Sint-Lucas School of Architecture, 2009.

Ockman, Joan. ed. *Architecture Culture 1943–1968. A Documentary Anthology.* New York: Columbia Books of Architecture and Rizzoli, 1993.

Portoghesi, Paulo. *Postmodern. The Architecture of the Post-Industrial Society.* New York: Rizzoli, 1983.

Solnit, Rebecca. *Recollections of My Nonexistence.* London: Granta, 2020.

Symposium The Practice of Architectural Research. 8 October 2020. https://www.youtube.com/watch?v=0dD6w294TEE&t=3392s.

Tafuri, Manfredo. *Progetto Et Utopia: Architettura E Sviluppo Capitalistico.* Bari: Laterza, 1973.

———. *Architecture and Utopia: Design and Capitalist Development.* Cambridge, MA: MIT Press, 1973.

———. *Theories and History of Architecture.* London: Granada, 1980.

Tschumi, Bernard. "Introduction." In *Architecture Culture 1943–1968. A Documentary Anthology,* edited by Joan Oackman, 11. New York: Columbia Books of Architecture and Rizzoli, 1993.

Vidler, Anthony. "Theories in and of History." November 2018. https://www.e-flux.com/architecture/history-theory/225183/theories-in-and-of-history/.

Roles and Challenges of the Hybrid Practitioner

Eireen Schreurs, Eva Storgaard, Marjan Michels

The chapters in this book developed out of an online symposium called The Practice of Architectural Research (8–10 October 2020), which examined a research field that operates between design practice and the formation of theory and history. As a consequence, it also explored – though largely implicitly – the character and legitimacy of the linking figure: the hybrid practitioner, who combines one or more academic or creative roles and activities. The special condition of hybridity as it came to the fore in the symposium dialogues is addressed in this text. While the many abstract submissions demonstrated a general interest in the theme, the symposium itself revealed a diversity in types of researchers. Even though most of the participants shared an education in an architecture school, individual career paths had subsequently diverged significantly. These range from academics with full time university careers, and architects writing and teaching while running an architectural office, to the majority operating somewhere in between. Together their variegated papers and presentations constituted a rich and divergent range of stances within, and reflections on, the field of "the hybrid practice."

The profile of this writing architect is compound and individual and far from fully established, either among academics or between writing and practising architects themselves.[1] If we look for the communalities among the symposium participants, we can confirm the definition of the "species" of the hybrid practitioner, as formulated in the introduction to the volume. First, there is a research relationship to the object that is operative, in the sense that the architect is using history and theory to reflect on and develop their own creative practice. This may directly influence their own work or function as a parallel narrative, but either way, it is embraced as a subjective teleology. Second, the hybrid practitioner has an empirical understanding of how things are made, which means that architectural objects are more readily perceived in their spatial and geographical context than their historical and temporal one, which is augmented by the preponderance of visual intelligence. Last, the hybrid practitioner takes on roles other than those in professional practice in order to write and communicate culturally – as teachers, lecturers, writers, publishers, and curators. To do this, the architectural practitioner draws from and interprets the skills of the academic in their awareness of a wider, deeper context and debate, a methodological approach to evidence and interpretation, the importance of the distant perspective, and an ambition to be scholarly.

What follows are three synthetic conversations, constructed out of fragments taken from the presentations and discussions at the symposium.[2] Revolving around the characteristics of the hybrid practitioner described above, the conversations focus on the different roles that emerge from their strategic positioning between practice and academia. They confront each of these hybrid practitioners with a number of critical questions and responsibilities that surfaced in the closing debate with Rolf Hughes and Hilde Heynen, which we have used here to set a preliminary agenda for the hybrid practitioner.

1. The Operative

The hybrid practitioner's attitude is operative: it is geared towards making history and theory productive by transferring knowledge from the confinement of the academic library to the reality of the office. Academic expertise can inform the actual production of architecture: by providing continuity and background to a personal oeuvre, while also allowing for the testing of theories and (re)introduction of design knowledge so that, ideally, academic knowledge develops and innovates practice. Having established that the work of the hybrid professional extends beyond the office, the knowledge thus generated can then enter the debate in lectures and discussions, it can serve as inspiration for exhibitions, and it can act as critical touchstone in themed journals and magazines.

However, a striking aspect of the symposium was the way participants ascribed the field of operation for their personal knowledge most commonly not in practice but in, one could say, the intermediate step of teaching – also those researchers with active practices. Several of the presentations recognised the relevance of the studio over the office, as a place where research results are shared: Wouter van Acker analysed John Hejduk's nine-square grid exercise as a way to develop and propagate design thinking. In his study on Álvaro Siza, Paulo Providência discussed the value of Siza's method of reiteration or tracing, acknowledging its value as a teaching tool. Knowledge transfer in the studio can surpass didactic relevance and can even become political, as Fatma Tanis demonstrates in her study of Turkish architect Sedad Hakki Eldem's teaching programme, which focused on the tacit knowledge embedded in Turkish vernacular architecture that was at risk of being lost.

The last example reveals that the work field of the hybrid practitioner also embodies the tension between the supposed scientific neutrality of academia and the various conflicts of interest that challenge practice. In one of the symposium discussions around the creation of knowledge, Wilfried Wang critically remarked: "Research is a process of abstraction, categorisation, and of ordering, asking of researchers – also the historians – a position: is all knowledge equally valuable?" Wang recognised a tendency in academia towards relativisation and a dissolving of categories, which raises the question of the position of the researcher and the use of research: What is being distilled and for what purpose? The reverse question is also relevant: Can the "subjective teleology" of the hybrid practitioner operate within the academic standards of the scholar? Several participants showed their concern: practitioner Simon Henley described an architectural culture that is at risk of becoming autonomous and invisible without common ground, while in his keynote lecture, Wang defined the responsibility of academia to help find a shared narrative for practice by defining good design. The criteria for this are much needed, Wang stressed in a point reiterated by Tony Fretton, in order to convince, among others, politicians, because practice today is under much political and economic pressure.

Hybrid practitioners certainly occupy a strategic position and embody an interest and concern for the future of practice, and their knowledge gained from academic research might have the authority to extend beyond the scale of the studio or their own design work. In the closing discussion of the symposium, after having counted the limited number of practising architects in the symposium proceedings, Hilde Heynen posed the critical question: "Would the next anthology on architectural theory include writing architects?" The answer would have to be a question to the hybrid practitioner: Why, or why not? As Caroline Voet formulated in the opening statement of the symposium: "Can 'design knowledge' find a more secure position within the academic field as an expertise to develop (critical) history and theory?" Of the participants, Wang was the only one who explicitly formulated this ambition.

2. Empirical Understanding

Knowledge also flows in the opposite direction: expertise and insights acquired in building practice can enter academia. The hybrid practitioner's embodied understanding of the practice of design supports the study of buildings as objects and places as opposed to the lens of the historian that centres the temporal. One of Caroline Voet's opening questions for the symposium was whether the classical canon, the authoritative voice of the architect, and the production of grand narratives can still offer relevant insights. This can be answered affirmatively, but the introduction of new lenses creates different depths of field. Jana Culek disclosed the utopian world of Ludwig Hilbersheimer not from the classical urban point of view, but from a comparison with literary utopias, using speculative drawing techniques. Cathelijne

Nuijsink bypassed Rem Koolhaas's built and written oeuvre to study a housing competition of which he was the single jury member. There is also a shift towards other projects, as demonstrated by Sepideh Karami's material and political dissection of a British colonial institute somewhere in Iran, or to objects such as the mysterious iron column resisting interpretation in Helen Thomas's keynote lecture.

Another discerning feature of hybrid practitioners, that of their visual intelligence, was omnipresent at the symposium. A number of participants used drawing as a tool, for the obvious reason that it is the central mode of communication in architectural practice. It contains a specific form of knowledge, as an irreplaceable primary source for the study of design, and it makes research accessible for exploration in the design studio: Rosamund Diamond detected activities and modes of inhabitation with her students, Tom Mayes recorded experiences, and Thomas Coward registered the inhabitation of space. During the discussions, it became apparent that while both the "reading" and production of drawings is second nature for those with a past in practice, it is not so for theorists and art historians, who often lack the skills to recognise and interpret drawings as tacit demonstrations of design knowledge. Here lies an opportunity for further exploration, to counterbalance the prevailing historical reading of plans, to advance alternative approaches, and to develop disciplinary knowledge.

Other methods available to unlock knowledge from the field of practice came to the fore in the discussion led by David Vanderburgh. Speech, the act of speaking, emerged as an underestimated tool in design communication, as it is a more direct alternative to writing, it is easier to share, and it can transmit both information and embodied expressions. Speech is directed to laypeople, to clients; it adapts itself to its political and social context and therefore its choices of vocabulary are influential and telling. Van Acker agreed that the academic focus on writing as the prevailing means of communication should be challenged, but remarked that other ways of communicating, such as poetry, fieldwork, writing as a visual act, and drawing, are less accessible. Via a different route, Pauline Lefebvre reached a similar conclusion in her research on a New York practice, which she observed and analysed through their development of a written position statement. The office discovered that words were more simply shared and also accessible for people, such as clients, who are not accustomed to reading plans. Lefebvre also identified specific vocabularies for different audiences.

In the concluding session, Hilde Heynen expressed her slight disappointment stemming from a lack of criticality that she perceived in the symposium. In many papers she detected a strong inward focus:

> It was about drawing, sketching, tracing, arranging, configurating, materializing, constructing – the poetical, the making, but for me that also meant

that the social and the political were slightly pushed to the background. Why all this introspection, what can the knowledge from inside offer the academic field beyond its own discipline? [...] One could possibly think of aiming for doing both: a critical analysis of the forms and the tools, on how we do architecture and at the same time really tease out the social content, the political meaning.

Heynen ended with a plea for academic interdisciplinarity so that architectural knowledge can become productive and relevant for other fields, in order to concern itself more explicitly with social and political issues.

3. The Ambition to Be Scholarly

In her keynote lecture, Thomas posed the question how hybrid practitioners with ambitions to be scholarly could position themselves in the reality of academia. This realm can seem like an internalised world or a self-sustaining reality, with its own separate rules, expectations, and hierarchies. The symposium contained several lively debates on the expanse of reality and how it relates to the standards of academic research. Lara Schrijver stated that academic reality does not pertain to a single centre, but rather engages and commits itself to an agreed framework of knowledge, which appeared to be a position shared by many of the participants. Patrick Lynch referred to the Aristotelian notion of friendship, reiterated by Rolf Hughes in the closing discussion: in friendship, a conversation establishes a mode of intersubjectivity while at the same time it opens up the discussion to enclose the social and political. Perhaps, Lynch proposed, this works in the production of architecture too, where shared concerns have shaped the city.

Hybrid practitioners enrich and sometimes even challenge academic epistemology, thanks to their accurate instinct for contemporaneity and their independent and entrepreneurial attitude. Much harder to resist is the dominant communication tool in academia, which remains writing. Its conventions, in the words of Hughes, "are geared towards serving an explanatory function with its codes of precision and justification and legitimacy." But, Hughes added, there are other forms of writing that explore artistic and tacit forms of knowledge, those that offer "immersive experiences, with degrees of opacity, density or complexity." Both types of writing require specific training, and for those initiated, the academic discourses open up, while for others, they remain closed. According to Birgitte Hansen, practitioners write and speak all the time, but she asked whether their kind of writing, their kind of language, counted in the academic arena. Additionally, she claimed that even some highly positioned practitioners in academia shy away from writing because they doubt their academic writing skills.[3]

Discursive modes of research need new platforms where exchange and discussion can take place unconditionally. Carlo Menon brings the little magazines to the table as the place for such interchange. He argues that these magazines embrace and gather together various practices – designing, teaching, writing, protesting, collecting, publishing – to produce hybrid kinds of architectural knowledge and, in doing so, offer an alternative platform for exchanging ideas in architecture. Menon continued: "They contribute to re-defining the practice of criticism in a non-prescriptive way: an intellectual position which can be considered as healthy in times when academic standards threaten to overrun and subsume other forms of practice, especially in the design studios." Other media, such as Instagram, also create new platforms. They have generated what Joseph Bedford describes as a "hyperawareness" in the discipline, and he pointed out the missed opportunity inherent in the broad tacit base that these media command but with little ambition to make this knowledge explicit.

4. To Conclude

When Heynen raised the question whether architects who write are a dying race, she also questioned whether it is possible to embrace and fulfil the multiple roles of this hybrid figure who simultaneously practises architecture, carries out research, and educates the next generation. Hybrid practices shift back and forth between worlds: between the problem-solving mode enforced by the conditions of practice and the questioning mode necessary for good academic research. Points of discussion in the symposium were the means of accomplishing this state, including the compartmentalisation of different interests, and whether it is indeed beneficial or necessary. In this volume, Christoph Grafe proposes that rather than problematising the division between practice and academia, it can be used productively as a place to monitor the discipline and to explore new modi operandi.[4]

There are voices within academia maintaining that the position of the writer is that of the historian and the theoretician, echoing the advocacy of Manfredo Tafuri of keeping an academic, critical distance. Others, like Heynen, prioritise a more active political and social role, stating that these aspects pose the essential "why" question for architecture: Why do we build? Architects have a civil role in decision-making about public space. Admitting to her modernist stance, Heynen defines one of the researcher's goals to acquire the knowledge that can attribute to a better future. There are yet other academics, such as Hughes, who regard the writing architect as implicitly critical, socially and politically engaged, prioritising the study of the tools, the materials, the poesis – the act of making: several of them were represented at The Practice of Architectural Research symposium. For them, the social and political is not central, but also not absent.

The symposium did not explicitly problematise the idea of the hybrid practitioner, which means not all its challenges have been addressed here. The discussions did reveal that the practice of architectural research is multifaceted and discursive. Even if they are often not aware of it, hybrid practitioners bring perspectives to the table that can refresh academic debate and challenge existing norms; they have knowledge and skills that deserve recognition. But with recognition comes responsibility. We can start from here, Voet concluded. "If we let go of the objective idea of overlooking everything, like drawing without preconceptions, and start not from one direction, but from the mess," then we can begin to discern the many identities of hybrid practitioners and their roles in and outside of academia.

Notes

1. An international symposium When Architects and Designers Write, Draw, Build?, held at the Aarhus School of Architecture in Denmark, May 2011, explored similar themes as The Practice of Architectural Research, but then focused on the education of the PhD students. Jørgen Dehs, Martin Weihe Esbensen, and Claus Peder Pedersen, *When Architects and Designers Write, Draw, Build? Essays on Architecture and Design Research* (Aarhus: Arkitektskolens Forlag, 2013)
2. All discussions of the symposium have been transcribed and serve as underpinnings for the article.
3. Hansen raised her concern in an email to the editorial team after the symposium.
4. Chistoph Grafe in this volume, 31.

Bibliography

Dehs, Jørgen, Martin Weihe Esbensen, and Claus Peder Pedersen. *When Architects and Designers Write, Draw, Build? Essays on Architecture and Design Research.* Aarhus: Arkitektskolens Forlag, 2013.
Grafe, Chistoph. "Hybrid Practices: A Few Thoughts on Organic Intellectuals in Architecture." In *The Hybrid Practitioner: Building, Teaching, Researching Architecture,* edited by Caroline Voet, Eireen Schreurs, and Helen Thomas, 29-36. Leuven: Leuven University Press, 2022.

PART 1

The Practice Perspective and Its Framework

Operating beyond a binary opposition to text-based history, the contributions of Part 1 offer six complementary perspectives on processes within architectural practice and their layered relation to architectural knowledge. Observing, designing, and writing are intertwined in different ways when "in the making," and history and theory are often "operative." In this sense, the processes of decision-making and reflective methods within and through architectural practice can be ahistorical and intentional. By hybridising the boundaries between theory and practice, the authors succeed in entangling genesis, transformation, and interaction, introducing novel research approaches to incorporate artistic emancipation in the creation of knowledge.

Christoph Grafe aims to find openings in the auto-construction of the profession, challenging the academic preconceptions of the discipline. He brings to the fore two monumental personalities in Flanders – André Loeckx and Christian Kieckens – to illustrate a *Möglichkeitsraum* for what it might mean to be an architect. The breadth of expertise, but also the refusal to become an expert with a narrow pitch, of these hybrid practices requires a certain accepting attitude, intellectual flexibility, and, as Grafe ruminates, a humble stubbornness. As such, he reveals the tension between the reality of architecture as service provision and instrument for monetary value creation and the architects' cultural aspirations, as well as the ambivalent attitudes between practising professionals and architects whose activities are confined to teaching.

The following three contributions examine the contemporary practice and its processes of decision-making by offering either a conceptual, pragmatist, or methodological perspective. Irina Davidovici starts from the conceptual perspective: artefacts are determined by an intentional contrast between orderly forms and their adjustment based on personal, opaque value systems. The rational basis for form has been challenged by the necessity for adjustment, most clearly so in the notion of *disegno*, or the transition from idea to drawing. As statements of artistic emancipation, these intuitive gestures underscore the same belief in the fundamental autonomy of the architectural work. As such, Davidovici argues for their equivalence as emancipatory practices, which highlight a common framework of authorial control. Pauline Lefebvre follows architecture in the making, offering a pragmatist view on otherwise established discourses. Through fieldwork, she analyses how architects at work in their office exchange and discuss their projects and motivations, aiming to "eclipse their discourse." Lefebvre shows that the architects are "crafting" their discourse with many other tools, materials, skills, gestures, etc., then writing words, testifying how a building "performs." Through focusing on the making of "values" within the architectural office, she considers them as a series of interconnected socio-material practices. Brigitte Louise Hansen analyses architectural thinking in practice through a methodological perspective, as such, including a discussion of the design paradigm: ways to interpret architecture and the role of designers in the development of projects. What Hansen proposes is a paradigmatic model – a methodological thinking tool – that can be used to analyse, interpret, and discuss the discipline of architecture from multifarious perspectives as a system of different knowledge fields.

The last two contributions involve different entanglements with historical perspectives, focusing on "reading" the city. Both examine the architect's position in relation to architectural history and theory so as to render these instrumental for architectural practice, while positioning contemporary developments. Sophia Psarra makes a plea for the consideration of architecture as the collective outcome of socio-economic processes over time. She criticises the dichotomy between artistic and scientific approaches, and from that perspective, she proposes ways to overcome these dichotomies, opening new possibilities for research based on multiple overlapping definitions of authorship and invention. Elke Couchez takes a historical approach to architecture's search for its own unique mode of intellectual work, framing the tool of reading in the disciplinary exchange between historians and architects in the 1960s and 1970s. Her text identifies the act of reading the city as a tool instrumentalised at the International Laboratory of Architecture and Urban Design, established in 1976 by Giancarlo De Carlo.

CHAPTER 1

Hybrid Practices: A Few Thoughts on Organic Intellectuals in Architecture

Christoph Grafe

The notion that the architect ought to be a "generalist," the only surviving specimen of the Humanist homo universalis is one of the most powerful constituents in the ideological auto-constructions of the discipline. One of the ardent and outspoken contemporary advocates of this proposal has been Kenneth Frampton, who advanced the architect as a person (so far, mostly, a man) who, as it were, single-handedly defies the prevailing tendency of an ever-increasing division of labour. Frampton identifies the expertise of assembling buildings within the perspective of tectonic culture as the "vestigially resistant core" of the architectural discipline, and the architect as an actor and author withstanding the drift towards efficiency and the wholesale economisation of everything.[1]

Frampton's proposition of the architect as a force of resistance sustains a position that may have its historical roots in the modern avant-garde of the early twentieth century or in the older concept of the Romantic and post-Romantic artist. Whether it was ever practicable for a profession that is essentially dependent on patronage, and thus on existing power structures, is doubtful. A certain degree of calculated naiveness, or opportunism, has probably always been as essential a character trait for an architect as perseverance and talent. An architect cannot exist outside the sphere of power, which is, in turn, affirmed by a profession, even if this profession views itself as a cultural avant-garde or force of resistance. These contradictions were probably never more inescapable than in the long twentieth century. As André Loeckx wrote in one of the introductory essays to the anthology *Dat is architectuur*:

> It is obvious that in a modernist view, in which nothing of the world is left to itself, the "genetic" contradictory nature of architecture will be fully stimulated by a social context full of tension. In such a situation, one can expect architecture to be rife with excitement and ambivalence: between art and utility, between the avant-gardist and the plumber, between aesthetics and everydayness, between the sublime and the banal, between autonomy and servitude, between poetry and politics, between theory and practice, between inside and outside, between powerlessness and ubiquity.[2]

The tension between the reality of architecture as service provision and instrument for monetary value creation and the architects' cultural aspirations would not seem to exist for architects whose activities are confined to teaching. The attitude of practising professionals towards those who are primarily active in universities – or those appointed in public planning – is therefore often ambivalent. On the one hand, one is aware of the need for a professionally trained young workforce that is also equipped with the necessary cultural baggage. Most practising architects will also understand the function of those representatives of the discipline whose expertise contributes significantly to ensuring that architectural considerations are incorporated into planning procedures. Nevertheless, a certain carefully cultivated mistrust of the tenured architect and the representative of public interests remains. The academic who operates within the comfort of the university may be seen as a moralist in the ivory tower or alternatively as an architecte manqué – or both.

The emergence of the architectural educator, as well as that of the public (often municipal) architect, closely follows the history of divisions of labour in the profession. As such, it is part of the overall development of the discipline and its professionalisation begun in the eighteenth century. Karl Scheffler, one of Germany's most influential architectural critics of the early 1900s wrote:

> The 19th century, mainly in its second half, created a situation for the art of building for which there are hardly any parallels. The master builder could no longer be a universalist, he could no longer assign his talents to a synthesis because he found himself forced to become a specialist.[3]

This evocation of the master builder had an echo in many publications of the time and, indeed, in Frampton's claim to cultural resistance – even if he probably rejected the cultural conservativism associated with the concept of the "master builder." Scheffler positioned this ideal master builder – "the artist, the scholar, the technician, the entrepreneur, the civil servant and the craftsman come together and are indissolubly united" – against another group whose distance from the practices of making and of craft also separated them from the operations and concerns of the discipline. Scheffler, an autodidact with no previous training either as architect or historian, who probably sustained a residual lifelong distrust of experts, continued:

> The representatives of the "higher building profession" had become a caste of architects monopolised by the state and entitled to a pension, who closed themselves off in mandarin fashion against the independent architects, against the economy that was driven by demand and supply, and against the "subaltern" building trade trained in building schools.[4]

Scheffler's verdict on the effects of the detachment of a caste of architects who have left or never been involved in practice is damning:

> this educated architect felt himself to be the imperial custodian of all that is immortally beautiful. He gained influence because he was appointed by the state to communicate his knowledge and opinions to the young. In consequence, the results of a barren stylistic science penetrated to the smallest workshop, even to the building speculator, to become base and mean in every sense of the word.[5]

The distinctions between practice and academia are not specific to architecture. Indeed, they seem to be fairly representative of more general normative ideas about the "proper division between the university and the professions."[6] In Donald Schön's view, this division, and the concomitant distinction between universities and trade schools, is an essential and defining aspect of development of academic institutions and value systems. For a discipline such as architecture, which is connected to a set of tangible professional expectations, separating cultural and societal expectations and value calculations from the more directly instrumental knowledge of design presents a problem: what is taught in architectural school may, indeed, not always be immediately useful when viewed from the angle of efficiency. At a more conceptual level, the opposite seems to be true: the requirements of objectivity, which characterise the positivist academic traditions of the universities where architecture is typically situated, are not immediately compatible with the complex, unstable, and diffuse context of architecture – both as a profession and as a discipline.

Could the division between architects working in practice and academia (and, in different ways, that between those working in private practice and those in public service) be used more productively than as an opposition? Might the existence of a group operating at a certain distance from the pressures and complications of acquisition, planning, and building not be an essential component, even a catalyst, in the continuous change that characterises the architectural discipline and the profession? Does not every expert culture need such a group that, exactly because of the distance, can explore new modi operandi – or revisit those the profession has forgotten – to the benefit of the entire discipline? In the architectural profession, change is perennial and continuous. Yet, particularly at a time when the model of the architect – as professional, as expert, as author, and as a human – is challenged from a variety of angles, the space of opportunity offered by working outside the profession may be of particularly great importance. As the discipline, and the profession, has to address new definitions of universality and new forms of subjectivity, and a new balance between participation and anticipation, the explorations of those not bound by perceived or real entrepreneurial necessities may perhaps have a new and urgent significance. Does the discipline not need its own "organic intellectuals" and hybrid practices in order to find ways out of self-imposed culs-de-sac of technocratic preoccupations and economic assumptions?[7] Let us explore these perspectives by examining the biographical experiences of two educator-architects, both operating within the context of Belgian academia.

Explorations of Grey Zones between Cultural Practices

How might the teaching of architecture in general, and of its theory and history in particular, position itself vis-à-vis practice? And how might it position itself within a university educating designers, and not (at least not primarily) publicists or historians?[8] The questions that arise from this understanding of the role of the university rarely provide for greater efficiency, but often create a necessary moment for critical examination. This would seem to be entirely compatible with academic value systems. Yet, academic policies often explicitly discourage the more culturally or artistically framed, and more poetically worded, types of research that intend to reflect the position of architecture as a discipline relating to the sciences as well as to the arts and humanities. Where institutes that originated in a beaux arts tradition have been subjected to academic modes of operation (as has been the case in Belgium), the tension between artistic approaches or practice-based research, on the one hand, and explicitly scientific methods, on the other, is particularly evident. Christian Kieckens, who for several decades shaped the identity of the Antwerp architecture school as one of its most respected teachers, has described the effects of so-called "academisation" with regard to the relationship between practice and science:

> on every level one can see that there is a division between the intellectual (thinking) and the feasible (doing). This is mostly visible in architectural education where the difference between the academic and the research at the universities splits from the practical design. Choosing one side means dissociating oneself from the other.[9]

In Kieckens's own practice, the questioning of a distinction, which may have been as necessary as it was artificial, materialised in explorations of grey zones. A substantial publishing activity, usually in culturally significant but seldom strictly academic journals, went hand in hand with working as a curator and impresario and a limited body of carefully selected building commissions. Formal research of generative principles in Roman baroque architecture appeared as a visual article in *OASE Journal of Architecture*.[10] Kieckens also took up the role of curator, bringing together multidisciplinary perspectives and positions of artists such as Peter Downsborough and David Claerbout. Precisely in allowing this multilayered presence of practices and approaches, Kieckens found a particular aesthetic precision that also permeated his personal work as a designer. As an educator, his teaching method could best be described as communicating cultural commitment, forging communities between artists, writers, and architects. The profundity of questioning disciplinary certainties, from a serious desire both to return to first principles and to explore new conceptual perspectives, shines through in one of the examination questions his students at Antwerp were invited to contemplate: "Is architecture a profession/ skill/craft that can be taught?"[11]

Examinations of the Awkward and the Generic

If Kieckens's trajectory between curating, writing, and teaching can be described as an examination of the space between different forms of creative practice – between "the arts" and architecture – Loeckx's position seems to be more clearly defined by his contribution to theoretical discourses. The earlier quote from *Dat is architectuur*, and indeed the very involvement in this monumental publication, illustrates the stance of an architect-author committed to the programme of improving conditions of society, not so much by means of architecture, but by understanding the role of the practice of space production within the realities of a capitalist society (without necessarily accepting them). Loeckx's practice has been one of collaboration and critical entanglement. Rather than being satisfied with the role of the detached academic, he has been involved: in juries for architectural competitions, as an adviser to the Flemish Government Architect (Vlaams Bouwmeester), and, probably instrumentally, to the Flemish urban policy unit (Vlaams Stedenbeleid). Providing advice to the newly established public bodies of the fledgeling Flemish administration, as it has developed since the 1980s, implies a practice that requires a distinct ability to negotiate and listen, and to accept doubt. As Loeckx himself noted in a conversation with three Bouwmeesters in 2013:

> What struck me was how impressed clients were with what you can meaningfully say about a design. [...] In other words, the jury session is also an intensive workshop for clients. And for jury members, because I learned as much as all the other participants. Capacity building of the highest order.[12]

It requires a particular openness to be able to learn from others, and to find compromise where no theory will lead the way.[13] The breadth of expertise, but also the refusal to become an expert with a narrow pitch, is palpable in Loeckx's publications, which range from critical analyses of urban projects in provincial Flanders to discussions of architectural projects, often with a strong social purpose.[14] It is in the latter that Loeckx also offers a statement of what architecture is for him. In describing an art installation on the roof of Hotel Min, a judicial

transit house for those (often ex-offenders) with a history of psychiatric problems, or (as the author calls it) "a house in the city to discretely help people, who
have unlearned the habit of living," he praises the building as "no heterotopia,
no bateau en route vers les colonies," but as a modern architecture restoring life
itself. For Loeckx, "That is architecture."[15]

Both these examples illustrate how hybrid practices can become essential
in opening up the concept of what it means to be an architect, to find openings
in the auto-construction of the profession, and to challenge the academic preconceptions of the discipline. These hybrid practices require a certain accepting
attitude, intellectual flexibility, and, probably, a humble stubbornness. In *Dat is
architectuur*, Loeckx asks: "Is the conspicuous insistence on pursuing the pure
and the true not to be understood as a cultural catharsis, as a medication against
the painful and essentially contradictory societal reality?"[16] In what are called
hybrid practices in this publication, a softer and realistically humanist approach
takes over where the purging impulse must fail. And the community of practice
that is architecture depends on organic intellectuals, who help to establish it, to
develop ethical and aesthetic values for an uncertain future.

Notes

1. Kenneth Frampton, *Studies in Tectonic Culture: The Poetics of Construction in Nineteenth and Twentieth Century Architecture*, ed. John Cava (Cambridge, MA: MIT, 1995), 377.
2. André Loeckx, "Het ambivalente denken, figuren van synthese en tegenspraak," in, *Dat is architectuur, Sleutelteksten uit de Twintigste Eeuw*, ed. Hilde Heynen et al. (Rotterdam: 010, 2001), 829.
3. Karl Scheffler, *Deutsche Baumeister* (Leipzig: List, 1939), 241.
4. Karl Scheffler, *Deutsche Baumeister*, 247.
5. Karl Scheffler, *Deutsche Baumeister*, 246.
6. Donald Schön, *The Reflective Practitioner: How Professionals Think in Action* (New York: Basic Books, 1983), 34.
7. The notion of the "organic intellectual" refers to Antonio Gramsci's *Prison Notebooks*, outlining the identity and role of a new form of intellectual embedded in emancipatory struggles. Gramsci demands that the "nuovi intellettuali," who rise from the status of professional organic intellectuals (traditionally within law, clergy, or medicine, but increasingly from industry), not limit themselves to "eloquence, the external and momentary mover of affections and passions," but "actively mixing with practical life, as a builder, organiser, 'permanently persuader.'" It is their "historical humanist concept" that allows the new intellectuals to assume a social and activist role on the basis of a cultural position and expertise. Antonio Gramsci, *Quaderni del carcere*, vol. III (Turin: Einaudi, 1975), 1550–1551. Cf. also Antonio Gramsci, *Selection from the Prison Notebooks*, ed. and trans. Quintin Hoare and Geoffrey Nowell Smith (London: Lawrence and Wishart, 1971), 9–10. The term is defined in Ian Buchanan, *A Dictionary of Critical Theory* (Oxford: Oxford University Press, 2010) as "An intellectual or someone of professional standing (i.e. a doctor, lawyer, or priest) who rises to that level from within a social class that does not normally produce intellectuals, and remails connected to that class [...] they are not upwardly mobile and their concern is for the conditions of their class as a whole, not for themselves." https://www.oxfordreference.com/view/10.1093/acref/9780199532919.001.0001/acref-9780199532919-e-499?rskey=SVb510&result=1 (accessed 11 June 2021).
8. Cf. mission statement Chair of Architectural History and Theory, University of Wuppertal: https://www.agt-arch.uni-wuppertal.de/en.html (accessed 16 May 2021).
9. Christian Kieckens, *LCTR_CKA_WW, Words on Works* (Brussels: CKA Books, 2012), 22.
10. Christian Kieckens, "Luce! dammi luce!" (introduction Job Floris), *Oase no. 86, Baroque* (2011): 118–123.
11. Kieckens uses the Dutch term "vak," which covers all the English terms. Christian Kieckens, *TXT_INT_CK* (Brussels: CKA Books, 2012), 451.
12. "Drie Bouwmeesters en de open oproep: proeve van oral history," André Loeckx in conversation with bOb van Reeth, Marcel Smets, and Peter Swinnen, in Vlaams Bouwmeester, *Open oproep – handleiding voor de publieke bouwheer* (Brussels: Vlaams Bouwmeester, 2013), 203.
13. The author experienced this when collaborating with Loeckx in the jury for the new headquarters of the Flemish broadcaster VRT in 2015. Unfortunately, the project was subsequently aborted for a variety of largely political reasons.
14. Cf. André Loeckx and Els Vervloesem, "Architectuur voor stadsvernieuwing," in Flanders Architecture Institute (ed.), *Radicale gemeenplaatsen*, Architectuurboek Vlaanderen no. 10 (Antwerp: VAi, 2012), 139–161.
15. André Loeckx, "The Architecture of the Awkward," in *The Specific and the Singular*, ed. Flanders Architecture Institute, 2010 edition of the Flemish architectural yearbook (Antwerp: VAi, 2010), 270.
16. André Loeckx, "Het ambivalente denken, figuren van synthese en tegenspraak," in *Dat is architectuur, Sleutelteksten uit de Twintigste Eeuw*, ed. Hilde Heynen et al. (Rotterdam: 010, 2001), 830.

Bibliography

Buchanan, Ian. *A Dictionary of Critical Theory*. Oxford: Oxford University Press, 2010.

Frampton, Kenneth. *Studies in Tectonic Culture: The Poetics of Construction in Nineteenth and Twentieth Century Architecture*, edited by John Cava. Cambridge, MA: MIT, 1995.

Gramsci, Antonio. *Quaderni del carcere*, vol. III. Turin: Einaudi, 1975.

——. *Selection from the Prison Notebooks*, edited and translated by Quintin Hoare and Geoffrey Nowell Smith. London: Lawrence and Wishart, 1971.

Kieckens, Christian. *LCTR_CKA_WW: Words on Works*. Brussels: CKA Books, 2012.

——. *TXT_INT_CK*. Brussels: CKA Books, 2012.

——. "Luce! dammi luce!" *OASE, Baroque* no. 86, 2011: 118–123.

Loeckx, André. "The Architecture of the Awkward." In *The Specific and the Singular, 2010 edition of the Flemish architectural yearbook*, edited by Flanders Architecture Institute, 267–284. Antwerp: VAi, 2010.

——. "Het ambivalente denken, figuren van synthese en tegenspraak." In *Dat is architectuur, Sleutelteksten uit de Twintigste Eeuw*, edited by Hilde Heynen, André Loeckx, Lieven De Cauter, and Karina van Herck, 829–843. Rotterdam: 010, 2001.

—— and Els Vervloesem. "Architectuur voor stadsvernieuwing." In *Radicale gemeenplaatsen, Architectuurboek Vlaanderen no. 10*, edited by Flanders Architecture Institute (ed.), 139–161. Antwerp: VAi, 2012.

Scheffler, Karl. *Deutsche Baumeister*. Leipzig: List, 1939.

Schön, Donald. *The Reflective Practitioner: How Professionals Think in Action*. New York: Basic Books, 1983.

Team Vlaams Bouwmeester. *Open oproep – handleiding voor de publieke bouwheer*. Brussels: Vlaams Bouwmeester, 2013.

CHAPTER 2

The Discipline of Concept and the Judgement of the Eye: Pedigrees of Form in Architectural Practice

Irina Davidovici

Contemporary architects often emphasise a conceptual basis for work as a matter of artistic integrity. Since the Renaissance, concepts have been theorized as a driving force to guarantee the coherence of formal, spatial, and material decisions. And yet, the rational basis for form has consistently been challenged by the necessity for adjustment, practiced by Mannerists as 'the judgment of the eye'. This countertendency remains visible in recent and contemporary architectural works. The appeal of the fully reasoned form is faced with the exercise of discernment as an integral, if often subliminal, part of the creative process.

1. A House of Stone and Paper

An emblematic early project of Jacques Herzog and Pierre de Meuron, the Stone House in Tavole was conceived in resistance to the formal excess of 1980s architecture. With its rugged masonry walls aligned into a perfect prism, this neo-archaic house was a profane temple: a primitive hut elevated by geometric purity. It declared timelessness instead of nowness, wholeness instead of fragmentation. A remote building in a remote village in a remote Ligurian valley, the Stone House nevertheless addressed an international community of connoisseurs, and was disseminated mostly through architectural photography. The abrasive materiality of the rough tactile surfaces became best known as printed on glossy paper, its mediatisation an indicator of cultural currency. In this way, the ostentatiously simple, defensively private Stone House claimed its place in the global professional discourse.

Thus, the architects' focus was not on the building's function as holiday retreat, nor on its material expression, nor on the legibility of reduced form. It was on its sophisticated conceptual pedigree: an intellectual edifice elaborated analytically, with no hint of nostalgia. The original sketches claimed the authority of art to bear upon on this modest structure.

As a result, the project's relation with its setting was deeply ambiguous. The architects memorably described the house as "an implosion of the landscape," channelling its semi-wild location with such concentration that it became alien to it.[1] The pictorial juxtaposition of dry masonry and in-situ concrete, contrasting raw materiality and precisely cut volume, was described by British critic Alan Colquhoun as an "endless text."[2] This comment – the mere fact of the international commentary – takes us to the other side of the coin. This private and inaccessible holiday home, concealed behind outgrown vegetation and property boundaries, was conceived to operate publicly through the autonomous channels of global cultural circulation.

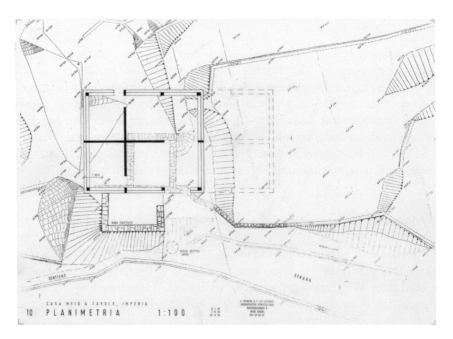

Herzog & de Meuron, Stone House, Tavole, Italy, 1982–1988. Site plan. The pure geometry is uncontaminated by the existing topography. © Courtesy of Herzog & de Meuron.

The images of architecture often reveal their hidden logic through the serial contexts in which they occur: sets of orthogonal projections, photographs on a film, the still frames of a moving image.[3] It is thus revealing that the architectural photography of the Stone House is almost exclusively external, its interiors barely and sparely documented, if at all. That this building is known almost exclusively by means of its exteriors suggests it was conceived primarily as an image. The physical existence of a small and rather unprepossessing structure in a remote part of Liguria was dwarfed by the ambition of its mediatised presence in the architectural discourse, as a house of stone and paper.

The iconic Stone House circulated internationally as part of a small pantheon of mostly secular temples built in similarly remote, scenic locations. An inordinate proportion of these was associated with 1980s and 1990s German Swiss architecture. The formally severe, materially sensuous projects of Herzog & de Meuron and other international Swiss protagonists – Peter Zumthor, Valerio Olgiati, Christian Kerez among others – were routinely circulated through the medium of print. In his 1996 text "Minimal Moralia: Reflections on Recent Swiss German Production," Kenneth Frampton placed this new phenomenon under the sign of architectural minimalism, establishing a binary contrast between Herzog & de Meuron's "art-like" (and thus seemingly dubious) practice and Zumthor's "craftsman"-like (and thus seemingly admirable) formation.[4] As the title suggests, the critique inscribed itself in a tradition of ascribing moral values to architecture.

The timing of Frampton's article is significant. By the mid-1990s, as the "recent Swiss German production" acquired an international following, its internal positions diverged considerably. The disintegration of this briefly monolithic construct undermined any credible claim to a nominal architectural-territorial identity. Not only did "regional culture" prove to be a slippery and heterogeneous construct, but the architects themselves claimed their work, not unreasonably, as a mark of artistic and ideological individuality. In this respect, as a Swiss artefact built in a remote Italian village for German clients, the Stone House illustrated the flimsiness of culturally or regionally determined claims. The rising international profile of its authors revealed the professional expertise and conceptual rigour involved as stateless commodities. Instead, the most stable ground available to architecture became the appeal to conceptual coherence, claiming an absolute, if ill-defined, sense of integrity. The physical territory in which the architecture operated only provided clues as to its appearance. What ultimately determined its formal and material expression was, nevertheless, immaterial. The basis for form was its capacity to be conceptually defined. In their architectural manifesto, "The Hidden Geometry of Nature" (1988), the architects wrote that the "project is, as its name denotes, a projection. A spiritual mental projection [...] from the body to the architect to new projected forms of appearance."[5]

Their view of architecture as primarily conceptual, rather than material, was disconnected from any specific formal language. Its purpose was to relieve the author from any signature style, to justify the production by removing it from gestures that could be perceived as subjective or arbitrary. This withdrawal from formal statements could be subsumed under the sign of an authorial decision: it was not the form, but the concept underlying it that could guarantee, as it were, the integrity of the architecture. These were the terms under which, in 2001, as recipients of the prestigious Pritzker Prize, Herzog & de Meuron presented their more recent, increasingly formally expressive, work:

> The sculptural and even seemingly accidental elements, the figurative and the chaotic, which have recently appeared in our work, are as much a consequence of conceptual strategies as our previously developed formal idiom and not the result of a singular artist [*sic*] gesture. This conceptual approach is actually a device developed for each project, by means of which we remain invisible as authors.[6]

2. The Stable Ground of Concepts

Already by the early 1990s, the insistence on the primacy of concepts had had a visible impact on the work of younger architects. The Kirchner Museum in Davos (1989–1992), by Annette Gigon and Mike Guyer, is a didactic illustration of an architectural concept at work. All aspects of the building are rigorously determined by the overall hypothesis of a correspondence between programme, spatial sequence, and material expression.[7] Every material and constructional aspect can be seen as a derivation of its plan. The plan itself – as orthogonal projection, an intellectual construct par excellence – has meanwhile acquired a distinct representational value, a sign autonomous from the building as such.

The dispersed galleries and interstitial circulations of the Kirchner Museum deliberately reversed the enfilade convention. In its questioning of established typologies, the plan closely referenced the "ideal museum" proposed by the conceptual artist Remy Zaugg in his 1986 lecture "The Art Museum of My Dreams," which reimagined the institution as a collection of "scattered rooms."[8] In their translation of Zaugg's abstract diagram to drawing, then to building, Gigon Guyer rendered an abstract ideal into concrete reality. This act of acknowledged conceptual appropriation achieved two aims. On the one hand, it materialised an idea. On the other, it allowed the architects to claim that the giving form had been removed from their own authorial volition, that no imposition of arbitrary aesthetic agendas had taken place: look, no hands.

A common condition in the Swiss architecture of the late twentieth century can be located in the collective rejection of arbitrary decisions – a culturally and intellectually justified rejection. An entire generation was enthralled to the primacy of concepts as a way of avoiding subjectivity, thus relying on the discipline of the idea as an objective ontological category. Christian Kerez named several of his projects after organising principles – House with One Wall, House with a Missing Column – indicating the concept as the main driving force.

Determined according to a predefined concept, the form of the architecture resulted from a matrix of self-imposed rules:

> To define architecture by a set of rules is to understand a building in a purely conceptual way. Rules establish a relationship between different parts, different elements of a building beyond any concern for aesthetic qualities, such as the shape of a volume or the size and proportion of an interior space. Rules understand a building as an entity beyond any narrative or anecdotal explanation. They are an attempt to overcome any personal taste for aesthetic decisions or any metaphorical use of architecture. This definition of rules refers more to the revelation of principles in architecture than to their invention.[9]

Kerez rightly pointed out that the principle of conceptual discipline was not new. The ordering of idea, programme, and site into the formal and material definition of the architectural artefact is inscribed in a rationalism that goes back to the classical tradition. In the later Renaissance, and already in fifteenth- and sixteenth-century art theory, the conceptual order as the rational basis for form was challenged by the necessity for adjustment, made most clear in the transition from idea to drawing, the *disegno*.

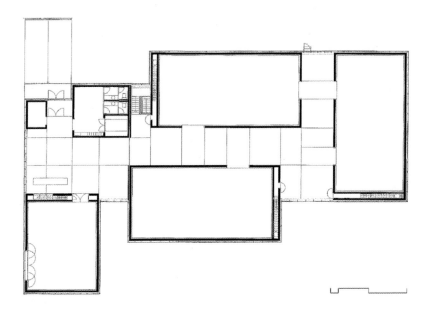

Gigon/Guyer. Kirchner Museum, Davos, 1989–1992. Showing the dispersed galleries and the typological innovation of the interstitial circulations, the plan has acquired an autonomous iconographic value. © Courtesy of Anette Gigon / Mike Guyer.

Sebastiano Serlio. *On architecture* Book I 'Geometry', 1584, page 10. Figure shows the geometric corrections necessary to maintain vertical proportions in relation to the distance from the eye. © Public domain.

3. Correcting Vision, Fine-Tuning Reason: A Renaissance Interlude

For Leon Battista Alberti, beauty in art was attainable "by a rational faculty which is common to all, and leads to a general agreement about which works of art are beautiful."[10] Unlike us, however, by "beautiful" he meant "the most usual, the most general, or the most typical" standards. Alberti conceived of architecture as the imitation of nature, replicating "certain general laws and orderly method [...] found in nature." Ancient architects, he claimed, had

> rightly maintained that nature, the greatest of all artists in the invention of form, was always their model. Therefore, they collected the laws, according to which she works in her production as far as humanly possible, and introduced them in their method of building.[11]

Architecture was justifiable as the replication of natural principles, which alone could guarantee, at the very least, appropriateness.

Alberti's fundamental contribution to architecture was to bring method into the construction of pictorial space. Based on mathematical foundations, perspective created an illusion of spatial depth through fully rational means. One-point perspective provided the tools for the representation of the ideal city as static and stable, composed according to Alberti's urban planning principles of decorum and civitas. Adjustments of reality to create ideals occurred, even more readily, in built architecture. According to Robert Tavernor, Alberti's design for the facade of Palazzo Rucellai was composed pictorially, bending the rules of classical composition, on account of the narrow street, so as to appear grander from constrained viewpoints.[12]

Late Renaissance theory increasingly emphasised the artist's capacity to correct nature. In Book I of his treatise *Tutte l'opere d'architettura et prospetiva* (1584), Sebastiano Serlio stipulated how the height of vertical elements, such as columns, should be taken into consideration when adjusting the proportions of facades: "If you want distant elements to appear the same size, you will have to make use of artifice."[13] During late Cinquecento, painters and architects increasingly bent the rules of perspective according to the *giudizio dell'occhio*, the judgement of the eye, defined as an "intuitive sense of proper proportions, the ability to create a harmonious and balanced composition out of disparate elements."[14] The objectivity of perspective was devalued by the imperative to demonstrate skill, inviting artists to represent more complex sets of conditions than the simple dichotomy of viewer's (actual) and represented space. As Massimo Scolari has noted,

> at the height of Renaissance perspective inquiry, many more examples of works bend the rules of linear perspective than adhere rigidly to them. And often they are more pictorially interesting, precisely because of the tendency

of perspectival representation to compromise the overall balance of the composition, plunging it into a cone-shaped catastrophe.[15]

The geometric rigidity of perspective was questioned by the greatest personalities of mature and late Renaissance. For Leonardo, who devoted tracts to the anatomy of the brain and vision processes, the judgement of the eye was necessary to mediate between perceived and rational reality, for "knowing to judge the truth concerning the breadth and length of things."[16] Later, Michelangelo was quoted as saying that "all the reasonings of geometry and arithmetic, and all the proofs of perspective, are of no use without the eye." He deemed more "necessary to have the compasses in the eye and not in the hand, because the hands work, and the eyes judge."[17]

By the end of the fifteenth century, Albertian reason was all but displaced by mystical faith. In the treatise *L'Idea de' Pittori, Scultori, et Architetti* (1607), Mannerist Federico Zuccaro decreed the *disegno interno* as the foundation of all intellectual activity, entangling illusion and reality, artifice and nature, the sacred and the secular.[18] As the manifestation of the divine into the human mind, Zuccari's *disegno* interno provided a licence for deforming proportions and blurring the boundaries between depicted and actual space, between manufactured artifice and natural formation. This tendency towards the formal convolution of established canons is identifiable throughout art history. Unsurprisingly, it recurs in recent architecture, which reflects the Mannerists' ambivalence towards rational form.[19]

4. The process-driven adjustment of concept

Contemporary architecture is beholden to concepts, which are perceived as guarantors of intelligibility, integrity, and cultural merit. In recent decades, a most widespread design method has generated form through the scanning of sites for formal and material clues, which are then, through logical steps, tied into satisfactory unity. Arbitrary gestures and formal preferences are avoided, formal expressions held in check by conceptual frameworks. At the same time, a generational shift is perceptible in newer works, which delight in the ambivalence of postmodernist conceptions of form and space. Unleashed upon the rational edifice, the true creative act consists of destabilising the conceptual equilibrium. Instead of a unifying, reductive severity, a new, ironic playfulness emerges.

Exemplifying this approach are the material and topographical explorations of Dutch architect Anne Holtrop. Fluid forms, merging with the landscape, are generated by art-inspired actions, such as pouring melted metal into sand, or flowing ink on paper, materialised through collaborations with skilled craftspeople. Holtrop's position deliberately resists a priori forms, relying on process for their definition:

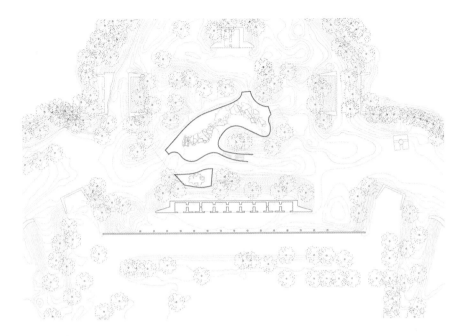

Anne Holtrop. Museum Fort Vechten, Utrecht, 2011, completed 2015. The plan shows how the underground part of the museum fits within the existing topography, which was nevertheless slightly adjusted. © Courtesy of Anne Holtrop.

> In my work I start with forms or material gestures that often come from outside the realm of architecture, in the conviction that things can always be re-examined and reinterpreted, and could in turn also be seen as architecture. [...] I try to look freely at material gestures and forms and let them perform as architecture.[20]

The method can be seen as a rebuttal of a priori or composed structures, by which form becomes the result of action. And yet, the rejection of preconceived ideas is itself preconceived. Starting the design process from a set of ground rules, without the exercise of conventional design actions such as sketching or measuring, refers to performance practices. Forms are "found" through open-ended processes, rather than through compositional or mimetic principles.

Studio Holtrop's earth-embedded Fort Vechten Museum is a case in point. Its volumes are determined by its siting among the sand dunes of the Nieuwe Hollandse Waterlinie (New Dutch Waterline), a nineteenth-century military defence system and national heritage site. Dug into the ground, the building's contours coincide with those of the topography. Yet the form-finding process is not simply the result of a logical sequence of steps, but also of moments of selection and readjustment.[21] While drawing the museum into the dunes

around the existing fort, a certain mound ruined the overall composition, so
Holtrop designed the plan as if this dune did not exist. We witness here a re-
versal of sorts; the concept was itself subjected to an unquestionably rational adjustment simply to make it work. This example highlights the exercise
of judgement as intrinsic part of the creative process. If personal judgement
intervened during the translation of concept into form, this translation was
mediated through the act of drawing – a simultaneity long ago encapsulated in
the Mannerist *disegno*.

5. Of Form and Life

By making intuitive adjustments to concept-driven forms, architects from different times and cultures have held in balance mind and eye, reason and senses,
knowledge and instinct, rigor and freedom. The pairing of rational concept and
intuitive judgement, each with its own implicit limitations and risks, shows
the necessity of processes of rationalisation and correction. Yet this oscillation
between discipline and adjustment, between the exercise of pure reason and of
subjective experience, is primarily attached to an understanding of architecture
as a primarily autonomous practice. All the projects mentioned above, while
existing in concrete settings and often taking these settings as the departing
premise of design, unfold their sequencing of conceptual logic and adjustment
in the bubble of architectural autonomy.

   To be sure, conceptual approaches encompass a balance between autonomous architecture as artistic gesture and heteronomous architecture as
socially engaged practice. On the autonomous side of the spectrum, projects are
primarily focused on forms and the cultural messages encoded within. At the
other end, the appeal of concepts resides precisely in their ability to incorporate
external considerations and speculate about the resulting buildings in terms
of their everyday use, contribution to the environment, and challenge to the
construction industry. They hint at the holy grail of modernism – the ability
of architecture to be political, reflect societal needs, and claim societal impact.[22]

   This offers a seemingly secondary, yet in fact fundamental, reading of the
Caritas Psychiatric Clinic in Melle, whose refurbishment by architects De
Vylder Vinck Taillieu can be seen as a typically conceptual project. The focus is
the original 1905 psychiatric centre, a pavilion whose planned demolition was
stalled by the simultaneous change in the clinic's direction and the discovery
of asbestos on the site. In dialogue with the clients, the architects developed an
alternative approach. They preserved the building as a lived-in ruin, a roofless,
open-air shell, inhabited by spaces for encounter and therapy shaped as small,
environmentally controlled glasshouses. A substantial landscaping, fit-out,
and gardening scheme complement the materially distinct refurbishment of
the existing architectural fabric.

The architectural interventions, as circumscribed by the architectural concept, established a deliberate contrast between the existing ruins, in a state of preserved decay, and the fragile, transparent enclosures. At the same time, independently of the architects' intentions, the visible repairs became incorporated in the way the building's users read it and, to an extent, identified with it.[23] In that respect, as observed by Bart Decroos, "Caritas appears as a blind spot in the strictly regulated and overly defined psychiatric campus, opening up a space of ambiguity beyond any conventional visions on what care should be."[24] The patients were encouraged to equate the reuse of architectural fabric of the building with its therapeutic programme. The refusal to destroy the old pavilion and the care and energy placed into small acts of patching up and restoring were seen to advocate for the integration of mental health patients into society. Valuing and pictorialising material repair, the building became a metaphor for the patients' condition, and thus a validation of their social status. This development indicates both the potentialities and limits of the architectural concept: when the project transitions from the control of the architect into whatever might be seen as "real life." Jan de Vylder and Inge Vinck acknowledge that "this project is not only about the project itself. But it is about a wider debate on the meaning of architecture and psychiatry. On space and life."[25]

de Vylder Vinck Taillieu, Caritas Psychiatric Centre, Melle, completed 2016. Interior sketch showing the inhabitation of the original shell, open to elements, and the insulated interventions introduced during refurbishment. © Courtesy of architecten de Vylder Vinck Taillieu.

What, then, of the architectural concept and of drawing as its own space of appearance? Drawing – the contemporary embodiment of the *disegno* – is central to the practice and teaching of Jan de Vylder and Inge Vinck:

> Usually a drawing prepares the way for a project. Or it represents a never (to be) realised project. Or simply an idea. Once ideas and projects are realised, drawings become redundant. Maybe that's what the architectural drawing is, in essence: a preparation for an approaching reality.[26]

Even if accepted in a dialectical fashion, the discipline of concepts seems by it-self ill equipped for the encounter between architecture and the "approaching reality." The adjustment, and sometimes interchangeability, of irrational and rational moments represents an acknowledgement of a more profound inade-quacy of architecture. Many contemporary architects who rely upon concepts to justify their work are absorbed by their inner coherence, and tend to disre-gard the wider reverberations of the built material form. They formulate rules from within architecture, and outside of the everyday practices of the city and citizenship, to find reasons for form. Whereas in socially engaged commis-sions, the creative process is more of a synthesis, largely moulded by factors outside the creative process, and impervious to conceptual justifications. The necessity for concepts and adjustments, pertaining to an intra-architectural discourse, transcends the dialectic of rational and irrational when they open towards the world at large. The potential of architecture to be appropriated, used, and transformed goes beyond the reach of the architect. By escaping the full control of concepts, the architectural form attaches itself to reality, and becomes part of life itself.

Notes

1. The architects quoted in Gerhard Mack, ed., *Herzog & de Meuron 1978–1988: Complete Works*, vol. 1 (Basel, Boston, and Berlin: Birkhäuser, 1997), 57.
2. Alan Colquhoun, "Regionalism 1," in *Collected Essays in Architectural Criticism* (London: Black Dog Publishing, 2009), 284. First published in *Postcolonial Spaces*, 1992.
3. Eve Blau and Edward Kaufman, "Introduction," in *Architecture and Its Image: Four Centuries of Architectural Representation: Works from the Collection of the Canadian Centre for Architecture* (Montreal: Canadian Centre for Architecture, 1989), 13.
4. Kenneth Frampton, "Minimal Moralia: Reflections on Recent Swiss German Production," *Scroope: Cambridge Architecture Journal*, no. 9 (1996): 19–25.
5. Jacques Herzog and Pierre de Meuron, "The Hidden Geometry of Nature (1988)," in *Herzog & de Meuron*, ed. Wilfried Wang (Zurich, Munich, and London: Artemis, 1992), 146.
6. Jacques Herzog and Pierre de Meuron 2001, "The Pritzker Architecture Prize 2001," *a+u Architecture and Urbanism* 2 (February 2002), *Special Issue Herzog & de Meuron 1978–2002*: 6–10.
7. Irina Davidovici, *Forms of Practice*, 2nd edition (Zurich: gta, 2018), 126.
8. Rémi Zaugg, *The Art Museum of My Dreams, or A Place for the Work and the Human Being*, ed. Hinrich Sachs and Eva Schmidt (Berlin: Sternberg Press, 2013), 50.
9. Christian Kerez, "Glossary," in Christian Kerez et al., *Christian Kerez 2010–2015, Junya Ishigami 2005–2015. El Croquis* vol. 182 (2016): 15.
10. Quoted in Anthony Blunt, *Artistic Theory in Italy, 1450–1600* (Oxford: Clarendon Press, 1962), 17.
11. Quoted in Anthony Blunt, *Artistic Theory in Italy, 1450–1600* (Oxford: Clarendon Press, 1962), 19.
12. Robert Tavernor and Leon Battista Alberti, *On Alberti and the Art of Building* (New Haven: Yale University Press, 1998), 89.
13. Sebastiano Serlio, Peter Hicks, and Vaughan Hart, *Sebastiano Serlio on Architecture* (New Haven: Yale University Press, 1996), 18.
14. William E. Wallace, "Verrocchio's 'giudizio dell'occhio,'" *Notes in the History of Art* 14.2 (1995): 7.
15. Massimo Scolari, *Oblique Drawing: A History of Anti-perspective* (Cambridge, MA: MIT Press, 2012), 27.
16. David Summers, *The Judgment of Sense: Renaissance Naturalism and the Rise of Aesthetics* (Cambridge: Cambridge University Press, 1987), 173.
17. Blunt, *Artistic Theory*, 74–75.
18. Blunt, *Artistic Theory*, 141–145.
19. See Irina Davidovici, "Onstoffelijkheid en zinsbegoocheling," *OASE*, no. 65, *Ornament. Decorative Traditions in Architecture* (December 2004): 100–137.
20. Anne Holtrop, https://afasiaarchzine.com/2016/04/anne-holtrop-11/, accessed 27 June 2021.
21. Anne Holtrop, lecture at ETH Zurich, 28 February 2019.
22. I am grateful to Hilde Heynen for her call to historians and architects, in the framework of the initial conference (9 October 2020), to reconsider and render explicit the acts and principles of architectural design as subservient to societal agendas. This encouragement opened the theoretical, strangely claustrophobic challenge of understanding architectural concept to a much wider and generous type of inquiry.
23. Douglas Murphy, "Frame of Mind: De Vylder Vinck Taillieu's Caritas Psychiatric Centre in Melle Brings the Outside In," *The Architectural Review* (London) 244, no. 1454 (2018): 26–29.
24. Bart Decroos, "Caritas, Text #2," https://architectenjdviv.com/projects/pc-caritas/ (accessed 21 May 2021).

25. Jan De Vylder and Inge Vinck, "Caritas, Text #5," https://architectenjdviv.com/projects/
     pc-caritas/ (accessed 21 May 2021).
26. Jan De Vylder, "Architecten De Vylder Vinck Taillieu," Drawing Matter, 7 September 2017,
     https://drawingmatter.org/architecten-de-vylder-vinck-taillieu/.

Bibliography

Blau, Eve and Edward Kaufman, eds. *Architecture and Its Image: Four Centuries of Architectural
     Representation: Works from the Collection of the Canadian Centre for Architecture.*
     Montreal: Canadian Centre for Architecture, 1989.
Blunt, Anthony. *Artistic Theory in Italy, 1450–1600*, 2nd imprint. Oxford: Clarendon Press, 1962.
Colquhoun, Alan. "Regionalism 1." In *Collected Essays in Architectural Criticism*, 280–286.
     London: Black Dog Publishing, 2009.
Davidovici, Irina. *Forms of Practice*, 2nd expanded edition. Zurich: gta, 2018.
——. "Onstoffelijkheid en zinsbegoocheling = Abstraction and Artifice: Mannerism in the
     20th Century." *OASE: tijdschrift voor architectuur = OASE: Architectural Journal* no. 65,
     Ornament. Decorative Traditions in Architecture (December 2004): 100–137.
Decroos, Bart. "Caritas, Text #2." https://architectenjdviv.com/projects/pc-caritas/. Accessed 21
     May 2021.
De Vylder, Jan. "Architecten De Vylder Vinck Taillieu." *Drawing Matter*, 7 September 2017,
     https://drawingmatter.org/architecten-de-vylder-vinck-taillieu/.
—— and Inge Vinck. "Caritas, Text #5." https://architectenjdviv.com/projects/pc-caritas/.
     Accessed 21 May 2021.
Frampton, Kenneth. "Minimal Moralia: Reflections on Recent Swiss German Production."
     Scroope: Cambridge Architecture Journal, no. 9 (1996): 19–25.
Herzog, Jacques and Pierre de Meuron. "The Hidden Geometry of Nature (1988)." In
     Herzog & de Meuron, edited by Wilfried Wang, 142–146. Zurich, Munich, and London:
     Birkhäuser, 1992.
—— and Pierre de Meuron. "The Pritzker Architecture Prize 2001." *a+u Architecture and
     Urbanism* 2 (February 2002), *Special Issue Herzog & de Meuron 1978–2002*: 6–10.
Kerez, Christian. "Glossary." El Croquis, vol. 182 (2016), *Christian Kerez (2010–2015) and Junya
     Ishigami (2005–2015)*: 1–15.
Mack, Gerhard, ed. *Herzog & de Meuron 1978–1988: Complete Works*, vol. 1. Basel, Boston, and
     Berlin: Birkhäuser, 1997.
Murphy, Douglas. "Frame of Mind: De Vylder Vinck Taillieu's Caritas Psychiatric Centre
     in Melle Brings the Outside In." *The Architectural Review* (London) 244, no. 1454
     (2018): 26–29.
Scolari, Massimo. *Oblique Drawing: A History of Anti-Perspective*. Cambridge, MA: MIT
     Press, 2012.
Serlio, Sebastiano, Peter Hicks, and Vaughan Hart. *Sebastiano Serlio on Architecture*. New
     Haven: Yale University Press, 1996.
Summers, David. *The Judgment of Sense: Renaissance Naturalism and the Rise of Aesthetics*.
     Cambridge: Cambridge University Press, 1987.
Tavernor, Robert and Leon Battista Alberti. *On Alberti and the Art of Building*. New Haven:
     Yale University Press, 1998.
Wallace, William E. "Verrocchio's 'Giudizio dell'occhio.'" *Source: Notes in the History of Art* 14,
     no. 2 (1995): 7–10. http://www.jstor.org/stable/23205625.
Zaugg, Rémi. *The Art Museum of My Dreams, or A Place for the Work and the Human Being*,
     edited by Hinrich Sachs and Eva Schmidt. Berlin: Sternberg Press, 2013.

CHAPTER 3

Values in the Making: Observing Architects Crafting Their Discourse

Pauline Lefebvre

The conference room of a Brooklyn-based architecture firm is where most of the action will take place (fig. 3.1). The walls are covered with printouts from the ceiling to the floor; a large screen hangs on one side. The remote control, a box of pins, a roll of tracing paper, and some pens are lying on a table designed and fabricated by the architects. Between 2016 and 2017, I immersed myself for eight months within this firm to conduct my research, sharing my time between my own desk and the various team meetings and presentations, mostly in the studio and the fabrication facility, but also visiting clients or the construction site. My aim was to describe architecture in the making, instead of studying the architects' production, once built or published.

Observing Architects at Work: Eclipsing Their Discourse?

Following the architects at work allows for the collection of material that is different from – and additional to – what is found when digging into existing documentation (writings, drawings, publications, monographs, press…) or conducting in-depth interviews. That material includes provisional, unstable elements, those that do not last or will not be saved and recalled: drafts, hypotheses, discussions, gestures, time spans, attitudes, hesitations, versions… Because this approach reaches – and favours – those aspects that are not directly accessible in documents or the architects' own recollections and explanations of their work, it tends to provisionally eclipse what architects have to say and emphasise material operations instead.

When I started this research, several studies had been published in the previous years that were based on following architects at work. Three of them are of a particular interest in the context of this paper because they display variations with regard to the role they grant to the architects' discourse, while having in common a "pragmatist" approach – which they situate as a prolongation of Bruno Latour's work in the field of Science and Technology Studies. In 2009,

Albena Yaneva published the results of her ethnographic study conducted at the Office of Metropolitan Architecture (OMA) in Rotterdam.[1] She is explicit about how adopting a "pragmatist approach" required excluding the architects' theories from her scope, to focus on following the architects in their daily activities and encounters:

> I follow designers at work also because I assume that there is much more logic in each piece of work executed by them, even in the apparently insignificant and unrelated design operations such as classifying models or reusing an old and forgotten piece of foam, than in the totality of their behavior or design philosophy.[2]

Yaneva explicitly aims to apply the actor–network theory to the field architecture.[3] That approach encourages the researcher to put on hold any attempt to explain the practice observed with the help of contextual elements or pre-established categories or theories. The social background of the actors, or society as a concept, for instance, are given no explanatory potential; they need to be explained with the help of the observations.[4]

The same year – 2009 – Sophie Houdart, an anthropologist who also studied with Latour, published another monograph based on ethnographic observations and descriptions, this one about Kengo Kuma's firm in Tokyo.[5] She also proposes to "forget for a moment the idea, the intention, not to visit the

Fig. 3.1 The conference room at the centre of the studio space of the Brooklyn-based architecture firm. Photograph: Pauline Lefebvre.

buildings."[6] She focuses on "ways of making that often have nothing special, that are considered daily, trivial by the architects themselves."[7] However, she maintains a closer connection to the architect's discourse: her intention is to depict how the intentions and concepts that Kuma develops in his writings are practically made to happen in built form through a long series of numerous unremarkable gestures. She shows the concrete work that these intentions entail and how materials eventually actualise them.

Finally, a third author, the sociologist Christophe Camus, also refers to Latour to explain his approach, which he calls a "constructivist"[8] one. Departing from what architects "actually do,"[9] he is less interested in depicting the design process than in showing how architecture is constructed as a discipline. His hypothesis is that architects' activities, products, and words continuously shape what architecture is. While Camus acknowledges the relevance of Yaneva's work as she insists on the material operations of design, he regrets the fact that her inquiry sets aside the architects' discourse, and therefore doesn't address their communication strategies. In his own fieldwork, Camus observed the amount of time the designers were spending on activities other than design, among which the communication of their work (brochures, portfolio, etc.) and the formulation of a discourse.

In a similar manner, this paper questions the tendency to dismiss the architects' words when focusing on their daily practice and, more importantly, to draw a line between their discourse and their work. Like Camus, my fieldwork made it impossible to ignore the time and resources spent by the firm on writing and discussing texts, and more generally on their branding and marketing efforts. Unlike Camus, however, I do not focus on how they establish contours for the discipline. My aim is closer to Houdart's when she attempts to bridge the architect's intentions with their realisations, by emphasising "all the little things through which their work in the making transits."[10] My research investigates more particularly the forms that architects' political or social engagements take within their daily practice, beyond the posture or values that they explicitly claim (whether with words or in built forms). However, as I will show in this paper, their claims cannot be eclipsed altogether; it is their multifarious articulations – in words, images, attitudes, artefacts, organisations – that matter.

I had chosen that particular firm as my object of inquiry because part of their discourse was precisely about favouring practice and making over thinking or theorising on what they do. When I started my research there, presenting my work to the founding partners, they made clear that they were not oriented towards working with words. One of the partners mentioned, for instance, that "if [the firm] was to make a monograph, it would definitely question the fact that books contain so much text."[11] They also explicitly refuse to set an agenda regarding the architecture they want to do before experimenting with the situation they are asked to deal with. In the "about" section of their website at the time, they stated:

> A deep engagement with the program and context of each project underpins an approach to design problems that favors the development of rule sets, processes and protocols over any particular stylistic or formal agenda.[12]

The firm engages in making and craftsmanship: they develop an experimental approach based on prototyping at a 1:1 scale, and the business model of the firm includes a fabrication department that allows them to take some of their projects all the way to construction. Earlier in that short text, they also emphasise their "social" engagements, in the form of participatory processes and architectural products that empower their users. These characteristics a priori exclude both the establishment of a given agenda and writing as a favoured medium. Yet, once in the firm, it was impossible to ignore the energy that the architects were spending on discussing and defining what they were doing and how to communicate about it, writing various forms of texts and constantly looking for the right formats and words.

Episode 1: Observing Architects Crafting Words

I propose to focus here on one particular episode. At the time of my observations, the founding partners and the marketing associate were engaged in
the renewal of the firm's communication strategies and supports. They had
hired a London-based graphic designer to renew their website but also their
visual identity entirely (e.g. logo, fonts, colours, portfolios, cards, general layouts). In that context, they also wanted to revise the texts about their work.
Ahead of a meeting with the web designer, two internal workshops took place
during which the partners and the marketing associate brainstormed and de-
bated in order to agree on a series of keywords to describe the work of the
firm (fig. 3.2). They called those their "values" and eventually established five
of them: "generative collaboration," "centrality of making," "multidisciplinary
craftsmanship," "radical pragmatism," and "impact." For each, the team also
wrote a short paragraph, phrasing and rephrasing them with precision in a
shared document, before integrating them as slides in the deck they would
present to the web designer.

Fig. 3.2   The whiteboard used to brainstorm keywords that could be used to describe the
firm's values, as captured after the meeting with the marketing associate and stored in the
dedicated folder on the server. Courtesy of SITU.

During that presentation, they read these words very quickly, showing signs of embarrassment. They pretended the texts had been drafted the night before and were not so important after all. Their reluctancy at that point was in sharp contrast with the energy they had – and would continue to – put into this effort. It confirmed their ambiguous relationship with writing. This episode is just one of a long series in which I observed tensions when the architects had to write about their practice: what was the right length and format of text and what exact words would be best. They had these discussions not only around their website, portfolio, and slide shows but also around every competition entry and bidding process, or around presentations to clients in the context of a project (What were the concepts put forward? What title for each section of the presentation? What captions on the images? How to name each component, piece of furniture, or room?, etc.).

The debates – about formats and content – revealed a major unresolved tension between two stakes: their values (what they cared about) and their message (what would allow them to do more, or more interesting, work). For instance, when defining their values, the need to emphasise their process, rather than the end products, came to be discussed:

> Partner 1: It would be helpful for us [...] to be able to go through our process through our message.
> Marketing Associate: My concern about that is [that] some people aren't interested in the process, and there are core attributes that aren't a part of the process. There are people who are just interested in the result – it needs to be quick [...]
> Partner 2: A number of clients *are* interested in that, and it sets us apart.

On the one side, the architects wanted to present their work in a way that was aligned with their affinities, what was important to them, and what they enjoyed doing: their process-driven, trial-and-error, experimental, and very material way of working. On the other side, they were compelled to target potential clients in order for the firm to keep growing – and survive on the highly competitive market of New York City – and therefore were balancing in favour of a presentation of themselves that would be quick, efficient, and more market oriented, leaving some of the experimental aspects aside.

In the context of the marketing effort in which they had engaged, writing definitely played a central role. It was so crucial that, after their first attempt to establish their five values, they hired a special branding consultant to help them with "how to talk about themselves" and with "the complexity to choose a few words." However, these words were never separated from the production and choice of images, nor from their actual practice as designers and fabricators. Texts were meant to take place among many other documents and media. The slides with their five values were, for instance, only a small part of a much longer presentation: a slide show presenting films, photographs, and a few drawings to attest to the various design and fabrication activities of the firm. The work they had put in that "branding deck" was substantial: selecting the projects, choosing and ordering the images, building a narrative, and so on. Their values as a firm are not contained in the slides presenting five concepts and their short description. Their values are built up throughout all the slides: in their carefully chosen order, the framing of the pictures, the choice of using film as well, the limited number of drawings, the very short, or absence of, captions, for example. The architects "craft" their discourse with many other tools, materials, skills, and gestures than writing words. One activity that was central in that regard was the pinning up of images, pages, or slides to reconfigure and fine-tune a narrative. For any kind of presentation, the architects were always printing out the slides, pinning them up, moving them from one place to another, clipping alternative versions on top of each other, annotating the content with markers, etc. Each wall in the office was dedicated to a specific process that was ongoing in the firm, the marketing and branding effort among a number of current design processes at various stages (fig. 3.3). The presence of all these images on the walls allowed the architects to constantly refer to past and current projects in conversations. With them, the building of a discourse was also made into a material and physical activity: moving corkboards, climbing on ladders, pricking one's fingers...

Fig. 3.3 Pin-up boards and table with models. Photograph: Pauline Lefebvre.

Episode 2: Observing Architects Dealing with Their Values

During the first brainstorming that the architects organised around their "values," a specific moment pointed to the entanglement between the operations of choosing words and selecting images. After one of the partners stated that "performance is an aspiration" for the firm, his colleague continued on that topic but shifted the focus, suddenly wondering "how can we document the project?" and declaring "you have to document how it performs—it needs to be used." In this sequence, performance – as a value – is at once something they wish to achieve with their work, an existing feature of their projects to be documented, and a guideline about how to capture this characteristic.

At the time the architects engaged in the renewal of their communication strategy, they had just delivered an important project, which they were about to document. These processes were interconnected: they wanted their communication to highlight this project in the best possible way, with the hope that it would bring them similar clients in the future. This project – hopefully a breakthrough – had been commissioned by the creative agency of a major tech company. It entailed refurbishing their office floor in Manhattan, including the design and fabrication of custom pieces of furniture. The discussions that took place around the organisation of the photo shoot of that workspace echoed those around describing their "values" with words, in particular in this case around "performance" being an aspiration. The photographs had to document how the space performed.

The architects were truly interested in how the employees of the creative agency were using their refurbished workspace. Parallel to the documentation of the project, the architects were conducting a short survey to understand successes and failures alike. For them, the fact that the employees freely reconfigured, or even "hacked," their design was a sign of success in terms of its performance. In a draft version of the slide show presenting the project, the following caption was, for instance, included (before it was judged too long and eventually removed):

> Within the first week of occupying their new space, [the] staff had re-arranged desks, walls and pods to support the needs of a diverse array of teams and projects. The conference room became an experimental VR lounge, while the "WarHall" transformed to host a team-wide potluck dinner. Designed to be responsive and reconfigurable, the space will continue to transform as projects take shape and the [...] community continues making it their own.

However, the discussions around the photo shoot showed how competing imperatives were at stake. The main issue was about the necessity, as mentioned earlier, to document the space as it is used. On the phone with the photographer in charge, the marketing associate explained: "a person looking at the photographs should want not just an architecture like this, but the kind of work that is done in there." The photographs would preferably show the space occupied rather than empty. One question that arose was the choice between staged photographs or more so-called embedded or journalistic images, which would require shooting while the employees were at work. The architects and the photographer liked the second option better. The latter admitted that architects usually asked him for staged views, taken before the clients occupy the space, to have more control over the images. Yet once this option had been dismissed, the participants in the meeting identified a few problems. On the one hand, the space was not yet occupied and used to its full potential at the time of the shooting. On the other hand, some parts of the space were already too messy, which wouldn't deliver the right message about its performance either. The architects decided that the occupation of the space had to be "curated" for the shooting. They wanted to organise an "embedded" rather than "staged" shooting, but eventually opted for a hybrid of the two.

Among the images to be produced, there was a time-lapse taken with a camera circulating on a rail mounted to the ceiling of the workspace (fig. 3.4). On the main day of the shooting, the architects had to make sure that all

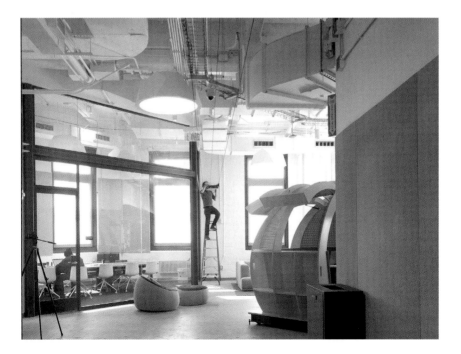

Fig. 3.4   Installation of the railing for the time-lapse in the creative agency's workspace. Photograph: Pauline Lefebvre.

rooms and custom devices were used, in particular the "WarHall," a flexible
space for impromptu meetings and other activities that was a central feature
of the project. During the shooting, they invited their own design and marketing teams to organise their work meeting there, pinning up on the custom
moveable boards. The time-lapse successively shows employees of the creative
agency at their desks and employees of the architecture firm in the flexible
meeting space. This hybrid solution was opportune on at least three different
fronts. It was first a solution to document the project fully used, despite the
fact that it was not so in reality. But it was also an occasion for some employees of the architecture firm to visit the project, turning the operation into a
team-building moment. Finally, it was a way for the architects to experience
for themselves – and thereby evaluate – how "performant" the space they had
designed was. They ended up very satisfied with the shooting, with the opportunity to enter the headquarters of this famous tech company, as well as
with the work sessions they held there, which they judged to be very prolific
– just as they hoped it would be for their clients. The result is the time-lapse
but also a series of photographs in which employees of both firms occupy the
space next to each other, such as this curious mise en abyme (fig. 3.5) where an
employee of the creative agency is coding on his computer next to one of the
architects who is busy working on his laptop, refining the documentation of
the very space in which that scene is captured.

The way the architects cherish "performance" is at work in their words
as much as in the production of images, but also in the way they concretely organise this documentation. Tracing their values at work demonstrates a
constant and complex overlap between the intentions that drive the architects,
the evaluation and communication of their built work, and their strategies to
reach out to new clients. There is no strict line between what guides the practice, what allows for its evaluation, what's central in the way it is presented, and
what serves as lures for new commissions. Yet these are distinct requirements,
which sometimes concretely contradict each other, and force the development
of fruitful compromises.

Describe Values in the Making

These observations offer an opportunity to track the making of what the architects called their values. In the case developed here, the architects' values
appear less as overarching moral imperatives, than as provisional descriptions of "what they care about." I depicted, for instance, how they cherish
their process-driven approach, or how they pursue performance as a quality
in their projects. When discussing their values, they are establishing what is
important for them in their work while evaluating what they are and have been
doing, and this effort comes entangled with other questions, such as how to

Fig. 3.5 Photography of the creative agency's workspace showing one of their employees (left) next to one of the architects (right), whose screen shows a view of the same workspace. © John Muggenborg.

best communicate about what they do and orient themselves in their present and future practice. Those entangled time frames bring me to conclude that the architects' values are not prior, nor external, to their practice and production, but rather themselves in the making through these very concrete things and processes.

When values are used as synonyms of "intentions" or "aspirations," they are considered as prior: they serve as guidelines during the design process so that its products (e.g. sketches, models, pieces of furniture, buildings) materialise them in the best possible way. In that scenario, the documentation process is understood as aiming to show how – or to evaluate whether – the end product actualises the intentions. However, such a linear sequence is not confirmed by the observations. Because the establishment of the values cannot be separated from the documentation of their past projects, it is impossible to decide once and for all whether the values explain or are explained by their work. Are the values illustrated by the projects the architects made, which means the values came first and the projects confirmed them? Or are the values written to summarise how these projects were made, which means that they were not prior principles that the architects followed? Being in the firm allows to bridge the gap between these two poles, intention and realisation, and circle this line back in a loop without a given direction. Moreover, the observations showed that the architects' values could not be considered independently of what they want to do in the future nor of the means to achieve these prospects. They are constantly making compromises between what they care about and what they feel is needed to get opportunities to continue doing their work.

Values are, at once, what they care about, what they do to achieve or sustain what they care about, and the evaluation of their undertakings. Such a definition echoes the one given by the pragmatist philosopher John Dewey in his "Theory of Valuation" (1939). He shows how valuation (a term he favours over "value") designates "both prizing, in the sense of holding precious, dear [...] and appraising in the sense of putting a value upon, assigning value to."[13] He demonstrates that valuation is an active, worldly process: when one values something, one takes care of it, acts in order to bring it into or maintain its existence. Moreover, any valuation can itself be evaluated, both in terms of its means and its ends. From a pragmatist perspective, values are not personal preferences, nor are they absolute moral imperatives.[14] They always relate to a given situation, and it is possible to investigate them, as they "are activities which take place in the world and which have effects in the world."[15]

Values are not merely made of ideas, words, or even attitudes.[16] The scenes depicted in this paper showed how material the establishment of a discourse actually is (how it is not made of words but of many other materials). Taking this one step further, my observations point to the fact that there is no strict a priori distinction between the material and the discursive. Following the philosopher of science Karen Barad, the "insistence on the materiality of meaning making [...] goes beyond what is usually meant by the frequently heard contemporary refrain that writing and talking are material practices."[17] Barad accounts for the intimate relationship that exists in knowledge practices between concepts and materiality, meaning and matter – or, in our case, between values and architectural production. She refuses to consider concepts as abstractions existing independently of their encounter with their objects or as concrete attributes to be discovered in the objects. Instead, she describes the processes through which both the concept and the attribute of the object emerge (and are delineated as two different kinds of things). Concepts (or values) are part of the world to which they apply instead of external to it. In the case of architectural design, projects are not mere representations of prior values, and values are not mere descriptions of the projects. Whereas the first idea turns the material side of the couple into "a passive and blank slate awaiting the active inscription of culture,"[18] the second deprives the values of any agency on the process. This paper aimed to show how the ways in which values circulate and are enacted in the studio exceed these restrictive definitions.

Observing the architects at work, one notices how their values manifest themselves in practice and how these values exist in the architects' decisions and acts on a daily basis. I chose to focus here on the documentation and communication process, but the same could be done with their design activity, tracing how their values manifest themselves in their work, for instance,

Fig. 3.6 Live-testing prototypes of the mobile pin-up walls for the workspace of the creative agency. Courtesy of SITU.

when the performance of a piece of furniture is live tested with prototypes rather than imagined and modelled in the studio (fig. 3.6). Values are not what explains architects' work nor what should be deciphered in their built production, but what needs to be explained thanks to the meticulous depiction of what architects do.

Acknowledgements

This research was supported by the Belgian American Educational Foundation and by Fonds National de la Recherche Scientifique. I am deeply grateful to the architects who allowed me to conduct my research in their firm.

Notes

1. Albena Yaneva, *The Making of a Building: A Pragmatist Approach to Architecture* (Bern: Peter Lang, 2009); Albena Yaneva, *Made by the Office for Metropolitan Architecture: An Ethnography of Design* (Rotterdam: 010, 2009).
2. Yaneva, *Made by the Office for Metropolitan Architecture*, 26.
3. Albena Yaneva, "Understanding Architecture, Accounting Society," *Science Studies* 21, no. 1 (2008): 3–7.
4. Bruno Latour, *Reassembling the Social: An Introduction to Actor-Network-Theory* (New York: Oxford University Press, 2005).
5. Sophie Houdart, *Kuma Kengo: une monographie décalée* (Paris: Éditions Donner Lieu, 2009).
6. Houdart, 38 (my translation).
7. Houdart, 186 (my translation).
8. Christophe Camus, "Pour une sociologie 'constructiviste' de l'architecture," *Espaces et sociétés*, no. 142 (2010): 63–78.
9. Christophe Camus, *Mais que fait vraiment l'architecte ? Enquête sur les pratiques et modes d'existence de l'architecture* (Paris: L'Harmattan, 2016).
10. Houdart, *Kuma Kengo*, 38 (my translation).
11. Unless otherwise specified, all the quotes attributed to the architects are from the notes I took during fieldwork.
12. Former "about" section on the architects' website, last consulted in August 2017.
13. John Dewey, "Theory of Valuation," *International Encyclopedia of Unified Science* (Chicago: University of Chicago Press, 1939), 5.
14. I discussed this aspect elsewhere, around "authenticity" as a value: Pauline Lefebvre, "'What the Wood Wants to Do': Pragmatist Speculations on a Response-able Architectural Practice," *Architectural Theory Review* 22, no. 1 (2018): 24–41.
15. Dewey, "Theory of Valuation," 19.
16. See also Nathalie Heinich, *Des valeurs. Une approche sociologique* (Paris: Gallimard, 2017).
17. Karen Barad, *Meeting the Universe Halfway: Quantum Physics and the Entanglement of Matter and Meaning* (Durham, NC: Duke University Press Books, 2007), 147.
18. Barad, *Meeting the Universe Halfway*, 150.

Bibliography

Barad, Karen. *Meeting the Universe Halfway: Quantum Physics and the Entanglement of Matter and Meaning*. Durham, NC: Duke University Press, 2007.

Camus, Christophe. *Mais que fait vraiment l'architecte ? Enquête sur les pratiques et modes d'existence de l'architecture*. Paris: L'Harmattan, 2016.

———. "Pour une sociologie 'constructiviste' de l'architecture." *Espaces et sociétés*, no. 142 (2010): 63–78.

Dewey, John. "Theory of Valuation." *International Encyclopedia of Unified Science*, vol. 2, no. 4, 1939.

Heinich, Nathalie. *Des valeurs. Une approche sociologique*. Paris: Gallimard, 2017.

Houdart, Sophie. *Kuma Kengo: une monographie décalée*. Paris: Éditions Donner Lieu, 2009.

Latour, Bruno. *Reassembling the Social: An Introduction to Actor-Network-Theory*. New York: Oxford University Press, 2005.

Lefebvre, Pauline. "'What the Wood wants to do': Pragmatist Speculations on a Response-able Architectural Practice." *Architectural Theory Review* 22, no. 1 (2018): 24–41.

Yaneva, Albena. *Made by the Office for Metropolitan Architecture: An Ethnography of Design*. Rotterdam: 010, 2009.

———. *The Making of a Building: A Pragmatist Approach to Architecture*. Bern: Peter Lang, 2009.

———. "Understanding Architecture, Accounting Society." *Science Studies* 21, no. 1 (2008): 3–7.

CHAPTER 4

Notes on Interpretation: Analysing Architecture from the Perspective of a Reflective Practitioner

Birgitte Louise Hansen

Definitions

This paper is about the interpretation of architecture in architectural research. It is a disciplinary discussion taking as its departure point that "what architecture is" depends on the position of the interpreter. In other words, several interpretations are possible. The concept of the architect – and what an architect does – reflects the ontological perspective. There is not "one architect" nor "an architecture." Instead, architecture could be seen as a number of knowledge fields, each with its own roles, responsibilities, and architectural means for an architect to use. To illustrate this point of view, a "methodological thinking tool" will be proposed through which architecture can be analysed and understood from multifarious perspectives. The approach has a performative quality, like walking through the same building several times but in another condition, thereby seeing different realities. It is not about defining an absolute truth or tools to design. It is about opening doors of perception for the purpose of demonstrating the complexity of the architectural discipline mapping out possible work fields and territories of thoughts for architects. The analytical strategy was developed within the framework and research of the dissertation "Architectural Thinking in Practice."[1] Written from a reflective practitioner's perspective, the aim was to bridge academia and practice. The interpretation of architecture exposed here is as such informed by experiential knowledge developed in practice.

While there is a strong methodological side to the argument made, the search to define an analytical framework for architects is not only abstract, philosophical, and didactic. It is derived from interactions with people in practice who made it clear that the territory of architects is challenged in today's world. Through liberalisation, competition from neighbouring disciplines, and a general lack of understanding of what architects "bring to the table" in the decision field, it is difficult for laypeople to assess the value of architecture and the role of architects in the development of, for example, large-scale complex building projects. Within the discourse on healthcare architecture – which was the subject of the dissertation – it is common to assume that an evidence-based practice is the way forward.[2] Despite that facts and figures indeed contribute to the narrative of a profession with a strong history of material evidence, this paper aims to put forward qualitative arguments to demonstrate the encompassing nature of architecture.[3] For this sake, "the object of architecture" should be scrutinised and discussed professionally – leaving behind the definition of the architect as primarily "the artistic genius" and instead generating plural interpretations and possible role models that practitioners can identify with. This is the potential power of the methodological thinking tool – to surface tacit knowledge in practice and make it accessible to the outside world.

Fig. 4.1   To the left in front, the interpreter – architect Eigil Hartvig Rasmussen – at the decision table. The other three people are not known. The image is evidence of the importance of spoken words. In fact, Krohn & Hartvig Rasmussen, in their work with the collaborating engineers, developed a lingua franca around the construction system, demonstrating how the two thought and knowledge fields were intertwined. Hvidovre Hospital archive, 1966. Photographer unknown.

The Analytical Foundation

The perception of architecture as a thought field that can be explored is informed by the notion "reflective practice" – meaning thinking about thinking. It is an important aspect of "practice-based professional learning"[4] as well as "experiential learning."[5] In the dissertation, it meant taking a critical stance towards how architects think but also, and more importantly, looking at how their thoughts are constructed in relation to a number of factors, of which some are internal and tied to the individual thinking, others related to external stimuli, contextual conditions, and the collective. The reflective perspective as such questioned the definition of the design paradigm, leading to three interpretations of the design world, as, a. the production of e.g. physical objects; b. the things architects make being the result of e.g. a relationship, a negotiation, a situation in which architects participate; and c. designing as the materialisation of culture and ideas within history. In terms of architecture analysis, this meant that architecture can be analysed in three ways, as I. a media, II. a decision-making process in which the architect is agent and actor, and III. an interpretation of the role of architects and the meaning of their work in culture and society.

The work of the American philosopher John Dewey,[6] the American theorist and philosopher Donald A. Schön,[7] and the British design researcher Nigel Cross[8] have been important for the way in which architecture is understood as a thought field. Complementary to the work of Donald Schön and Nigel Cross – which is primarily about how architects and designers think in the making – the research represented here is about how architects are informed in their thinking and act accordingly. From an academic point of view, the distinction between the two approaches corresponds to the split in architectural education between teachers who teach design studios and those who teach architecture analysis and research, architecture history and theory.[9] In an ideal world, the artistic and often tacit research done by practitioners would be connected with the more scientific and academic attitude, leading to a communal definition of architectural means, possible roles and positions, and the classification of meaning. This type of work is important for the understanding of architecture, for people in practice as well as in education, where students in, for instance, architectural research long for a knowledge platform that they can use to develop their own thinking.[10]

The Research Strategy and Analytical Procedure

The development of the methodological thinking tool is an example of the potential of merging practice related research with academic analytical and reflective activities leading to – in this situation – a contemplative model for architectural research. It is derived from the practice perspective of the dissertation research, which provoked questions such as: How to describe what architects do, how they operate, how they think? What is architecture, and how is this made manifest through the architectural means through which an architect works? With whom do architects work? Who are the decision makers in the development of buildings? And what are the roles of the architects? This meant that the "design thinking" of particular architects was analysed, situated, and understood in relation to the way in which they were informed, with whom they worked, as well as what was going on in the surrounding society and culture.

The area of research was the development of hospital architecture within the Capital Region of Denmark over a period of one hundred years. Historical inquiries mapped the situation in which hospitals emerged in relation to a wide range of historical facts and societal changes. The information was sought in overview literature and translated into timelines. Methodologically speaking, the timelines were an analytical tool to record the most important moments in time – not only what happened but also the reason why. While the buildings on the timelines could be read as historical documents, each building also bears witness to the views, ideas, and values of the people within society who made them happen. From a qualitative point of view, the buildings were cultural artefacts. As a result, the case study research then became an archival study of who, how, and why the people involved acted and thought as they did. As public intellectuals and agents for people within society, architects were one group of citizens in the development of these buildings. The research aimed to unravel the role these architects had next to the clients and maybe also the users. As a consequence, material about the development of specifically Kommunehospitalet by Christian Hansen (1863), Bispebjerg Hospital by Martin Nyrup (1913), and Hvidovre Hospital by Krohn & Hartvig Rasmussen (1976) was collected and studied to trace how the architects related to the historical context and societal situation in which they worked. Next to this, an architectural analysis was made to see how they had translated their thoughts into actions and how their deeds materialised in buildings, drawings, images, models, and texts.

When ordering, analysing, and comparing the data, certain notions started to appear, and specific ideas became central to the perception and reading of the material. This made it possible to structure the source material thematically into conceptual categories, which could be written about and grouped visually.[11] Inevitably, this was a repeated process in which tests were made to see whether it was reasonable to proceed this way. The analytical process and coding procedure was paralleled by an independent, academic, methodological literature research in classification.[12] The interaction with students in architectural analysis played an important part in this work. The classroom was, so to speak, an analytical laboratory. In the classroom, models of interpretations were discussed, and new analytical categories came to the fore, while others already established were adjusted, changed, or confirmed. The "methodological thinking tool" at some point surfaced as a stratified model for thought: a way of structuring information and research, which makes it possible to discuss the discipline of architecture as the combination of five different knowledge and thought fields. Together, they portray how architects can operate within several thought and knowledge fields simultaneously.

The Methodological Thinking Tool

The five knowledge fields in the methodological thinking tool were derived from the previously mentioned conceptual categories that could be used to order and analyse the case study data: 1. Public Building, Representation, Imagery; 2. Building Culture, Materialisation, Constructional Spaces; 3. Use, Organisation, Distribution of Activities; 4. Social Relations, Hierarchy, Power, and Bonds; 5. Experience, Imagination, and Memory. Each of the categories represents a specific research paradigm and analytical perspective: an epistemological and philosophical discussion about ways of seeing and being in the world.[13] Per paradigm, an "interpretive lens" was defined, as were analytical parameters and the outline for a classification system. Concordantly, the in-depth analysis of the work of Krohn & Hartvig Rasmussen on Hvidovre Hospital confirmed how architecture is a complex field of interrelated thought and knowledge fields. It showed how large-scale complex building projects have, since the end of the 1960s, been organised and performed by a team of architects, each with their core qualities and roles in the decision-making process – not one "master builder."[14] It was (and is) nevertheless still primarily the image of "the design architect" that is represented in the literature on architecture – as confirmed in the press, magazines, films, literature – not the other possible architects. This gives a distorted reflection of the discipline.

In an academic setting, in classes on architectural analysis and research, the interpretive lenses do not only operate as a pedagogical device with which students can position themselves ontologically while researching and designing. It trains them to become critically aware of their own discipline, terminology, and means. In an international student population, the interpretive lenses can also act as a tool to bring to the surface different perceptions of reality, space, place, behaviour, and sense-making, of which some are more known in one part of the world than others. An example is the discussion on "the social aspect of architecture" (lens 3) or "the experiential aspect of architecture" (lens 5). Conversations with students and their analytical work demonstrate how doors, windows, passages, and thresholds are not interpreted the same way depending on the cultural background and lay perspective of the person perceiving. They are architectural means that can be used to articulate and address specific aspects in the material culture. This is an indication of how necessary it is to include qualitative and cultural parameters in architectural analyses and research.

Finally, the analysis of the role of architects in the decision field uncovered patterns of behaviour and roles in practice not visible to an outsider. When architects talk and write about their work, they most often concentrate on "the object of architecture": the product.[15] This means that their role in the development of the project – and in society – is left out. As a consequence, what constitutes the everyday life of practising architects is invisible. And so evaluation, negotiation, critique, discussion, and debate usually are not presented as part of an architects work, and neither is research, analysis, nor experimentation. Pragmatic planning procedures, calculation, reading laws and regulations, administration, and steering the production process are most often also not included. The result is that the experiential knowledge developed in practice – about being a practitioner – is not being recorded and voiced. This is a missed opportunity to show people outside the architectural field what it means to be a practising architect. To make this change, the design paradigm needs to addressed in the architectural discourse.

The Interpretive Lenses – Lens 5

Seen from a methodological perspective, lens 5 – "the experiential aspect of architecture" – questions the translation between qualitative data and its conceptualisation in the methodological thinking tool. Is there any such thing as objectivity? Where and how does subjectivity enter the scene? And how do these abstract analytical ideas relate to the practice of architects? Within the classification system of the methodological thinking tool, reality – in the world view of lens 5 – is seen as a projection of imagination, memory, and experience: a place where humans are intuitive, emotional, and sensing beings.[16] The hypothesis is that architects refer to this paradigm when they express the impression or effect they think their architecture will have on people or the poetic quality of their work. An analysis from the perspective of the experiential frames how these thoughts are articulated through different architectural media such as spoken and written word, drawings and photographs, models and buildings. Next to this, the analysis looks at how different architectural expressions merge with sociocultural beliefs as well as with interpretations of the architects.

A common interpretation of experience in architecture is to see it as the sensorial and perceptual space of, for example, sounds, smells, contrasts between light and dark, colours, rhythm, proportion, and tactility.[17] Even more so, experience in architecture is often interpreted as something fantastic – the sublime, the beautiful, the poetic.[18] While this view is present in the articulation of lens 5, the analytical approach in the dissertation was fundamentally different, as it included considerations about the synergy between "spatial characters and effects" and the "conditions" of the people experiencing the spaces.[19] In other words, it dissected how architecture can possibly support the existential processes of people like patients, medical staff, and hospital visitors. An analysis of the experiential aspect of architecture therefore necessarily contains a study of whether the architect(s) incorporated thoughts about being – in an existential sense – in, for example, the design of a building. The study thereby relates to the knowledge field of anthropology, environmental psychology, and the field of philosophy. It also relates to the world of art, theatre, literature, and film, in which human conditions and the sense of life often are used, described, and explored as part of the work field.[20]

The 1963 competition proposal by Krohn & Hartvig Rasmussen for Hvidovre Hospital – represented by the two drawings included (fig. 4.2) – will be used for a short demonstration of the enactment of lens 5. The proposal author is one of the partners, Eigil Hartvig Rasmussen, who was known for his artistic qualities, his sensitive spirit, and kind nature.[21] In the analysis – while investigating the experiential aspect of the projects means and accompanying decision process – it concordantly comes to the fore how Eigil Hartvig Rasmussen was the most explicit in addressing the life condition of ill patients. As he did not write much, his drawings are an important source for analysis. They bear witness that his thoughts were primarily tacit – expressed in his humanistically informed perspectives – but most importantly in the content and spatial character of the competition project. To give an example, the competition proposal includes a large roof garden outside – in addition to winter gardens and patio gardens inside. This was not an obvious solution in 1963, and the competition brief did not mention any green recreational areas. The garden is an example of Eigil Hartvig Rasmussen's idea of agency: that sick people should have access to nature. In the competition proposal, he, in a few words, therefore also expresses how being in gardens is essential for patients.[22] He refers to an experiential aspect of gardens demonstrating an awareness for the tranquillising effect of nature. This view was not based on scientific evidence but on a personal preference and cultural belief.[23] The gardens were a means of association and memory.[24] It was about reminding people of where they came from – their natural surroundings in the suburb of Hvidovre – much like a door, but then in the imagination. In that sense, the gardens were a place for mindful physical presence, where one could transcend reality, as the bed in the patient room could be a place for daydreaming.

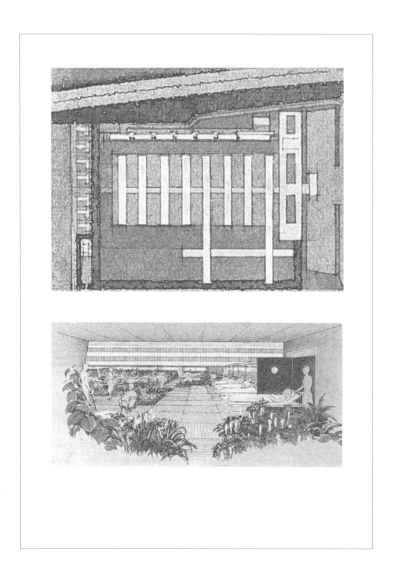

Fig. 4.2 Two drawings from the Hvidovre Hospital competition proposal in 1963, by architect Eigil Hartvig Rasmussen. The urban plan depicts an abstract composition of building blocks. It seems to communicate that the white strings of patient wards – together with the large block of service facilities – will stand out, whereas the large rectangular treatment facility below the wards, coloured in grey, will blend in with the ground. The perspective adds to this impression by suggesting that the roof of the treatment facility is a patient garden. The drawing visualise how the garden will be a place of rest, plants, flowers, and maybe of pleasure being outside despite being bedridden or walking with crutches. Seen from a cultural perspective, the drawings are cultural artefacts and agents of their own. The handmade strokes of pencil on paper might even emphasise that this is a place of poetry. *Arkitekten*, no. 18 (1963): 336–337. Drawing: Eigil Hartvig Rasmussen.

The Connection Interpreter: Interpretation

The open-ended procedure and the practice of coding is characteristic to qual-itative research and shares similarities with the approach of "grounded theory" – a way of thinking about and conceptualising data – developed by the two soci-ologists Barney Glaser and Anselm Strauss.[25] While one of the main purposes of the Grounded Theory methodology was to challenge the hypothetico-deductive approach within sociology demanding precise theories and/or hypotheses be-fore data collection can take place, neither Glaser nor Strauss believed in what is called "naïve empiricism". On the contrary, seeing itself is a theory-laden undertaking. An "open mind" should therefore not be confused with an "empty head." Glaser and Strauss name the ability to see data "theoretical sensitivity."[26] It shows how methodological reflection is related to a deeper philosophical discussion about interpretation.[27] Qualitative research is not only about gaining knowledge – in a rational sense – it is about being-in-the-world. This indicates that practising (concrete examples of real-world phenomena) informs theoreti-sation (abstract models of real-world phenomena) and vice versa. In relation to the case analysis presented above, it also cannot be excluded that an interpretive interference occurred. Seen from a historiographical perspective, it might even be argued that one cannot talk about "experience in architecture" in a project from 1963, as this type of awareness was not explicitly part of the architectural discourse before the late 1960s or early 1970s.[28] While this critique is relevant, lens 5 provides an example of an architect who had an intuitive and cultural understanding of the role and responsibility architects have in designing for people. This exemplifies how architects in practice can introduce and reintro-duce ideas in society as actors for a greater good, while at the same time being agents for deeper culturally derived values and myths.[29]

Seen from the point of view of the interpreter–interpretation interrelation-ship, it is nevertheless obvious that the interpretive lenses are not neutral con-cepts. Their "coming into the world" is informed by a "theoretical sensitivity," which was developed over many years. What is more, the idea that different knowledge fields exist is derived from an epistemological position that several worlds coexist depending on the interpretation. Fundamental to this type of "interpretive research" is that it is neither possible nor desirable to establish a value-free objectivity.[30] It is about solidifying arguments for the qualitative aspect of architecture. The classification system of the five interpretive lenses can be used to think systematically about data and to relate data in complex ways. As the definition of the lenses are intertwined with the coding procedure, it works in a similar manner as Strauss "paradigm model." The lenses refer to a specific research position and also theory about the world, thereby constituting the link between theory and method. Whether the "paradigmatic model" of the five interpretive lenses is the result of an inductive or deductive process is difficult to say. Another possibility is to see them as the result of the "hybrid position" of a reflective practitioner combining practice, research, writing, and teaching. On a deeper experiential level, they are related to a philosophically driven curiosity to question, explore, and understand what it means to be a human and subsequently an architect, the modus operandi.

A Critical Reflection of the Outcome

Essentially, this paper stresses the importance for researchers in architecture to involve themselves with methodological research. Contrary to disciplines such as sociology or the natural sciences, there is no exact characterisation in the discipline of architecture on research methodology. While there is inspiration to be found in the neighbouring disciplines such as history or anthropology, which seem to have no problem addressing the issue of architecture as well as architectural practice in their research,[31] it is less obvious, whether – or how – their methodological procedures and theoretical insights correspond with the architectural knowledge field and the discipline of practice itself. For this reason, this paper make a plea that practitioners entering the academic arena reflect upon practice itself, thereby constructing a bridge between the world of academia and the world of practice, between research (thinking) in and about architecture.

Seen from a practice perspective, it is evident that practitioners bring with them their own knowledge into the world of academia when doing research. In this light, the methodological thinking tool and the definition of interpretive lenses could be seen as the creative output of a "designer" doing research. As Nigel Cross stressed in his work, designing is a process of pattern synthesis, rather than pattern recognition.[32] What is more, the experiential knowledge from being a practitioner is unconsciously or consciously translated into the research mindset and method in academia. To give an example, the idea of space as an enactment in time is informed by the work done as a designer in the field of site-specific performance art and multimedia.[33] Having to design in the context of people and places furthermore introduces architecture as a complex field of diverse values, views, and interests – the sociocultural aspect of designing – where architectural knowledge interacts with the knowledge of other discipline.[34] Thus, the interpretation of the design paradigm is informed by experiential learning in the field.

While the analytical framework of "the methodological thinking tool" and "the interpretive lenses" has reached some solidity, it is still experimental in character and not complete. It has been – and still is – an ongoing learning process open for future explorations and developments. The purpose is not to provide a rigid solution to design and thereby scare off intuitive practitioners. The methodological thinking tool is an analytical device, but it is also a mirror and an invitation for practitioners and academics to revise how they think, act, and formulate their thoughts on practice: unlocking new paths for interpretation. The intention is to offer a critical and reflective frame of thought, systems of interpretations, and examples of different attitudes and types in the discipline. It can help make the complexity of the discipline known. Finally, it could be seen as the starting point for a discussion of the relationship between practice and academia, between practice and education, or all three of them.

Fig. 4.3 The photograph illustrates how the project for Hvidovre Hospital was conceived collectively by many voices. The building almost disappears in the natural surroundings of leaves, trees, and ground cover. It is an example of the interplay between architecture and garden, just as Eigil Hartvig Rasmussen envisioned. The architectural proposition of Hvidovre Hospital was creatively and productively reinterpreted by other actors in the decision field – here, the Danish landscape architects Morten Klint and Knud Lund-Sørensen. Source: *Landskab*, no. 6 (1984): 126. Photograph: Henrik Fog-Møller.

Notes

1. Birgitte Louise Hansen, "Architectural Thinking in Practice," (PhD diss., TU Delft, 2018).
2. Birgitte Louise Hansen, "An Interview with Kirk Hamilton," in *All Designers Use Evidence* (Utrecht: Innovatieplatform Architecture in Health and Platform GRAS, 2009).
3. This view is informed by reseach done before the dissertation. Published in Birgitte Louise Hansen, "Is meten weten?, Notities over Evidence Based Design vanuit ontwerpper-spectief," in *AU!, Bouwen aan de architectuur van de zorg*, ed. Peter Michiel Schaap et al. (Rotterdam: College bouw zorginstellingen, Stimuleringsfonds voor Architectuur, and Atelier Rijksbouwmester, 2007); and Birgitte Louise Hansen, ed., *Beyond Clinical Buildings* (Delft: Het Stimuleringsfonds voor Architectuur and TU Delft, 2008).
4. For example, the work of the American theorist and philosopher Donald Schön.
5. Learning through experience is an old philosophical concept. In education, the American education theorist D. A. Kolb used it to define his "experiential learning model'" in which the main elements are concrete experience, reflective observation, abstract conceptualisation, and active experimentation.
6. John Dewey, *How We Think* (Boston: D.C. Heath, 1910).
7. Donald A. Schön, *The Reflective Practitioner* (London: Basic Books, 1983, 1991).
8. Nigel Cross, *Design Thinking* (London and New York: Bloomsbury, 2011).
9. This view is based upon participant observation at different schools and universities since 1995.
10. This view is informed by my role as a teacher in architecture analysis and research since 2000.
11. The practice of coding will be discussed later. Initially it was informed by culture anthropo-logical methods described in Kirsten Hastrup et al. *Kulturanalyse: Kort fortalt* (Frederiksberg: Samfundslitteratur, 2011).
12. It goes beyond this paper to discuss the literature study. The work of the Danish art historian Lise Bek was of particular importance methodologically: "Arkitektur som rum og ramme – en analysemodel," *Rumanalyser* (Aarhus: Fonden til udgivelse af Arkitekturtidsskrift B, 1997).
13. The epistemological discussion relates to "Chapter 3: Systems of Inquiry and Standards of Research Quality" in *Architectural Research Methods*, ed. Linda Groat and David Wang (Hoboken: John Wiley & Sons, 2002), 21–43. It also relates to the course Research Methods and Design Practices initiated by Tom Avermaete at the TU Delft, 2013 in which a number of "epistemes" were discussed based upon the book *The Order of Things* by the French philosopher Michel Foucault (London and New York: Routledge, 2005; published in French, 1966).
14. Dana Cuff in *Architecture: The Story of Practice* (Cambridge, MA: The MIT Press, 1991) also emphasises how architects work in collaborative settings.
15. There are exceptions to this. One example is Reinier de Graaf, *Four Walls and a Roof: The Complex Nature of a Simple Profession* (Cambridge, MA: Harvard University Press, 2017).
16. Birgitte Louise Hansen, "Architectural Thinking in Practice" (PhD diss., TU Delft, 2018), 58–59.
17. Think of Steen Eiler Rasmussen, *Om at opleve Arkitektur* (Copenhagen: Gads, 1959).
18. Think of the phenomenological writings by e.g. Juhani Pallasmaa, in *Oase # 58*. (Rotterdam: naio10, 2002); Klaske Havikin *Oase #91* (Rotterdam: naio10, 2013); or Peter Zumtor's book *Atmospheres* (Basel, Boston, Berlin: Birkhäuser, 2006).
19. This particular focus relates to Kim Dirckinck-Holmfeld and Lars Heslet, "Rummets og Kunstens Metafysik," in *Sansernes Hospital* (Copenhagen: Arkitektens Forlag, 2007), 260–261. It also relates to research in i.e. "The role of gardens and parks in rehabilitation" (Swedish University of Agricultural Sciences, Sweden, 2005–2006), as well as it resonates with my own experiential learning as a human and courses in psycho therapy
20. This was the subject of the conference (and publication) Beyond Clinical Buildings (TU Delft, 2007).
21. Birgitte Louise Hansen, "Interview with Flemming Skude," Copenhagen, 1 March 2016.

22. Eigil Hartvig Rasmussen, *Københavns Hvidovre Hospital, Beskrivelse af konkurrenceprojektet* (Copenhagen: Krohn & Hartvig Rasmussen, 1963).
23. Eigil Hartvig Rasmussen grew up in a nursery and was very fond of gardens. In an interview with his daughters, they explained how he, in dark moments of his own life, would sit outside. In the study of the jury report, the hospital gardens were mentioned as typically Danish.
24. The memory referred to here is not only individual and subjective but also collective embedded in Danish culture. The historical study, for example, showed how hospital gardens have a history in Denmark.
25. Linda Groat and David Wang, *Architectural Research Methods*, 2nd ed. (Hoboken: John Wiley & Sons, 2013), 235–239.
26. Udo Kelle, Copenhagen: Krohn & Hartvig Rasmussen, "'Emergence' vs. 'Forcing' of Empirical Data? A Crucial problem of 'Grounded Theory' Reconsidered," *FQS: Forum: Qualitative Social Research* vol. 6, no. 2, (May 2005).
27. Think here of Martin Heidegger's "'Hermeneutic Circle'" describing interpretation as a circular process.
28. For example, the books by the Danish couple psychologist Ingrid Gehl and architect Jan Gehl, respectively: *Bo-Miljø* (SBI-rapport. Copenhagen: Statens Byggeforskningsinstitut, 1969) and *Livet mellem Husene* (Copenhagen: Arkitektens Forlag, 1971).
29. The experiential – as well as the symbolic – cultural historical meaning of gardens in Denmark is discussed in Hansen, "Architectural Thinking in Practice."
30. Linda Groat and David Wang, *Architectural Research Methods* (Hoboken, NJ: John Wiley & Sons, 2002), 33.
31. An example is the work of British anthropologist Albena Yaneva *The Making of a Building: A Pragmatist Approach to Architecture* (Bern: Peter Lang, 2009). Within history, e.g. Spiro Kostof, *Architect: Chapters in the History of the Profession* (London and Los Angeles: University of California Press, 2000; originally published by Oxford University Press, 1977)
32. Nigel Cross, "Designerly Ways of Knowing," *Design Studies* 3, no. 4 (October 1982): 223–224.
33. Some is published in Theil, Per, Kirsten Dehlholm, and Lars Qvortrup, *Hotel Pro Forma* (Copenhagen: Arkitektens Forlag, 2003).
34. Think here of e.g. engineers, technicians, construction workers, furniture makers, gardeners, etc.

Bibliography

Avermaete, Tom. Msc 1 course: "Research Methods and Design Practices." TU Delft, 2013.
Bek, Lise. "Arkitektur som rum og ramme – en analysemodel." In *Rumanalyser*, edited by Lise Bek and Henrik Oxvig, 9–44. Aarhus: Fonden til udgivelse af Arkitekturtidsskrift B, 1997.
Cross, Nigel. *Design Thinking*. London: Bloomsbury, 2011.
———. "Designerly ways of knowing." *Design Studies* vol. 3, no. 4 (October 1982): 221–227.
Cuff, Dana. *Architecture: The Story of Practice*. Cambridge, MA: MIT Press, 1991.
de Graaf, Reinier. *Four Walls and a Roof: The Complex Nature of a Simple Profession*. Cambridge, MA: Harvard University Press, 2017.
Dewey, John. *How We Think*. Boston: D.C. Heath, 1910.
Dirckinck-Holmfeld, Kim and Lars Heslet. "Rummet og Kunstens Metafysik." *Sansernes Hospital*, 251–289. Copenhagen: Arkitektens Forlag, 2007.
Foucault, Michel. *The Order of Things: An Archaeology of the Human Sciences*. London and New York: Tavistock and Routledge, 1970/1989.

Gehl, Ingrid. *Bo-Miljø*. SBI-rapport. Copenhagen: Statens Byggeforskningsinstitut, 1969.

Gehl, Jan. *Livet mellem Husene*. Copenhagen: Arkitektens Forlag, 1971.

Groat, Linda N. and David Wang. *Architectural Research Methods*, 63–100. Hoboken, NJ: John Wiley & Sons.

Hansen, Birgitte Louise. "An interview with Kirk Hamilton: I believe that all architects are making hypotheses – it is just mental and you never state them – you never write them." In *All Designers Use Evidence*, edited by Joram Nauta and Peter Michiel Schaap, 14–24. Utrecht: Innovatieplatform Architecture in Health & Platform GRAS, 2009.

———. "Architectural Thinking in Practice." PhD diss., TU Delft, 2018.

———, ed. *Beyond Clinical Buildings*. Stimuleringsfonds voor Architectuur & Architectonisch Ontwerpen-Interieur, TU Delft, 2008.

———. "Interview with Flemming Skude." Copenhagen, 1 March 2016 and 18 January 2010.

———. "Interview with Elsbeth and Karen Speyer." Copenhagen, 10 March 2016.

———. "Is meten weten? Notities over Evidence Based Design vanuit ontwerpperspectief." In *AU!, Bouwen aan de architectuur van de zorg*, edited by Peter Michiel Schaap et al., 142–148. College bouw zorginstellingen, Stimuleringsfonds voor Architectuur, Atelier Rijksbouwmeester, 2007.

Hartvig Rasmussen, Eigil. *Københavns Hvidovre Hospital, Beskrivelse af konkurrenceprojektet*. Copenhagen: Krohn & Hartvig Rasmussen, 1963.

Hastrup, Kirsten, Cecilie Rubow, and Tine Tjørnhøj-Thomsen. *Kulturanalyse, Kort fortalt*. Frederiksberg: Samfundslitteratur, 2011.

Havik, Klaske, Hans Teerds, and Gus Tielens, eds. *OASE # 91*. Rotterdam: 010, 2013.

Kelle, Udo. "'Emergence' vs. 'Forcing' of Empirical Data? A Crucial Problem of 'Grounded Theory' Reconsidered." *FQS: Forum: Qualitative Social Research* vol. 6, no. 2 (May 2005). Artikel 27.

Kostof, Spiro. *Architect: Chapters in the History of the Profession*. Los Angeles: University of California Press, 2000.

Pallasmaa, Juhani. "Lived Space. Embodied Experience and Sensory Thought." *OASE # 58*. Rotterdam: nai010, 2002.

Rasmussen, Steen Eiler. *Om at opleve Arkitektur*. Copenhagen: GEC Gads Forlag, 1959.

Robinson, Julia William. "The Form and Structure of Architectural Knowledge: From Practice to Discipline." In *The Discipline of Architecture*, edited by Julia William Robinson and Andrzej Piotrowski, 61–82. Minneapolis: University of Minnesota Press, 2001.

Schön, Donald A. *The Reflective Practitioner*. London: Basic Books, 1983, 1991.

Theil, Per, Kirsten Dehlholm, and Lars Qvortrup. *Hotel Pro Forma*. Copenhagen: Arkitektens Forlag, 2003.

Yaneva, Albena. *The Making of a Building: A Pragmatist Approach to Architecture*. Bern: Peter Lang, 2009.

Zumtor, Peter. *Atmospheres*. Basel, Boston, and Berlin: Birkhäuser, 2006.

CHAPTER 5

The Building within the City: Contingency and Autonomy in Architectural Design and Research

Sophia Psarra

Introduction: Two Historic Questions in Architectural Research

Architecture is often defined by the humanistic idea of authorship and the individual creativity of the designer. In contrast, the large body of buildings and cities where social life takes place is seen as the collective outcome of socio-economic processes over time. This difference separates the social purpose of individual architectural works from the collective architectural and urban production, fragmenting architecture into different fields of knowledge. Used to signify buildings and cities as the collective outcome of society, the notion of the "built environment" characterises scientific, behavioural, or computational approaches to knowledge, which are increasingly gaining strength in architectural research due to advancements in behavioural data, algorithmic design, and machine learning. The field of architectural design, on the other hand, is primarily defined as artistic and aesthetic practice.

This paper argues that the dichotomy between artistic and scientific approaches separates individual intent from the collective constructions through which we recognise buildings and cities. It furthermore proposes ways by which to overcome these dichotomies, opening new possibilities for research based on multiple overlapping definitions of authorship and invention.

The division between architecture as the product of creative intention and buildings and cities as the unconscious products of society is deeply rooted in Western thinking about our relationship to the world and human production. This gap is often embedded in the trajectories of educational programmes and pedagogical cultures. The background to this paper reaches back to my post-graduate years in the Unit of Advanced Architectural Studies (AAS)[1] at the Bartlett School of Architecture at University College London in the late '80s and early '90s. The AAS unit was one of the research groups established by John Musgrove in 1967 as a direct result of Richard Llewelyn-Davies' promotion of research as director of the Bartlett in 1960.[2] Taking up the Chair of Architecture in 1960 at the Bartlett, Llewelyn-Davies set out to develop a research-based foundation for architectural education in close connection with the social sciences, material sciences, and environmental sciences. My personal experience of the changes that took place in the department at the turn of the '90s further illuminates this study. From 1961 to 1991, the research heritage of the Bartlett was firmly set on a rational epistemological system. When the pioneering architect Peter Cook took up the position of the Chair of Architecture in 1990, he radically changed the direction of the school from a scientific rational approach to an experimental educational culture, and from the horizontal system of year cohorts to the vertical microcosms of the atelier or units.[3]

Cook's radical changes were not isolated phenomena. The distinction between the humanistic idea of architectural creativity and the idea of buildings and cities as socio-economic processes leads to different educational and research frameworks through the arts and humanities, on the one hand, and the social and environmental sciences, on the other. At the Bartlett School, a number of research programmes in the areas of building science, city science, and spatial morphology adopt the empirical method and epistemology. Inaugurated around 2000, the Design PhD programme[4] at the School of Architecture defines design through architectural and interdisciplinary research and design practice. In essence though, it is also characterised by the artistic–humanistic paradigm rather than the empirical model of science. Such divisions fragment architectural education in many schools around the world, where each side in the debate often thinks it has the right approach, or at least a better approach than the other.

Binary opposites construct oscillation between two irreconcilable notions, critically opening questions such as the following: How is the architectural work conceived? Are architectural knowledge and authorship found outside conscious architecture, or are they actively invented from within? These questions translate to: What is the source of the architects' knowledge? How can we define authorship in architectural work? I will explore these questions by looking first at the logical paradoxes inherent in them. Next, I will use the examples of Venice and projects by Le Corbusier and Carlo Scarpa that are informed both by Venice and the individual imagination. These projects are Le Corbusier's Venice Hospital, Scarpa's Olivetti Showroom in Piazza San Marco, and his extension to Museo Canova in Possagno.

If we support the view that architecture is autonomous, we accept that ideas originate within the architect's thinking internal to design practice. If, on the other hand, we believe that architecture is solely contingent on external factors, such as socio-economic conditions, material and historical influences, or sociotechnical innovation, then it remains impervious to the discipline of the designer. None of these positions alone seems sufficient to provide a convincing account of the source of architectural ideas. As Mark Gelernter asserts, "if a theory can explain the role of the creative author in the generation of form, then it cannot explain how individuals seem to fall under the coercive influence of a prevailing style or a dominant ideology."[5] Equally, if a theory accounts for how architects attend the idiosyncrasies of context, it cannot explain why they often generate versions of familiar forms throughout history for many different functions and contexts.

For Gelernter, such problems originate in our philosophical heritage and arise from a conceptual paradox deeply embedded in the Western system of knowledge.[6] Known to philosophers as the "subject-object" problem or the "body-mind" problem, this dualism is responsible for similar confusions in many other fields, including psychology and the philosophy of science. It is beyond the scope of this text to explore the philosophical dimensions of this problem, but it is useful to explain that it suffers from a dualistic conception of the individual as a creative subject and as an object in the physical world governed by universal laws. Designers identify themselves with the creative side of this equation, epistemologists with the opposite. The underlying ambiguity of this subject has often allowed for the fusion of these sides. There are theories of creation resembling theories of knowledge and vice versa.[7]

The Humanistic Idea of Modern Authorship

The divisions underlying the autonomous-contingent problem were accentuated by the humanist idea of authorship. Marking the beginning of modernity in the Renaissance, the theories of Alberti, Serlio, and other Renaissance architects established two things: first, the superior status of the design original to the collective, non-designed, and tacit systems through which cities and buildings are produced without conscious design intention. Second, the superiority of the design original to variations, to which the original might otherwise be subjected through use over time.[8] For Alberti, design might have a fluid state, but when revisions stop, they should stop forever.[9] Yet the Albertian model has deeper and wider repercussions than this. It confers the superior status of architectural design to buildings and cities as found, because they are mosaics of accidents, adaptations, adjustments, additions, subtractions, revisions, and other errors, most significantly by lacking an identifiable author. A clear demonstration is Palladio's *Four Books*, in which the adjustments he made to some of his built projects so as to meet site contingencies are corrected to match an idealised version of design.[10]

We recognise the problem of designed and collective architectures in Rem Koolhaas's 2014 International Architecture Exhibition Biennale in Venice.[11] Presenting doors, windows, and other architectural components, this exhibition implied that architecture is an assemblage of standardised elements over and above architectural intention. The same idea underlines Koolhaas's *Delirious*

New York, reading Manhattan as a self-organised framework of investors' capitalism that optimises the economic and programmatic potential of skyscrapers.[12] Discussing the skyscraper island as an empirical cityscape without a manifesto and privileging aggregate building production over individual architects and their designs, Koolhaas put forward a view of architecture as a system that is blind to the final outcome of design. In contrast, the model of architecture developed by Alberti is clear in its design intention but blind to evolutionary process. Equally passionate about Manhattan's evolved diversity was Jane Jacobs, describing New York as an empirical framework of organised complexity.[13] A similar idea was introduced by Alison Smithson's idea of "Mat-Building," defined as the aggregate configurations of the anonymous collective.[14]

The idea of architecture as authored, autonomous object concerns the imaginative processes of inventing. In contrast, the approach to buildings and cities as empirical processes is at the core of scientific inquiry, such as the rationalisation of life and work patterns, scientific management, behavioural studies, or morphological and typo-morphological analysis. Using quantitative research of observable phenomena, these approaches seek models that can support decisions in design. Architects generate designs using intuition, imagination, and personal experience. They often call upon their subjective interpretations of factual evidence, spaces, and events, assigning attributes to places that real-world phenomena might not intrinsically possess. Empirical analysis, on the other hand, enables research to identify patterns from ground up that can be generalised to explain larger worlds of phenomena. Yet, clearly set apart from design conceptions, scientific approaches disregard possible alternative configurations that form the core principle of design. These differences define architecture either as the mysterious possession of the creative individual or as an analysable system subject to the scientific process.

Venice, Le Corbusier's Venice Hospital, and the Works of Carlo Scarpa

In *Delirious New York*, Koolhaas adopts the literary metaphor of the "ghostwriter" of Manhattan that writes its retroactive manifesto in order to grasp it theoretically. I will use the metaphor of the archaeologist excavating Venice, a city that, in appearance and form, is unlike Manhattan, but like the twentieth-century metropolis, has for centuries provided a mythical laboratory for invention. Having remained intact since the fourteenth and fifteenth centuries, Venice offers archaeological evidence about the processes that shaped the city. Venice is chosen for two additional reasons: first, it is the outcome of evolutionary urban growth and conscious design intention expressed in the medieval urban fabric, the monuments, and major public spaces of the city. Second, it was the centre of Vitruvian studies, decisively opening to the Renaissance and architectural authorship in the fifteenth century. So it can illuminate the interaction of architecture as autonomous field with socio-economic factors that are external to the conceptual operations of design. Le Corbusier, in his hospital, and Scarpa, in most of his buildings, were influenced by Venice, and so they help to explain the origin of creative ideas, that is, whether they originate in the mind or are discovered in buildings and cities as found.

If we look at the dense network of spaces in Venice, we see that the squares, or *campi*, are densely interconnected through alternative pathways and intersecting circular paths (fig. 5.1).[15] The majority of the squares are directly accessible from a canal and the alley network, which seems to suggest that they work as nodes in the intersection between the two movement systems. This property captures the memory of Venice as evolutionary process from an archipelago to a compact city.[16] The squares with their churches were the social nuclei of parish islands, semi-autonomous community centres that had a market servicing communication between islands by being directly accessible by the lagoon's waters. The *campi* were also centres of water collection through wells located at the centre of each square. The continuous network of routes shows that

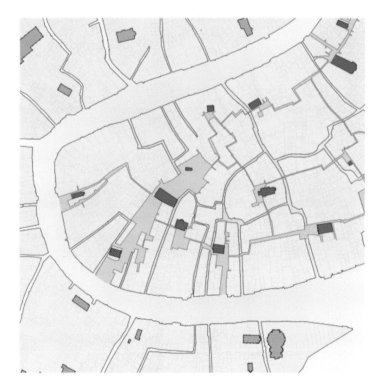

Fig. 5.1   Interconnected squares in Venice. Figure: Gustavo Maldonado.

the bridges that connect islands were built to link the squares with each other, forming a network of multiple interconnected centralities. As the city developed new land, local functional needs, such as dual access from land and water, and social needs, such as the redistribution of land ownership and privileges of physical access, led to the system of interconnected squares with large-scale consequences for the organisation of the city as a whole. Another fundamental characteristic of the squares is that they consist of a combinatorial system of urban elements: square-church-well-canal-bridge-loading steps. From the most modest squares at the fringes of the city to the magnificent Piazza San Marco, the *campi* of Venice comprise these recurring composite structures.[17] The repetition of these elements in the squares of Venice, the repetition of the squares themselves in the fabric of the city, and their interconnections through the alley-canal networks lead to a recognisable order without conscious intention.

The combinatorial structure of these elements and the evolutionary logic of the city's networks influenced Le Corbusier's hospital as well as Scarpa's designs. A closer look at the Venice Hospital reveals an analogical relationship between the building and the networks of Venice through a system of pathways (which Le Corbusier calls Calle, in a direct analogy with the alleys of Venice) intersecting at the centre of Unité de Battise (which Le Corbusier calls Campiello in an analogy with the squares of Venice) (fig. 5.2). So the architects of the hospital interpreted the processes that formed the city in a new designed reality.[18]

Circulation and Surgeries　Treatment　Patient Beds　Outside space　Church

Fig. 5.2　Le Corbusier, Venice Hospital, third floor. Figure: Sophia Psarra.

If Corbusier's hospital is an analogical expression of the networks of Venice, Scarpa's work presents a different case altogether. His projects are not shaped like a network, but adopt a lot, first, from the ways in which Venice's streets and canals relate to one another, shaping bodily movement and, second, from the evolutionary growth of Venice, reconciling various stages and styles of built form through a logic of accretion. In the Olivetti Showroom for example, we encounter a series of techniques that split a narrow site into three long and narrow strips (fig. 5.3). To see the entire layout, the visitor has to turn direction ten times, defining a complex pattern of circulation for such a small space. Circumnavigational movement is linearly accentuated and contrasted by the long axial vistas travelling from front to back. Yet, by extending circumnavigation through these twists and turns, Scarpa contrasts the synchronic views with the sequential progress of the viewer through the interior. By punctuating the floor, the ceilings and the horizontal and vertical surfaces with different types of materials and details, he creates distinct thresholds, such as the terrazzo floor made of pieces of red glass on entering, the stone slabs of the staircase, and the timber lattice shutters of the windows. The linear progression through space is thus staged as a sequence through clearly demarcated episodes or chapters.

A circumnavigational course is a characteristic of other works by Scarpa, as in the Castelvecchio, meandering back and forth along the linear extension of the building but also around the exhibits, as it is never possible to confront them frontally or survey all the works all at once. This can be also seen in Scarpa's Gipsoteca in Possagno: the long axis in the original gallery, where statues of similar height are symmetrically positioned on either side of the axis, contrasts the organisation of space and display in the extension to the museum (fig. 5.4). In the extension, there are objects of different types and scales placed on differently shaped pedestals. Some works portray reclining figures, others seated ones; some are busts while others represent full bodies. Instead of being tacked against the wall as in the old building, they are set at different points throughout the room, some floating close to the wall, others situated near the corners. Furthermore, each of the statues looks towards a different direction. The two reclining female figures address opposite-facing walls; the seated male figure faces away from the visitor, looking towards the bust on the wall. The varied positions of the statues requires the visitors to walk around them, crossing their own paths multiple times. The scale of the work in the linear gallery is also varied, with two major large pieces, a reclining statue at the beginning, and the other – the three Graces – at the end of the view framed by the garden. There are also small figurines inside vitrines, designed by Scarpa, to hold the smaller pieces. The changes between galleries and floor levels are marked by the changes in the ceiling and by different configurations of windows. There are vertical glazed surfaces on the right and at the far end of the gallery, clerestory windows and irregularly spaced square windows, defining a varied set of experiences.

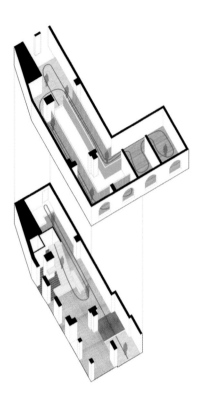

Fig. 5.3 a, b: Carlo Scarpa, Olivetti Showroom, Venice. Figure by Gustavo Maldonado; photograph by Sophia Psarra

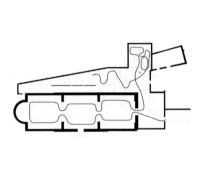
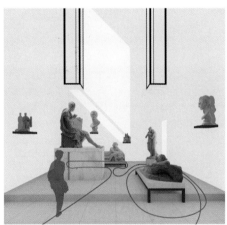

Fig. 5.4 a,b: Carlo Scarpa, Canova Museum in Possagno Extension. Figures by Gustavo Maldonado; photograph: Sophia Psarra.

In all three Scarpa's works, the source of inspiration is Venice. The linear splicing of space in the Olivetti Showroom, the narrow mezzanines, the sculptural staircase, and the water located in the central zone are mediated references[19] to that great catalogue of forms that is Venice – with its narrow passages, *fondamentas*, *sottoporticos*, bridges stretching over the water, water flooding the edges of space, all featuring as chains of reference to the aquatic city where Scarpa spent his life (fig. 5.5). The organisation of seeing and moving in these projects is analogous to the ways in which seeing and moving take place in Venice, where views extending over the linear stretches of the canals link places that are reached only indirectly, by the meandering and intersecting canals and alleys.

Fig. 5.5   Streets and canals of Venice. Photograph: Sophia Psarra.

Critics interpret Scarpa's work as being about metonymic articulation of found fragments. This can be best understood by Nelson Goodman's third category in terms of how buildings mean, that is, "exemplification" by metaphoric or metonymic expression, defining properties not possessed by a work, but expressed by the work.[20] Scarpa's tectonic poetry was brought into being by the growth of a tradition within modernity. This tradition was based in the Venetian constructive practice to merge discrete building elements of disparate origin and building spoils that came from their trade routes. A clear example is the facade of San Sebastiano in Venice facing a narrow triangular *campo* (fig. 5.6). The upper columns are shorter than those on the ground floor, and they are raised on pedestals so that the two floors have matching heights.[21] This is because the columns on the upper level were found objects that came from another structure.

Scarpa left behind no iconic abstract plans but a series of layered drawings that worked as mechanisms for his thoughts rather than a set of instructions to builders for a finished object. Richard Murphy explains that, for Scarpa, there was no sequence of thought or organisation ordering a project from general design concept to detailed construction.[22] While representing a unity of craft and design, this approach has been criticised as attacking the building details at the expense of an overall unifying concept. The preference for iconic abstract drawings is a preference the historiography and theory of architecture have developed since the time of the Renaissance treatise, alongside the concepts of authorship and authorial control over the wholeness of form as a relationship between parts and whole. For Scarpa, Venice and architecture were a storehouse of forms, a laboratory of combinatorial tectonic possibility, untouched by the academic tradition for the part-whole relationship and compositional impulse.

Fig. 5.6 San Sebastiano, Venice.
Photograph: Sophia Psarra.

Conclusion: The Need for a Different Conceptual Model for Architectural Research

Coming to the first question raised at the beginning of the chapter regarding the source of architectural knowledge, the examination of Venice and these works help illuminate the origin of architectural ideas. The sources of form in the projects discussed are neither in the internal operations of the architects' mind, nor on external influences, but in the interrelationship between the individual imagination of the architect and the world of collective imagination. Architects retrieve the logic of designed and non-designed artefacts and innovatively interpret them in new designs.

The second question raised in this chapter is how we can define authorship in architecture. The analysis of the three artefacts shows that they all have a formal logic based on a pattern of combinations that is either recursive, as in Venice's squares and the hospital; or based on metonymic tectonic translations; or on spatial translations of bodily movement, as in the case of Scarpa's projects. They can explain morphogenetic processes that work from the ground up and from the part to the whole and vice versa. The morphological affinities between these works point to two basic ideas: first, the idea of authorship as creative translation across formal systems. The second idea refers to multiple, heterogeneous, intersecting forms of authorship influencing each other. The concepts of creative translation across systems and alternative intersecting forms of authorship can explain how society and culture enter designed and non-designed artefacts, built and environments, empirically understood and mentally accessed structures. The examples of Le Corbusier's Venice Hospital and Scarpa's work help us see how cities like Venice inspire architects and what they can draw out of architecture and buildings.

Returning to the discussion introduced at the beginning of this text, the split between the imaginative processes of the designer and the evolutionary processes that give rise to cities and buildings leads to irreconcilable world views about the origin of our architectural knowledge. As this analysis shows, architectural knowledge travels from material contexts that are collectively produced to the designer's mind and vice versa, through the combined effects of evolutionary logic and creative invention. When architectural research and education are exclusively rooted in the model developed by Alberti or the empirical model of science, it is not possible to bridge individual and collective imagination. Perpetuating the elitist definition of architecture as high art or the mechanistic functional order of empirical evidence, without recognising the hypothetical dimensions of human minds, removes the capacity of architecture to actively contribute to the creative, social, and political processes of everyday life. We need new educational and theoretical models for architectural research, the seeds of which are contained within the educational heritage of many schools but are trapped in separate institutional and epistemological traditions.

Notes

1. The Advanced Architectural Studies Unit (AAS) was directed by John Musgrove followed by Bill Hillier, who, alongside Julienne Hanson and colleagues, pioneered an approach to the morphological description of space in close connection with social activity and cultural meaning. Bill Hillier and Julienne Hanson, *The Social Logic of Space* (Cambridge: Cambridge University Press, 1984).
2. Amalie H. White, "The Bartlett, Architectural Pedagogy and Wates House: An Historical Study," *Opticon1826* 16 (2014): 1–19, DOI: http://dx.doi.org/10.5334/opt.ci.
3. White, "The Bartlett, Architectural Pedagogy and Wates House: An Historical Study," 1–19.
4. Directed by Professor Jonathan Hill.
5. Mark Gelernter, *Sources of Architectural Form: A Critical History of Western Design Theory* (Manchester: Manchester University Press, 1994), 18.
6. Gelernter, *Sources of Architectural Form.*
7. Gelernter, *Sources of Architectural Form.*
8. Mario Carpo, *The Alphabet and the Algorithm* (Cambridge, MA: MIT Press, 2011).
9. Mario Carpo, *The Alphabet and the Algorithm.*
10. Andrea Palladio, *The Four Books on Architecture*, trans. Robert Tavernor and Richard Schofield (Cambridge, MA: MIT Press, 1997).
11. Rem Koolhaas, *Elements of Architecture*, ed. James Westcott and Stephan Petermann (Cologne: TASCHEN 2018).
12. Rem Koolhaas, *Delirious New York* (New York: Monacelli Press, 1994).
13. Jane Jacobs, *The Death and Life of Great American Cities* (New York: Random House, 1961).
14. Alison Smithson, "How to Recognise and Read Mat-Building: Mainstream Architecture as It Has Developed Towards the Mat-Building," *Architectural Design* (September 1974), 573–590.
15. These interconnections are computed by calculating the shortest paths between all pairs of streets and spaces. This analysis shows that the network of shortest paths in Venice crosses the squares indicating their strategic position in the pedestrian and aquatic system of movement. Sophia Psarra, *The Venice Variations: Tracing the Architectural Imagination* (London: UCL Press, 2018).
16. Sophia Psarra, *The Venice Variations.*
17. Sophia Psarra, *The Venice Variations.*
18. Sophia Psarra, *The Venice Variations.*
19. Nelson Goodman, "How Buildings Mean," *Critical Inquiry* 11, no. 4 (1985): 642–653.
20. Nelson Goodman, "How Buildings Mean," 642–653.
21. Marco Frascari, "Architectural Traces of an Admirable Cipher: Eleven in the Opus of Carlo Scarpa," *Nexus Executivo* (19 January 2004), 9-16.
22. Richard Murphy, Marherita Bolla, and Kenneth Framptom, eds., *Carlo Scarpa and Castelvecchio Revisited* (Edinburgh: Breakfast Mission Publishing, 2017).

Bibliography

Carpo, Mario. *The Alphabet and the Algorithm*. Cambridge, MA: MIT Press, 2011.

Frascari, Marco. "Architectural Traces of an Admirable Cipher: Eleven in the Opus of Carlo Scarpa." *Nexus Executivo* (19 January 2004), 9:16.

Goodman, Nelson. "How Buildings Mean." *Critical Inquiry* 11, no. 4 (1985): 642–653.

Gelernter, Mark. *Sources of Architectural Form: A Critical History of Western Design Theory.* Manchester: Manchester University Press, 1994.

Hillier, Bill and Julienne Hanson. *The Social Logic of Space*. Cambridge: Cambridge University Press, 1984.

Jacobs, Jane. *The Death and Life of Great American Cities*. New York: Random House, 1961.

Koolhaas, Rem. *Delirious New York*. New York: Monacelli Press, 1994.

———. *Elements of Architecture*, edited by James Westcott and Stephan Petermann. Cologne: Taschen, 2018.

Murphy, Richard, Margherita Bolla, and Kenneth Frampton. *Carlo Scarpa and Castelvecchio Revisited*. Edinburgh: Breakfast Mission Publishing, 2017.

Palladio, Andrea. *The Four Books on Architecture*, translated by Robert Tavernor and Richard Schofield. Cambridge, MA: MIT Press, 1997.

Psarra, Sophia. *The Venice Variations: Tracing the Architectural Imagination*. London: UCL Press, 2018.

Smithson, Alison. "How to Recognise and Read Mat-Building: Mainstream Architecture as It Has Developed Towards the Mat-Building." *Architectural Design* (September 1974), 573–590.

White, Amalie H. "The Bartlett, Architectural Pedagogy and Wates House: An Historical Study." *Opticon1826* 16 (2014): 1–19, DOI: http://dx.doi.org/10.5334/opt.ci.

CHAPTER 6

Architects Who Read, ILAUD, and Reading as Direct Experience

Elke Couchez

The city does not tell its past, but contains it like the lines of a hand, written in the corners of the streets, the gratings of the windows, the banisters of the steps, the antennae of the lightning rods, the poles of the flags, every segment marked in turn with scratches, indentations, scrolls.
—Italo Calvino, *Invisible Cities*

Introduction

This paper takes a historical approach to architecture's search for its own unique mode of intellectuality in the mid-1970s by focusing on the debate of reading as direct experience.[1] The tool of "reading" the city was central at the International Laboratory of Architecture and Urban Design (ILAUD), established in 1976 by Spazio e Società's founder Giancarlo De Carlo (1919–2005). This educational laboratory – an extension of Team X – invited students and acclaimed practitioners from different Western universities to rethink urban form. During ILAUD's formative years, the physical and social environment of Urbino functioned as a laboratory. All participants were invited to develop strategies for urban interventions based on a thorough understanding of the marks left by social, historical, and topographical transformations on the physical space.

It was a Monday evening: 29 August 1977. A group of students gathered in a room packed with white drawing boards and vacant exhibition walls (fig. 6.1). They had just flown in from different countries in Europe and from the United States, and they were welcomed with a generous wine and cheese party by the

ILAUD staff members. Throughout the year, all of the students had engaged in so-called 'permanent activities' and were now ready to start a highly ambitious eight-week residential summer course organised in situ in the Italian town of Urbino (fig. 6.2). Wearing wide-legged jeans, they waited for Giancarlo De Carlo to address them and to kick off the summer school.

In his opening speech, De Carlo vividly talked about the historical town of Urbino, which he knew like the back of his hand from his experience drafting the master plan of the city and the region (fig. 6.3–6.5). He briefly introduced the central themes of the summer school: "reuse" and "participation."[2] Some students might have noticed his agitation when he talked about the recent post-war developments in the city. Predominantly residential zones, as he told them, were jeopardised by an uncontrolled mix of developer-, state-, and university-sponsored buildings and consequently were disconnected from the historical town centre and the surrounding rural areas. De Carlo told them how such transformations of the physical space always reflect changes in society. He warned his public of mere historicism in the revitalisation of a historic city centre – and encouraged the students to enter into a dialogue between the history of the place and the users' needs. Urban form, he emphasised, could not be separated from social awareness.

The first four weeks of the residential course in Urbino were devoted to the exercise of "reading," which allowed the readers to extend their perspectives as much as possible:

> If one can read the great palimpsest of the city and the territory one is able to understand everything: the events that occurred through time, the history, the social and cultural development, the sense and the role of the organisational systems and of the architectural forms. But in order to read one needs to be able to look in the depth of the stratifications, to discover and select critically the most significant signs; one needs to design. Our design is "tentative," meaning that it does not seek for univocal solutions but to match confront the project area with series of hypotheses that unveil its substance and open up the process of its transformation; at the same time they "tempt" it and drive it to talk about its capacity of resisting to change, of how it can be changed in order to attain structures and forms that are appropriate to the circumstances and corresponding to the expectations.[3]

Reading thus was the proposed method to unravel an intricate web of relationships in the physical environment. The role of the designer, according to De Carlo, was to empathetically engage with – or read – the pre-existing layers of meaning and relationships and to articulate them through the activity of drawing.

Fig. 6.1 The ILAUD design studio.Archivio ILAUD, Biblioteca civica d'arte Luigi Poletti, Modena.

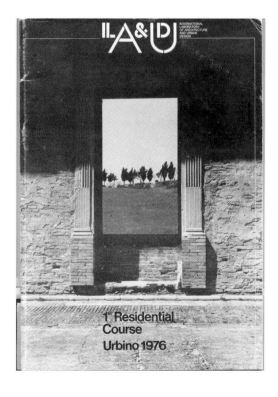

Fig. 6.2 Cover of the first ILAUD yearbook. Giancarlo De Carlo, *International Laboratory of Architecture and Design, 1st Residential Course Urbino 1976* (Urbino: ILAUD & Università di Urbino, 1977).

with the cultural atmosphere that could well form the corner-
stone for the Commune's economic recovery.

Apart from the main highways outside the city and the urban
street pattern itself, there is also a fragile network of secondary
roads serving the rural districts and linking Urbino with other
small communes nearby. In many places the roads are unsur-
faced and impassable in bad weather, thus isolating various parts
of the district even further and cutting off outlying communities
from the possible use of facilities the city has to offer. Poor road
communications also discourage provision of amenities in rural
areas, since to be an economical operation, community services
must be readily accessible to a sizeable number of people and
hence to a sufficiently large area in this era of rural depopulation.

**Elementary Education
Facilities**

Elementary-school facilities are a clear illustration of this last
problem. Throughout the Commune these institutions conform
with Italian legislation which requires compulsory attendance at
elementary school. In fact, no settlement is more than four kilo-
meters, as the crow flies, from a school. In recent years, the local
administration has made every effort to fill the major gaps in
school facilities, and superficially the situation might appear to

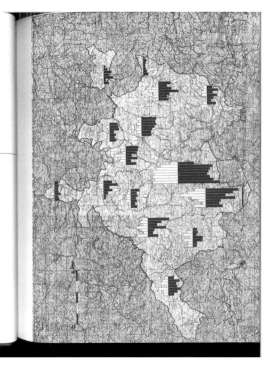

Survey of the territory

The south front of the Ducal Palace

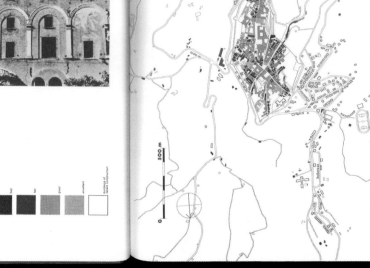

500 m

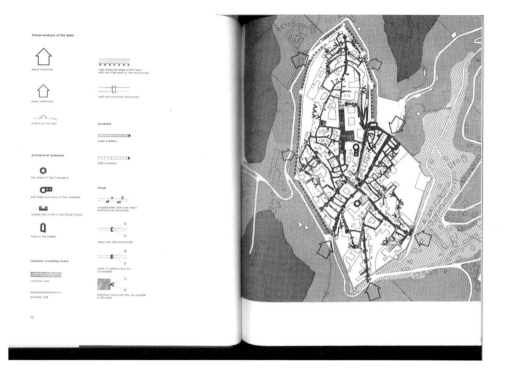

Fig. 6.3–6.5 Spreads from the book Giancarlo De Carlo, *Urbino. The History of a City and Plans for Its Development* (Cambridge MA: MIT Press, 1970). De Carlo's developed his master plan for Urbino from 1958 to 1964. First, De Carlo sent out a housing survey to Urbino's inhabitants to better view property, use, and activity of individual buildings. The housing survey results were then combined in a series of highly effective visual maps of the city and its region, showing the uses, needs, and "problem areas" at a glance. Finally, based on his maps, De Carlo made recommendations for mixed use of some areas and for which sections of the city should be renewed, with actions going from absolute preservation to renewal of individual buildings to renewal of group of buildings to demolition and rebuilding or demolition without rebuilding.

1. Challenges to Intellectual History

In the introduction of this volume, the editors make a plea for the understanding of architectural practice as a hybrid phenomenon, moving between observing, designing, and writing or between design and discourse. As pedagogical experiments played a crucial role in shaping architectural discourse, this paper travels to the heart of design education to analyse De Carlo's reading tool. Architecture historians have often been wary of studying the myriad of experiments and activities in the studio because, as James Elkins noted in *Our Beautiful, Dry, and Distant Texts: Art History as Writing*:

> personal and largely inarticulate discoveries made in the studio do not seem applicable to finished works that exist in history. Studio talks are riven by ungrammatical arguments, illogic, and nonverbal communication by gestures and marks that conspire to make it nearly illegible to philosophical inquiry.[4]

This paper argues that, if we want to understand architecture as a hybrid practice, we should not only look at how architects produce knowledge through design and writing but also through the day-to-day activities – such as teaching and reading – that structure architectural research and practice. As Edward Baring (2011) argues, these activities remain a relatively untapped and yet immediate context in intellectual history.[5] Though these activities are often overlooked in the core narratives of architectural theory – which primarily focus on published and finished texts – these activities have always been part and parcel of architectural practice. As Jorge Otero-Pailos rightly noted, there is no "mother tongue" in architectural intellectuality:

> Before the rise of what we now call architecture theory, these practices [practices of interpretations in the form of written documents, drawings, pictures or photo essays, movies, scaled models, full-scale buildings, exhibitions, class syllabi, teaching curricula, and countless other forms] were included in what was considered legitimate intellectual work in architecture, not something secondary to mental acts but as their primary source and governing standard."[6]

By looking at the tools developed in the design studio, the intellectual historian faces a massive challenge of mining work that is not finished and embracing the contingencies of architectural thought. This paper will unpack the tool of reading the city, not by looking at how students made it operational in their design proposals[7] (fig. 6.6–6.7), but by exploring the intellectual arena in which the tool was deployed. De Carlo's tool of reading the city first of all tied into a post–World War II debate on the illegibility of towns. Second, the tool enabled

and represented a critical stance vis-à-vis the figure of the architectural historian and traditional "linear" historiography. What can we learn from looking at
the role of the architect as a reader, rather than seeing the architect merely as a
producer of knowledge from a vanguard position?

2. Reading as a Design Act: From Reading to Legibility

In reassessing the design tool of reading the city, we must, first of all,
acknowledge that Giancarlo De Carlo's reflection on how to read urban form
in architectural education evolved within the post-war discourse on the
European city and the region.[8] Prompted by a general dissatisfaction with
universalistic modernist functionalist planning models and the imposition
of a priori visions upon the city – which arguably disregarded human needs
and neglected the existing historical, physical, and topographical factors of an
area – he, together with other architects, theorists, and educators turned to
the urban "real." [9] As a consequence of the modernist reductive functionalist
approach, the city had become "illegible." According to Nan Ellin in her review on post-war theories of urban design, this lack of legibility of post–World
War II landscapes "incited a desire for the familiar and issued a call for designing 'contextuality' with regards to historical and local contexts."[10] This
quest for contextuality was defined from different perspectives. European
neo-traditionalists resorted to a pre-industrial time – thus avoiding change –
whereas others made a strong call to "re-everything – rehabilitate, revitalise,
restore, renew, redevelop, recycle, renaissance, and so forth."[11] Thus, the tool
of reading was a method to "re" the illegible city and functioned as a corrective
to the blindsiding of urban problems in architecture. De Carlo felt comfortable
with the second perspective.

Though De Carlo showed a strong affinity with the Team X discourse and
invited its members – such as Peter Smithson and Aldo van Eyck – as keynote
speakers at ILAUD, the tool of reading can only be fully comprehended by
looking at the discourses of the interlocutors who were not invited to the summer school. The Italian proponents on the new urban dimension were notably
absent. As Micha Bandini noted in his reflection on architectural approaches
to urban form, "reading" was a central attitude in the 1960s and '70s debate
on urban morphology.[12] Proponents of the Venice School such as Aldo Rossi
and Carlo Aymonio developed a typo-morphological reading in which they
analysed the grammar of the city:

> trying to find "the fundamental types of habitat: the street, the arcade, the
> square, the yard, the quarter, the colonnade the avenue, the boulevard, the
> centre the nucleus, the crown, the knot [...] So that the city can be walked
> through. So that it becomes a text again. Clear. Legible." (Delevoy, 17)[13]

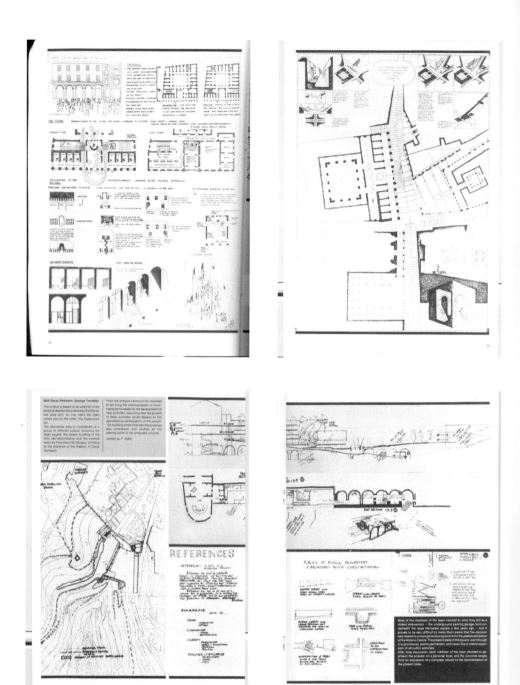

Fig. 6.6–6.7 Student works during the first Residential ILA&UD course in Urbino, illustrating the different implications of reading the city. Spreads from Giancarlo De Carlo, *International Laboratory of Architecture and Design, 1st Residential Course Urbino 1976* (Urbino: ILAUD & Università di Urbino, 1977).

Rather than imposing a model or lingua franca upon the city – as the modernists had done – these educators invited their students to read, decode, and interpret local types – or dialects as it were – and trace their historical formations. Yet, Giancarlo De Carlo carefully barred the work of these neo-nationalists from the ILAUD summer schools based on a semiotic discussion. Whereas for Rossi, types were timeless and could house different, consecutive functions, De Carlo instead believed that any change in function would also alter the type itself. [14] De Carlo thus criticised Rossi's readings of the city, for he too exclusively focused on the denotative level of signs – recognising their spatial existence – and ignored the intangible values or meanings attached to types. For De Carlo, the symbolic meaning thus had a continued existence over the functional meaning of a building.

Following from this semiotic argument, De Carlo held a different opinion on how these types should be made operational in design. Though Rossi and De Carlo both approached the city as a "living palimpsest" of past processes that could be traced or read, reading for De Carlo was not only an analytical tool but also a hermeneutical process at the basis of any design process at the basis of any design proposal. As Mark Blizard wrote:

> In practice, reading – an attempt to decipher the traces and marks within the landscape – was active and reciprocal. It involved not only analytical inquiry, but also the formulation of tentative propositions. Each proposal was provisional in that it took the form of a question that was founded on the gathered insights. These, in turn, furthered the investigation. By its very nature as dialogic, this process unfolded differently with each project undertaken. Essentially, it was a research strategy that was also, and at the same time, an engine for forming and testing provisional design solutions. [15]

3. Reading as Direct Experience: Epistemological Claims

Next to being a research strategy and a directive for design, De Carlo's reading tool also epitomised a 1970s disciplinary tension between architects and historians. We can, for instance, deduce this from De Carlo's statements on reading as a design approach: "It is an extraordinary proposition that a study of the places we inhabit offers a much truer and fuller tale than all the words which we conventionally define as 'history.'" [16] And he continued: "There are events that are not recorded in the archives and yet are embedded in the architectural forms and testify to the lengthy layering process over centuries." De Carlo – finding a theoretical bedrock in the writings of Christian Norberg-Schulz, who was a welcome guest speaker at the ILAUD residential courses – preferred the analysis of existing urban complexes through direct experience above the interpretation of maps or archival sources. Though he admitted that oral accounts or written documents had their value in architecture and planning processes, for him, these sources were subjective and fixed in the past. Urban form, he argued, could be registered in the physical realm directly and could give clues as to how to design for future use. [17]

Echoed in De Carlo's quotes is the nineteenth-century pedagogical concept of "lived" or "direct experience," which, as Zeynep Çelik wrote, reveals a deep-rooted belief in the existence of "a nondiscursive, nonconceptual way of knowing that could nonetheless compete in its rigour with reason realised through language, concepts or logic."[18] Reading was an attempt to retrieve an "essence" that was believed to be "truer than history or words," and thus involved a search for an architectural knowledge that was embedded in architectural and urban form. By promoting the tool of 'reading," De Carlo made a claim on history from within design practice and indirectly demoted textual history. It can thus be argued that this experiential tool of reading enabled and represented a critical stance vis-à-vis the figure of the architectural historian and traditional "linear" historiography. Herewith, De Carlo joined postmodernist discourses that gave rise to such historical awareness in the 1970s and 1980s and influenced architectural education at large.[19] Different architectural histories could now be sources of influence to the designing architect.

This disciplinary consciousness did not only play out in written texts but also in the tools which were used to understand urban form. In the works of De Carlo's contemporaries such as Alison and Peter Smithson, Aldo Rossi and Vittorio Gregotti, direct analyses of urban form through plans often displaced texts.[20] As Andrew Leach wrote:

> History is not removed from the spectrum of concerns for the fields of criticism aligned with planning, but rather treated as a present contextual condition, along lines similar to the treatment of history by modern architecture, but without the confusion introduced by the manufactured detachment of its writers. They interrogate the past as one dimension of a specific site of enquiry in present in order to propose an idea for the future from a thoroughly considered present. Urban typology and the conception of architectural form are thus drawn together in practice where analysis informs the plan.[21]

For De Carlo, engaging with history through architecture was not without obligation. Underlying this focus on "direct experience" was a solid hope to develop architectural projects committed to matters concerning society at large. De Carlo, whose line of thought can be related to anarchist thinking of, for instance, Colin Ward, had stressed that history "does not concern itself with the past but with the present and it gives direction to the future."[22] In fact, the Italian scene was strongly marked by this question to which extent history had the potential to "be committed." As Karla Keyvanian noted, the 1960s and '70s architectural discourse in Italy was strongly coloured by the left-wing ideas of Gramsci and Benedetto Croce, who demanded a history that was "alive" or aimed at social change. This idea permeated all De Carlo's work, and especially his educational project in Urbino.[23]

Conclusion: The Predicaments and Dialectics of Reading

De Carlo's approach to reading can be interpreted as emblematic for what Tafuri called "operative history" in his 1968 work *Theories and History*. The risk of this approach is that the reading would deform or distort the past to achieve future goals. Tafuri, at all costs, would say that there is no ready-made solution for urban form to be found in its history. How, then, should we evaluate this tool of reading in an educational context?

Architectural Knowledge Is Mediated by the Tools We Employ

De Carlo's understanding of traditional history is dubious. He denounced the positivistic faith in the truthfulness in archival documents, but replaced it with a faith in the truthfulness or "essence" of urban forms. De Carlo seemed to succumb to the temptation of replacing one way of gaining knowledge with another. The implied opposition between contemplative intellectual pursuit fixated on the past and design action oriented to the future is untenable in today's discourse where architecture is instead seen as a hybrid practice able to overcome such contrived divides. As Çelik Alexander wrote, even tools based on the notion of direct experience are "accompanied by strict protocols that dictated another kind of order and syntax upon what was imagined as unmediated lived experience."[24] In other words, even direct experience is mediated by the tools we employ. There is thus a need to critically reassess the pedagogical tools in our studio-based education and to question their implied knowledge claims and embodied disciplinary tensions and divides.

Reading Stimulates an Empathetic Design Approach

Having zoomed in on the intellectual Italian context in which the tool of reading could emerge, reading can be considered a response to the alienation engendered by post-war urban environments. Staged in binary opposition to textual history, the tool and its underlying pedagogy of direct experience upheld a promise of a more democratic and participatory way of perceiving the built environment. De Carlo's aim for ILAUD was not to develop clear-cut solutions for problem areas in the city of Urbino but to test tools for urban inquiry in order to evolve to a committed or empathetic architectural practice. It is this coupling of reading and empathy that can inspire educators in today's studios.

In Giancarlo De Carlo's speech, the relation between reading and architectural design remained unresolved. The tool of reading did not offer the students
a toolkit for design – or for the "writing" of place. I would go as far as to say
that the educational potential lies precisely in this conundrum between reading and writing. Almost simultaneous to the organisation of the first ILAUD
summer schools, Roland Barthes, Michel Foucault, and Umberto described
reading as a dialectical and interpretative process.[25] The meaning of the text,
they argued, could no longer be reduced to the author's intentions but is plural.
Or, as Barthes wrote in 1977:

> The Text is not a co-existence of meanings but a passage, an overcross-
> ing; thus, it answers not to an interpretation, even a liberal one, but to an
> explosion, a dissemination. [...] What he [the reader] perceives is mul-
> tiple, irreducible, coming from a disconnected, heterogeneous variety of
> substances and perspectives: lights, colours, vegetation, heat, air, slender
> explosions of noises, scant cries of birds, children's voices from over on
> the other side, passages, gestures, clothes of inhabitants near or far away.
> All these incidents are half-identifiable: they come from codes which are
> known but their combination is unique, founds the stroll in a difference
> repeatable only as difference.[26]

The tool of reading enables an empathetic attitude in today's design education.
Empathy, as Sarah Robinson noted, is the capacity to

> perceive the experience of others through the tissue of our own bod-
> ies – regardless of whether those others are persons, creatures, places or
> things – is a dynamic pattern of relationship that extends our awareness
> of the multi-layered emotional latency inhering in the situation. Empathy
> expands the domain of the personal to encompass the felt experience of
> the other.[27]

As a pedagogical tool, reading thus stimulates a gentler and contextually responsive design. It can be applied as an exercise in recognising cultural and historical
diversity and in identifying the intangible values of urban forms in the city's
text. There is no writing before reading in architectural practice.

Notes

1. A first version of this text was presented at the SPACE International Conference on 20 November 2020 and published in the e-proceedings: https://spacestudies.co.uk/product/ebook-e-proceedings-space-international-conferences-november-2020/. This chapter is a heavily revised and extended version. I wish to thank the editors of this book for their suggestions for improving this chapter.

2. Giancarlo De Carlo, "Introduction: Comments on the Design Work," in *International Laboratory of Architecture and Design, 2nd Residential Course Urbino 1976* (Urbino: ILAUD and Università di Urbino, 1977), 5.

3. Giancarlo de Carlo, quoted in https://www.ilaud.org/category/about/ (accessed 8 May 2021).

4. James Elkins, *Our Beautiful, Dry and Distant Texts: Art History as Writing* (New York: Routledge, 2000), 13.

5. Edward Baring, *The Young Derrida and French Philosophy, 1945–1968* (Cambridge: Cambridge University Press, 2011), 223. I also developed this argument in a paper that I wrote together with Rajesh Heynickx and Hilde Heynen: Elke Couchez, Rajesh Heynickx, and Hilde Heynen, "Tracing the Avant-Texte of Architectural Theory: The Paul Felix Case," *History of Intellectual Culture* 11 (2016): 2–27.

6. Ibid., xii.

7. This was the focus in another paper: Elke Couchez, "Reading the City by Drawing. Tentative Design as an Educational Tool for Urban Regeneration in the 1977 ILAUD Summer Course," *OASE 107 - The Drawing in Landscape Design and Urbanism*, edited by Bart Decroos, Frits Palmboom, and Bruno Notteboom (2020): 39–48. This paper showed the different and often contradictory implementations of this method of reading by drawing. Reading by drawing was by no means a self-contained analytical tool that covered all layers of complexity, but a deliberately tentative design approach that fed from the hinge between interpretation and projection.

8. For a deeper discussion on the theoretical debates on the urban in architecture, see Mary Louise Lobsinger, "The New Urban Scale in Italy," *Journal of Architectural Education* 59, no. 3 (2006): 28–38.

9. Benedict Zucchi and Giancarlo De Carlo, *Giancarlo De Carlo* (Oxford: Butterworth Architecture, 1992), 5.

10. Nan Ellin, *Postmodern Urbanism* (New York: Princeton Architectural Press, 1999), 16.

11. Ellin, *Postmodern Urbanism,* 18.

12. Micha Bandini, "Some Architectural Approaches to Urban Form," in *Urban Landscapes: International Perspectives*, ed. J. W. R. Whitehand and Peter J. Larkham (Hove: Psychology Press, 1992), 115.

13. Ellin, *Postmodern Urbanism*, 23. The focus on defining a typology of the city was also central in the work of Kevin Lynch, who tried to improve the legibility of the city by making it imageable. The student works developed during the formative ILAUD years show a strong affiliation with this Lynchean approach. See Couchez, "Reading the City by Drawing."

14. See Nesbitt's introduction to Rossi's text "An Analogical Architecture," in Kate Nesbitt, *Theorizing a New Agenda for Architecture: An Anthology of Architectural Theory, 1965–1995* (New York: Princeton Architectural Press, 1996), 345. Whereas Rossi would take a structuralist view on morphological types as for instance expressed by Claude Lévi-Strauss, De Carlo rather followed Eco's semiotic approach.

15. Mark Blizard, "Discursive Design: The Discourse of the Built Work of Giancarlo De Carlo in Urbino, Italy," *The International Journal of the Constructed Environment* 9, no. 1 (2018): 40.

16. John McKean and Giancarlo De Carlo, *Giancarlo De Carlo: Layered Places* (Fellbach: Edition Axel Menges, 2004), 48.

17. McKean and De Carlo, *Layered Places*, 48.
18. Zeynep Çelik Alexander, *Kinaesthetic Knowing: Aesthetics, Epistemology, Modern Design* (Chicago University of Chicago Press, 2017), 11.
19. In his manifesto *Complexity and Contradiction* (1966), Robert Venturi for instance advocated for an architecture that was "more historically informed but not addressed to history per se." This attitude was only one among a diversity of attitudes towards the past, as became clear during the Venice Biennale *Presence of the Past* of 1980. For further reading, see Léa-Catherine Szacka, "Historicism Versus Communication: The Basic Debate of the 1980 Biennale," *Architectural Design* 81, no. 5 (1 September 2011): 98–105.
20. Andrew Leach, "Choosing History: A Study of Manfredo Tafuri's Theorisation of Architectural History and Architectural History Research" (PhD dissertation, Ghent, UGent, 2005), 78.
21. Leach, "Choosing History," 78.
22. Raman P.G., "Libertarian Themes in the Work of Giancarlo De Carlo," *Ekistics* (July/August–November/December 1998): 104.
23. Carla Keyvanian, "Manfredo Tafuri: From the Critique of Ideology to Microhistories," *Design Issues* 16, no. 1 (1 March 2000): 3–15.
24. Çelik Alexander, *Kinaesthetic Knowing*, 22.
25. Michel Foucault, "Qu'est -Ce Qu'un Auteur?," 1969, http://1libertaire.free.fr/MFoucault319.html; Roland Barthes, *Image Music Text* (London: Fontana Press, 1977); Umberto Eco, *The Role of the Reader: Explorations in the Semiotics of Texts* (Bloomington: Indiana University Press, 1979).
26. Barthes, *Image Music Text*, 159.
27. Sarah Robinson, "Boundaries of Skin: John Dewey, Didier Anzieu and Architectural Possibility," in *Architecture and Empathy* (Espoo: Tapio Wirkkala – Rut Bryk Foundation, 2015), 48.

Bibliography

Bandini, Micha. "Some Architectural Approaches to Urban Form." In *Urban Landscapes: International Perspectives*, edited by J. W. R. Whitehand and Peter J. Larkham, 133–162. Hove: Psychology Press, 1992.

Baring, Edward. *The Young Derrida and French Philosophy, 1945–1968*. Cambridge: Cambridge University Press, 2011.

Barthes, Roland. *Image Music Text*. London: Fontana Press, 1977.

Blizard, Mark. "Discursive Design: The Discourse of the Built Work of Giancarlo De Carlo in Urbino, Italy." *The International Journal of the Constructed Environment* 9, no. 1 (2018): 37–56.

Çelik Alexander, Zeynep. *Kinaesthetic Knowing: Aesthetics, Epistemology, Modern Design*. Chicago: University of Chicago Press, 2017.

Couchez, Elke. "Reading the City by Drawing. Tentative Design as an Educational Tool for Urban Regeneration in the 1977 ILAUD Summer Course." In *OASE 107 – The Drawing in Landscape Design and Urbanism*, edited by Bart Decroos, Frits Palmboom, and Bruno Notteboom, 39–48. Rotterdam: OASE Foundation, 2020.

Couchez, Elke, Rajesh Heynickx, and Hilde Heynen. "Tracing the Avant-Texte of Architectural Theory: The Paul Felix Case." *History of Intellectual Culture* 11 (2016): 2–27.

De Carlo, Giancarlo. "Introduction: Comments on the Design Work." In *International Laboratory of Architecture and Design, 2nd Residential Course Urbino 1976*. Urbino: ILAUD and Università di Urbino, 1977.

———. *Urbino. The History of a City and Plans for Its Development*. Cambridge, MA: MIT Press, 1970.

Eco, Umberto. *The Role of the Reader: Explorations in the Semiotics of Texts*. Bloomington: Indiana University Press, 1979.

Elkins, James. *Our Beautiful, Dry and Distant Texts: Art History as Writing*. London: Routledge, 2000.

Ellin, Nan. *Postmodern Urbanism*. New York: Princeton Architectural Press, 1999.

Foucault, Michel. "Qu'est -Ce Qu'un Auteur?" 1969. http://1libertaire.free.fr/Mfoucault319.html.

Keyvanian, Carla. "Manfredo Tafuri: From the Critique of Ideology to Microhistories." *Design Issues* 16, no. 1 (1 March 2000): 3–15.

Leach, Andrew. "Choosing History: A Study of Manfredo Tafuri's Theorisation of Architectural History and Architectural History Research." PhD dissertation, UGent, 2005.

Lobsinger, Mary Louise. "The New Urban Scale in Italy." *Journal of Architectural Education* 59, no. 3 (2006): 28–38.

McKean, John and Giancarlo De Carlo. *Giancarlo De Carlo: Layered Places*. Fellbach: Edition Axel Menges, 2004.

Nesbitt, Kate. *Theorising a New Agenda for Architecture: An Anthology of Architectural Theory, 1965–1995*, 1st ed. New York: Princeton Architectural Press, 1996.

Raman, P.G., "Libertarian Themes in the Work of Giancarlo De Carlo," *Ekistics* July/August–November/December (1998): 391–393.

Robinson, Sarah. "Boundaries of Skin: John Dewey, Didier Anzieu and Architectural Possibility." In *Architecture and Empathy*, 42–63. Espoo, Finland: Tapio Wirkkala – Rut Bryk Foundation, 2015.

Szacka, Léa-Catherine. "Historicism Versus Communication: The Basic Debate of the 1980 Biennale." *Architectural Design* 81, no. 5 (1 September 2011): 98–105.

Zucchi, Benedict and Giancarlo De Carlo. *Giancarlo De Carlo*. Oxford: Butterworth Architecture, 1992.

PART 2

Reciprocal Negotiations: Teaching Architecture

In Part 2, the demands of teaching involve identifying a curriculum, that is the subject matter and skills to be imparted, and also the pedagogical methods for doing this. Each of the first three essays in this section are written by an architect who is also a teacher, and the subjects and approaches they take give insights into their creative practice. They explore how the two-way communication between teacher and student evolves into a fertile negotiation around the subjective interpretations of drawings, objects, and processes of design. Using their course Structural Contingencies as a subject, Caroline Voet and Steven Schenck develop a deep historical context for their teaching, which proposes a rereading of the material and structural details of architecture in defining the atmosphere and character of the spaces they enclose. Acknowledging the importance of Christian Kieckens, this exploration of the relationship between sensuous experience and conceptual understanding uses his concept of "Buildingness" to link research to design practice. Rosamund Diamond looks at examples used in her own teaching when she identifies three different drawing types as tools for design and communication. These are the figure-ground drawing as embodied in the Nolli Plan, 1748; the figure-ground projection using an example by Rafael Moneo, 1984; and Eileen Gray's developed surface drawings from the late 1920s. By constructing concepts that associate the intentions and tasks of their progenitors with their potential uses in pedagogic and design contexts, she proposes new meanings for and ways of understanding the drawings in relation to the objects they represent. Thomas Coward makes connections between consultation strategies used in his own architectural practice, which involve conversations around memory and everyday objects, and how these inform his teaching in relation to a reading of his lived experience of Charles Moore's Unit 9, where he used observation and drawing to record how different subjective spatial and temporal realities can resonate in the objects they contain.

Chapters 10 and 11 start not from a written argument, but from a series of sketches and models as tools that anchored theoretical reflections within the design studio. "The Unfinished Sketch" was written following a series of conversations between Louis Mayes and Philip Christou, former co-director with Florian Beigel of the Architecture Research Unit (ARU). A hand-drawn sketch by Beigel of a Korean *Pojagi* formulates the lines of thought through which the cyclical relationship between design and theory unfolds towards a new design and towards the student work in the design studio. The paper explores how this form of drawing remains inherently a product of both the hand and the mind – an intuitive response of the designer that may encompass the key concepts, histories, and spatial qualities of the project. Sereh Mandias gives an insight into the tools of her and Tomas Dirrix's studio at the Chair of Interiors Buildings Cities at TU Delft, unfolding an intimate encounter with a series of 1:5 large models. The models are used as an instrument to examine the architectural qualities of the existing Museum Boijmans van Beuningen in Rotterdam and subsequently as a basis for architectural interventions within the museum. Neither detail nor space, the tactile approach of the 1:5 scale fosters empathy with the museum ensemble.

CHAPTER 7

Lost and Found: Intuition and Precision into Architectural Design, Studio Structural Contingencies KU Leuven, 2016–2021

Caroline Voet, Steven Schenk

Architecture is the essential being of building.
Other forms come into being, they are not created.
—Christian Kieckens (1951–2020), "Buildingness," 2002[1]

Ever since Leon Battista Alberti's conceptualisation of architectural design in the fifteenth century, according to which a building is an identical copy of the architect's design,[2] the role of analytical drawings or preliminary design sketches and models to explore principles of a space, a building, or a city remained crucial. The designing architect who analyses, sketches, and makes models is not merely a creator of spaces that elicit aesthetic responses. The act of designing is equally a research trajectory where the architect tries to capture social relations, as such, enabling the building's position within contemporary society and architectural culture. The constant fostering of one's own intuition as well as the critical questioning of a defined precision within this research is at the heart of the KU Leuven research platform and Master Studios Structural Contingencies.[3] Its members' PhD subjects, such as Dom Hans van der Laan (Caroline Voet), Kunio Maekawa (Hera Van Sande), Henri Labrouste (Eireen Schreurs), Sigurd Lewerentz (Steven Schenk) or Paul Neefs and Alfons Hoppenbrouwers (Laura Lievevrouw), embark on unravelling the processes of designing architects. To position the approach of the Structural Contingencies programme within architectural research, more specifically the studios led by the authors Caroline Voet and Steven Schenk, this paper critically explores its roots and traditions on architectural imagination and creation, mediating between sensuous experience and conceptual understanding. Although intuition is cherished as an instinctive feeling that drives the designing hand as a primary tool, designing in the studio is not a merely artistic

Fig. 7.1 Design for a funerary chapel, digital collage of model photography, by Joke Oelbrandt, student in the Studio Territory of Imagination II. Ma2 Structural Contingencies 2019–2020. Starting from Scarpa's architecture, the building engages in an ambivalent relationship between structure and space.

Fig. 7.2 Design for a funerary chapel, model of inner spaces, scale 1:20, by Matthis Adam, student in the Studio Territory of Imagination I. Ma2 Structural Contingencies 2018–2019. The shifting angle of the layered interior spaces is based on the changing perspective in the Abbey of Thoronet. This gradual shift cannot be seen when moving through the inside; it can only be perceived.

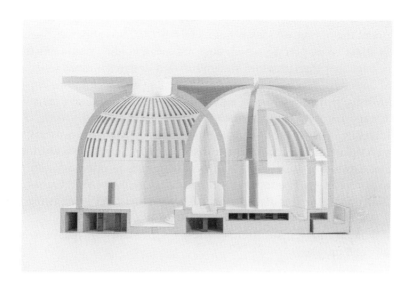

Fig. 7.3 Design for thermal baths, a model as section, scale 1:20, by Tigone Priem and Lore Delputte, students in the Studio Territory of Imagination I. Ma2 Structural Contingencies 2018–2019. Interlocking geometrical spaces, creating irregular interlocking thresholds, based on John Soane's Bank of England.

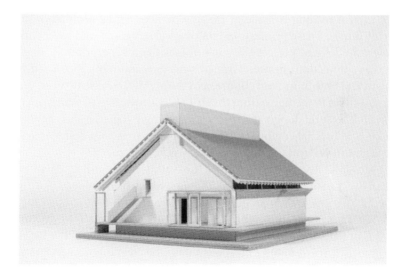

Fig. 7.4 Design for a museum for architecture, model scale 1:20, by Wietse De Cooman, student in the Studio Territory of Imagination I. Ma2 Structural Contingencies 2018–2019. Architectural elements are objectified to create a new language, inspired by Heinz Bienefeld.

activity, and the output we seek is not merely artistic. It is about architecture and it is about being precise, which does not mean holding onto one's frame of knowledge that then provides straightforward design solutions to straightforward questions. Precision means the sharpening of one's intuition through the knowledge gained by reading and looking, which creates an extensive internal library that feeds the imagination with hybrid analogies.

Addressing the influence of our mentor Christian Kieckens, we start with his abstract plan analysis of Borromini in relation to Scarpa. It is ahistorical, but it belongs to a tradition, one that now continues in our work and especially in our teaching. The input of Otto Friedrich Bollnow, Paul Frankl, and James Ackerman, as well as dialogues with Eireen Schreurs, Wilfried Wang, and Sophia Psarra throughout the process of editing this book, have stimulated new lines of thought and insights. Architecture is a secret language that we seek to demystify and unravel.

Reading Architecture I. The Autonomous, Abstract Composition

The focus of the Structural Contingencies programme is on architectural language and involves the rereading of material and structural details in their relation to the experience of the spaces they enclose. Students work from the structural detail and the interior to the urban fabric, by (re)drawing and (re)modelling. To formulate design strategies, whether for new buildings or for reuse, a careful reading is made of existing pioneering, vernacular, or primitive architectures. These primary and ontological structures and spaces aim to fuel new attitudes and projects through mimesis and superposition. The aim is to reveal connections between design strategies and tools abstracted from their historical time frame and culture, and the architectural structures, spaces, and atmospheres that emerge from them. This ahistorical lens, which operates through architectural design and its creative methodologies, is then applied in the design studios, challenging students to develop a conscious design intention. How does intuition work, and where does precision come in?

The studio is deeply rooted within the tradition of the Belgian architect Christian Kieckens's approach of Buildingness, which he developed as a design attitude, linking research to architectural practice.[4] Architecture as a practical process is granted a certain autonomy from cultural considerations, and in this sense, it is understood as an ontological structure and a space to live in. From that perspective, it is granted its responsibility: the creation of an architectural identity as a cultural object. Identity has nothing to do with style or form but with the circumstances of "place" and "attitude," nor is it an "alien" expression but rather the recovering of an authentic material language. To operate beyond personalised contradictory formal(istic) themes – self-referential as well as unique or formalistic – the studio fosters an awareness of design traditions

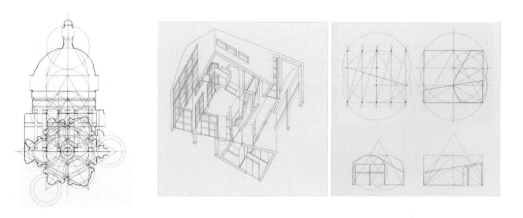

Fig. 7.5 Left: Christian Kieckens, superimposition of a symmetrical aerial photograph and a precise line drawing of a geometric analysis of Francesco Borromini's San Carlo alle Quattro Fontane, 1983. Right: Christian Kieckens, first proposal for the house in Baardegem (1990). Pages from: Christian Kieckens, "Form is One Function too" (1993): 8, 14–15.

throughout history. From this, critical insights in linguistic expressions are generated: new programme typologies, materials, techniques, and the workings of space. This expertise provides a building with its form through a dialogue with existing conditions and ideas, from an accurate engagement with facts and things and from the specificities of a place and society at large. The language of architecture disposes of an inherent logic and structure linked strongly to an awareness of it within building. "Every intelligent handling of data, every further reform from a rediscovery, results in the essence of the concept of 'traditio': a further development based on existing achievements. Building on that tradition is what architects should do," was fundamental for Kieckens: "Building is dealing with accuracies, of material, of proportion, of the relationship with the earth, of technology, of a span. Architecture is the result of an intelligent handling of that accuracy."[5]

Kieckens's observations on architectural space, from that of Borromini to Scarpa, are based on an analysis through the abstract image of plan, section, and facade. This type of architectural analysis has its roots in the idealist criticism and gestalt psychology of German late nineteenth-century philosophy. The historical line of spatial concepts that developed from there starts with art and architecture critic Heinrich Wölfflin's *Renaissance und Barock* (1888) and continues through to his pupils Paul Frankl's *Principles of Architectural History* (1914), Rudolf Wittkower's *Architectural Principles in the Age of Humanism* (1949), Sigfried Giedion's *Space, Time and Architecture* (1941), and then to Wittkower's pupil Colin Rowe, who in his turn influenced theorists like Richard Eisenman through publications including "The Mathematics of the Ideal Villa" (1947) and "Transparency, Literal and Phenomenal" (1963).[6] Each in their own

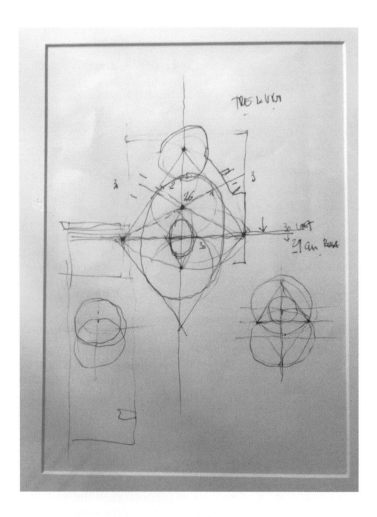

Fig. 7.6 Tre et Uno Assieme (plan, section, and facade as one) by Christian Kieckens and geometric pattern of the San Carlo alle Quattro Fontane by Francesco Borromini. Starting from a 26:30 proportion, two triangles are drawn. From the centre of their perpendiculars, two inscribed circles are defined. From the same anchor points, two overlapping circles are drawn, which define the inscribed geometry of the whole Borrominian systematic. Sketch with black pen on A4 paper, made for an interview with MA students from KU Leuven, Faculty of Architecture Studio Fragile, 19 December 2014, tutors: Caroline Voet and Carl Bourgeois. See: "The Thinking Hand," in Caroline Voet, Sofie De Caigny, Lara Schrijver, and Katrien Vandermarliere, eds., *Autonomous Architecture in Flanders. The Early Works of Marie-José Van Hee, Christian Kieckens, Marc Dubois, Paul Robbrecht and Hilde Daem* (Antwerp: Flanders Architecture Institute, 2016): 44–47. Sketch: Caroline Voet, private archive.

right revolutionised our understanding of geometry, modular pattern, and the ways in which plans are used to explain the work of an architect. Disinvested from the complexities of history, they invested in an abstract and intellectual approach towards the work of a given architect who could offer a coherent investigation surrounding perspective, proportion, geometry, and the advent of ideal form in architecture.

Within the vocabulary of the designing architect, applying this technique of reading an existing building gradually becomes incorporated, superimposed, or translated within their own design ideas. Where the schemes are directed towards a certain precision in composition, measurements, and proportion, their essential nature comes into being through the intuitive understanding of how the space works and functions. Reading a building or a drawing takes time. The slow process of going beyond looking towards actually understanding as an architect spans successive sessions of measuring, sketching, digital drawing, photographing, or model making. In the same way, when trained, a swift sketch by hand has the power to grasp the essence of a building with only a few defining lines. Only when this process is superimposed with attempts to name what one sees in order to find the right terminology that describes what it is, how it functions, and why, this type of close reading bridges artistic and scientific research.

In this sense, the process of reading a building is not so different from the process of creating one. Buildings are mosaics of accidents, adaptations, adjustments, additions, subtractions, revisions, and other errors.[7] But where drawings of abstract, autonomous building principles are often directed towards an idealised version, the design process is a messy one. One of the oldest demonstrations is Palladio's *The Four Books on Architecture*, in which the adjustments he made to some of his built projects so as to meet site contingencies are corrected in the new drawings to match an idealised version of design.[8] In the same manner, the archetypal models of walls, rooms, and buildings in Dom Hans van der Laan's book *Architectonic Space* exemplify philosophical spatial concepts.[9] His design sketches and building plans obsessively follow exact hierarchies with units and proportions that culminate in measurements specified in centimetres. Even when drawing a building of 175 metres long, each single centimetre mattered. Nevertheless, Van der Laan's models do not demystify the way his buildings draw you inside when you experience them. Clarity and a visible hierarchy between the whole and the parts seem to disappear within a never-ending layered composition made through an austere materiality, elementary colours, or precise daylight infiltration.[10] Besides composition, they equally formulate the syntax, the language of architectural form. Questions arise around its treatment of mass and surface, and of light, colour, and other optical effects in relation to spatial concepts that capture experience and have meaning and engagement with society at large.

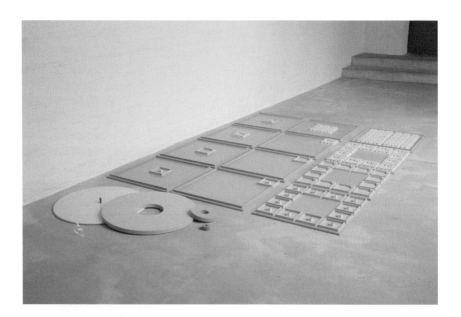

Fig. 7.7 Dom Hans van der Laan, Wooden models, 1982, made for the travelling exhibition starting at Bonnefanten Museum Maastricht. © Van der Laan Archives. Van der Laan sought for the space that we involve in our existence through movement. The scale and hierarchy of architectonic space is constructed as such that it is in a superposition with the intuitive thresholds of one's experience. Three experience fields surround one's body: the workspace (the length of one's body projected outwards, the scale of one room), the walking space, and the visual field. Van der Laan translated these directly into architecture: cella, court, domain. These become architectonic when one arises through the other.

Fig. 7.8 Dom Hans van der Laan, Roosenberg Abbey in Waasmunster, Belgium, 1974. Oblique perspective from one of the dark interstitial spaces towards the cloister. Rotation in plan is based on a mathematical figure extending the wing by root 26:5. See Caroline Voet, *Dom Hans van der Laan. A House for the Mind. A design manual on Roosenberg Abbey*. (Antwerp: Flanders Architecture Institute, 2017). © Photograph: Jeroen Verrecht.

Reading Architecture II. Sensing Hidden Anatomy

All the senses are engaged intensively when moving through Dom Hans van der Laan's Roosenberg Abbey. In a similar way, Sigurd Lewerentz's St. Peter's Church draws its inhabitant into its presence through techniques of deformation and inclination inflicted upon the walls and the floor of the church. The result is the experience of a simple, archaic space despite, or unerringly through, the specificity of these well-chosen elements, carefully drawn by hand in series of detailed drawings.[11] These ingredients constitute this space as an autonomous and whole entity with an appearance that is absent of expression, appearing as a condensed and essential simple cube-like space. Lewerentz seems to have found the precision in these elements' expression and intensity to allow the human mind to conceive of their effects in a way that they are active, but at the same time remain silent. They do not become overtly present within the observer's consciousness, unless actively sought. Lewerentz worked with details that are conceived and made with great precision, and do not contribute to a more excessive or ornamented and distracting whole. How can we understand this sublime experience of architecture that made Lewerentz into the mystic architect he is known for?

Answers to this question can be sought in the lived experience of the space and how materials and light appear at different times of the day. The character of darkness and the attitude of light in the interior space of the church generate a framework for the reduction of detail.[12] Here, the light is not a Louis Kahn–like substance that lets the space come into being through its material quality, but it is flattening the hierarchy between source and surface so that they become equal players. Because of this performance in simultaneity, the idea of the building as a whole can relate to a much larger area of our perception. If all elements appear similarly important, our kinaesthetic selves immediately take over from our eyes and read the floor more strongly. The visual is no longer the primary sense through which the building is experienced, and the other senses are stimulated by the building in a special way.

To give an example, in the drawings of Swiss architects Raphael Zuber and Helena Brobäck a sophisticated detail can be seen, in which the bricks of the top lights are laid askew so that no light enters the church directly. This creates a contrast to the windows on the walls, which create a backlight so that the contours of the walls dissolve, and the ceiling and space as such, as a spiritual place, become more important.[13] This effect is emphasised by the almost centred steel column that reinforces the central movement and builds a contrast to the more directional character of the ceiling.

All these details are something else when they are seen without context and become something different when they are all experienced simultaneously. Moreover, they interact with each other through their contradictions and tensions so that, for example, the position of the observer, but also sensual stimuli like music or change of light due to time and weather, can make a whole different building.[14] The fact that Lewerentz was frequently present at the construction sites is due to his endeavour to tacitly understand subtle elements as being built parts, as well as their mutual relationship to the whole. This interest in the training of the senses is evident in Lewerentz's earlier experimental photographs taken during his trip to Italy seventy-five years earlier. [15]

Fig. 7.9   Sigurd Lewerentz, Sankt Petri Kyrka, Klippan Sweden, 1968. This building is a manifesto in the way it is made: the connection between walls, floors, and ceilings are micro-topographical worlds of excessive craftmanship. The ceiling reveals a sympathy towards local vernacular farm buildings. The church becomes a space with linear and directional character, because the inclination is given a sense of organisation. © Steven Schenk.

Fig. 7.10 Slightly shifted from the middle of the space stands the steel column, which, depending on the location of the observer, has the potential to influence the directional character of the ceiling and give the space a more central movement. © Steven Schenk.

Fig. 7.11 Masonry detail, St. Mark's Church, Bjorkhagen Sweden, 1960. Experimenting with deformation from a straight to a vaulted expression. © Steven Schenk.

But let us focus on the potential of contradiction that these details or ingredients have. If we are affected by the slightest change in their appearance, it is the active character of our interpretation that can radically reorient each understanding of the whole. This active collaboration between observer and building affects the intimate coexistence of our senses in such a way that the result can communicate instantly different realities from the same source. If architecture is the separation between interior and exterior, there is no thinner line able to contribute to something more versatile. It becomes a mechanism that creates multiple perceptions from only one stimulus, as the famous duck-rabbit drawing that amazed Ludwig Wittgenstein so enormously. The light in the building – made by the building – becomes a part of the architecture itself, as it is removed from the conditions of time. It seems that, in this place of enchantment, the territory of our reality dwells.

Within our own architectural practice and our teaching, we seek these occurrences that reveal the discrepancies between our senses that cannot be grasped directly in analytical plan drawings. We wonder how these ingredients can be found, and why they seem ineffable within our present-day methodical tools in architecture. Our design studio starts from this notion of *sense* as a way to read and understand existing phenomena and classify their potential by judging their relationship with our imagination. We try to study them through modelling, photography, drawing (by hand), and collage. We go on a quest to understand why, how, and when these things appear in order to collect and compare these ungraspable encounters. How can we reveal their hidden anatomy, and how to revive them actively in producing architecture?

This element of architectural learning and education plays a crucial part in the creation of an architecture rooted in the dialogue between our imagination and the real. To formulate new architectural strategies, the studio challenges a dialogue with tradition by framing mysteriousness with directness (and intuition with precision). It is directly asking the students to reveal the potential relevance of a given phenomenon in reality for our imagination. When designing, architecture is about discovering, recovering, uncovering, and about recognising the potential in images and drawings without a dislocation from its potential in built reality. This "return to the object" of the past addresses its logos, gravity, stratification, and tectonics through experience first, and from that precision, it addresses functional or cultural considerations. It aims at engendering a deep reading of the complexities of expression. Students search for buildings that embody these other ingredients, aiming to describe the immediate causes for the deliverance of architectural spaces that foster this reality. As such, they frame and redraw the etymological base and linguistic approach and *Stimmung, m*eaning mood and atmosphere at the same time, rooted in a place. Seen from its own context of techniques, construction, and materials, the contextual phenomenon is reconstructed in its idea and relocated in a more universal pattern of thought.

Fig. 7.12 Folded beam of a roof structure, model in concrete. Cultural Centre Lokeren, competition design, not executed, Architect Juliaan Lampens, approx. 1960. "Auto-stability" (as defined by structural engineer Guy Mouton in a studio critique, February 2020): the structure is not added; it is embodied in the form itself. Human shelter at its most basic form. When the architectural detail is not decided yet, deciding upon that exact ontological moment amid a myriad of structural contingencies. Course leaders: Caroline Voet, Eireen Schreurs. Students: Wouter Persyn, Marie Van Parys, Guillaume Bernard. From a workshop in concrete modelling with Tomas Dirix as part of Meesterproef Structural Contingencies 2019-2020.

Fig. 7.13 Eglise Saint-Jacques te Conzac in Saintogne, concrete model grasping the building's ontological Roman structure, by Maxim Lefebre and Reinout Vervaet, students in the Studio Territory of Imagination II. Ma2 Structural Contingencies 2019–2020.

To re-expose possible frameworks of productive thinking, we place our research within the frame of the primitive beginnings of human reasoning, where theories were derived from the sensory form of what was perceived or imagined. Equally sought out are examples that still hold this quality. Case study examples are the tomb of Hor-Aha in ancient Egypt (thirty-first century BC), the Stoa of Attalos in Greece (second century BC), but equally the Cistercian Abbey of Le Thoronet in France (twelfth and thirteenth centuries) or John Soane's Bank of England (1971–1833). Those early explorations of nature are central in the studio, as they can reveal the relevance of some conceptual processes of discovery and invention that are still relevant in architectural production. The ability to focus on the senses requires an explicit training in recognising and understanding. It is by explicitly looking for these ineffable and sometimes forgotten elements that our design assignment focuses on the relationships between our senses. The studio and its educational approach intend to analyse the specific strengths and weaknesses of the ways in which sensory modalities interact and identify what entails the constituent of an intimate cooperation between proportions, materiality, and light as modulating this interaction.

Making Architecture

From the two frameworks of mapping described above, absorbing and using the ineffable and elusive qualities through the two-dimensional drawing and the three-dimensional model, photograph, collage, or sketch, we try to build up an act of recognition without dislocation by the use of our methodical apparatus. If the "analytical approach" and the "sense-awareness approach" focus on our general urge to understand ourselves and our surroundings, it is this double build-up framework that allows a focus on the potential of our perceptive self as a methodological body.

From the relationship between our innate ability to recognise and to imagine, we try to envision new potential. The studio builds up an inner world generated largely from these conscious experiences in the studio and of the individual's personal repertoire, which is not limited to their reproduction. By talking about these ingredients, and by understanding drawings as figures that actively share these ingredients so that we can judge their potential, we try to activate the imagination. This way of producing architecture avoids any dislocation from space and its possible impact or reduction of our thought processes. Sharing our work in the studio, we try to grasp the mechanisms of the creative process, aiming to reveal how widely human beings explore and comprehend by acting and handling rather than by mere contemplation.

From this perspective, we and our students make models and drawings by hand that range from precise geometries obtained with a scaled ruler to intuitive patterns of space. The sketches and models seem to be of autonomous

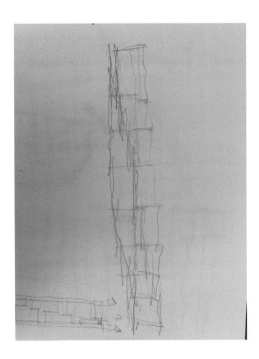

Fig. 7.14 Drawing possibilities of presence and absence of spatial elements. Pencil drawing by Schenk Hattori, 2017. © Schenk Hattori.

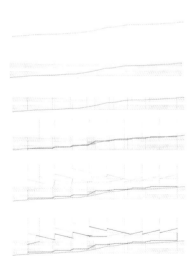

Fig. 7.15 Sequential sections mapping the topography of the building and its surroundings, Chorley Elementary School by Paul Rudolph (1969, demolished 2012), by Kristof Bonny and Lise Brusselmans, students in the Pioneering Morphologies, MA1 Structural Contingencies 2018–2019.

structures as no context is drawn. Nevertheless, they grew out of embedded tacit knowledge and aim to be expressions of a sensitivity to that precise context. The patterns executed by the drawing hand are lines of association and memory, grown from the empathic immersion of the author within the project, their personal perspective and cultural background. The potentials of a possible built space are creatively explored. The lines of inquiry are synthetic, expressing humanistic perspectives of use, life conditions, human relations and experiential aspects, the context and spatial character of the envisaged building.

The seemingly opposing skills of precision and intuition are brought into play with each other, fostered and trained through creative practice, study, and experiment. Whether making abstract analytical schemes or rough design sketches, they both embody what was and what could be without trying to represent something other than themselves. In this, precision is not only present within the exact analytical scheme, and intuition is not only part of the creative sketch by hand. When the analytical mechanism is as creative as the design sketch, through the fostering of an emphatic relation with the object of research, this lens can offer lost keys for understanding the building. Equally, the sketch can embody a layered content of precise observations beyond mere representation.

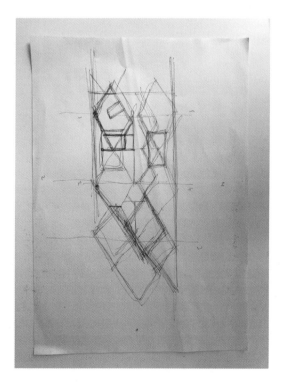

Fig. 7.16 Possible pattern of rooms at Roosenberg Abbey by Dom Hans van der Laan. Pen drawing on loose A4, Caroline Voet, 2021. © Caroline Voet.

Notes

1. From the studio brief of Diploma Unit 9, The Architectural Association London, 2001–2001. Tutors: Christian Kieckens and Caroline Voet.
2. This argument is taken from Mario Carpo, *The Alphabet and the Algorithm. The Rise and Fall of Identical Copies: Digital Technologies and Form-Making from Mass Customization to Mass Collaboration* (Cambridge, MA: MIT Press, 2011). Also see Psarra Sophia, Chapter 5, 83.
3. The research platform and Master studios Structural Contingencies is part of the Faculty of Architecture at KU Leuven and is based at Campus St.-Lucas in Ghent. Coordinated by Caroline Voet, it got its start in 2018. Its members carry the hybrid profile of practising architect, educator, and researcher. Most of them have obtained a PhD or are in the course of conducting one. Members are Caroline Voet, Hera Van Sande, Klaas Goris, Eireen Schreurs, Steven Schenk, and Laura Lievevrouw. See also: www.structuralcontingencies.be.
4. The notion of "Buildingness," according to Christian Kieckens, originates in a conversation with the American artist Dan Walsh. Kieckens elaborated it further in 1999 as a plea for the coexistence of building, structure, image, and space as one inseparable whole. It evolved as the theoretical and conceptual framework for a studio brief implemented at the Technical University of Eindhoven (1999–2002) and the Architectural Association in London (2000–2002), which was taught with Caroline Voet. Both authors of this article have worked within Kieckens's office, learning the craft of close observation and precise design skills. Steven Schenk graduated in his studio at the University of Antwerp in 2009. Christian Kieckens, "Buildingness," *Zoeken, Denken, Bouwen* (Ghent: Ludion, 2001), 116.
5. Christian Kieckens, "Buildingness," *Zoeken, Denken, Bouwen* (Ghent: Ludion, 2001), 116
6. Heinrich Wölfflin, *Renaissance Und Barock* (Basel and Stuttgart: Schwabe, 1888, reprint of 1965); Paul Frankl, *Principles of Architectural History. The Four Phases of Architectural Style, 1420–1900*, ed. and trans. James F. O'Gorman (Cambridge, MA: MIT Press, 1968, originally published in 1914 under the title *Die Entwicklung der neueren Baukunst* [Stuttgart: Verlag B. G. Teubner]); Rudolph Wittkower, *Architectural Principles in the Age of Humanism* (London: Warburg Institute, University of London, 1949); Sigfried Giedion, *Space, Time, Architecture* (Cambridge, MA: Havard University Press, 1941); Colin Rowe, "The Mathematics of the Ideal Villa, Palladio and Le Corbusier Compared," *Architectural Review* (March 1947); Colin Rowe and Robert Slutsky, "Transparency, Literal and Phenomenal," *Perspecta* 8 (1963): 45–54.
7. Psarra Sophia, Chapter 5, 81–94.
8. Andrea Palladio, *The Four Books on Architecture*, trans. Robert Tavernor and Richard Schofield (Cambridge, MA: MIT Press, 1997).
9. Dom Hans van der Laan, *De Architectonische Ruimte* (Leiden: Brill, 1977), translated in 1983 as *Architectonic Space*.
10. For an insight into Dom Hans van der Laan's design practice, see www.domhansvanderlaan. nl. Also see, for example, Caroline Voet, *Dom Hans Van Der Laan: A House for the Mind - A Design Manual on Roosenberg Abbey* (Antwerp: Flanders Architecture Institute, 2017).
11. For Lewerentz's drawings, see, for example, Claes Dymling and Wilfried Wang, eds., *Architect Sigurd Lewerentz. Vol. I-II. Photographs of the work - Drawings* (Stockholm: Byggförlaget, 1997).
12. On shadow and light, see Jun'ichiro Tanizaki, *In Praise of Shadows. Translated from the original Japanese text from 1933* (Sedgwick, ME: Leete's Island Books, 1977).
13. "… sondern es [das Licht] bricht regelrecht ein und steigert die Dunkelheit der umgebenden Mauerflächen," in Christoph Wieser, "Vielschichtig, bedeutend, sinnlich: die Kirche Sankt Peter in Klippan (1962–1966) von Sigurd Lewerentz," *Werk, Bauen+Wohnen* (9/2005): 45.

14. Interesting in this context is the never built church in Växjö that was solely designed as a moonlight-catcher. See Colin St. John Wilson, "Sigurd Lewerentz. The Sacred Buildings and the Sacred Sites," in *Sigurd Lewerentz. 1885–1975*, ed. Nicola Flora, Paolo Giardiello, and Gennaro Postiglione (Milan: Electa, 2001), 32.

15. Cf. Nicola Flora, Paolo Giardiello, and Gennaro Postiglione, "Journey to Italy," in *Sigurd Lewerentz. 1885–1975*, ed. Flora, Giardiello, Postiglione (Milan: Electa, 2001), 39.

Bibliography

Carpo, Mario. *The Alphabet and the Algorithm. The Rise and Fall of Identical Copies: Digital Technologies and Form-Making from Mass Customization to Mass Collaboration.* Cambridge, MA: MIT Press, 2011.

Dymling, Claes and Wilfried Wang, eds. *Architect Sigurd lewerentz. Vol. I-II. Photographs of the work – Drawings.* Stockholm: Byggförlaget, 1997.

Flora, Nicola, Paolo Giardiello, and Gennaro Postiglione, eds. *Sigurd Lewerentz. 1885–1975.* Milan: Electa, 2001.

Frankl, Paul. *Principles of Architectural History. The Four Phases of Architectural Style, 1420–1900*, edited and translated by James F. O'Gorman. Cambridge, MA: MIT Press. 1968.

Giedion, Sigfried. *Space, Time, Architecture.* Cambridge, MA: Harvard University Press, 1941.

Kieckens, Christian. "Buildingness." In *Zoeken, Denken, Bouwen*, 116. Ghent: Ludion, 2001.

Palladio, Andrea. *The Four Books on Architecture*, translated by Robert Tavernor and Richard Schofield. Cambridge, MA: MIT Press, 1997.

Rowe, Colin. "The Mathematics of the Ideal Villa, Palladio and Le Corbusier Compared." *Architectural Review*, March 1947.

—— and Robert Slutsky. "Transparency, Literal and Phenomenal." *Perspecta* 8 (1963): 45–54.

St John Wilson, Colin. "Sigurd Lewerentz: The Sacred Buildings and the Sacred Sites." In *Sigurd Lewerentz. 1885–1975*, edited by Nicola Flora, Paolo Giardiello, and Gennaro Postiglione, 64–87. Milan: Electa, 2001.

Tanizaki, Jun'ichiro. *In Praise of Shadows*, translated by Thomas J. Harper and Edward G. Seidensticker. Sedgwick, ME: Leet's Island Books, 1977.

van der Laan, Dom Hans. *De Architectonische Ruimte.* Leiden: Brill, 1977.

Voet, Caroline. *Dom Hans van der Laan: A House for the Mind – A Design Manual on Roosenberg Abbey.* Antwerp: Flanders Architecture Institute, 2017.

——, Sofie De Caigny, Lara Schrijver, and Katrien Vandermarliere, eds. *Autonomous Architecture in Flanders. The Early Works of Marie-José Van Hee, Christian Kieckens, Marc Dubois, Paul Robbrecht and Hilde Daem.* Antwerp: Flanders Architecture Institute, 2016.

Wieser, Christoph. "Vielschichtig, bedeutend, sinnlich: die Kirche Sankt Peter in Klippan (1962–1966) von Sigurd Lewerentz. " *werk, bauen + wohnen* 9 (2005): 40–49.

Wittkower, Rudolph. 1949. *Architectural Principles in the Age of Humanism.* London: Warburg Institute, University of London.

Wölfflin, Heinrich. 1888, reprint 1965. *Renaissance und Barock.* Basel and Stuttgart: Schwabe.

CHAPTER 8

Architecture from Drawing:
A Brief Inquiry into Three Types

Rosamund Diamond

It is the actual drawing that forces the artist to look at the object in front of him, to dissect it in his mind's eye and put it together again.
—John Berger, "Drawing"[1]

For artists and architects, drawing is a vehicle of discovery through iteration, not simply one of translation. In architectural practice and the teaching studio, the skill of designing depends on repeated drawing and the way the drawing is made, for example, as a plan or an isometric projection. This affects how a design arises, enabling the design process, and training the architect how to look. Preliminary architectural studies in which ideas are processed contribute significantly to final designs and their drawings. They are equivalent to John Berger's distinction in art between a "working drawing and a 'finished' work," but in architecture, they can be indistinguishable. This paper looks at how three different types of drawing have been used, initially in my own architectural practice, and then in my studio teaching in Degree Unit 3A at the University of Nottingham School of Architecture, to reveal ways in which the process of making these drawings affect how different kinds of configurational decisions of architectural form are made. In my architectural practice, the process of design involves investigative research, ranging from spatial morphology to detailed construction, in which drawing is used as an analytical methodology. Three recurring types used in this research – the Nolli figure-ground plan, the axonometric projection, and the developed surface drawing – have evolved into teaching instruments to study underlying architectural strategies. As the teaching focus of Unit 3A is on the physical and material reality of architecture, drawing plays an essential role in the critical development of student projects.

Treating the drawing type as its own precedent study, this paper discusses each in relation to its original form and the students' interpretations. The mechanism of redrawing that they were asked to undertake revealed underlying methods in the case studies, resulting in a potential reciprocity in students' designs. A question arises as to whether certain drawing types are applicable to specific kinds of projects; for example, in my practice research, I used redrawing to understand the spatial effects of architectural interventions on the same plan form in the Louvre Museum or making dynamic plans and sections of Eileen Gray's moveable fixed furniture to understand the effects of her mechanical fixing techniques on her spatial design.[2] Less familiar drawing types, such as the ones proposed here, are useful when they disrupt conventional ways of looking at projects and challenge preconceptions about the purpose of different drawing systems.

In tasks associated with urban propositions, individual building designs, and their inhabitable spaces, the students of Unit 3A, and Nick Haynes's and Laura Hanks's mArch Studio 4 students, recorded the contemporary city by applying Nolli's urban plan type; my students used James Stirling's and Rafael Moneo's versions of the sectioned axonometric to draw existing conditions or parts of their projects, and they referenced Eileen Gray's version of the developed surface interior drawing to explore interior spaces. Initially, the types were chosen because of their respective associations with context, tectonic form, and inhabitation, yet each contains parts of the others. We found that by using three drawing types disconnected from a linear working method that moves from large to small scale, we could disrupt the preconception about working from overall form to detailed design.

Type 1: Giambattista Nolli's Map of Rome (1748)

For the architect, recording context is a primary design action that is difficult to effect in a single drawing. The interplay of topography, time, personal experience, access, and the conditions of the existing fabric requires multiple representations. To a certain extent, this issue of overlaying multiple data in one drawing is overcome, or at least acknowledged, in Giambattista Nolli's 1748 map of Rome (the Nolli plan), which is based on a drawing system used to investigate ground-level urban activity while acknowledging built form. (fig. 8.1) For some teaching studios in the United Kingdom and the United States, this representational method became the eponymous recording technique of the postmodern era, but applying it to the post-industrial contemporary city is complicated, since it is fractured by disruptive infrastructures and strategic ideological interventions. This year, Unit 3A's design brief was sited in Nottingham's city centre, which is currently undergoing radical changes. The Nolli plan type was used to investigate and analyse Nottingham's public space, identify potential sites and interstitial gaps, and specifically engender discussion around the redevelopment of a large, derelict 1970s shopping mall.[3]

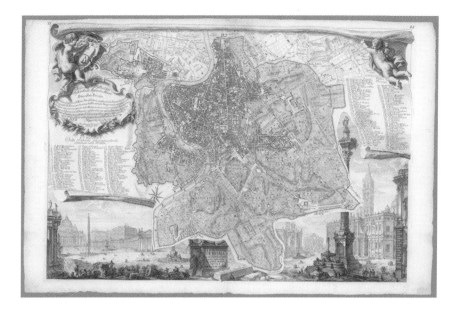

Fig. 8.1:   Giambattista Nolli La Piante Grande di Roma ("the great plan of Roma"), 1748, extract, version illustrated. La Topografia di Roma di Gio Batta Nolli Dalla Maggiore in Questa Minor Tavola Dal Medesimo Ridotta. © Courtesy, Barry Lawrence Ruderman Collection, David Rumsey Map Center, Stanford Libraries. http://purl.stanford.edu/jt810vk7350.

Distinct from the drawing system of depicting building blocks as black figures on white ground representing exterior space, Nolli's map depicts external and internal open space as an urban continuity.[4] Generated from a meticulous survey of Rome, it records a city centre whose form has changed little in the subsequent 270 years. The accuracy of the plan is such that it continued to be used as the basis for Rome's maps until the 1970s, when most of the public spaces depicted remained open.[5] Derived from Leonardo Bufalini's 1551 printed map of Rome, it was one of the first ichnographic city maps (previously, cities had been depicted using bird's-eye perspective). [6] Whereas Bufalini's city is a line-drawn network of spaces and built fabric, the Nolli plan records building blocks as solids, with a consistent morphology of internal public spaces carved from them and depicted as white, equalising them with the surrounding urban network of streets and public squares. Almost for the first time, it presented building interiors as part of a continuous network of accessible urban space.

How Nolli came to do this remains unexplained. His map of Rome demonstrates how a plan can convey ideology by graphic means. In Bufalini's map, the topography and large structures of the ancient city are dominant features. Topography and the presence of ancient Rome are integrated into Nolli's representational system, in which he portrays the extant ancient city within the contemporary form. Ancient Rome's structures are shown as discrete elements, fragments in the surrounding vineyards, or integrated into city centre blocks, with a sense of their spatial inhabitation. The idea that the city's mapping could include its fabric's historic vestiges may have led Nolli to choose to depict public internal spaces with their enclosing structures as a way of describing the fusion of the old and contemporary cities in one period. In the network of space Nolli represents, his attachment of building structure to the principal spaces of churches, scholastic orders, hospices, and palazzi interweaves Rome's social order into his contemporary city. His portrayal equalises exterior and interior public spaces, irrespective of their relationships to the block, presenting to us the idea that a city could be a continuously inhabited organism. Nevertheless, while Rome was ordered by its institutions, many of these, as the map shows, were ecclesiastical and would have had controlled access. Nolli's graphic method of using dots through the middle of streets to define Rome's governing structure of *rioni* or districts, for which the map was commissioned, does not interrupt its concept of inhabitable physical space transcending civic structures. Unlike this paper's other drawing types, it was made as a statutory document for dissemination. Composed of twelve engravings, its indisputable accuracy and printed form gave it authority.

In distinguishing between built form and external or internal public space, the Nolli plan presents a useful way of observing urban morphology as a ground-level phenomenon. In Unit 3A, the type has been used to discuss notions of civic space and relationships to building form, ownership, and public access, questioning whether Nolli's method is applicable to the contemporary city. What appeared to be a clear system for denoting all public space is complicated, because as public access changes, single mappings do not present a definitive record. Trials carried out by Unit 3A, and mArch Studio 4A,[7] adapted Nolli's graphic methodology to the contemporary city by making mappings at different times of all public interior spaces. As a preliminary experiment, Unit 3A students speculatively mapped part of the Via de Condotti, Rome, and part of Nottingham's Low Pavement, extending Nolli's mapping of interior public space to include shops, bars, and restaurants as interior public space. mArch Studio 4 mapped three main Nottingham city centre squares – Market Square, St Peter's Square, and Nottingham Contemporary (fig. 8.2) – investigating whether their public spaces are extended by the surrounding public interiors. Publicly accessible space appears to have grown in the daytime, but as a phenomenon detached from architectural form. Both question the relationship of public space to land ownership. Redrawings of Nolli's Rome map for different times would distinguish the spaces of institutions that would have had controlled access. The contemporary history of interior public spaces in the United Kingdom is one attempt to manipulate them for private commercial gain at the expense of their democratisation and coherent urban form.

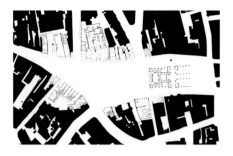

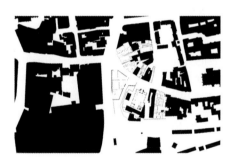

Fig. 8.2: Nolli plans of squares daytime Nottingham city centre, from top Market Square, St Peter's Square, Nottingham Contemporary. © School of Architecture M Arch Studio 4 Group 2 students Bethan Crouch, Brady Hill, Georgina Ley, 2020. The mappings have indeterminate outcomes and some intriguing findings in relation to Nolli's plan of Rome. While a typology of spaces equated to inhabitable building volumes is discernible in Nolli's map, the public spaces drawn in these three Nottingham mappings are generally detached from architectural form and without hierarchy, apart from the churches and the exchange building. Large shop interiors appear spatially endless without the ordering structures of their buildings. The difference between the contemporary public city and its Roman predecessor also appears to be the condition of continuous public frontages on block exteriors. The perimeter shops convey more about a commercially driven market than a spatially ordered urban structure.

Type 2: The Axonometric Projection

The axonometric projection type conjoins two and three dimensions, making it a critical design and representational tool within Unit 3A, alongside physical model making. Oblique projection can simultaneously represent a building and its construction, applying figuration in the depiction of built form, as a complete or partial portrayal. The axonometric, including the bird's-eye or worm's-eye view as whole or cutaway views, is capable of conveying spatial volume grounded in context or as an abstraction. Using as precedents hand-drawn versions by Auguste Choisy, James Stirling, and Raphael Moneo, these variants of the type have been used in Unit 3A to describe composition, tectonics, and inhabitable space, focusing on one while investigating its interaction with the others.

The versions of the projection type derived from Choisy, which became synonymous with Stirling's practice, could impart the interdependency of form and construction. As Chris Dyson, who worked in Stirling's office, has observed,

> The plan was the originator – initially quite diagrammatic, it was then fleshed out using the axonometric, the worm's eye, the split up view and the single-point perspective. [...] The axonometric [...] enabled measured massing and form to be tested in contextual drawings. The split up view [...] enabled the viewer to understand the hierarchy of spaces within the building.[8]

In using axonometric techniques, which were relatively new at the time, to describe ancient construction, Choisy understood how worm's-eye-view drawings were simultaneously capable of conveying construction and spatial character.[9] His worm's-eye oblique partial projections showing interior volumes resulting from a building's ordering system are equivalent to placing of oneself inside a physical model. The worm's-eye view effectively represents inhabitable architectural space perceived while floating in space. In Stirling's projects, axonometric representations, showing buildings without context, privilege their formal concepts. In the studio, this has become a means to discuss a project's abstract intention, temporarily suppressing context in favour of the figure. In Stirling's designs, such as the Staatsgalerie Stuttgart and the unbuilt North Rhine–Westphalia Art Collection Dusseldorf, the worm's-eye projection (fig. 8.3), in which volumes and elements are drawn floating without context or registering their actual scale, convey form and route, simultaneously enabling the viewer to envisage themselves standing in the spaces of the building and moving through them while reading the architecture as an abstract concept.

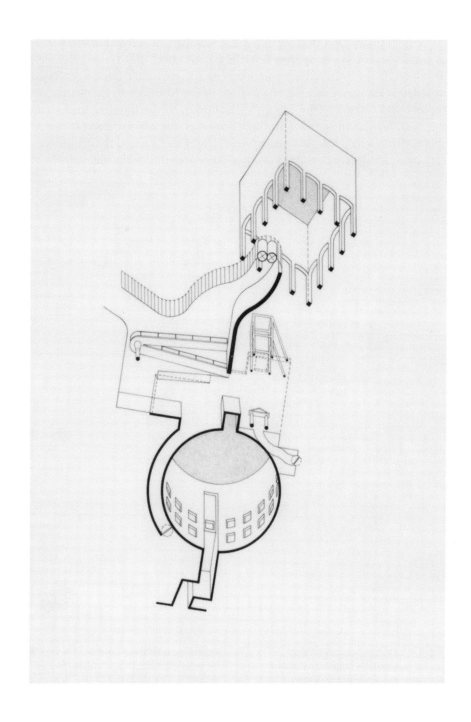

Fig. 8.3: James Stirling Northrhine-Westphalia Art Collection Dusseldorf worm's-eye axonometric, 1980. James Stirling/Michael Wilford fonds Canadian Centre for Architecture © CCA.

A preliminary Unit 3A study of some of Nottingham's urban elements, such as arcades and canopies, appropriated the axonometric type to reinterpret their definitions in the fractured contemporary city. A survey of the canopy generated its redefinition on a route starting in front of the Nottingham Contemporary Gallery and extending the canopy's description to the tramline undercroft (fig. 8.4). Similar to some of Stirling's drawings, the canopy study connects spaces defined by a load-bearing structure, floor surface, and the art gallery's canopy, a cantilevered volume hovering like an exterior baldachin.

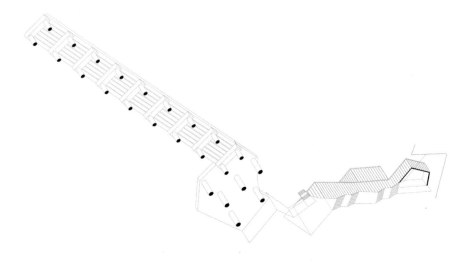

Fig. 8.4: Nottingham city canopy worms-eye view Nottingham School of Architecture B Arch Unit 3A Group 2, 2019. © Oliver Skelton. The worm's-eye axonometric described the possibility of inhabiting spaces so that the fragmented components would reassemble themselves into a discernible urban route. It draws the potential for infrastructural elements superimposed on the city's steep topography to be recomposed into a more coherent urban form. Nottingham School of Architecture B Arch Unit 3A Group 2 Oliver Skelton (drawing), Imogen Clark, Nida Hannan, Jessica Hollis, 2019.

Moneo uses another type of cutaway axonometric projection, notably on the National Museum of Roman Art Mérida, 1980–1986, in which the building is shown partially, with its ground floor and the street context. The expressive drawing technique, used to impart the construction with the overall spatial concept, conveys the building's atmosphere.[10] (fig. 8.5) It imparts the idea of the brick arched form overlain on the museum's archaeological level like an ancient construction while simultaneously showing slim walkways taken through the walls and the contemporary, linear roof lights.[11] In its portrayal of the building system, and the black drawn-cut sections, it recalls Nolli's spatial representation integrating the ancient city into his contemporary plan of Rome. The cutaway axonometric offers Unit 3A a more legible drawing type to describe structural form and construction detail than the standardised large section and dismantles distinctions between working and finished drawings.

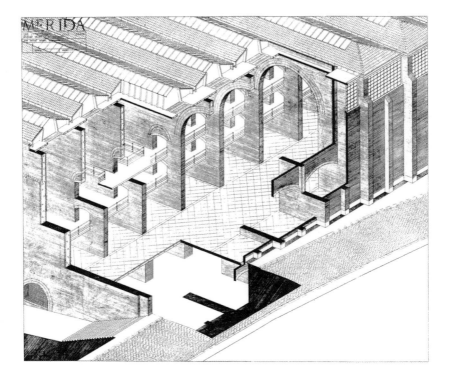

Fig. 8.5: Raphael Moneo, National Museum of Roman Art Mérida axonometric, Enrique de Teresa 1980. © Rafael Moneo arquitecto Madrid.

Type 3: The Developed Surface Drawing, Eileen Gray

If the axonometric can be characterised as a drawing capable of conveying inhabitation, the type of orthographic projection used by the designer and architect Eileen Gray to depict interior space, by projecting elevations around a floor plan, can be seen as the most complex to read spatially. She applied her unique version of an eighteenth-century drawing type to the design of buildings, notably the two houses E.1027 and Tempe á Pailla, which were her most realised works and for which she made multiple projection drawings. The two houses, which are works of total design, are the result of her multifaceted skills and the way she was able to fuse them through a consistency of spatial concepts, applied to each component, including their purpose-designed fixed and loose furniture, carpets, and lighting. At the same time as she started designing buildings, she was working on interior commissions. Gray worked almost entirely alone,[12] making all her own drawings. They were working examples of her parallel design practices of architecture, furnishings, graphics, collage, and sculpture.

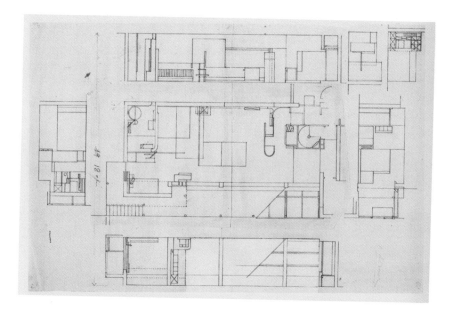

Fig. 8.6:   Eileen Gray E.1027 plan and internal elevations of salon c. 1929. © *National Museum of Ireland*. Gray appears to use the same line weight as she constructs layers of spaces from the assemblages of parts and imagines their inhabitation, equivalently indicating building elements such as her unique folding terrace doors, screens, daybeds, rugs, and adjustable furniture, such as pivoting bedside tables.

Gray's drawing technique is a version of an eighteenth-century type referred to by Robin Evans as "the developed surface interior," used to represent
room interiors, as "a way of turning architecture inside-out." A technique used
by Robert Adam to individualise rooms by showing their figured and embellished walls was adopted by Gray to represent interconnected interior space.[13]
Gray had also seen how members of the De Stijl group, for example, Theo Von
Doesburg, described their spatial ideas in wall patterns. Gray's versions are
complicated by the interaction of the building envelope, exterior space, interior
partitions, and furnishing elements. She treated space in the configuration of
her houses, and their tectonic forms, in the way she had in the evolution of her
furniture. From the mid-1920s, at a time when she was also starting to design
buildings, her loose furniture transformed: tables and chairs were conceived
as free-standing pieces with less predetermined uses, and the tables were accessible and useable from all sides. They supported the idea of the informal
occupation of rooms.

Gray's development of adjustable fixed furniture coincided with her adaptation of her adjustable block screen into a wall lining and the idea that both
could construct or moderate space. This starts to explain why the technique of
the developed surface drawing, in which she could integrate building elements
and furniture, suited her design methods. The interior and spatial compositions
imagine inhabitation intimately. Her drawing of the salon in E.1027 (fig. 8.6),
in which fixed and loose furniture and fittings are flattened onto line-drawn
elevations, visually equalising all the elements, suits the equivalence with which
she constructed space in her buildings and furniture. The elevations can appear as abstract compositions, yet simultaneously, layers of space are implied
by the overlaying of the parts. More than recalling their eighteenth-century
predecessors, these drawings reference cubist space, with its repetition of objects viewed from different angles, and particularly Marcel Duchamp's version,
"elementary parallelism."[14] It is hard to know the extent to which the drawing
type assisted Gray's approach, but the complex assemblies almost describe her
thought processes. She had evolved a way of treating space in the configuration
of her houses and their tectonic forms, in the way she had in the evolution of
her furniture, from recognisable forms to adaptable, free-standing pieces.

In Unit 3A, the brief for the first student project asked groups to imagine
how actions of inhabitation could create atmosphere by designing rooms using
the developed surface drawing, first in order to unpack room precedents. By
using the unfamiliar drawing type, the intention was to disrupt preconceptions
associated with plan and elevation drawings, and a conventional architectural hierarchy leading from building tectonics and the enclosure, to its fitting.
Groups used the drawing type together with developmental models to test
composition, the design of fittings, and changing atmospheres generated in
their interior spaces resulting from occupation. A group designing a space for
the actions of cooking and eating (fig. 8.7) investigated spatial characteristics

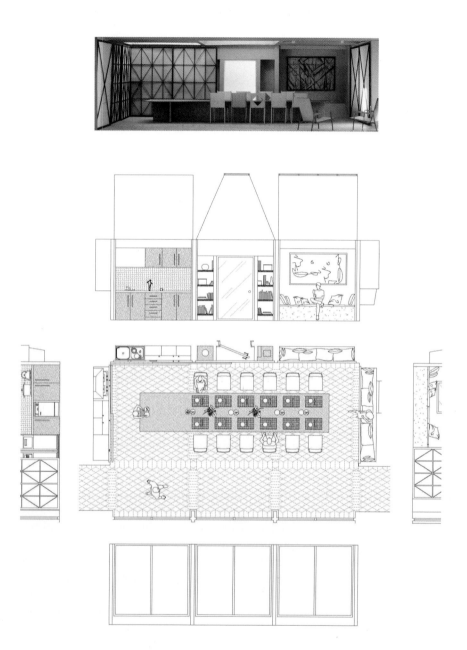

Fig. 8.7: Nottingham School of Architecture B Arch Unit 3A Group 2 "A Room of One's Own, cooking and eating," 2020. © Tonia Constantinou, Dona De Vas Gunasekera, Rhys Jamieson-Prince, Oliver Skelton. The group experimented with moving screens and space dividers to create and hide alcoves and subsidiary spaces. Yet tectonic and material qualities enhanced by light and the extruded rooflights visible in photographs of their 1:20 scale model were not translated into the drawings.

generated by volumetric forms and daylight control, approaching the room interior as they would a building design. However, the drawings tended to privilege surface and furniture over spatial experiment. While the model conveys the room's changing atmosphere, the drawing portrays the room as static. In Gray's projection drawings, spaces of modestly sized rooms, unconfined by conventionally structured enclosure, extend to balconies and exterior terraces, implying atmospheric differences from changes in daylight. What we should have done was to try to understand her methods by redrawing, using multiple plans and elevations to interrogate the layers.

Conclusion

Architectural design depends on drawing to activate ideas from which concepts develop, and then drawing conveys them as physical entities and inhabitable space, as John Berger points out: "A line, an area of tone, is not really important because it records what you have seen, but because of what it will lead you on to see."[15] The purpose of architectural drawing often proceeds unquestioned in practice and the school design studio, where it can relate to the need for production but not necessarily investigation.

In investigating how abstract concepts can prevail, as detailed projects are developed in the teaching studio, three kinds of drawing, treated as types and associated with specific tasks, were used as methods to disaggregate parts of a linear design approach in which drawing scales are often equated with particular stages of a design's development. Our strategy was to ask students to work simultaneously and equally on interior inhabitation, tectonics, and contextualised form. The developed surface interior drawing was used with versions of the axonometric to develop interior spaces and atmospheres, while at the same time, other versions of axonometrics were used to depict tectonic form or networks of interior volumes. In Nolli plan drawing exercises, projects were superimposed on their contexts as public ground-floor interventions and constructional forms. The purpose of using the three types of drawing as investigative tools was also not to distinguish between making drawings to present designs or to construct.

By superimposing tectonic form on an urban figure ground, the Nolli plan led the students to represent their building designs in an urban context, in which the city is not defined at ground level by individual building form but as a continuous network of public access. By conjoining the section and the elevation, projected from the oblique plan, which conveys space from a standing viewpoint, the axonometric of a building whole or a fragment enabled students to materialise their formal ideas, simultaneously observing relationships of the individual to the city. Using the drawing technique of the developed surface interior, spaces were investigated as dynamic entities, their atmospheres altered by changes of light and their occupation. While not completely resolved, the students' examples demonstrated how the drawing types could be used to integrate design concepts into developed projects, overcoming tendencies to separate drawings made to represent ideas from construction descriptions. While the studio drawing experiments, in cases such as the Nolli plan, have not led directly to design answers, they have shown their value as provisional tools, exposing some of the uncertainties accompanying the design process.

In practice and teaching, a common assumption exists that distinguishes between what are characterised as working and presentation drawings: if both are concerned with description, it should be possible to convey construction and its appearance simultaneously. A floor plan may seem the obvious drawing to describe an entire complex, and a section the drawing to describe construction, but more is required of a drawing to comprehend meaning or even to understand how to construct something. What might be needed to conflate ideas and fabrication are drawings that combine more than one kind of geometrical projection. Nolli's plan of Rome, Stirling's and Moneo's axonometrics of parts of their designs, and Gray's developed surface interior drawings of her houses are exemplars in which their architects have simultaneously conveyed formal concepts, fabrication, and inhabitation in a single drawing. The problem of the neorealist render, now such a familiar school of drawing, and one also used in our teaching studio, is its focus on surface, which fixes a proposition on one view and one moment in time. By dissecting the drawing as an integral device of research and approach in my architectural practice and in the teaching studio, it has again become central to design. It makes us and our students conscious that the way we draw affects how we design.

Notes

1. John Berger, "'Drawing' from *Permanent Red*, 1960," in *John Berger Selected Essays*, ed. Geoff Dyer (London: Bloomsbury, 2001), 10.
2. Rosamund Diamond, "Too Many Objects and Not Enough Bathrooms," (MSC thesis, unpublished, 1997); Rosamund Diamond, "Five Easy Pieces - Technical Shifts and Spatial Ideas in Eileen Gray's Architecture," (Conference paper presented at Eileen Gray and the Making of Modernism, October 2006).
3. The Broadmarsh shopping centre, which covers a 2.5 ha site in Nottingham's city centre.
4. Giambattista Nolli Nuova pianta di Roma, 176 x 208cm, consisting of twelve copper-plate engravings, 1748. The survey was started in 1736. It was made in response to Pope Benedict XIV's commission to demarcate fourteen *rioni*, or districts, of Rome.
5. Its accuracy is confirmed by overlays of Rome's contemporary satellite image. This is demonstrated in the digital remastering of interactive maps by the University of Oregon, presented on its Nolli Map website, http://nolli.uoregon.edu/.
6. Nolli acknowledged the importance of his predecessor Leonardo Bufalini's printed map of Rome of 1551 by including it with his 1748 map. Bufalini's was the first ichnographic (orthogonal) map. Nolli's map is also differentiated by its north–south reorientation.
7. Unit 3A students Yasmine Dahim, Felix King, and Chloe Marples, MArch Studio 4 *"Territories of Transformation,"* students Bethan Crouch, Brady Hill and Georgina Ley, tutors Nick Haynes and Laura Hanks.
8. Chris Dyson, "No House Style: The Drawings of Stirling and Wilford," *Architects' Journal*, 13 October 2015, https://www.architectsjournal.co.uk/practice/culture/no-house-style-the-drawings-of-stirling-and-wilford.
9. Hilary Bryon, "Measuring the Qualities of Choisy's Oblique and Axonometric Projections," in *Auguste Choisy (1841–1909): Proceedings of the International Symposium held in Madrid*, eds. Francisco Girón Sierra and Santiago Huerta Fernández (Madrid: Instituto Juan de Herrera, 2009).
10. Drawing made by Enrique de Teresa September 1980. A second, worm's-eye version was made by Stan Allen May 1984, after the building's completion.
11. Stan Allen, "Drawing with Raphael Moneo Madrid 1984," *Drawing Matter*, 14 March 2019, https://drawingmatter.org/stan-allen-on-drawing-with-rafael-moneo-madrid-1984/.
12. Apart from some collaboration with Jean Badovici, the architect and editor of *l'Architecture Vivante*.
13. Robin Evans, "The Developed Surface: An Enquiry into the Brief Life of an Eighteenth-Century Drawing Technique," *9H No. 8, On Rigour* (London, 1989), 120–147.
14. Rosamund Diamond, "Eileen Gray and the Influence of Cubism," in *E.1027 Eileen Gray*, eds. Wilfried Wang and Peter Adam (Tübingen: Wasmuth, 2017), 52–61.
15. John Berger, "'Drawing' from *Permanent Red*, 1960," 10.

Bibliography

Allen, Stan. "Drawing with Raphael Moneo Madrid 1984." *Drawing Matter*. 14 March 2019, https://drawingmatter.org/stan-allen-on-drawing-with-rafael-moneo-madrid-1984/.
Berger, John. "'Drawing' from *Permanent Red*, 1960." In *John Berger Selected Essays*, edited by Geoff Dyer, 10. London: Bloomsbury, 2001
Bryon, Hilary. "Measuring the Qualities of Choisy's Oblique and Axonometric Projections." In *Auguste Choisy (1841–1909): L'architecture et l'art de bâtir*, edited by Francisco Javier Girón Sierra and Santiago Huerta Fernández, 31–62. Madrid: Instituto Juan de Herrera 2009.

Diamond, Rosamund. "Eileen Gray and the Influence of Cubism." In *O'Neil Ford Monograph 7 E.1027 Eileen Gray*, edited by Wilfried Wang and Peter Adam. Tübingen: Wasmuth, 2017.

——. "Five Easy Pieces – Technical Shifts and Spatial Ideas in Eileen Gra's Architecture." Conference paper Eileen Gray and the Making of Modernism, October 2006.

——. "Too Many Objects and Not Enough Bathrooms." MSc thesis, University College London, 1997.

Dyson, Chris, "No House Style: The Drawings of Stirling and Wilford." *Architects' Journal*, 13 October 2015.

Evans, Robin. "The Developed Surface: An Enquiry into the Brief Life of an Eighteenth-Century Drawing Technique." *Translations from Drawing to Building, and Other Essays*, 202. London: Architectural Association, 1996.

Maier, Jessica. "Leonardo Bufalini and the First Printed Map of Rome: 'The most beautiful of all things.'" *Memoirs of the American Academy in Rome* vol. 56/57 (2011/2012): 243–270. http://www.jstor.com/stable/24616443.

Tice, Jim and Steiner, Erik. *The Nolli Map Website.* © 2005–2021. University of Oregon. http://nolli.uoregon.edu/.

Verstegen, Ian and Ceen, Allan, eds. *Giambattista Nolli and Rome Mapping the City Before and After the Pianta Grande Studium.* Rome: Urbis, 2013.

CHAPTER 9

Time in Unit 9: A Comparison between the Projected Life of the Drawing, the Residues of Living, and Lived Experience

Tom Coward

This is an exploration of what happens after a study visit to a building, an encounter that pulls at the root of architectural practice. Responses to time spent at Charles Moore's Unit 9 at Sea Ranch in California provide the opportunity to draw together the various strands that constitute my personal form of hybrid practice. Writing and research enable a critical and self-reflective understanding of my trajectory through the discipline, which I enact as the director of a business and architectural practice called Agents of Change (AOC) and through my role as year leader and design unit tutor in the master's course at the Kingston University Department of Architecture and Landscape (KSA). In this sense, a building visit is the qualification of critical theory, it is the source of experience that fuels practical production, and it gives currency to the conversation between students and tutors, brought together from diverse backgrounds and with different experiences.

The paper will explore the relationship between the practice of architecture and academic activities by analysing what each offers the other through the self-conscious experience of architecture that takes place during a building visit. The focus on lived experience reflects the architect's core responsibility, which is the translation of culture into a form that somehow carries human experience. In my practice and in my teaching, the role of everyday objects in this process is fundamental. In his material engagement theory, Lambros Malafouris describes a world of "enactive things": objects as containers of memory and as cognitive extensions of the human body. [1]

A Practice-Based Perspective

Over the last decade, AOC has become increasingly involved with objects as well as with rooms, buildings, and landscapes. A recent project, called the Reading Room, involved the permanent refurbishment of a double-height gallery on the second floor of the Wellcome Collection's headquarters in London.[2] This accommodates a public library and museum space that blurs the distinction between gallery and academic research library and is suitable for all ages and interests. The challenge was to conceive of a spatial layout and furniture design that would encourage individual engagement with a large collection of varied content in an inclusive way. The brief was to foster communities of knowledge, meeting somewhere in between the format of the popular temporary exhibitions that the Wellcome Trust have successfully hosted in the past and the dense content of the reference library, frequented principally by academics.

Curators and architects worked fluidly around a shifting but shared sense of the collection and its value, developing an understanding of how object-based learning,[3] archival analysis of exhibition form, and spatial trials could direct the hand of decision makers (the client's development team and trustees), pushing the proposition away from conventional notions of museum exhibition design. A pedagogical aspect within the project related to broader discussions around person-centred learning[4] and how hybrid spaces such as this could contribute to the quality of social learning.[5] In simple terms, this became a careful rearticulation of the everyday nature of tables and chairs to meet, present, and work around.

The completion of the Reading Room at the Wellcome Collection in 2015 led to conversations with a wide range of potential clients interested in the way that AOC design through engagement. This process shows that the shared institutional imagination of a place can be interpreted through its objects – the collection – to the same extent as it is represented by its community, its stakeholders, the building, or its spatial context. One of the outcomes of these conversations was a commission for a design research project around dementia. Working as part of a diverse team, AOC developed a household model of care for a new care home. Our research was based on a concern for the arrangement of things, and design work was carried out using a method devised to "curate memories."

The proposed care home was organised into households formed around eight people, with staff as equal family members. Each interior adapts to meet changing needs, creating a therapeutic environment that enables people. Each household has a generous provision of open display and closed storage; the open display in a range of areas provides opportunities to fill up the household with the stuff of life – with props, music, and life themes made available from each individuals history.

Our fieldwork included significant periods within care home settings. It revealed standard practice in using props (media, clothes, food, tasks) to support activity and to encourage reminiscence. Some props were borrowed and bartered by staff over time to produce what we called a "constructed domestic" that suited the residents' alternate realities. More significantly, each family member is encouraged to bring furniture and fittings with them when they move into a home, and a story of each resident's life is developed and shared day to day in a memory box located at the threshold to each private bedroom.

In existing care homes, families often help their loved one settle in and become situated. And the range of spaces created in typical private rooms is truly remarkable: white cube galleries for a model car display; rooms layered and filled with the best china, a library, and family portraits; even contrived facsimiles of entire flat layouts condensed to replicate the previous trip from home to the day-care centre across the road. In making smaller integrated households, it became harder to facilitate the autonomous moments described, so the question from the work became how to establish the right responsive encouraging aesthetic that could make individual lifeworlds (all the immediate experiences, activities, and contacts that make up the world of an individual or corporate life) redolent in the same household. Our intention was to develop an aesthetic of architecture that would support these acquired everyday collections with ease. A successful architectural solution would put things in all the right places to make suggestive and enactive situations and to enable the performance of dementia care (a stage set to support players and requiring direction). It would be generous in deployment to trigger an expanded imagination of thought, where memories are accessed through engagement with physical things.

The Interrelationship of Things

In 2019–2020, the unit I run at KSA explored the concept of "Our Health," enacted through a professional collaboration set up by AOC with Pembroke House, a settlement located in Walworth, Southwark. Our project was based in The Walworth Living Room, an experimental space set up by the settlement to examine social prescription and community health (or well-being) in a semi-derelict Victorian church hall. Students joined a weekly residency gaining hands-on experience of live design while helping to run a community social prescription service. The eight-week period provided a unique context for students to test and develop ideas around managing objects in space. This experience in the field was supported by a field trip visiting the built work of Charles Moore, focusing on his collaborative process as a way to consider community co-design in a more global context.

The design unit subscribes to the concept of "thinking through making,"[6] which considers the production of drawings, models, and eventually buildings, for example, as situated acts that gain affordance[7] through the previous lived experience of buildings. This consideration lies at the heart of decision-making in both my professional practice and my teaching. At the school of architecture, the evaluation of iterative work is often carried out through conversation, either in a formal review or an informal tutorial. This conversational "to and thro" reflective process fosters the development of personal judgement, which itself grows through the self-conscious experience of architecture. The thinking works beyond object or building consideration to "place-making" and at all scales of work is overtly active rather than abstract or purely formal. As a design process, it considers material as an enactive sign and includes the everyday as relevant in contributing to perception or transformative cognition – the content within can be equivalent to geometry and light in a survey of space. The approach requires careful observation, addressed in teaching through a material survey – a tool developed similarly in architecture and archaeology, used to both capture the past and predict the future use of material.

In February 2020, I took my students to visit Condominium One in Sea Ranch, a place important for me as a pedagogic, historical, and creative subject. Sea Ranch was designed by Moore, Lyndon, Turnbull, and Whitaker and completed in 1966. Charles Moore kept a home in Unit 9 there until his death in 1993, and it remains a tantalising record of the architect's imagination not only writ large but expanded and reiterated as a lived everyday reality. The home adapted to Moore's shifting needs and persuasions and became filled with objects gleaned through his life and travels. As such, Unit 9 is ripe for exploration as a pedagogic and creative subject for analysis of "contented space."[8] Moore, who was also an architect and an educator, helped instigate a still popular architectural idea, where the "poetic image" of an architecture "as found," in other words its phenomenological effect on the individual, is considered more important than its location in history.[9]

Unit 9 remains much as it was when Moore died in 1993, filled with his objects, and in this state is available for holiday let; taking advantage of this, we spent three days living there. This strange situation is augmented by the existence of archival material on the space, from the design process to media coverage, to photographs taken over the years of its occupation. Among these papers, Moore's own words on well-being can be found:

> Inhabiting [...] is a basic human endeavor, not far behind eating and sleeping, though to my mind far less universally achieved. While touted theoretical or linguistic abstractions have been the basis for some architects' houses, I've tended toward the idea that a house can be a stage where the inhabitant can act out his or her life [...] For me it has involved establishing as potently as I could manage a sanctuary not only for me but for

my possessions, trying to evoke the feeling of well-being that Indonesian dancers call being centered.[10]

Working Forwards and Backwards

I was first introduced Sea Ranch Condominium One during my undergraduate studies, and visual memories from it have remained with me ever since, so the opportunity to visit Unit 9 was the personal realisation of a twenty-odd-year desire. These lasting impressions include the different scales of the building, from its silhouette as a diminutive "wooden rock"[11] fitting into the Californian coastal landscape, its somehow diaphanous facade with careful apertures, the layers of space internally making houses within houses, and finally, the collections of knick-knacks revealed in the images shown as orchestrated cones of vision. Harry Mallgrave highlights various studies suggesting that the processes of remembering the past and imagining the future share a common brain network centred in the hippocampus.[12] This area of the brain is crucial in "scene construction theory," used not only in creating memories but also in the imagination and projection of the future, which is essential to the act of design.

In contrast, the design studio activities carried out in the Walworth Living Room became the practice of an architecture with immediate feedback. For example, a 09:00 meeting with project stakeholders – a dancer, a service designer, a project manager – would involve discussion of student-led changes to the spatial layout. By 11:00, the space would be reorganised, and locals would start to arrive. Such a day would be dominated by lunch and the tea for children after school, which was, for many, their best access to either conversation or good food that day. By 16:00, after a day of joining in, each student would have an observed understanding of how the space had been used and what had worked better for whom, ready for the next week. In our time in the Walworth Living Room, we came to understand the significantly varied social outcomes possible through the weekly rearrangement of things within a fixed architectural formal space.

In advance and following our field trip to California, this process was reversed – we wanted to unpick the evolution of the architecture as found through historical drawings and photos to understand the relationship between architectural form and its content. The same presentation drawings are used in most publications – the Rizzoli-published monograph on Moore[13] reviewed on-site revealed that the Unit 9 plan and internal elevations deviate significantly from the readily available published book record – the drawings perhaps drawn for presentation prior to completion. A famous internal perspective[14] reveals the volumetric concept, its spatial invitation, and its capacity to hold domestic fixtures and fittings, which can be understood as a presentation drawing developed in design as a promise of the space to come. Unit 9 as experienced became the corollary of that: an opportunity embellished by the life and times of Moore. Reference to the online archives[15] suggests that final site decisions may well have significantly affected the character of the space – and as one of ten similar but different units, Unit 9 is not specifically represented in the final representations. The fieldwork research we undertook suggests that Unit 9 as built is not part of the drawn record – in publications or readily accessible archive records.

Across a history of photography, the accretion and movement of objects across the space can be traced. The mirror, moose head, and lighthouse model have remained in place a long time, but the Indian fabric paintings, the wall-hung Spanish ceiling stuffed with prancing horses and abalone, and the goat sculpture all are later additions. These change the atmosphere of the space, along with the refreshment of upholstery and painted supergraphics.[16]

Our Lived Experience

And everywhere are shelves jammed with books and objects – awash with objects – and that is its most notable characteristic. All of these things, souvenirs of places I have visited, miniature cities and scenes with staggering leaps of scale, all of these things contribute by default to the ornament of my house. [17]

We arrived late in the day after the drive from Santa Cruz and pizza in Gualala and left early on the fourth day for San Francisco. We lived in Unit 9 for around sxity hours. This occupancy served as a study of the form of things; it was an attempt to register the building through everyday and architectural acts, like getting up, eating, going to bed, socialising, and reading, but also through making a survey, which involved walking the surroundings (fig. 9.1) – Black Point, the beach, the coastline up to the Meadow (all important spaces in the Lawerence Halprin led master plan and design process) – and conversations with Donlyn Lyndon and Maynard Lyndon[18]. Of those sixty hours, 30 per cent of my time was spent in slumber, 20 per cent was spent on excursions around Sea Ranch, and 25 per cent was spent surveying the Condominium One and its vicinity – 80 per cent of that survey time was spent inside Unit 9.

More revealing were the cycles of activity. We rose early to watch the sun emerge and light up the home; we went walking south-east in the morning, north-west in the afternoon; and we experienced a cool blue morning was followed by a bright orange sunset in the "saddlebag" bay window – mornings in, afternoons out. Throughout, the bed tent glowed with either the sun or electric light. That first morning after getting our bearings, we surveyed Unit 9, revealing its simple manufacture. We undertook a number of photo surveys of

the space that mapped the changing illumination. My own photo survey captured seventy-nine object groupings, including Moore's own drawing board
in the cleaning cupboard. While being a mix of things, with recent additions,
a majority can be seen somewhere in the historic picture archive. More than
half the objects are either representations of animals or architecture. Half the
objects are arranged on or in furniture, while an additional quarter were hung
on that internal structural frame. Around one third of the objects adorn the
double-height space of the main living area and the bay window (fig. 9.2).

Fig. 9.1   An afternoon walk across Black Point © Tom Coward.

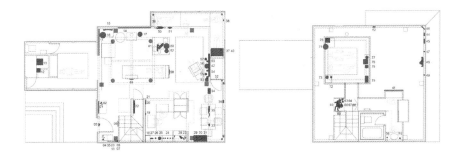

Fig. 9.2   Annotated survey plans measured in situ show the locations of objects on open
display during the visit. © Tom Coward.

Inventory and Its Relationship to Material Engagement Theory

The collective survey process made with the students became a resource for my own reflections. The first step was to construct as built drawings of the space in plan section and elevation. The photos were used to determine the timetable of actions and the object list. Next, the plans were used to plot the object list. Then, returning to the internal design perspective of Unit 1 as a guide, I constructed an object model of the actual location of objects as they were found in Unit 9. The aim was to recreate that propositional perspective through a reverse process; the auditing of the collection, decor, fixtures, and fittings revealed dialogues in material space and an approach to revealing participation within everyday collections (fig. 9.3).

This pedagogical and personal experience raised questions pertinent to my own design practice, around the purposes of visiting and surveying a building for study, gathering immediate spatial information but also perhaps considering deeper content, searching for a continuance of architectural culture through the material of the buildings themselves. If we explore buildings to perceive our shared culture of architecture – then our musings are not far from a socio-cultural anthropology.

Fig. 9.3   The reimagined internal perspective of unit 9 prepared from survey drawings revealing the lived reality following on from the original propositional perspective. © Tom Coward.

Archaeological illustration can be described in discrete parts: surveying to produce accurate records of sites through plan, section, elevations, and axonometric projections; artefact illustration to record objects using agreed conventions to allow further study; and interpretive reconstruction illustration visualising the results of fieldwork in a way that is meaningful and visually appealing to as many people as possible.[19] These aims and means resonate with the architectural practitioner; they are the tools of the trade in describing design work for various audiences throughout the process of conspiring a future building. The role of drawings then, from scratchy fieldwork notes to glossy visualisations or even photographs is to put out feelers speculatively into both our past and into our future and to evidence a cultured position into the material world of things.

The premise of material engagement theory, mentioned at the beginning of this discussion in referring to "enactive things," helps draw together different threads of my personal hybrid practice. Enactive signification as a dynamic between material and mind makes sense to architects – it is the imagination within the recombination of the "poetic image," but it also leads to positive qualities being maintained within physical standards (material, technological, and geometric). In Moore's Unit 9, the syncopation between envelope aperture and the structural figure does much to determine its architectural, that is geometric and material, appeal. But this was also the mechanism in which Moore constructed his lived cognitive centring: it determined the potential for deployment of things within the space. There is a clear distance between the project at conception, in its making, and in its current reality. Moore's "centring" evolved to maintain a spatial image of his own thinking – the orchestration of things in space and light to construct his view of the world – a spatial reinforcement of a good feeling.

The material engagement theory as an explanatory path is based on three interrelated working hypotheses: first, the extended mind is a condition in which cognition is intertwined with material culture; second, enactive signification is a dynamic interaction between material and mind enacting and bringing forth the world; and third, material agency, which is not generated just from the mind, is a product of situated activity. This approach facilitates an understanding of the significance of contingencies in our thinking,[20] of situated action, where all action is a product of the context in which it is taken, and affordance, being what the environment offers the individual.

The provocation is that designers can only design by thinking through their lived experiences, or, in other words, that design is a cultured form of mirroring.[21] The correct analysis of any architectural precedent, on paper or even better in tangible reality, is arguably one of assimilation, and the actions one goes through in occupying any architecture are the primary way to understand its worth. I finish with the words of Tim Ingold,[22] who suggests reversing the architect's "building perspective," or plan for occupation, by considering the "dwelling perspective," allowing us to think of the house as something that arises "within the life process itself [...] the forms people make or build [...] arise within the current of their involved activity, in the specific relational contexts of their practical engagement with their surroundings."[23] To spend any period of time in Unit 9 might give a sense of this dwelling perspective – and remind one of the spatial primacy vital within architectural education, the development of practice, and in criticism – to ensure that you are experienced in the experience of architecture or its "situatedness,"[24] and that buildings last a very long time beyond their original ideation to become only better – and better to inspire others.

Notes

1. Lambros Malafouris, "Part II Outline of a Theory of Material Engagement," in *How Things Shape the Mind: A Theory of Material Engagement* (London: MIT Press, 2013), 57–148.

2. The Wellcome Trust runs the Wellcome Collection, a public venue based in a 1930s neo-classical building at 183 Euston Road, London.

3. Amy Edmonds Alvarado and Patricia R. Herr, "What is Object-Based Enquiry," in *Inquiry-Based Learning Using Everyday Objects: Hands-On Instructional Strategies That Promote Active Learning in Grades 3–8.* (Thousand Oaks: Corwin Press Inc. 2003).

4. Louise Embleton Tudor et al., "Freedom to Learn," in *The Person-Centred Approach: A Contemporary Introduction* (Basingstoke: Palgrave Macmillan, 2004), 163–183.

5. https://www.britannica.com/science/social-learning (accessed 25 April 2021).

6. Tim Ingold, *Making: Anthropology, Archaeology, Art and Architecture* (London: Routledge, 2013), 69 and 115, but also as an ethos within Kingston School of Art: https://archive.ica.art/whats-on/thinking-through-making-140-years-kingston-school-art-panel-discussion (accessed 24 April 2021).

7. James J. Gibson, *The Ecological Approach to Visual Perception* (Boston: Houghton Mifflin Harcourt, 1979), 127.

8. Content can be defined as everything that is included in a collection and that is held or included in something. Contentedness can be considered as the state of being contented with your situation in life. I am interested in the combination here – everything that is included in a collection to be content with your situation.

9. Jorge Otero-Pailos, "Chapter 3: LSDesign Charles W. Moore and the Delirious Interior," in *Architecture's Historical Turn: Phenomenology and the rise of the Postmodern* (Minneapolis: University of Minnesota Press, 2010), 134–139.

10. Kevin P. Keim, "Chapter 10. My Own Houses," in An Architectural Life: Memoirs & Memories of Charles W. Moore (New York: Bullfinch Press, 1996), 169.

11. Charles Moore, Gerald Allen, and Donlyn Lyndon, "The Sea Ranch," in *The Place of Houses: Three Architects Suggest Ways to Build and Inhabit Houses* (New York: Holt, Rinehart and Winston, 1974), 41.

12. Harry Francis Mallgrave, "New Models of Perception," in *From Object to Experience: The New Culture of Architectural Design* (London: Bloomsbury Visual Arts, 2018), 81.

13. Eugene J. Johnson, *Charles Moore: Buildings and Projects 1949–1986* (New York: Rizzoli, 1993).

14. View of a characteristic unit volume in section perspective. Drawing by Edward B. Allen, 1965, accessible at College of Environmental Design Archive, UC Berkeley: http://searanch.ced.berkeley.edu/s/sea-ranch/item/649#?c=0&m=0&s=0&cv=0&xy-wh=-425%2C-83%2C2848%2C1648 (accessed 25 April 2021).

15. For example, http://searanch.ced.berkeley.edu/s/sea-ranch/page/condo-one-as-built (accessed 25 April 2021).

16. In 1968, Yukio Futagawa took photographs for GA Documents that were published in 1970. Fifty years later, his son Yoshio Futagawa revisited Sea Ranch to reshoot the project. The subsequent reissue of the GA special publication mixes resources from the original with new photography. See Yukio Futagawa, *GA Residential Masterpieces 29 Paperback – MLTW – The Sea Ranch, California 1963–* (Ada Edita Global Architecture 2019).

17. Kevin P. Keim, "Chapter 10. My Own Houses," in *An Architectural Life: Memoirs & Memories of Charles W. Moore* (New York: Bullfinch Press, 1996), 181.

18. Donlyn Lyndon is one of the four principal architects making up MLTW, architect of the scheme. Both he and his brother Maynard were involved in the construction of the project and currently live at Sea Ranch.

19. https://en.wikipedia.org/wiki/Archaeological_illustration (accessed 23 September 2020).

20. Lambros Malafouris, "Understanding the Effects of Materiality on Mental Health," in *BJPsych Bulletin* (2019): 1.

21. The nineteenth-century conception of empathy (feeling-into-form) has much in common with the neuroscience theories of mirroring and affordance. Harry Francis Mallgrave, "New Models of Perception," in *From Object to Experience: The New Culture of Architectural Design* (London: Bloomsbury Visual Arts 2018), 67–68.

22. As provoked by Harry Francis Mallgrave, *From Object to Experience: The New Culture of Architectural Design* (London: Bloomsbury Visual Arts, 2018), 51.

23. Tim Ingold, *The Perception of the Environment, Essays on Livelihood, Dwelling and Skill* (London: Routledge, 2000), 186.

24. Dalibor Vesely, "Towards a poetics of Architecture," in *Architecture in the Age of Divided Representation, the Question of Creativity in the Shadow of Production* (Cambridge, MA: MIT Press, 2004), 387.

Bibliography

Alvarado, Amy Edmonds and Patricia R. Herr, "What is Object-Based Enquiry." *Inquiry-Based Learning Using Everyday Objects: Hands-On Instructional Strategies That Promote Active Learning in Grades 3–8*. Thousand Oaks: Corwin Press, 2003.

Tudor, Louise Embleton, Keemar Keemar, Keith Tudor, Joanna Valentine, and Mike Worrall. "Freedom to Learn." *The Person-Centred Approach: A Contemporary Introduction,* 163–183. Basingstoke: Palgrave Macmillan, 2004.

Futagawa, Yukio, ed. "MLTW / Moore, Lyndon, Turnbull and Whitaker, The Sea Ranch, California, 1963–1966." *GA Global Architecture*, no. 3 (1970):1-40.

Gibson, James J. *The Ecological Approach to Visual Perception*. Boston: Houghton Mifflin Harcourt, 1979.

Ingold, Tim. *Making: Anthropology, Archaeology, Art and Architecture*. London: Routledge, 2013.

———. *The Perception of the Environment, Essays on Livelihood, Dwelling and Skill*. London: Routledge, 2000.

Johnson, Eugene J., ed. *Charles Moore: Buildings and Projects 1949–1986*. New York: Rizzoli, 1993.

Keim, Kevin P. *An Architectural Life: Memoirs & Memories of Charles W. Moore*. New York: Bullfinch Press, 1996.

Malafouris, Lambros. *How Things Shape the Mind*. London: MIT Press, 2013.

———. "Understanding the Effects of Materiality on Mental Health." *BJPsych Bulletin* (2019): 1–6, doi:10.1192/bjb.2019.7.

Mallgrave, Harry Francis. *From Object to Experience: The New Culture of Architectural Design*. London: Bloomsbury, 2018.

Moore, Charles, Allen, Gerald, and Lyndon, Donlyn. *The Place of Houses: Three Architects Suggest Ways to Build and Inhabit Houses*. New York: Holt, Rinehart and Winston, 1974.

——— and Toshio Nakamura. *The Work of Charles W. Moore: A+U, Architecture & Urbanism*. Tokyo: A + U, 1978.

Otero-Pailos, Jorge. *Architecture's Historical Turn: Phenomenology and the Rise of the Postmodern*. Minneapolis: University of Minnesota Press, 2010.

Turnbull, William Jr. and Donlyn Lyndon. "MLTW/Moore, Lyndon, Turnbull & Whitaker, The Sea Ranch, California 1963–69." *GA Residential Masterpieces*, no. 29 (25 October 2019).

Vesely, Dalibor. "Towards a Poetics of Architecture." *Architecture in the Age of Divided Representation, the Question of Creativity in the Shadow of Production*. Cambridge: MIT Press, 2004.

CHAPTER 10

A Dialectical Sketch: The ARU Studio by Florian Beigel and Philip Christou, London, 2000–2018

Louis Mayes, Philip Christou

This essay was written following a series of conversations between Louis Mayes and Philip Christou, former co-director with Florian Beigel of the Architecture Research Unit (ARU). From 1974 until 2017, ARU was a laboratory for testing the relationship between design, research, and teaching. This text examines some connections between the design process and the pedagogical approach of ARU.

Introduction

The relationship between practice and theory is complex. Inherently, one depends on the other – design decisions are often based on some form of reference from the past. In this way, design and theory can have a cyclical relationship, an approach that the late Florian Beigel, director of ARU, consistently referred to from the late 1970s onwards as "design as research"[1] – a proponent to a widespread approach that has become increasingly popular in both teaching and practice in recent years. Within ARU, this is a method of practice incorporating design, drawing, and writing that allows the project to develop in a thoughtful and critical manner. We would like to explore how one influences the other and reconsider how we define theory, as we interrogate alternative approaches to the use of references.

I

The hand-drawn sketch can often be identified as the starting point of a scheme. This form of drawing remains inherently a product of both the hand and the mind – an intuitive response of the designer that may encompass the key concepts, histories, and spatial qualities of the project. Often, it is also the first time that the designer begins to transcend the schism between two- and three-dimensional spatiality of a project or, to use Peter Märkli's term, the point at which composition becomes gestalt.[2] Whether it represents a reference image or a site plan, the sketch can be read as a tangible summary of the primary thoughts of the designer.

By taking a close look at a hand-drawn sketch by Beigel of a Korean *pojagi* (fig. 10.1), a textile made from patches of fabric traditionally used to wrap and transport food – we can explore the idea of design as research. The ambiguity of Beigel's pencil drawing can be described as "beautifully unsure," relaying essential characteristics of the irregular and seemingly unconcerned way in which the original textile is sewn together.

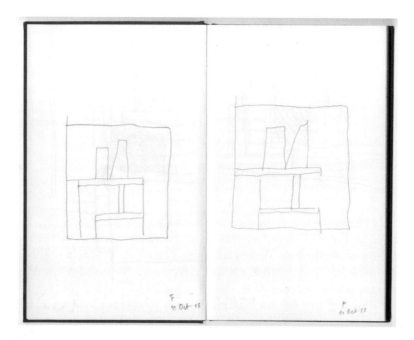

Fig. 10.1   Florian Beigel, two pencil sketches of a *pojagi*, 11 October 2013.

This particular drawing was produced after the completion of the building but can still be used to explore the manner in which Beigel has used the sketch to summarise the reference. Over two facing pages of a sketchbook (slightly narrower than A4 size), there are two interpretations of the same piece of cloth – gentle and uniform pencil lines delineate a series of shapes that seem to correspond to each other but differ in scale and to some extent proportion. Both are dated on the same day.

The sketch on the right has one extra line. The fact that Beigel drew the same subject in two similar ways suggests that he was aiming to portray a quality beyond simply representing the subject. He often said that he tried to draw "without preconceptions," and the sketch of the *pojagi* is a highly selective and reduced representation of the fabric; Beigel has drawn out the essential characteristic qualities as he sees them.

Despite being created subsequently, Beigel's drawing of the *pojagi* is significant in explaining ARU's approach during the design of the Pojagi Building (2004, fig. 10.2 -10.3), a scheme built by ARU in Korea housing a jazz café, a gallery for fabrics, and a house.[3] A central element of this scheme are the lightweight polycarbonate pavilions that sit gently above the solid plinth of the café,

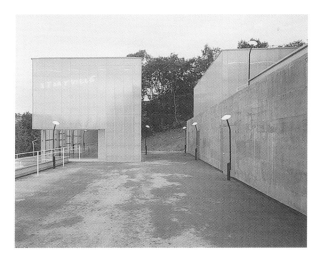

Fig. 10.2–3 Florian Beigel and ARU with Kim Jong Kyu and MARU, Pojagi Building, Heyri, Korea, 200. Photographs: Kim Jong Oh.

supported by a visible steel structure and a slightly skewed timber subframe. It is the relationship between the skewed timber members and the original fabric of the *pojagi* that lends the building its name. A series of developmental drawings from different stages of the design (fig. 10.4) consistently show the character of this frame as it evolves from concept to construction – all of which are related to the original sketch. Through this process, the open-ended qualities of the sketch can be translated into a project – the built work has become less "finite."

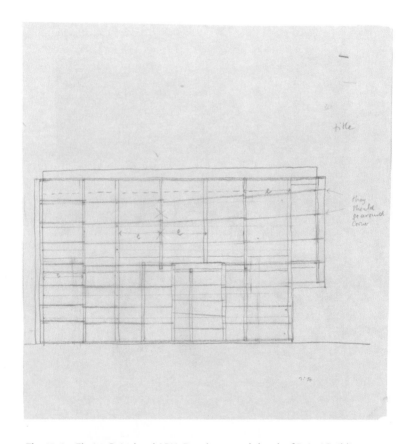

Fig. 10.4   Florian Beigel and ARU, Developmental sketch of Pojagi Building.

The design sketch translates the original reference of the *pojagi*, aligning it with the final timber structure. It adopts the inherent ambiguity of its reference, allowing a non-finite quality and a variety of interpretations. Adopting the characteristics of the cloth observed through Beigel's first sketch, the uncertainty of the pencil lines relates to the original reference while also allowing a certain amount of interpretation. As such, the idea of the "beautifully unsure," inherent to Beigel's indistinct pencil lines, conveys the way in which the building is constructed. In this way, a sketch of a reference can become part of the design – a process that Beigel describes as "an intelligent understanding of the past."[4] This allows the designer to reinterpret history within the design process through a reappropriation of the original object.

II

To understand the importance of the sketch in relation to ARU's work, we must first contemplate what the aim of the sketch was – and what we can learn from it. This begins with a comparison of the conceptual and the theoretical.

The etymology of the word "concept" consists of "take" (*capere*) and 'with' (*con*). This suggests a conjunction of ideas, in the same way that thoughts are gathered together at the *inception* of a project, or how a *receptacle* unifies different elements into a single place. A "theory," however has a far more removed relationship with the design process and comes from the idea to consider or to look at ("spectator" – *theōros*) – sitting in line with a set of ideas perceived retrospectively.

We could therefore align the idea of the concept with a certain amount of temporality and flux, whereas theory has a more static dimension. The distinction between the two is made clearer in the context of their definitions when we suggest that the concept isn't easily made tangible, whereas a theory can often be associated with something that can be seen and described, for instance through realised buildings.

In his writing on suprematism, Kasimir Malevich proclaims that "essence has always been destroyed by the subject."[5] In many ways ARU's design approach follows this idea, where the open-ended and interpretive concept is used to guide the choice of form, material, or colour. As with Beigel's sketch, an early drawing often succinctly defines the key concept or architectural articulations relevant to a project, and in the case of Beigel's *pojagi* sketch, the subject is less important than the ability of the sketch to convey a concept. Perhaps the design process used by ARU could be called *operative theory*; the sketch is a vehicle for understanding the design, and, at the same time, it defines the premise of ARU's theoretical approach in a more general sense.

In addition to this, it is evident that the drawing of the *pojagi* allows other concepts to be applied – for example, the idea of the tension between the solid and the void of the original cloth. It is the void and its element of uncertainty and ambiguity that lends this sketch its poignancy. Whether it is made before or after, the sketch is a developmental tool whose open-endedness allows the project to be understood. The lines define a concept; the voids in between represent the potential for changefulness; the solid and void are in tension. In this manner, the sketch acts as a medium that can be interpreted in various ways. It becomes not only a carrier for a concept relevant to a particular project, but equally formulates spatial ideas that resonate through ARU's work.

III

How has this working approach informed the way that students are guided in their design projects? The point is to come to an understanding of the principal spatial and tectonic relationships of a given reference and to use this understanding as a guide when searching for a spatial concept in a project without imitating an image or a style. In the following students' work, characteristics true to ARU's pedagogical approach are conveyed without relaying a specific stylistic norm. Design is a synthesis process that requires a certain sense of risk and a few stabs in the dark before it begins to come to life and begins to have its own internal logic. One can use an existing architectural example as a reference or inspiration during the design process. It is there to strengthen and focus the spatial ideas as they are developing in the design. In the end, it is a matter of having a good eye.

Urban Figures – Soho, London, 2007, MA student Alex Bank

Initially, Bank made a careful study of the "hôtel particulier" building type that were built during the seventeenth and eighteenth centuries in France. He studied the Hôtel de Beauvais (1660) and the Hôtel Carnavalet (1548), both in the Marais district of Paris (fig. 10.5–10.8).[6]

The Hotel de Beauvais, built within a dense and awkwardly shaped site in the city, has a beautiful regular void figure as a courtyard, a powerfully theatrical space embedded within the city block. At the first-floor level, there is a garden courtyard asymmetrically positioned to the main courtyard. Alex studied and drew this obsessively (fig. 10.9). He selected a similarly dense site in central London, where he made intelligent translations and interpretations of the hôtel particulier typology (fig. 10.10).

He designed a series of public courtyards – urban figures as voids. Similar to Hôtel de Beauvais, the entrance to the main courtyard is through a passage, and the garden courtyard is located on the first level.

Fig. 10.5 Urban Figures, model studies of the design proposal (left), the Hôtel de Beauvais (middle), and the Hôtel Carnavalet (right) all at the same scale, Alex Bank.

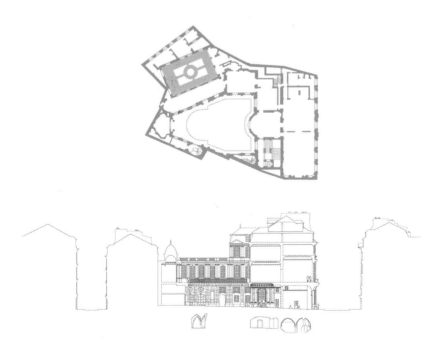

Fig. 10.6 Hôtel de Beauvais, Paris, (1660), first-floor plan and section studies, Alex Bank.

Fig. 10.7 Courtyard of the Hôtel de Beauvais. Photograph: Alex Bank.

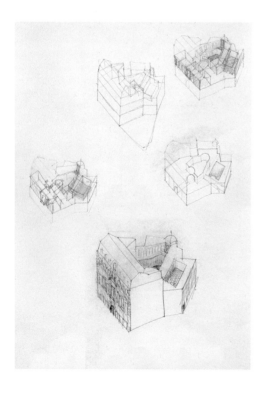

Fig. 10.8 Hôtel de Beauvais, Paris, pencil sketch studies, Alex Bank.

Fig. 10.9 Sketch study of the design proposal with courtyard voids as figure.

Fig. 10.10 First-floor plan in the context of the existing city block.

A Good House, Beyond Object-ness – Quinta da Malagueira, Évora, Portugal, 2015, Jasmine Low

In this next example, one corner of a field of patio houses within Álvaro Siza's design of the Quinta da Malagueira urban landscape project in Évora, Portugal has been reconfigured with several public void spaces. Public and domestic activities are in close proximity. A public hall, like a small tower house, builds an active relationship with Siza's overhead infrastructural ducts and the horizon. The concept plan drawing is filled with spatial tension and potential (fig. 10.11–10.12).

What we can see from the two students' work is that they have developed different schemes through a range of different mediums. Yet there is a thread that draws the two together – an underlying set of concepts that can be explained through the project – the relationship between the solid and the void, or the ability to make drawings that are open to interpretation and reflect the essential characteristics of the design proposal. This is the manner in which ARU has worked with students – a propositional approach based on spatial concepts. In this way, ARU's approach to design as research, or operative theory, can be seen in the way they work as architects and how they convey ideas to their students.

Fig. 10.11 Design concept plan drawing of figure and void, Jasmine Low.

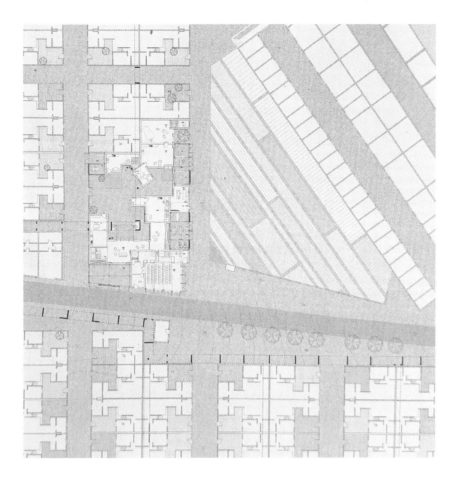

Fig. 10.12   Design plan, Jasmine Low.

Conclusion

Throughout ARU's work there is an element of duality, a dialectical relationship that exists: solid and void, infrastructure and inhabitation, hand and
mind. Once viewed outside of the design process, these can be seen as theories associated with the works of ARU. In this way, concepts are drawn out as
theories providing a framework to understand ideas. Theory and practice in
this case are intrinsically related and self-defining at the same time – the two
are distinct, yet intimately reliant on each other. In the words of Beigel, "The
world has become quite complex. Things are no longer one thing or another,
they are both."[7]

Notes

1. Florian Beigel and Philip Christou, "Engaging People To Love Architecture (Far Amare L'Architettura)," *DOMUS*, no. 991 (May 2015): 9.
2. Florian Beigel and Philip Christou, "Peter Märkli's Spatial Gestalt," in *Everything one invents is true: The architecture of Peter Märkli*, edited by Pamela Johnston (Quart Publishers: Lucerne, 2017), 228–233.
3. Florian Beigel and Architecture Research Unit, London in collaboration with Kim Jong Kyu and MARU, Seoul. House, Jazz Hall and PoDjaGi Gallery, Heyri Art Valley, South Korea, completed August 2004. See Andrew Mead, "Pojagi Gallery and Jazz Club Story Ville," *The Architect's Journal* issue 241 (September 2004): 24–33.
4. Florian Beigel and Philip Christou, *Baukunst 01: The Idea of City* (London: Ajand, 2013), 22.
5. Charles Harrison and Paul Wood, *Art in Theory 1900–2000* (London: Blackwell Publishing, 2010) 175.
6. See Florian Beigel and Phlip Christou, "Introduction," in Sam Casswell, Gemma Drake, and Tom Graham, eds., *Urban Figures* (London: Architecture Research Unit, 2011). Design research study publications of historical and contemporary architectural projects made by diploma students of architecture at the London Metropolitan University tutored by Florian Beigel and Philip Christou include *Urban Figures* (2007), *Landscape as City* (2008), *City Structures* (2009), *Architecture as City* (2010), *Baukunst 01* (2011), *Cultivation and Culture* (2012), *Beyond Object-ness: A Good House* (2015, unpublished), *Time Architecture, Palace of the People* (2016, unpublished).
7. Florian Beigel, "Exteriority and the Everyday, Materiality, Towards Invisibility," *Korean Architects* issue 141, (May 1996): 189; and Florian Beigel, "Paisajes Urbanos, Urban Landscapes," *Quaderns D'Arquitectura i Urbanisme* issue 216 *Form and Place* (1997): 41.

Bibliography

Beigel, Florian. "Exteriority and the Everyday, Materiality, Towards Invisibility." *Korean Architects*, Issue 141 (May 1996): 189.
——. "Paisajes Urbanos, Urban Landscapes." *Quaderns 'Arquitectura i Urbanisme*, 216 *Form and Place* (1997): 41.
—— and Philip Christou. *City Structures*. London: Ajand, 2009.
—— and Philip Christou. *Architecture as City: Saemangeum Island City*. Vienna and New York: Springer, 2010.
—— and Philip Christou. "Introduction." In *Urban Figures*, edited by Sam Casswell, Gemma Drake, and Tom Graham. London: Architecture Research Unit, 2011.
—— and Philip Christou. *Cultivation and Culture*. London: Architecture Research Unit, 2012.
—— and Philip Christou. *Baukunst 01: The Idea of City*. London: Ajand, 2013.
—— and Philip Christou. "Teaching Through Design." *JOELHO*, no. 04 (April 2013): 24–33.
—— and Philip Christou. "Engaging People to Love Architecture (Far Amare 'Architettura)." *DOMUS*, no. 991 (May 2015): 6–9.
—— and Philip Christou. "Peter Märkl''s Spatial Gestalt." In *Everything One Invents Is True: The Architecture of Peter Märkli*, edited by Pamela Johnston, 228–233. Quart Publishers: Lucerne, 2017.
——, Philip Christou, and A. Gore. *Landscape as City*. London: Architecture Research Unit, 2008.

Malevich, Kasimir. "From Cubism to Futurism to Suprematism: The New Realism in Painting."
     In *Art in Theory 1900–2000*, edited by Charles Harrison and Paul Wood, 173–183. London:
     Blackwell Publishing, 2010.
Mead, Andrew. "Pojagi Gallery and Jazz Club Story Ville." *The Architect's Journal* 241
     (September 2004): 24–33.

CHAPTER 11

The Building Is Present: The 1:5 Model as a Way of Seeing, TU Delft, Chair Buildings, Interiors, Cities, 2018–2019

Sereh Mandias

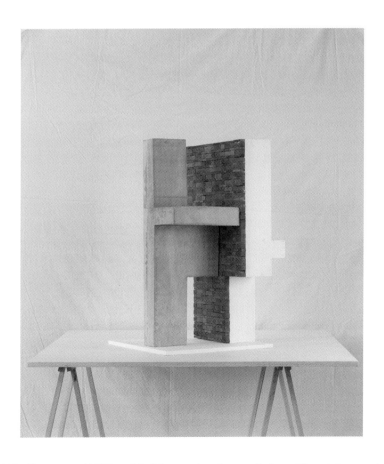

Fig. 11.1 Concrete and MDF model of the meeting of two walls from different times, scale 1:5, by Riccardo Garrone and Sam Stalker. Photograph: Bas Leemans.

The object is both large and small. It stands before us on a makeshift table, at eye level.

There are two parts, pushed together to create a three-dimensional figure: a composition of two walls, three openings, and two cantilevers. We can further dissect it on the basis of its colours and materials. A white painted volume bears a surface of what appears to be tiny bricks, painted in shades of deep red and brown and assembled in a bond of alternating rows of narrow and wide bricks. It is created as cladding, as such depriving its host of structural logic. And a concrete element, which is cast in one piece, meets the brick surface in the middle, while distancing itself at the top and the bottom. As an autonomous object, it is small; its rows of small bricks allow us to read it as a miniature. But as a model, it's large. One has to walk around it to see it from all sides. Even without lifting it, one senses its weight.

We are looking at a model at 1:5 scale of a fragment of the Museum Boijmans van Beuningen in Rotterdam. It was made by two students out of a group of thirteen during a design course in the spring of 2019 in the Chair of Interiors Buildings Cities at TU Delft.[1]

Fig. 11.2 Presentation of the fragments, with a foam and paper model of a monumental stairwell in the original museum, scale 1:5, by Chen Zhu and Seongchul Yu. Photograph: Sereh Mandias.

Museum Boijmans van Beuningen is an extraordinary ensemble of different building parts from different times. In opposition to a harsh and large-scale renovation plan, the course intended to address possible shortcomings of the current museum by departing from what was already there. Through a close reading of the architecture of the ensemble, the students explored a sensitive and intimate way of thinking about the transformation of more and less monumental pieces of architecture.

An Intimate Encounter

The 1:5 model anchored the course. Over the course of eleven weeks, it was used as an instrument to examine the architectural qualities of the building and, subsequently, as a basis for architectural interventions within the museum.

Rather than seeing the museum as something abstract, represented through drawings or digital models, the intention was to foster a kind of empathy with the museum ensemble. The 1:5 model focused the attention of our students on the physical and intimate encounter with the building – as a tactile experience.

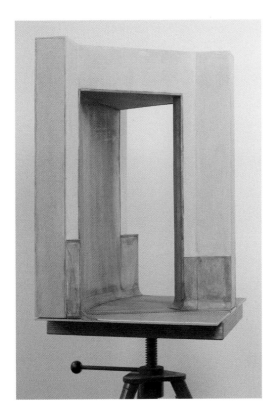

Fig. 11.3 MDF and veneer model of a passage in the original museum, scale 1:5, by Shamila Gostelow and Silja Siikki. Photograph: Shamila Gostelow and Silja Siikki.

The approach and design of the course sprung from a collective interest at the Chair of Interiors Buildings Cities in exploring the notion of intimacy in architecture. It was initiated and taught by Tomas Dirrix and myself, who have both been educated in this Chair and now teach there. Its culture is characterised by a sustained attention to the things that surround us, an attention to the bodily experience of architecture, the specifics of materials and their assembly, the atmosphere of spaces, and the construction of this atmosphere.

This is reinforced by Tomas Dirrix's research into vernacular construction and its materials as a practising architect and my own training in philosophy, which has led me to attempt to translate the precision one acquires in philosophy in dealing with language into the discipline of architecture.[2]

We visited the building. Construct a model at scale 1:5, we asked our students, of a fragment of the museum that captures your experience of the building, of the body in relation to specific architectural moments. And choose and build it in such a way that the model itself becomes a potent physical object.

One of these moments is situated within the original museum of 1935 by the architect Adrianus Van der Steur and concerns the transition between gallery spaces. Here, the wall widens, and in this thickened wall, a passage is carved out. The wooden wainscoting extends to clad the entire opening, making it stand out against the light grey walls of the gallery. If one steps from the linoleum of the galleries onto the wood of the passage, one suddenly hears one's own footsteps.

Fig. 11.4 MDF and veneer model of a passage in the original museum, scale 1:5, Shamila Gostelow and Silja Siikki, detail. Photograph: Bas Leemans.

The model isolates this moment from the sequence of spaces that it is a part of. In plan, it is shaped like a truncated triangle, but not all sides have been treated the same way. The opening and its adjacent surfaces have been clad in stained veneer and grey paint. On other sides, the thin boards of MDF with which it is constructed remain visible. In doing so, it brings into focus the way the wall opens up and becomes a deep threshold between one gallery and the next.

Fig. 11.5   Concrete model of the meeting of two extensions from different times, scale 1:5, Ananta Vania Iswardhani and Coen Gordebeke. Photograph: Bas Leemans and Tomas Dirrix.

Intentional Abstraction

The 1:5 scale posed an interesting challenge, as we found that it is, at this scale, almost always possible to exactly replicate the existing structure. Abstraction is no longer a necessary consequence of the format, but becomes a deliberate choice. The most interesting models hovered between exact representation and intentional abstraction.

The brick and concrete model is one such example. The students chose as their fragment the meeting of an exterior wall of the original museum with the 2003 extension by Paul Robbrecht and Hilde Daem. Their model is a precise representation of the meeting of the two surfaces. Van der Steur's 1935 brick wall is reconstructed using bricks cut from MDF, which are painted with ecoline, in a very near approximation of the colour of the original wall, and then assembled in Van der Steur's characteristic bond. Robbrecht and Daem's extension is abstracted to the rough concrete of the construction and poured using actual concrete. The window frames inserted by Robbrecht and Daem next to the original wall are left out, abstracting this moment to the meeting of the two materials.

Fig. 11.6 Concrete and MDF model of the meeting of two walls from different times, scale 1:5, Riccardo Garrone and Sam Stalker, detail. Photograph: Bas Leemans.

This model was both a highly accurate and vibrant representation of the material expression of the fragment and, at the same time, an abstraction focusing on the specific way that the architects of the extension explicitly expressed the meeting between new and old. In doing so, they were able to identify the confrontation of different building parts from different times and the way these moments of confrontation are negotiated within architecture, as a core characteristic of the museum's architecture.

Fig. 11.7   Foam and polyester model of a fragment of the facade by Robbrecht and Daem, scale 1:5, Mees Wijnants and Tommaso Tellarini. Photograph: Bas Leemans.

Neither Detail, Nor Space

The 1:5 scale poses restrictions to the size of the fragment that can be extracted from the building and therefore in large part determines what becomes significant. The fragments are neither detail nor space, but rather experiential and material moments within the building. They teased out specific architectural themes and made them explicit: from the way that the relation between the museum and the city is negotiated through the facade to the particular way that the meeting of old and new is staged or the idea of the museum as a series of thresholds.

As a result, we came to locate the essence of the building at the scale of the fragment. In doing so, our way of working proposes the identification of the "significant architectural moment" as a way of analysing what is valuable in a building. It is a specific way of looking, one that locates architectural themes within the material fragment.

Fig. 11.8   Concrete model of a proposed intervention, scale 1:5, by Shamila Gostelow and Silja Siikki. Photograph: Bas Leemans.

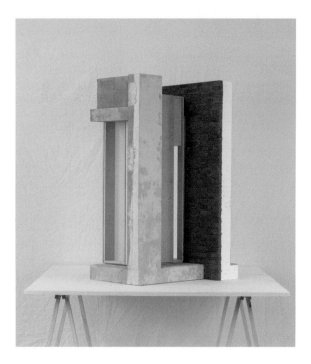

Fig. 11.9   Concrete and MDF model of a proposed intervention, scale 1:5, by Riccardo Garrone and Sam Stalker. Photograph: Bas Leemans.

On the basis of the themes they identified when building the 1:5 fragments of the museum, the students went on to develop interventions into the museum.

One of the results was a pink column. It was made by the builders of the passage between two gallery spaces, who continued their research by interpreting the museum as a collection of thresholds. They proceeded to address one especially problematic threshold: the transition from the entrance area of the museum to the museum space proper, an awkward and slightly chaotic way of entering the galleries.

The precise position of the column reorganises and highlights the moment of passing through. It has a slightly rectangular footprint, and the side facing the entrance has a different texture from the others. It was developed from a series of experiments with casting concrete models to explore texture, colour, and tactile qualities. Referring to the playfulness of other art objects in the entrance hall, the intervention oscillates between architectural object and artistic intervention. It is a small project, but as it reorganises the entrance area of the museum, it has an impact beyond its physical limits.

The Resistance of Materials

Working on the 1:5 scale was instrumental in retaining the focus on the small scale and made it possible to discuss the tactile and material qualities of the evolving designs within the studio setting. It made students aware of the resistance of materials, of how things are constructed while designing them, and enforced a kind of concreteness and precision into the analysis and design.

The duo examining the meeting of different building parts from different times expanded their research into the theme of the architectural joint. They focused their intervention on another, more complicated, and currently less successful joint: a small patio next to a narrow landing, between the original building and one of its extensions. The intervention proposes to eliminate the patio in favour of extending the landing, making it a more generous space when entering the galleries on the first floor. The proposed structure, crafted out of timber, repeats the move of visually distancing the new from the older as a clearly legible addition by detailing this extended threshold as a piece of wooden furniture within the gallery space.

Beyond demonstrating the value of small-scale interventions, these projects show how one can develop a contextual and precise approach to adjusting existing architecture. The 1:5 scale makes it possible to develop this approach in a concentrated way, without having to immediately address the complexities of the entire building. Just as the 1:5 fragment of the building can tease out a critical moment and stands for a specific interpretation of the museum, each intervention is a highly suggestive example of a specific approach.

Fig. 11.10   Foam and polyester model of a fragment of the facade by Robbrecht and Daem, scale 1:5, by Mees Wijnants and Tommaso Tellarini. Photograph: Mees Wijnants and Tommaso Tellarini.

In setting the terms of the project, we suspected there might be value in creating a collection of beautiful material pieces to represent the museum. During the design process, when the fragments were present within the studio at all times, these models worked as highly concrete reminders of the experience of the building. It was not allowed to recede into the distance, but remained a character in the room.

Notes

1. The students' names are Ananta Vania Iswardhani, Chen Zhu, Coen Gordebeke, Dinand Kruize, Helen Cao, Jakub Wysocki, Mees Wijnants, Riccardo Garrone, Sam Stalker, Seongchul Yu, Shamila Gostelow, Silja Siikki, and Tommaso Tellarini.
2. The Chair Interiors Buildings Cities, previously run by Tony Fretton and now by Daniel Rosbottom, and where Mark Pimlott is a continuing presence, has a tradition of working with large-scale models. Varying from courses in which conventional types of models of various scales make an appearance to design courses in which one specific type of model serves to anchor the course as a whole. However, the 1:5 scale had not been explored like this before.

PART 3

Different Worlds and Other Places

What the essays in this part have in common is that they each offer a perspective that challenges mainstream academic thinking. Post-colonisation theories question the universal applicability of Western paradigms and are able to make sense of conditions that are so chaotic and conflicting that the idea of a single comprehensive reading loses all relevance. New materialist ideas developed in the fields of philosophy and political sciences stress the agency of inanimate things, helping researchers to see humans as part of a larger (and vulnerable) ecosystem, evaluating our endeavours through the lens of non-humans. In addition, feminist perspectives interrogate the power structures underlying our understanding of architecture through storytelling and engagement with alternative experiences of the production of architecture.

In her piece, "The Mysteries Encountered when Finding Reality," Helen Thomas describes the search in the 1960s and '70s for viewpoints that opposed the then dominant Western research traditions in their use of history. Joseph Rykwert's master's course set up at the University of Essex in 1968 challenged the distance between architectural history and practice. The architects Fernand Pouillon and Yasmeen Lari both put history as building practice to work, Pouillon in accessing the history of stone, Lari in developing a "reset vernacular." All three demonstrate "new realities" that reveal themselves through history as a source. The transgression of academic borders also opens a route to alternative viewpoints that are capable of perceiving alternative worlds. The playful imagination that storytelling introduces is one such tool. Starting from the reality of the object, in this case a deserted school building in an Iranian oil town, Sepideh Karami uses photographs and fictional narratives to make sense of "the mess," in this case a postcolonial setting, allowing her to speculate on pasts that might not reveal themselves otherwise. Entire speculative worlds come to life in Jana Culek's alternative understanding of the architectural utopia. Culek compares architectural and literary utopias, with the aim of including the underlying social processes and conditions, all of which are revealed in series of drawings presented at different scales to question the "form" of utopia. Yet another way of capturing social processes is developed in the project Growing up Modern, in which Julia Jamrozik looks for the meaning of architectural culture beyond the professional debate. The oral histories she has collected paint a colourful picture of life in iconic buildings from a child's perspective. By turning not to the clients, but to their children, the buildings reveal their function as social spaces and places of memory, which have left a surprisingly strong mark on some of their occupants.

CHAPTER 12

The Mysteries Encountered When Finding Reality

Helen Thomas

One day in December 2019, I travelled from the Barbican in London to the Copyright Bookshop in Ghent to celebrate the publication of Marie-Jose Van Hee's book about her work. It was here that William Mann introduced me to Caroline Voet, but in a way, we had already met. I had recently been using her book on Hans Van Der Laan with my students at Kingston University; she had been reading my article on Joseph Rykwert and his time at the University of Essex, which she had come across in her initial research for this book. Our meeting in this room lined with books – the captured thoughts of our peers and mentors – was an apt place to begin discussing the practice of architectural research. This activity had produced the myriad desirable publications that surrounded us and had caused us to come together in the type of social encounter that researchers actively seek – the incidental juxtaposition of different perspectives. But underlying this inquiry into what constitutes research, especially as embodied in this relationship between designing as a dynamic creative process, and history as legacy and provocation, is another question, which is *why* do we research?

There are three overlapping spheres of action within which the researcher potentially operates, which are explored here through the work and milieu of three architect-writers. Two of these spheres, which are the *social* and the *political*, rely on collaboration, competition, and hierarchy, and are communal. The third, called here the *creative*, reverts to the individual. It is a way for the subjective and the intuitive to connect to the consensus and order of the social and the political, and specifically to embrace the collaborative nature of design. Searching for a starting point of the current tensions between the conceptual work of academia and the hands-on work of the practising architect, and which also provides a rich site for identifying the interplay between the social, the political, and the creative, is the early pedagogy of architect and historian Joseph Rykwert.

Joseph Rykwert and the Problem of Institutional Reality

A shift in the productive relationship between the design process as experience and action towards its possible future, and history as a repository waiting to be mined, was embodied in the master's course in the history and theory of architecture set up by Rykwert. His proposal to the University of Essex in 1967 stated that "[t] here is at present no course of this nature being offered at any school of architecture or university in this country; or indeed anywhere else that I know of."[1]

In the autumn of 1968, just four years after the University of Essex had opened its doors to around 120 students, three men arrived at the Department of Art History in the School of Comparative Studies. These were Rykwert's founding students, each of them with architectural training, as stipulated in the prospectus, which stated that "[t]he scheme of study will be a self-contained programme for students who are familiar with the basic notions of planning and designing, and who also have some experience of architectural and design office practice."[2] At the time, history and theory were not integral to the education of the architect, and in the words of an early student called John McKean, "no-one was teaching history of architecture in schools, far less ideas. There wasn't any kind of philosophical debate in my experience and I think for the people around."[3] Cultivating the embodiment of architectural history and theory into design thinking was fundamental to Rykwert's plan, and also for his colleague Dalibor Vesely, who Rykwert had invited to teach with him.

Rykwert is well connected and has many friends. McKean's course notebook, for example, reveals that, in finding ways to apply his thinking to present-day architecture, Rykwert introduced the work of Aldo van Eyck, who had published *The Idea of a Town* in his journal *Forum* in 1963, Giancarlo De Carlo, who he knew through his travels through Italy during the 1940s, and Hassan Fathy. Each of these architects is an example of the thinker-practitioners that Rykwert and Vesely were training their students to become. The most important educational process for them to carry this out was the intense study and discussion of historical and philosophical texts. Rykwert's written description of his seminar course, Theoretical Literature of Architecture Before 1800, explicitly stated that "[p]articular weight will be given to the implications of theory for contemporary practice." McKean's notebook records the following advice, given during his first meeting on this course – "it" being the text: "First, read it, then second, make it clear that you understand it. Third, add commentary and fourthly include your own attitudes, any ideas, feelings etc, however way out." Another student, Helen Mallinson, remembered that during "four, six weeks we looked at one paragraph of Alberti [...] I was completely taken aback by the whole thing, by the intensity of it."[4]

The ambitions acted out through teaching the master's course were also political, a term understood here to have several implications, one of them being the radical intent that underlies so much of research practice as an activity and its outcomes as a goal and catalyst. This is the ambition to reflect on and change the way that we ourselves and others think about and ultimately engage with the world, or to contribute to a larger movement whose objectives we are sympathetic to.

The setting of the researcher can influence the nature of the political expression. It might be hierarchical and internalised within the institutional context of academia, or practical and economical within the commercial world of practice. For Rykwert and Vesely, there were two political issues at stake within their academic context. One was the intellectual challenge to the rationalist foundations of modern architecture and the hegemony of Enlightenment thought and its influence on architectural education. According to their student Alberto Perez Gomez, they used a pincer action: "For me their approach worked very well together," he told me, "Joseph went 'forward' from Vitruvius to the eighteenth century, Dalibor 'backward' from phenomenology to the nineteenth century ending with Semper."[5]

The second issue was the invention of a productive and symbiotic connection between the practice of architecture and the transformation of academic knowledge through discussion and research.

Unfortunately, this dream did not align with the politics of the institution in which it was set. The master's course became untenable at the University of Essex. Within this newly established education and research institution, the Department of Art History was modelled not on an art or design school, but on the Courtauld Institute of Art. This was where the establishment framework of art history and connoisseurship reproduced itself. Michael Podro, who came from the Courtauld to Essex shortly after Rykwert, told me he came because the department needed someone with superfluous "reading lists." Cast out of the academy, the master's course and its participants were obliged to become peripatetic.

By 1973, seminars were being held in the basement kitchen of the Soane Museum in London, around the kitchen table. Removal from an established setting and institutional frameworks defined a situation that relied on social relations enacted around a table and dependent upon ritual. These nomadic circumstances could be described as incorporating an intense version of the social relations underlying research practice. Belonging to a group bound by common knowledge and codes provides a setting for individual work. This work can then be tested, validated, and ranked within the context of these shared values. The master's course depended upon the charismatic presence of its two main teachers – Rykwert and Vesely. Mallinson told me that she got the feeling that "Joseph was the stable person who set up not just the administration but the fact that you had tea, and that someone was always organised to bring biscuits. There was the sense of civilization, an order of business that Joseph was very responsible for," she said. "There was a kind of ethos to the way one was expected to participate." Mallinson took part in seminars hosted in Hugh Casson's office at the Royal Academy and was joined by David Leatherbarrow. He remembered that just as important as the Royal Academy was Fortnum and Mason across the street. "At the first meeting of the seminar," he said, "Joseph took the whole group there to select and buy all the apparatus for making coffee. The context we had was limited to those who participated in the seminar."[6]

The table at the centre of a select group of people hosted more that simple tea parties, however. Enactment of the texts themselves was also ritualised – they were read aloud and they were dissected with the same intensity as poetry. For some of the participants of the seminars, this experience of exchange and shared interpretation of complex texts became embedded in forms of architectural practice. The outcomes of these new practices were not necessarily buildings. Students also became teachers and writers. Drawing as a practice was inspired by the teachings of the course, and a well-known practitioner in this sense was Daniel Libeskind, recognised until the turn of the century through his Micromegas and Chamber Works series.

Mysterious Reality

The Iron Pillar of Delhi is a mysterious column that was cast sometime in the fourth century, now located in the courtyard of the Quwwatul Islam Mosque in Delhi's Qutub Minar complex. It has resisted oxidation for 1,600 years, and although its chemical composition has been analysed, the technological knowledge of the metallurgists who created it remains enigmatic. The column bears history in another way, through the inscriptions that cover it. Nevertheless, it is a secretive object that ultimately withholds the processes of its construction and the intentions behind its manufacture from the researcher. Its past is inaccessible – both in the sense of its material origins, even where it was made, and also in its cultural meaning over time. As an object, it has an oracle-like quality. As an utterance and an agency, its messages are ambiguous and obscure. In this sense, it resonates with a translation of a quote from Friedrich Nietzsche's text "On the Uses and Abuses of History for Life," which states: "When the past speaks it always speaks as an oracle: only if you are an architect of the future and know the present will you understand it."[7] This powerful phrase is open to many interpretations that spring from the relationship between the past, present, and future that it suggests. In most architectural histories, this relationship today differs from that of the twentieth century, for example, when the role of the architect, or the builder, in making the future corresponded with a Western belief in technological progress that corresponded to the dream of utopia that had motivated colonisers and modernists.

Rykwert and Vesely's use of historical and philosophical texts, their moving backwards and forwards through time, was a precursor to today's questioning

Fig. 12.1   Iron Pillar, Quwwatul Islam Mosque, Delhi © Indrajit Das.

of the legitimacy of Western ideas of technological progress and its outcomes. As researchers, we are engaged with finding and also creating narratives of the past that are useful for the present and which provide a field of action for the future, but the utopias of the twentieth century are no longer available. The academic institution favours the scholarly above all other forms of narrative. Scholarly, in this instance, is the verifiable and rigorously sourced, the peer reviewed and firmly located within existing traditions of thought and structures of knowledge; it accretes. But if design and architectural practice are introduced into the equation – that is, an engagement and response to an uncontrollable world, with unpredictable ways of thinking and acting that exist outside the academic system – the narratives connecting history, theory, and practice cannot be seamless and objective, purely scientific, or theoretical. This questioning of the once-dominant themes of modernism – technological advancement and the novelty it engenders, mass production and industrialisation – which enabled the coining of terms like first world and third world, and a view of the future as a superior present, will be explored next through the approaches of two very different architects to the realities of their historical, geographical, and cultural situations.

Fernand Pouillon's Use of History

> He who, without betraying the constraints of the modern programme or materials, produces a work that seems always to have existed – that is, in a word, banal – may consider himself a man well satisfied.
> —Auguste Perret, 1952

French architect Fernand Pouillon (1912–1986) was a man with a biography so vivid that it overshadowed his presence as an architect in the French cultural imagination for many years. He was a prolific builder, developer, teacher, and also a writer, whose form was fiction. While languishing in prison for fraudulent bankruptcy,[8] Pouillon passed his time writing, and he was abundant and talented. In addition to his autobiography, he wrote a novel set in thirteenth-century Provence. It is narrated through the diary of Guillaume Balz, who is the master builder of the Cistercian abbey of Le Thoronet, but also of course, the embodiment of Pouillon himself. In French, this book is called *Les Pierres Sauvages*, which has been translated into English as *The Stones of the Abbey*. On the English cover, we learn from Umberto Eco that this is "a fascinating contribution to the understanding of the Middle Ages," as if it were a minutely researched and scholarly publication. I would argue that, on the contrary, this is a fascinating contribution to the understanding of the mid-twentieth century, or at least a corner of French culture in a small part of France. Pouillon's narrative is not academic or scholarly but fictional. The site of research was not external, but

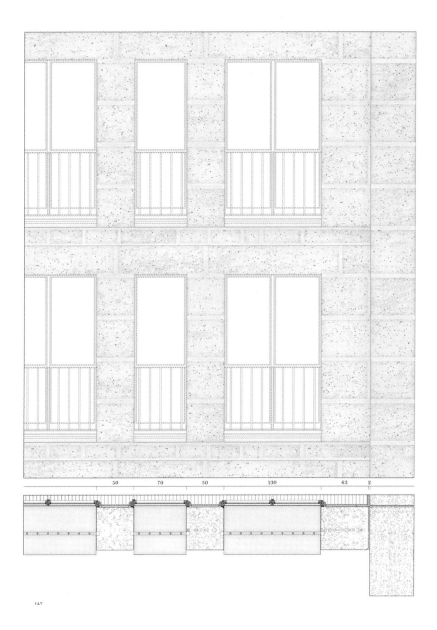

Fig. 12.2 Details of limestone façades, Pantin Estate, Paris, 1955–1957 © Chair of Adam Caruso, ETH Zurich.

internal and drawing from his latent knowledge. Much of this knowledge was
gathered through practical experience as an architect and developer.

His architectural ambitions were grandiose, described in his autobiography
as the capability to build

> Two hundred housing units at 200 metres from the city, built in 200 days,
> for 200 million francs. [...] I planned the construction in cut stone, a
> Pouillon system of flooring, a Pouillon method of load-bearing walls, a
> Pouillon vaulted structure. All this represented a housing development of
> simple invention, achieved at a cost as low as possible and within a time
> frame that nobody thought possible.[9]

The research processes he carried out to achieve this objective were practical, managerial, and technical. His theory of architecture is implicit within
his novel. Unlike his modernist counterparts, and explicitly his nemesis Le
Corbusier, he never wrote manifestos, treatises, or tracts. It is through the voice
of the master builder that Pouillon revealed his ideas about architecture as a creative and cultural force, and these incorporate a belief in the presence of the past.

Although the narrator tells the story, it is the hard limestone that is the
protagonist in Pouillon's novel. Much of the action revolves around the management of the workforce – a combination of lay brothers and priests who threaten
mutiny over the time-consuming and difficult approach to the construction's
mining, cutting, laying, and dressing, which was required for stones that had
to be "roughly finished and delicately assembled."[10] The master builder finds
himself justifying this work to himself and his colleagues. Quoting his voice
from the book, he said: "Thus we began our discussions about the exterior
facings, laid with dry joints, that is, without mortar [...] standard practice in
the days of antiquity."[11] "This method of laying, my method, will give a touch
of richness to what is otherwise austere: it will weave a design on every wall, a
net of variously shaped mesh or an open lacework of dark threads."[12]

The master builder's monologues give rare insight into Pouillon's processes
of design and into the way that he makes connections between the past and
the present in which he was building. There are hundreds of possible passages
that could be quoted here, as he details the reasons, both practical and poetic,
for his decisions.

> Although I have given the abbey its proportions and harmony, it is the
> stone alone that will preserve the independent soul of the place; when it is
> reduced to order, it will remain as beautiful as a rough-pelted wild beast.
> That is why I do not want to use mortar or daub it with lime; I want to leave
> it a little freedom still, or it will not live.[13]

Pouillon knew the quarry that was mined for the construction of Le Thoronet through his relationship with the Fontvieille quarry near Arles in Provence. He had started using stone from this quarry when he was running the Vieux-Port project for Auguste Perret in Marseilles during the 1950s. The building site required a large supply of stone, and the owner of this quarry had developed special cutting machines for rapid extraction. He would use this stone throughout his life, including in his large Algerian projects.

In terms of his architectural milieu, his social sphere, Pouillon was an outsider. For example, in May 1953, the ninth International Congress of Modern Architecture was held in Aix-en-Provence. The topic under discussion was the Housing Charter, and Roland Simounet presented his studies on the Mahieddine shanty town in Algiers. Pouillon was too busy to attend. At the beginning of the month, he had met with Jacques Chevallier, the new mayor of Algiers, and he was already at work for a large housing development in the city. The foundation stone was laid four months later. Another factor that set him apart was his aim, not for originality, but to achieve the commonplace, or a banality derived from continuity with the past. On several occasions, he quoted his master Perret, with the words cited above.

Yasmeen Lari's Practical Approach to Reality

A return to an earlier observation, made in relation to Rykwert's questioning of Western ideas of technological progress, brings the discussion to the work of Pakistani architect Yasmeen Lari (1941–). Her fifty-odd-year career as a professional architect has transformed in reflection of Pakistan's own history and its relationship with the west. During the 1960s, around the same time that Rykwert was introducing history and theory into the architectural curriculum, Lari was training as an architect at Oxford Polytechnic, now Oxford Brooks University. She returned to Karachi to work for a British construction company, but soon after founded her eponymous practice. As a member of the elite, she had access to many prestigious commissions. She approached these with the brutalist style she had learned in Britain, including the house that she built for herself and her family in Karachi in 1973.

During her brutalist years, Lari collaborated with Hungarian Canadian architect Eva Vecsei, who was based in Montreal, on the design of the Finance and Trade Centre, Karachi, completed in 1989. During one of Vecsei's visits to Pakistan, she was accompanied by Lari's husband, Suhail Zaheer Lari, who had been photographing rural architecture as part of a wider heritage project, to the provincial city of Thatta with which had been the medieval capital of Sindh. Fig. 3 shows a traditional house illustrating the use of wind catchers to corral air for passive cooling, which was a strategy that they used in the Finance and Trade Centre.

Fig 12.3   Wind-catchers,
Traditional Architecture of
Thatta © Suhail Zaheer Lari.

In 1980, Lari and her husband set up the Heritage Foundation, through which she developed strategies for protecting the ancient and historic buildings of Pakistan's cities. Lari researched and wrote about the traditional architecture of places like Thatta, using her husband's photographic record of these buildings and other key vernacular structures to publish books on the subject and to carry out various projects. More unusual strategies for preservation included the celebration of specific buildings in ceremonies accompanied by bands, speeches, plays, and comedy shows. Later, she organised a programme of cleaning and mural painting by students and schoolchildren. This was also the moment that the political and social quality of her work began to flourish. Lari told me:

> The problem with architectural practice is that you are so isolated from the reality of the country. You are busy doing work for the corporate sector or for others, and you never get the chance to really work with people. I had never sat on the street before in my life, and then my heritage work taught me that I could be with and come close to people.

Lari's research in places like Thatta was important to her, as she pointed out: "having been trained as an architect in the West, there was a period of unlearning as I tried to relate to the reality of the country and roamed our amazing historic towns for inspiration."[14] The intimate relationship between research and practice that Lari's work with Pakistan's architectural heritage bears comparison with that of Pouillon and the medieval architecture of Provence.

Fig 12.4   The Pakistan chula © The Heritage Foundation of Pakistan.

In 2005, a huge earthquake in the north of Pakistan caused Lari to change tack. She went into the field and started to put her historical and theoretical knowledge of vernacular architecture to work in the service of emergency housing and other essential provisions for impoverished and now homeless rural communities. One of the ways that the past permeates the buildings of Lari and Pouillon is through the construction materials that they use and the simpler technologies that they employ. As in the work of more conventionally modernist architects, these have been used at the service of mass production, and explicitly mass housing. But unlike the modernists, they have sought historical continuity in terms of the materials and methods of construction that they use.

As we have seen in Pouillon's housing developments in Paris, and in fig. 4, which shows Lari's reinterpretation of the rural *chula*, or open stove, their use of tradition does not mean a repetition of historic form and technique, but rather a responsive interpretation for the present. Where Pouillon used stone, Lari uses bamboo, mud, and lime plaster, whose techniques she has researched and modified. She is proud of the zero-carbon character of these materials, which are readily available and whose construction methods are familiar to the self-builders who use them.

Lari calls her reconfiguration of traditional structures and technologies "barefoot architecture." Another way of describing it is as a reset vernacular. Where the traditional *chula* was built on and in the ground, a new prevalence for flooding meant that this method was no longer viable. The different, wilder natural environment that results from a changing climate requires that the traditional design must change to accommodate it. Lari's solution is simple. The stove is raised on a platform, which now creates an outdoor room of variable extent. It can incorporate storage and space for socialising or simply remain a place for cooking.

Rykwert, Pouillon, and Lari come from very different worlds, socially and politically: the fringes of 1960s establishment Britain, a deliberate position outside the mid-twentieth-century French avant-garde, and the heart of Pakistani high society, which, by definition, is a postcolonial nation. Nevertheless, the relationship between writing and action – whether teaching, building, or activism – is a common thread, where the plausibility of received realities is always challenged.

Notes

1.   Joseph Rykwert, "Proposed MA scheme in the History and Theory of Architecture to begin in October 1968," University of Essex (UoE) archives, 17 February 1967.
2.   Introduction to 1967 prospectus for the School of Comparative Studies at the UoE, UoE archives, probably written by Joseph Rykwert.
3.   John McKean, interview with author (4 July 2002).
4.   Helen Mallinson quotes are from an interview with the author (3 July 2002).
5.   Alberto Perez-Gomez, email interview with author (29 July 2002).
6.   David Leatherbarrow, email interview with author (7 October 2002).
7.   Laurence A. Rickels, ed., *Looking After Nietzsche* (New York: State University of New York Press, 1990), 226.
8.   In 1961, Pouillon was charged with fraud and bankruptcy, partly due to his dual role as architect and developer. He was in prison for eighteen months before escaping to Italy and then to North Africa. Upon returning to France in 1963, he was imprisoned again, and this is when he wrote *Les Pierres Sauvages*, which was published 1964.
9.   Fernand Pouillon, *Mémoires d'un architecte* (Paris: Éditions du Seuil, 1968), 141.
10.   Fernand Pouillon, *The Stones of the Abbey*, trans. Edward Gillott (San Diego: Harcourt Brace Jovanovich, 1985), 71.
11.   Pouillon, *The Stones of the Abbey*, 69.
12.   Pouillon, *The Stones of the Abbey*, 67.
13.   Pouillon, *The Stones of the Abbey*, 78.
14.   Yasmeen Lari, interview with author (7 January 2020).

Bibliography

Lari, Yasmeen, *Traditional Architecture of Thatta*. Karachi: The Heritage Foundation, 1993.

Pouillon, Fernand. *Mémoires d'un architecte*. Paris: Éditions du Seuil, 1968.

———. *The Stones of the Abbey*, translated by Edward Gillott. San Diego: Harcourt Brace Jovanovich, 1985.

Rickels, Laurence A., ed. *Looking After Nietzsche*. New York: State University of New York Press, 1990.

CHAPTER 13

Starting from the Mess: The "Environment-Worlds" of Architectural Research and Design

Sepideh Karami

Fig 13.1 Bells on top of the Abadan Technical Institute. (Source: Obodon.com)[1]

Chimes are reverberating through the city. The thick smell of oil hangs in the hot, humid air, seeping forwards with every gentle breeze around the palm trees that line the pathway that leads to the Technical Institute of Abadan. The tap of black leather shoes ascending the steps at the building's entryway rhyme with the chimes, enriching them with layers of curiosity, uncertainty, untold stories, and unseen dreams. The students rushing through the corridors bring in the lazy smell of oil. Sweaty bodies drift into the cooled-down classrooms; they are ready to learn all about oil, that black viscous substance that has brought the British Petroleum Company to this land.

The Technical Institute of Abadan was designed and built in 1939 by the British architect James Mollison Wilson – the architect of the British Petroleum Company – in Abadan in south-west Iran. On top of the building are three bells made by Gillett & Johnston Bell and Clock Manufacturing in Croydon, Surrey, in England. The bells used to be heard over the city of Abadan when they welcomed new students on the first day of every academic year. The bells continued to chime even after the nationalisation of oil and the dismissal of the British Petroleum Company in 1951, but they stopped after the 1979 Iranian Revolution. While students have continued to be educated at the institute, in the vicinity of these dormant bells, dictatorship, imposed wars, and external and internal colonisation have created what Hélène Frichot calls an "environment-world"[2] in which the architecture nearly disappears in a series of complex relations.

Abadan is the border city in the province of Khuzestan, and it is the home of the Middle East's first oil refinery – one of the biggest in the world. Built and developed on oil economy after William D'Arcy's team of engineers and geologists discovered oil in the outskirts of nearby town Masjed Soleyman in 1908, the city played an important role in British history in the Second World War, as well in Britain's living standards from the 1920s to the 1940s, facilitating the move from coal to oil and paving the road for the arrival of modernity. Highlighting the role of Iranian oil in British history, Stephen Kinzer writes: "British cars, trucks and buses ran on cheap Iranian oil. Factories throughout Britain were fuelled by oil from Iran. The Royal Navy, which projected British power all over the world, powered its ships with Iranian oil."[3]

The prominent role of Iranian oil in Britain is what made Winston Churchill call it "a prize from fairyland beyond our wildest dreams." Churchill's prize was a curse for the Iranians, however: it brought the country under the colonial rule of British Petroleum (or what was then called Anglo-Persian or Anglo-Iranian Oil Company) for more than forty years. As in every other colonial example, the colonisation didn't stop at the exploitation of resources; a system of political manipulation was also needed to guarantee the monopoly over those resources. In his recent documentary *Coup 53*, Taghi Amirani shows how the colonisation of oil by Britain and its manipulation in the political system with the United States destabilised Iran forever. After the nationalisation of oil by Mohammed Mosadegh in 1951 and the dismissal of British Petroleum soon after, MI6 and the CIA choreographed a coup d'état in 1953 to remove Mosaddegh from the political scene and to regain access to oil; the coup brought an end to the project of democracy in Iran and the Middle East and resulted in a tragedy and a mess that has been escalating since.[4]

This mess is where the Technical Institute of Abadan is situated. The building was created as an element in a larger constellation of built infrastructures to support forces of colonisation and exploitation of oil resources. Constructed at the intersection of social and political complexities in this context, it has not only lived and transformed along with political events, but has also actively played a role in them. Besides being a historical building that has remained in operation on the site for nearly a century, it serves as evidence of how colonisation, through exploitation of natural resources, changes the course of history of a region and the life of its people forever. In this mess of colonisation, the exploitation of natural resources, various wars, dictatorship, ecological crisis, and social injustice, the institute, as a piece of colonial architecture, disappears and reappears in various instances. While the building inevitably carries its colonial legacy, its elements escape that legacy at critically political events, causing it to step back and fade into the background. In those moments of escape, the building becomes vulnerable, gives up its monumentality in service of a colonial period, and becomes an anti-monument to coloniality.

To examine the possibility of transforming a colonial piece of architecture into a decolonising infrastructure, I investigate how to expand those vulnerable moments during which the building becomes the antidote to its oppressive legacies and invites the multiplicities of narratives that are silenced or marginalised through colonisation processes. To do this, I apply two methods: watching the photograph, borrowed from Ariella Azoulay, and storytelling. The complex stories that buildings hold are not easily readable from looking at their photographs; one must delve deeper into the details that are inscribed in them over time. To be able to read those stories, we should start watching the photographs instead of looking at them, as Azoulay suggests, and expand the frame to the unframed and to what is not included in the photograph.[5] While "watching" instead of looking at photographs animates a finished event and opens up a closed frame to new possibilities, storytelling changes the course of the colonising grand narratives and brings in other (hi)stories.

In the Disappearance of the Object

In her *Creative Ecologies: Theorizing the Practice of Architecture*, Hélène Frichot invites us to turn around an object-oriented and frontal approach to architecture that is carefully "framed and curated" and instead to allow "its facilitative background" to emerge and make architecture "near indistinguishable from these surroundings." She writes: "This would be to allow the environment-worlds of architecture to be considered, as well as the minor characters who work away quietly at the periphery."[6] She describes the environment as what surrounds and supports all living things, where they do not passively exist but "reciprocally 'environ[s]' its local scenes through modes of action particular to its capacities."[7] She then expands these living things beyond living humans and non-human creatures to include "institutional arrangements and technological infrastructures."[8] These environments form the background when looking through the lens of architecture as object, where a contained and controlled environment is separated from its background. However, to challenge such a view and to assist the "background" in taking over, one needs to contextualise the building in broader political and social relations of the site that have not only played roles in the creation of the building but have also had roles in how it has been transformed materially and institutionally. Through such a lens, one might wonder where the building starts and where it ends. This question renders a piece of architecture as more than a discrete object and expands it into a site, where the logistics of material movement, construction, labour, and the organisations involved in the creation of the building and its operation become part of architecture.

The methods through which we encounter, critically read, and inhabit architectural projects and sites play a significant role in making new trajectories and shifts in practices of architecture design and research. They also reveal what we mean by practice and what it can and cannot do in response to the social, political, and environmental crises. In her "Expanding Modes of Practice," Bryony Roberts questions the "one-way street" architecture designers take "from idea to drawing to building" and dismantles this linearity by bringing in the "mess of labor, money, site conditions, trade collisions, political squabbling and occupancy," asking: "What if that mess were the starting point?"[9] To start from the mess, both in giving a critical reading of a piece of architecture and in designing one, is to embrace the complexity of the site and its environment-worlds and to interact with it. Staying with the mess throughout the process of design or critique would allow us to address the multiplicity of voices that construct the environment-worlds of architecture.

In reading an existing piece of architecture, storytelling is one way of staying with the complexity of the site that can make architecture as object fade in the cacophony of the mess that is integrated in its environment. Buildings carry evidence and are therefore storytelling creatures. Stories are inscribed in the building's material and in its structure. Telling stories is to capture what is outside the perfect frame of architecture as an object and to pertain to the complexity of the context. Architecture has always been a powerful instrument in the discussion of colonisation, to represent the colonial power and to mark the land. To reverse the process, architecture and building could be an anchor for the story of decolonisation. To reconstruct the environment-world of a building for the project of decolonisation, we should make a choice about what stories we want to tell and which voices we want to be amplified and by means of what tools. In this text, the photograph is applied as the main material to reconstruct the story of Technical Institute of Abadan in order to tell decolonising stories.

In her *Memoirs of Hadrian*, Marguerite Yourcenar writes that "[t]o reconstruct is to collaborate with time gone by, penetrating or modifying its spirit, and carrying it toward a longer future."[10] There is a gap between the moment in which a photograph is taken and the time when one looks at it. "The photograph," writes Ariella Azoulay, "exceeds any presumption of ownership or monopoly and any attempt at being exhaustive."[11] There is more to read from a photograph than how it is captioned. From a photograph, "some other event can be reconstructed," "some other player's presence can be discerned through it, constructing the social relations that allowed its production."[12] Azoulay writes in *The Civil Contract of Photography*:

> One needs to stop looking at the photograph and instead start watching it. The verb "to watch" is usually used for regarding phenomena or moving pictures. It entails dimensions of time and movement that need to be rein-scribed in the interpretation of the still photographic image.[13]

Following Azoulay, the act of "watching" opens up an image to new meanings and (hi)stories to extract potentials and to reconstruct, not the event that the photograph bears, but the political ground that it suggests. In this text, the story of oil and colonisation is complicated by watching the two photographs of the institute: one as a monument of colonisation, claiming domination over the city via its form and elements, perfectly framed in a postcard, and the other a low-resolution picture of the semi-demolished building in the war that is stepping back from being a monument and representing a colonial knowledge institution; a building that emerged through colonisation suddenly becomes an open-ended story in the corridors of which the multiplicity of voices echoes.

Watching the photographs of the Technical Institute of Abadan in these two situations animates the building's many stories and situates it in a complex historical, political, and social context. It connects these two photos to many others, documented or undocumented, taken or never taken. By watching a photograph, one creates a storyboard, many frames of which are missing from the colonial narratives and the grand narratives of the state. Those undocu-mented, vanished, or silenced frames become glitches in the animated story of one photograph; they can be found, exposed, or imagined and reconstructed by the act of watching. This is to assist the building's "background" in taking over the building as an object, in making the framed pictures of the building and its architect disappear, and then reappear differently.

The language that I use to describe the building of the institute during the colonial period is deliberately different from the language in the story of the building during the war. In the former, the absence of a specific character al-lows us to look at it from a distance and thereby map the building in a broader context. In the latter, the introduction of a character, a soldier, brings us as close to the building as possible. The choice of a semi-demolished, abandoned. and empty building allows the soldier – who can also be imagined as a former student of the Technical Institute – to daydream while wandering through the building and extract the many stories that are buried within its walls.

The Postcard: From Retaining Knowledge to Appropriation through Material Intervention

When British Petroleum formed a contract with Iran and founded the Anglo-Iranian Oil Company in 1909, most of the workers were either from other colonies, such as India, or were British technical staff. Iranians were not even considered a local workforce, since they were mostly employed as servants. The staffing strategy was obviously a way to secure the monopoly of the oil industry in British hands. Over the years, however, there was increasing pressure on the company to employ local workers as well as to create chances for Iranians to gain technical skills. The Abadan Technical Institute was an initial response to give Iranian apprentices basic technical skills. But, as Katayoun Shafiee writes in her book *Machineries of Oil: An Infrastructural History of BP in Iran*, seven years after the establishment of the institute, in 1945, only 1,700 Iranians had received training. As a strategy, the company "sought to minimize the number of Iranians sent for university training and maximize the number sent for trade training" in the United Kingdom, as it would block the threat of returning Iranians with superior skills stirring up trouble among the workers.[15]

Fig 13.2   A postcard depicting the Technical Institute of Abadan (Source: mizenaft.com)[14]

The Technical Institute thus becomes an interesting case as an institution in the context of colonisation, as it played a role in who could have access to knowledge and to what extent. While knowledge ownership was used to retain control over natural resources and the benefits thereof by enforcing dependency on a foreign source, the architecture also supported such dependency through material intervention and manipulation, to enroot colonial power. Such dependency was visible in general in Wilson's work – not only in terms of architectural style and models of urban planning and design but also in the building process and building material. For example, in Wilson's other work, Taj Cinema, also in Abadan, the London red brick that was used in construction of the building was imported from England to Abadan as ballast.[16] Injecting foreign material in a place is a symbolic way of appropriation. In his *Appropriation Through Pollution*, Michelle Serres writes about how polluting and leaving traces in a place enforces appropriation. The examples to support his argument vary from a wedding ring, marking ownership over the other's body, to how animals territorialise by urinating and leaving odour.[17] Similarly, as one of the most powerful material practices, architecture also assists colonisation and the appropriation process.

The dependency on a foreign source and symbolic appropriation by means of material intervention is also present in the Technical Institute of Abadan. Besides the bricks and the Indian teak wood flooring, the two more animate elements in the building – the clock and the three bells made by Gillett & Johnston Bell and Clock Manufacturing in Croydon and imported to Abadan from England – take the material manipulation to a different level. Bells and clocks are both living elements that manipulate time and the rhythm of not only the building but also the town. At present, while the bells are dormant, the clock is still working and visible as a colonial monument in Abadan. But perhaps the dormant bells are an anticolonial gesture, a silenced sound of colonisation over the town.

War-Torn Institute: Mess in the Death of Democracy

The photograph depicts the war-torn Technical Institute of Abadan, vulnerable and about to vanish from the frame. Smog obscures the view over the Arvand Rud river. The sun is blurring in its own heat, painting the slightly bowed palm trees orange. Palm trees, beheaded, half burned, cast their shadows over the building and the site. The orange shade stretches itself over the bricks and the dusted and broken windows. The arches and brickwork, once designed and drawn by the architect of the British Empire and British Petroleum Company James Morrison Wilson, are partially destroyed in the photographs; the walls have been hollowed and destroyed by the rockets and bombs. Wilson's commitment to symmetry[18] is overthrown by the asymmetrical mechanism of war.

Fig. 13.3   The Abadan Technical Institute at the time of war between Iran and Iraq.
Source: neconews.com.

The lower windows are cushioned by sandbags piled on top of wooden planks, each supported by two empty oil barrels; the structure is supposed to protect the fragile building material against the blast waves. The breakage in the upper windows, with dark irregular shapes, reveals the emptiness of an interior, an interior itself left in a mess upon evacuation at the onset of war in 1980 and later covered with the dust of frequent blasts that found their way in by smashing the windows. The photo partially frames the war-torn institute, which is just one of the many buildings demolished in south-west Iran during the war between Iran and Iraq, which started just after the 1979 Iranian Revolution and lasted for eight years. This war-stricken building in the photograph, however, points to longer and much more complex histories and stories.

Weary soldiers could have passed by this building. Perhaps they leaned against its walls, lit cigarettes while playing with pebbles on the ground with the tip of their boots. They exhaled the smoke into the air and watched it disperse against the sunset. Perhaps they remembered the chime of the bells when the Technical Institute was still in operation. They might have imitated the bells chime in their heads and rhymed it with the punch of bombs and the barrages. Weary soldiers might have lifted the sling of their rifles off their shoulders and have felt momentary relief from the weight of war.

One weary soldier might have stepped into the building on a quieter day of war to escape the burning heat of the southern sun. His steps might have echoed in the empty corridors, punctuated with pieces of glasses, stones, smashed bricks, pens, pencils, debris. The weary soldier might have opened the door to that famous, small lecture hall, called the Churchill Room by the petroleum students. Perhaps he blew the dust off the desk in front of him and looked through the obscured view of the lecture hall, recalling the photos of Churchill's war rooms in London. The weary soldier might have looked around at the mess and murmured: "This is the English job." Perhaps he laughed out loud at his own thought.

The weary soldier, like most other Iranians and those familiar with the history of the political relationship between Iran and Britain, knows the phrase: "This is the English job." It has turned into an ironic phrase that suggests that, behind every unexplained malfunction or sabotage, there is probably an Englishman. The saying has even become the title of a book by Jack Straw that explains why Iran distrusts Britain. Such a conspiracy theory has moved beyond the political realm into the realm of everyday life: a pipe breaks in your bathroom, and you could think "this is the English job." The phrase is from one of the most popular Iranian TV series of the '70s, called *My Uncle Napoleon*, based on an eponymous graphic novel by Iraj Pezeshkzaad. The story takes place in a garden in Tehran around which different families live. The community is dominated by the protagonist Uncle Napoleon, a paranoid patriarch who believes that foreign countries – specifically Britain – are responsible for any unfortunate events that happen in Iran. Such social satire is not mere paranoia, however, and the weary soldier knows that it is rooted in a long history of colonisation and manipulation of politics in Iran by Britain.[19]

The story is long, and the weary soldier remembers the opening line of a bedtime story that his father used to tell him: on the dawn of Tuesday, 26 May 1908, the dormant ghosts of oil were awakened by William D'Arcy's team of engineers and geologists.[20] They had come from an island far, far away called England, and they found the oil in Masjid Souleyman near Abadan. From that day forwards, the curse of oil has never left us.

The weary soldier still remembers the smell of oil on his father's big rough hands. And a blast wave wakes him up from daydreaming in the corridors of the Technical Institute of Abadan.

Notes

1.   Bahram Mahtabi, "A History of Technical Institute of Abadan (Shahid Tondgooyan Oil University)," 2007, http://www.obodan.com/%D8%A7%D9%85%D8%A7%DA%A9 %D9%86-%D9%88-%D9%85%D8%AD%D9%84%D8%A7%D8%AA/39.

2.   Hélène Frichot, *Creative Ecologies: Theorizing the Practice of Architecture* (London: Bloomsbury, 2019), 7.

3.   Stephen Kinzer, "BP and Iran: The Forgotten History," CBS News, 2010, https://www. cbsnews.com/news/bp-and-iran-the-forgotten-history/.

4.   Taghi Amirani, *Coup 53*, 2020.

5.   Ariella Azoulay, *The Civil Contract of Photography* (New York: Zone Books, 2008), 14.

6.   Frichot, *Creative Ecologies: Theorizing the Practice of Architecture*, 7.

7.   Frichot, *Creative Ecologies: Theorizing the Practice of Architecture*, 19.

8.   Frichot, *Creative Ecologies: Theorizing the Practice of Architecture*, 20.

9.   Bryony Roberts, "Expanding Modes of Practice," *Log 48* (2020): 11.

10. Marguerite Yourcenar, *Memoirs of Hadrian* (iBooks, 1981), 182

11. Ariella Azoulay, *The Civil Contract of Photography* (New York: Zone Books, 2008), 12.

12. Ariella Azoulay, *The Civil Contract of Photography*, 12.

13. Ariella Azoulay, *The Civil Contract of Photography*, 14.

14. "Oil Postcards," میز، نفت 2015, Accessed 15 July 2020, http://www.miz-enaft.com/gallery/9536/1/%DA%A9%D8%A7%D8%B1%D8%AA-%D9%BE%D8%B3%D8%AA%D8%A7%D9%84-%D9%87%D8%A7%DB%8C-%D9%86%D9%81%D8%AA%DB%8C-%D9%86%DB%8C%D9%85-%D9%82%D8%B-1%D9%86-%D9%BE%DB%8C%D8%B4.

15. Katayoun Shafiee, *Machineries of Oil: An Infrastructural History of BP in Iran* (Cambridge, MA: MIT Press, 2018), 138.

16. Rasmus Christian Elling, "Abadan: Unfulfilled Promises of Oil Modernity and Revolution in Iran," *Ajam Media Collective*, 2015, https://ajammc.com/2015/02/26/ abadan-the-devastated-harbor/.

17. Michel Serres, *Malfeasance: Appropriation through Pollution* (Stanford: Stanford University Press, 2011).

18. Barry Joyce, "James Mollison Wilson: Architect of Empire," *RIBAJ*, 2017, https://www. ribaj.com/culture/james-mollison-wilson-architect-of-empire-baghdad.

19. Iraj Pezeshkzad, *My Uncle Napoleon*, trans. Dick Davis (New York: The Modern Library, 2006).

20. Leonardo Davoudi, *Persian Petroleum: Oil, Empire and Revolution in Late Qajar Iran* (London & New York: I. B. Tauris, 2020), 95.

Bibliography

Amirani, Taghi (director). *Coup 53*. (Documentary by Amirani Media) 2020.

Azoulay, Ariella. *The Civil Contract of Photography*. New York: Zone Books, 2008.

Davoudi, Leonardo. *Persian Petroleum: Oil, Empire and Revolution in Late Qajar Iran*. London and New York: I. B. Tauris, 2020.

Elling, Rasmus Christian. "Abadan: Unfulfilled Promises of Oil Modernity and Revolution in Iran." *Ajam Media Collective*. 2015. https://ajammc.com/2015/02/26/abadan-the-devastated-harbor/.

Frichot, Hélène. *Creative Ecologies: Theorizing the Practice of Architecture*. London: Bloomsbury, 2019.

Joyce, Barry. "James Mollison Wilson: Architect of Empire." *RIBAJ*. 2017. https://www.ribaj.com/culture/james-mollison-wilson-architect-of-empire-baghdad

Kinzer, Stephen. "BP and Iran: The Forgotten History." *CBS News*. 2010. https://www.cbsnews.com/news/bp-and-iran-the-forgotten-history/.

Pezeshkzad, Iraj. *My Uncle Napoleon*, translated by Dick Davis. New York: The Modern Library, 2006.

Roberts, Bryony. "Expanding Modes of Practice." *Log, no 48*. 2020 : 9-14.

Serres, Michel. *Malfeasance: Appropriation Through Pollution*. Stanford: Stanford University Press, 2011.

Shafiee, Katayoun. *Machineries of Oil: An Infrastructural History of BP in Iran*. Cambridge, MA: MIT Press, 2018.

Yourcenar, Marguerite. *Memoirs of Hadrian*, translated by Grance Frick in collaboration with the author. London: Secker & Warburg. 1974: 134.

CHAPTER 14

Examining Utopias: Comparative Scales as a Transdisciplinary Research Method

Jana Culek

An Extended Introduction: On Curiosities – Utopias and Transdisciplinarity

Developing my work between the boundaries of what is considered a traditional architectural practice and academic research, my curiosities begin with one of the most prominent tools of the architectural discipline – the drawing – specifically, the ways in which drawings can be used as critical tools, as methods of creating, containing, and transmitting knowledge, and as objects that develop architectural narratives. But while some architectural drawings can accomplish these tasks by using their own visual elements, often they are accompanied by texts that deepen and develop the message they convey. The interest in the interrelation of drawings and text, and how they can be used to develop architectural thought, present architectural ideas, and create critical positions has led me to investigate a specific set of projects – utopian ones. Having (mostly) no intention of being built, these projects employ various affordances of drawings and texts to convey their fictional yet critical proposals. Utopian architectural projects are envisioned as a collection of ideals, working together to provide a theoretical testing ground. In the same way that utopian literature is not meant to provide an applicable script for an ideal society, utopian architecture does not intend to provide blueprints. Their aim is not one of realisation or total implementation, but rather one of providing a reflection and critique to their historical environments. In the context of my research, utopia is seen as a critical and speculative method, an unattainable ideal not meant to be achieved, but rather serves as an ever-moving goal towards which we stride. Utopia serves as a means for social imagination and as a hope for a better future.

But architecture is not utopia's primary field. Utopian projects produced in architecture mostly model themselves on a tradition already established in the literary field, where ideas of ideal societies and environments that enclose them have existed at least since Plato's *Republic*. The official history, as well as the name of the genre begins with Thomas More's 1516 fictional, political book *Libellus vere aureus, nec minus salutaris quam festivus, de optimo rei publicae statu deque nova insula Utopia* or, shortly, *Utopia*. Since then, the nomenclature signified a fictional work that, through directly or indirectly reflecting on various societal events and conditions, proposes alternatives. Due to the fictional character of the genre, these alternatives can (and have) also been far removed from their historical reality. While the literary field allows for more radical proposals to be developed, given that the limits imposed on them are only those of imagination, architectural utopias tend to be slightly more realistic. The environments they depict are often constrained by laws of physics or practice. However, the elements that they propose to change, or ones they highlight, are indicative of the societal issues present in the moment of their creation. Some of the issues addressed by the utopia's long history are still relevant today; others have become less important, irrelevant, or outdated.

To better understand and identify the tools and the critical and speculative methods architecture uses to produce its utopias, my research compares the architectural utopias with ones from the literary field. This allowed me to approach a more diverse and open field of knowledge and has prompted me to move past the boundaries of my own discipline to track possible roots and correlations of the ideas that utopias propose. Through a transdisciplinary approach that builds upon the traditional tools and practices of the architectural discipline, and by enriching them with tools, practices, and methods from other disciplines – in this case, primarily the literary one – new insights are produced.

This paper examines a research method I have developed for the purposes of my own doctoral research. Being both an architectural practitioner and researcher, I have developed a method that is a heterogenous blend of architectural design tools and scientific research methods. It involves not only a historical examination of the different architectural and literary utopian works but also a process of creative discovery through text and drawing, in which the imaginative and projective nature of the architectural discipline plays a strong role in understanding and reconstructing the utopian worlds. Building upon the complexities and multifacetedness of the architectural discipline, the research does not look at these utopian proposals only as enclosed wholes, in the manner of a historical overview. My interests also grew to include several more architecturally rooted questions: How and with what formal and conceptual elements are these fictional worlds were constructed? How did these elements respond or relate to "real," historical ones? What were the most common social and spatial forms used in the utopian projects? What types of changes do they propose or instil in our environment, and do these elements differ in architecture as opposed to literature? The method will be demonstrated through one of the case study pairs that I have been working with, namely that of Ludwig Hilberseimer's urban proposal Metropolisarchitecture,[1] and Yevgeny Zamyatin's novel *We*.[2] Looking not only into the proposed utopian elements but also how they relate to same-scale elements of their historical contexts allows us to see what types of utopian changes[3] lead to what types of results with the aim of identifying which social and spatial forms shape utopian worlds and which forms are, in turn, shaped by utopias.

The Problem of Different Fields: On Architectural and Literary Utopias

One of the first problems I encountered through my research was that, by examining works from two different fields – architecture and literature – the methods traditionally used in either were insufficient in bridging the transdisciplinary gap. The reason for this was mostly due to the differences in the approaches and outputs of the works, as well as differences in what is considered a utopian work. Literary utopias are created as fictional texts, with rarely any graphic representation. To describe the imagined world, the various changes the utopian work proposes in relation to our "reality" are depicted on the level of social interactions and spatial conditions, while the built environment is described throughout the narrative, as a set in which the plot unfolds. Architectural utopias, conversely, are presented mostly through drawings and generally focus on spatial changes of different scale, with the population described in toto within the accompanying texts, and in relation to their interaction with the built environment.

To build the framework around what is considered a utopian project, I relied on the definitions of two architectural historians and theorists: Françoise Choay and Nathaniel Coleman. In her book *The Rule and the Model* (1997), Choay offers a definition of seven features that make a work utopian, which she based on Thomas More's *Utopia*. Architectural historian and theorist Coleman proposes to view the architectural project not as utopian per se, but rather as having "utopian potential" or a "utopian dimension."[4] By combining their definitions, the most general aspects that define utopian works across both fields is that they propose a critical and innovative alternative to their historical conditions, which is built through a strong presence of both social and spatial elements or forms. Proposing both spatial and social changes goes to show how our environments have an effect on us, and conversely, how our social systems can have a direct effect on our spatial surroundings.

Having a way of clearly defining which architectural projects and literary works fall within the utopian genre did not, however, mean that the works would propose similar worlds. Although the pairs of architectural and literary utopias that I use throughout my research were generally created roughly in the same historical and geographical context, and often discuss and critique similar societal conditions, they don't always do so through the same lens. Certain historical conditions can be perceived completely differently across the fields. A concept that is considered positive and productive and is manifested as a utopia in literature can be considered negative and destructive and consequently manifested as a dystopia in architecture. Taking a direct example from one of my case studies – namely Metropolisarchitecture and *We* – both dealing with the implications of industrialisation and mass production on society, each author positions themselves differently. While Hilberseimer, a modernist architect and urbanist, sees order, control, and repetition as productive and welcome results of mass production, allowing him to propose a new city for the new metropolitan man, Zamyatin sees order, repetition, and uniformity as negative and dangerous concepts when applied to the population. What is also interesting when observing these case studies as reflections of their historical contexts, but from today's perspective, is that the notions of what is considered utopian or dystopian changes over time. In the period of its creation, Metropolisarchitecture was considered a utopian project, demonstrating all the possibilities of architectural modernism. From today's perspective, however, the popular opinion regarding this project is more closely related to the viewpoints of Zamyatin – which goes to show that what is considered utopian or dystopian is historically relative. Therefore, it is important to note that, in my research, I do not necessarily differentiate utopian and dystopian projects in a traditional manner. Both subtypes are investigated equally, since both are seen as a manifestation of an imaginary world or society which is informed by reality and creates a critique of a given historical context, regardless of whether this manifestation is built upon and based on desire or fear.

The Problem of Comparing: What to Compare?

An architectural approach to analysing utopian works traditionally starts from a formal analysis of the objects the project produced. A similar approach exists in comparative literature, where a traditional "formal analysis" or a "close reading" means "interpreting all of the formal techniques of a text as contributing to an overarching artistic whole."[5] But to avoid these traditional methods of both fields, which focus only on the produced elements themselves and not on how they correlate with the context in which they were produced, I have used a method proposed by literary theorist Caroline Levine in her book *Forms: Whole, Rhythm, Hierarchy, Network*. She proposes "broadening our definition of form to include social arrangements," which in turn has the effect of dissolving "the traditional troubling gap between the form of the literary texts and its content and context."[6] As a way of introducing a new method for looking at forms in comparative literature, Levine proposes to observe the affordances inherent in all forms. Based on James Gibson's term from his theory of perception, she defines affordances as "a term to describe the potential uses or actions latent in materials and design,"[7] stating that these ways of use or action can be multiple and parallel in each form. As a result of the different sets of affordances, she proposes four overarching groups of forms: (1) the (bounded) whole, (2) rhythm, (3) hierarchy, and (4) network. While affordance often refers to physical attributes of forms (or objects), what Levine adds with the inclusion of "social arrangements" are the different social conditions and events that these forms engender. For instance, the transparency of glass buildings in Zamyatin's One State leads to a complete lack of privacy, and consequently complete social control, which would not be possible with other, non-transparent materials.

Levine's specific differentiation of forms was not a direct way to structure my research, but her approach has been helpful in identifying the various elements that I have consequently analysed and compared. While a formal analysis is not a novelty in the architectural field, the inclusion of social elements and experiences into the overarching terminology of "form" certainly is. By combining both social and spatial elements, I was able to bridge the gap between the two fields. Utopian works of architecture and literature propose both social and spatial changes, but the traditional methods of analysis from each field rarely look at both. Even though both fields investigate "forms" of the works (forms of text in literature and physical form in architecture), they rarely look into how these forms perform – which is where Levine's inclusion of "social arrangements" becomes instrumental. The "forms" of both fields become substantiated with the societal effects they engender, creating a more complete picture of the critique which the utopian work poses.

Including both social and spatial aspects of the works, the method allowed for the identification of various isolated or overlapping "building blocks" that could be compared. From an architectural perspective, this allowed me to not only identify the spatial elements proposed through the drawings and described through the texts but also the societal consequences these spaces impose. It also allowed me to analyse how these elements overlap and influence each other. For instance, Hilberseimer's large-scale repetitive building blocks can be looked at not only as mass-produced elements that form the image of the city but also as structures that influence the daily rhythm of the lives of their inhabitants, as "bounded wholes" that enclose numerous other repetitive wholes, as a distributed network that shapes the entire city, or as elements forming the vertical transportation system. So, while the literary utopias perhaps lack precise visual descriptions of the spatial elements building the utopian worlds, and while architectural utopias lack the narratives that explore the implications of the proposed environments on the inhabitants, through our disciplinary knowledge and imagination, and through observing the affordances of specific forms, we can attempt to reconstruct the missing elements.

Interpreting both literary and architectural works as a collection of different generative forms, each responding or relating to a specific historical context, has allowed me to further level the playing field between architectural and literary utopias, as well as their contextual relationships. This way, instead of performing an immense historical overview that, in the end, only positions the works within their contexts, I identify and juxtapose a constellation of ideas – "real" or "fictional," social or spatial – that were brought forwards either within the works or within their respective contexts. These ideas build a collection of forms that have, in one way or another, shaped our social and spatial environment.

The Use of Drawings

Aside from assisting in bridging the gap between the two fields, breaking down the utopian works and identifying the various elements has also opened the possibility of visualising them. Drawing then becomes an integral part of the comparison, working together with text to depict and interpret the conditions surrounding the different forms. Through a "reconstruction" of missing elements, based on the affordances of the differing social and spatial forms, I was able to perform a visual and textual juxtaposition of different utopian "building blocks" (fig. 14.1–14.3, p. 218–223). While the juxtaposition of textual parts focused on the written narratives and related historical, philosophical, literary, and architectural writings, the visual analysis was created using both newly created analytical and interpretative drawings as well as original drawings created by the utopian authors, which accompanied the projects. Using drawing – as one of the main tools of the architectural discipline – and the architectural and spatial affordances of all the social and spatial forms that were described in the works only through limited written narratives, I created a series of images to reconstruct and depict the various elements that build up the utopian worlds. To visualise the changes that the utopian works proposed in relation to their historical contexts, the contextual forms were also reconstructed and drawn.

Comparative Scales: Small, Medium, and Large

Acknowledging that the various social and spatial forms I have identified within the works differ in size – both on a purely spatial level as well as on the scale within which they operate – I divided the compared elements into three predominant scales: small, medium, and large. The small scale focuses on the individual and their surroundings; the medium scale looks at communities, groups, and other forms of human organisations; and the large scale is focused on larger populations such as those of nations or even the global scale. And while it may seem that distributing various utopian and contextual forms throughout different scales would go against the possibility of understanding them and how they are connected, correlated, or overlap, it is in fact the opposite (fig. 14.4, p. 224). Taking as an example the children's book *Cosmic View: The Universe in 40 Jumps* (1957) by the Dutch author Kees Boeke, or perhaps the more well-known *Powers of Ten* (1977) film by Charles and Ray Eames, we see that distributing objects throughout different scales allows us to see their correlation. Boeke's aim was to "find a means of developing a wider and more connected view of our world and a truly cosmic view of the universe and our place in it."[8] Both the book and the film show a series of images that, through a progression of scales, show different elements. Zooming out from a 1:1 scale of a human, each subsequent larger (or smaller) scale puts the previous one into perspective. Showing a wider view allows one to visualise where the smaller element is placed and which other such elements it is surrounded by.

A Comparative Demonstration

Applied to the Hilberseimer and Zamyatin case study pair, and through situating them in their historical context, the scale analysis is as follows.

Beginning with the small scale, the analysis focuses on individuals living in three separate conditions: one located in a 1920s European metropolis, one living in Hilberseimer's High-Rise City, and one inhabiting Zamyatin's One State. While the written analysis focuses on the notions of alienation and takes the blasé[9] individual as a contextual anchor point, the visual analysis examines the living conditions of all three "metropolitan" subjects. The historical individual lives in a tiny apartment, crowded with unfunctional furniture and suffering from bad hygienic standards, but the conditions of his two utopian counterparts are quite different. Hilberseimer's "shadowy figure"[10] lives in a spacious modernist apartment, equipped with central heating, indoor plumbing, and cross ventilation, while Zamyatin's "number" lives alone in his transparent glass room, with amenities shared with the rest of his building block. The most obvious difference across all three conditions is the use of materials – the most radical one being Zamyatin's, where the room itself, as well as all its objects, are created out of glass. However, Zamyatin shares a similar scale as well as the notion of shared facilities with the condition of the historical context. Both Zamyatin's and Hilberseimer's individuals are dressed in uniforms – while Zamyatin's is an actual uniform, Hilberseimer's is the "uniform" of the capitalist metropolitan subject – a nondescript suit and a cylinder hat (fig. 14.5, p. 225).

The medium scale investigates the building types present in the three "cities" and the notions of multiplication, repetition, and typology (both on an architectural and human scale). The contextual streetscape contains various differing typologies, created in different historical styles, usually lacking any uniformity. The streets are narrow and not suitable for the increasing amount of traffic; the air is usually polluted due to the proximity of industry and

Yevgeny Zamyatin, *We*, 1921

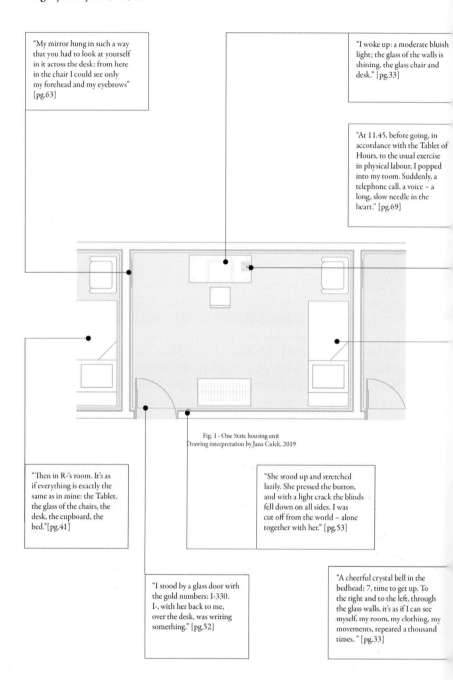

"My mirror hung in such a way that you had to look at yourself in it across the desk: from here in the chair I could see only my forehead and my eyebrows" [pg.63]

"I woke up: a moderate bluish light; the glass of the walls is shining, the glass chair and desk." [pg.33]

"At 11.45, before going, in accordance with the Tablet of Hours, to the usual exercise in physical labour, I popped into my room. Suddenly, a telephone call, a voice – a long, slow needle in the heart." [pg.69]

Fig. 1 - One State housing unit
Drawing interpretation by Jana Culek, 2019

"Then in R-'s room. It's as if everything is exactly the same as in mine: the Tablet, the glass of the chairs, the desk, the cupboard, the bed." [pg.41]

"She stood up and stretched lazily. She pressed the button, and with a light crack the blinds fell down on all sides. I was cut off from the world – alone together with her." [pg.53]

"I stood by a glass door with the gold numbers: I-330. I-, with her back to me, over the desk, was writing something." [pg.52]

"A cheerful crystal bell in the bedhead: 7, time to get up. To the right and to the left, through the glass walls, it's as if I can see myself, my room, my clothing, my movements, repeated a thousand times. " [pg.33]

Fig. 14.1 Small Scale – Visual and textual analysis and reconstruction of the living unit based on the Hilberseimer-Zamyatin case study pair. Original drawings by Ludwig Hilberseimer and reconstructed drawings © Jana Culek.

Ludwig Hilberseimer, *Metropolisarchitecture*, 1920s

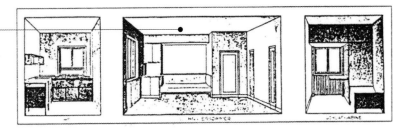

Fig. 2 - Metropolis housing unit interiors
Ludwig Hilberseimer, Wohnstadt, 1923

"Metropolisarchitecture
is considerably dependent
on solving two factors: the
individual cell of the room and
the collective urban organism."
[pg.270]

Yevgeny Zamyatin, *We,* **1921**

"On the avenue, when I'd already crossed over to the other side, I looked back: in the glass light block of the building, shot through with sunlight, there were, here and there, the grey-blue, opaque cells of dropped blinds – cells of rhythmic, Taylorized happiness. On the sixth floor my eyes found R-13's cell: he had already lowered the blinds."[pg43]

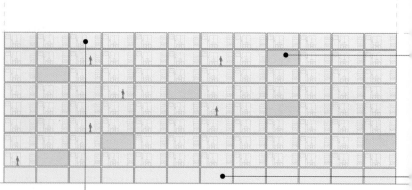

Fig.1 - One State Housing
Drawing interpretation by Jana Culek, 2019

"There are no more buildings: the glass walls have dissolved in the mist like crystals of salt in water. If you look from the pavement, the dark figures of people in the buildings are hanging, like suspended particles in a fantastical milky solution, low down, and higher, and higher still – on the ninth floor."[pg.69]

"Downstairs in the vestibule, at the desk, the inspector, throwing glances at the clock, was noting down the numbers of those coming in." [pg.50]

Fig. 14.2 Medium Scale – Visual and textual analysis and reconstruction of the housing slab based on the Hilberseimer-Zamyatin case study pair. Original drawings by Ludwig Hilberseimer and reconstructed drawings © Jana Culek.

"In an apartment block or high-rise, the window is entirely divested of this significance as an autonomous building element. As a result of its frequent occurrence, the window no longer contrasts with the surface but instead begins to assume some of the surface's positive functions: it becomes a part and component of the surface itself. The window no longer interrupts the surface but rather invigorates it evenly." [pg.272]

Fig. 2 - Metropolis Housing - Vertical City
Ludwig Hilberseimer, High-Rise City (Hochhausstadt) - Perspective view.
East - West Street, 1924, © Art Institute of Chicago

"Through the organization of individual rooms in the floorplan, the functional building that encompasses an entire street block is born." [pg.270]

Yevgeny Zamyatin, *We*, 1921

"To carry out the doctor's prescription I deliberately chose a route not along the hypotenuse, but along the two cathetuses. And here was the second cathetus already: a circular road by the foot of the Green Wall." (p.90)

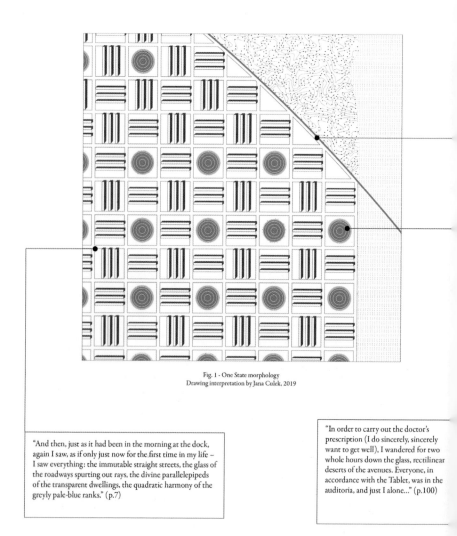

Fig. 1 - One State morphology
Drawing interpretation by Jana Culek, 2019

"And then, just as it had been in the morning at the dock, again I saw, as if only just now for the first time in my life – I saw everything: the immutable straight streets, the glass of the roadways spurting out rays, the divine parallelepipeds of the transparent dwellings, the quadratic harmony of the greyly pale-blue ranks." (p.7)

"In order to carry out the doctor's prescription (I do sincerely, sincerely want to get well), I wandered for two whole hours down the glass, rectilinear deserts of the avenues. Everyone, in accordance with the Tablet, was in the auditoria, and just I alone..." (p.100)

Fig. 14.3 Large Scale – Visual and textual analysis and reconstruction of the city morphology based on the Hilberseimer-Zamyatin case study pair. Original drawings by Ludwig Hilberseimer and reconstructed drawings © Jana Culek.

Ludwig Hilberseimer, *Metropolisarchitecture*, 1920s

"Rational thinking, accuracy, precision, and economy - until now the characteristics of the engineer - must become the basis of the new architectonic. All objects must be complete in themselves, reduced to their ultimate essential forms, organized reasonably, and led to their ultimate consummation." (p.268)

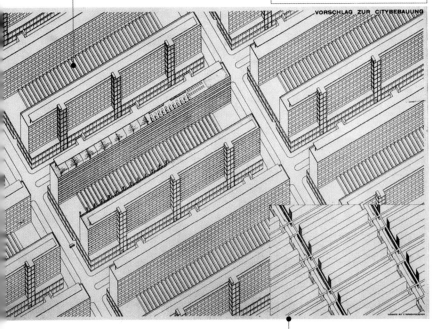

Fig. 2 - Metropolis morphology
Ludwig Hilberseimer, Berlin Development Project, 1928, © Art Institute of Chicago

"The simple cubic bodies - boxes, and spheres, prisms and cylinders, pyramids and cones, purely constructive elements - are the fundamental forms of every architecture" (p.268)

Matrix

Scale / Category		Social		Spatial
S 1:1 / 1:10	individual	individual, human or other, close-knit family unit or group	unit	interior, house, living unit, (objects)
M 1:100 / 1:1 000	group	social, religious, political, work, interest groups, institutions	building	housing, public buildings, public space, production facilities, institutions
L 1:10 000 / 1:100 000	society	citizens, nations, species, races, society	city	city quarter, city, city-state, country, (continent, planet)

Social Scales

Scale	Context	*Metropolisarchitecture*	*We*
S	liberated individual	working individual	number Mephi
	alienated individual	family with children	state mandated interactions
M	voluntary associations	living and working in same location	state mandated groups
	the crowd	moving with the market	informal, dissident groups
L	Gemeinschaft to Geselschaft	cities and individuality	One State
	modern globalization	unification through urban planning	Mephi

Spatial Scales

Scale	Context	*Metropolisarchitecture*	*We*
S	small, clustered units - unimportant	individual family unit - apartment	single unit / room
	condensed, bad living standards	unit as building block of city - tenement building	room as visible building block
M	Kunstwollen + buildings for power	housing and office/ commerce	housing and main building block
	speculative building with no planning	entire city centre out of one typology	other functions evenly distributed
L	modern metropolis - chaotic and fragmented	centralized and compact city	isolated domed city
	move from rural to urban areas + attachement to history	urban planning as base for growth	life beyond the dome

Fig. 14.4 Comparative scale matrix with elements and illustration through the Hilberseimer-Zamyatin case study pair.

Fig. 14.5 Small Scale – Interior scenes (from top): 1920s Berlin working-class apartment, Hilberseimer's apartment*, Zamyatin's room*. Images reconstructed by Jana Culek.

production. But Hilberseimer's and Zamyatin's streetscapes are both repetitive and uniform. They are structured mostly out of housing units and follow an endless rhythm of geometric multiplication. The materiality of the three is one of the greatest differences once again, given that Zamyatin's One State is constructed exclusively out of glass. Both utopian cities have systems of underground transportation networks running underneath an orthogonal grid of streets. There is no individuation in either streetscape. But the hygienic quality of life seems to be improved compared to the historical context. The wider streets, better orientation, and functional zoning (which is explicitly present only in Hilberseimer's proposal) create vastly different conditions. The public open spaces in the utopian proposals are also much larger than those in the historical metropolis, either to accommodate the political structures or to offset the scale of the buildings themselves (fig. 14.6, fig. 14.7).

And finally, the large scale investigates the three "metropolitan" conditions themselves, on the scale of the city and the city state. On a social level, the three cities are very different, ranging from post-war European capitals to a mass-produced and industrialised metropolis and finally an authoritarian, technocratic city state. The historical city is once again a heterogenous accumulation of functions and typologies, growing mostly in an organic way and with no overarching geometric plan. Both Hilberseimer's and Zamyatin's cities are entirely based on a strong and repetitive grid system. But while Hilberseimer's metropolis is one that could, in theory, be repeated ad infinitum, Zamyatin's One State is bounded within a glass wall, separating it from the rest of the planet, which has been reclaimed by nature and the wilderness (fig. 14.8).

The analysis demonstrates that, while the different social scales mostly focus on living beings and their interactions, they also include elements of ordering and arranging these interactions. Aside from looking at people (or other beings), the social scales examine formal and informal groups (political, religious, administrative, working, etc.), collective and societal systems (educational, political, etc.), as well as societies and societal structures in general. The analysis of social scales also uses abstract notions related to societal and individual interactions and states of being (alienation, fragmentation, commodification, capitalism, etc.) to describe the conditions of the examined elements. Each social scale has its spatial counterpart, which embodies the environment in which the social forms take place. Therefore, the small scale focuses on the habitus and immediate surroundings of the individual such as the house or the apartment, the medium scale investigates more complex forms of architecture encompassing not only housing but also various types of public buildings and spaces intended for human interaction, and the large scale investigates the city, either as a confined, bounded whole, or as an endless system of repetition.

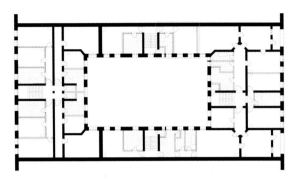

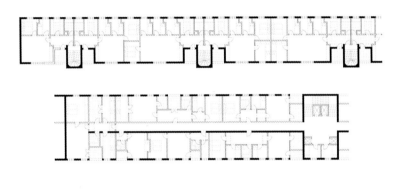

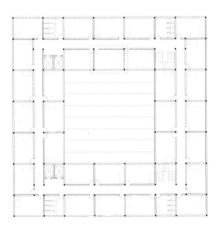

Fig. 14.6 Medium Scale – Housing (from top): 1920s Berlin tenement, Hilberseimer's housing (v1&v2), Zamyatin's building block. Images reconstructed © Jana Culek.

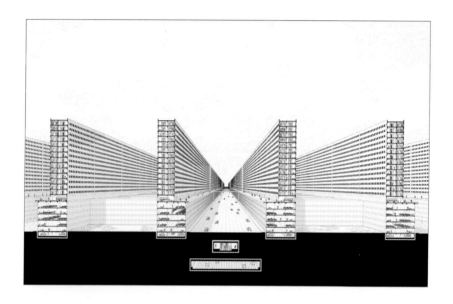

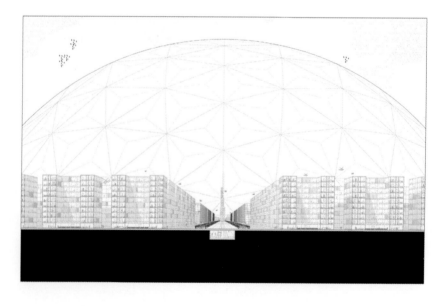

Fig. 14.7 Medium Scale – Utopian streetscapes: Hilberseimer's metropolis*, Zamyatin's One State*. Images reconstructed by Jana Culek

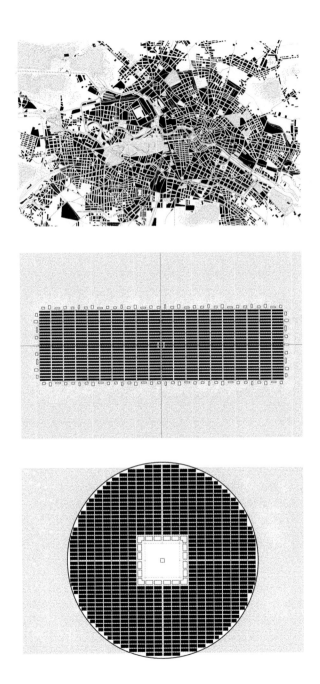

Fig. 14.8 Large Scale – City maps (from top): 1920s Berlin, Hilberseimer's metropolis, Zamyatin's One State. Images reconstructed by Jana Culek.

Conclusion: Architectural Tools from a Literary Perspective – And Back

Performing transdisciplinary research is challenging from the start, especially in a situation where one discipline develops knowledge not only through texts but also through drawings. Consequently, working with utopian works from two different fields is even more complex given that, aside from being produced through two different mediums (drawing and text), the works are also strongly based on imagination in their creation of new worlds that have not been described or depicted before. However, combining tools and methods of analysis from both the architectural field and the field of comparative literature has allowed me to develop an approach that enabled a productive comparison. Breaking the utopian works down to their building blocks has allowed me to identify the changes that occur throughout different scales and in different intensities. Performing an analysis on each scale separately has also allowed me to understand how the elements correlate and how they form intricate spatial and social systems.

And while this paper discusses some of the literary origins that influenced the development of my approach, its basis has always been innately architectural. What started as a traditional, formal, and typological analysis of the different forms and spaces proposed in utopian architectural projects has developed to also include what we would today call a "post-occupancy study" – in other words, how the buildings and spaces that were produced influenced its inhabitants and vice versa. What started as a visual analysis through different scales of space developed into an analysis and definition of various scales in which humans (or other imaginary beings) operate within a society. By identifying similar tools in both disciplines, which operate in a like manner, what initially seemed as a problematic task of comparing the textual world of literature with the visual and speculative world of architecture becomes an exciting task of filling in the missing pieces of the puzzles. Understanding that literature also produces images, albeit in a less directly visual form, allows us to use the established tools of architectural research to cross-disciplinary boundaries and produce new approaches and new forms of knowledge. Taking a cue from literature, and embracing both textual and drawing-based narrative approaches, has enabled architects to create different types of projects that focus not only on solving the brief, but also critically position themselves to their historical contexts and speculate on possible future scenarios of use, while investigating different ways in which the projects could have an effect on their societal contexts.

Notes

1. Ludwig Hilberseimer, "Metropolisarchitecture," in *Metropolisarchitecture and Selected Essays*, ed. Richard Anderson (New York: GSAPP Books, 2012), 264–304.
2. Yevgeny Zamyatin, *We*, trans. Hugh Aplin (Richmond: Alma Books, 2009).
3. The utopian change is referred to as a change of a specific condition/form/element in relation to its historical context – i.e. different political system is proposed, a new architectural type is devised, etc. – the results they lead to is the effect that these changes incite both in the utopian projects/narratives and in the historical contexts themselves.
4. Nathaniel Coleman, "The Problematic of Architecture and Utopia," *Utopian Studies* 25/1, (2014): 8.
5. Caroline Levine, "Introduction: The Affordances of Form," in *Forms: Whole, Rhythm, Hierarchy, Network* (Princeton: Princeton University Press, 2015), 1.
6. Levine, "Introduction," 2.
7. Levine, "Introduction," 6.
8. Kees Boeke, *Cosmic View: The Universe in 40 Jumps* (New York: John Day Company, 1957), 7.
9. The blasé individual stems from the blasé outlook introduced by Georg Simmel in his 1903 essay "The Metropolis and Mental Life." He defines it as an internal mechanism through which one deals with the overstimulation of senses.
10. Cameron McEwan, "Ludwig Hilberseimer and Metropolisarchitecture: The Analogue, the Blasé Attitude, the Multitude," *Arts* 7/92 (2018): 12.

Bibliography

Boeke, Kees. *Cosmic View: The Universe in 40 Jumps*. New York: The John Day Company, 1957.
Coleman, Nathaniel. "The Problematic of Architecture and Utopia." *Utopian Studies* 25, no. 01 (2014): 1–22.
Hilberseimer, Ludwig. "Metropolisarchitecture." In *Metropolisarchitecture and Selected Essays*, edited by Richard Anderson, 264–304. New York: GSAPP Books, 2012.
Levine, Caroline. "Introduction: The Affordances of Form." *Forms: Whole, Rhythm, Hierarchy, Network*. Princeton: Princeton University Press, 2015.
McEwan, Cameron. "Ludwig Hilberseimer and Metropolisarchitecture: The Analogue, the Blasé Attitude, the Multitude." *Arts* 7 (2018): 92.
Zamyatin, Yevgeny. *We*, translated by Hugh Aplin. Richmond: Alma Books, 2009.

CHAPTER 15

Growing Up Modern: Lessons from Childhoods in Iconic Homes

Julia Jamrozik

Writing about architecture can transport us to another place and time to understand not just the intricacies of architectural design and production, but more significantly to contextualise and frame the built as a cultural and social project. To understand what it was like to grow up in an early Modernist villa or housing estate, our creative documentation research project Growing up Modern, undertaken my myself and Coryn Kempster, looks directly to a group of individuals who were the first inhabitants of radical Modernist domestic spaces as children.[1]

Did living in such settings change children's attitudes? Did these radical environments shape the way they look at domestic space later in life? Were children in Modernist homes self-conscious about their avant-garde surroundings, or proud of them?

To answer these questions and others, we documented their memories in an effort to understand the impact, or lack thereof, that these buildings had on our interlocutors at the time, as well as the influence, if any, they continue to have on their adult selves. Moreover, we wanted to understand the buildings themselves from the perspectives of their users – not as sterile monuments or architectural visions, but as places that harboured life, and in many ways continue to do so. The stories gathered offer an aggregation of individual memories that differ in circumstances, intensity, and details, and which have all inevitably faded with the passage of time. They nevertheless paint a uniquely intimate portrait of Modernism.

To speak with the children who first inhabited these buildings, and not the adults, was crucial for us. Beyond the practical impossibility of speaking to residents who have long since passed away, the adults chose either to commission or to live in the avant-garde settings and might therefore be partisan to them.[2] Instead, we sought the perspectives of their children, who we imagined were more open-minded and less inhibited. We were fortunate to interview Rolf Fassbaender, Ernst Tugendhat, Helga Zumpfe, and Gisèle Moreau, original inhabitants, respectively, of a row house by J. J. P. Oud in the Weissenhof Estate, in Stuttgart, Germany (1927); the Tugendhat House, by Ludwig Mies van der Rohe, in Brno, Czech Republic (1930); the Schminke House, by Hans Scharoun, in Löbau, Germany (1933); and Le Corbusier's Unité d'Habitation apartments in Marseille, France (1952). As part of the project, we also visited our interlocutors' childhood dwellings and documented them through photographs that reflect their recollections.

Much has been written about the Modernist architects' claims of bringing about social change and the fulfilment (or failure) of these lofty ambitions. Our aim is neither to prove nor disprove the success of these buildings in this context; our project is not a quantitative study of the influence of architecture on its inhabitants,[3] nor an assessment of Modernism's wider social effects. Rather, it is an attempt to record the personal, unique, and fleeting memories of people whose childhood surroundings, through luck or the directed efforts of their parents, were unconventional. While it may be difficult to divorce the impact of architecture from its socio-economic or cultural contexts or the ideals of those who inhabited it, it is nevertheless worthwhile to examine these buildings from a point of view, that of the user, that has not been commonly represented in architectural history.[4]

The stories allow both architects and those interested in architecture to view these iconic buildings from another perspective, prompting readers to imagine design through the eyes of children and more generally through the eyes of the user. The goal of the research behind Growing up Modern has been to challenge ourselves, and our audience, to better understand the visionary and political agency of architecture, not by denying the fact that architectural spaces are functional – that their histories are multifaceted and not controlled by the architect – but precisely by embracing this reality.

"Oral history interviews might have the capacity to puncture through architecture's professional mask and bring to the fore unauthorized, polyphonic, human, and social narratives," Naomi Stead and Janina Gosseye suggest.[5] By giving voice to not only the architect but also others involved in the processes of producing and using architecture, Stead and Gosseye argue for the value of oral history as a methodology in the writing of deeper and broader architectural history. While many institutions have accumulated interviews with significant architects and landscape architects,[6] the perspective of the user has typically remained uninvestigated.[7] In the book Speaking of Buildings, Gosseye, Stead, and Deborah van der Plaat argue that "by documenting the experience of and interactions with buildings over time, oral history can give a dynamic fourth dimension to (what are generally thought of as) static three-dimensional structures."[8]

Using oral history methods,[9] our research consisted of a close reading of dialogues and material artefacts. It acknowledges the personal and subjective impacts of the interaction between narrator and interviewer; our individual and collective biases are more or less willingly tangled into the narratives, just as they are present in the framing of each photograph. The circumstances of the informal conversations, the language barriers or errors of translation, the ambiguity of unspoken gestures and implied connotations – all are embedded in the stories. The material is marked by the imperfections of this method, yet we believe it is also greatly enriched by them, ultimately allowing for a fresh and intimate look at these iconic structures.

The conversations we had pointed to no uniform conclusion, no consistent takeaway (nor universal love of white stucco walls and flat roofs). To attempt to define one single lesson would be much too simplistic and deny the richness of our interactions and the uniqueness of each narrator's circumstances. Nevertheless, these interviews did yield knowledge that might benefit students and designers as much as historians.

Rolf Fassbaender's happy childhood in a row house in the Weissenhof Estate had a lot to do with the proximity of other families with children and the spaces of the estate, which allowed freedom of play (fig. 15.1).[10] The variety of types of houses and housing in the community, calibrated by Ludwig Mies van der Rohe to respond to the different financial statuses of its inhabitants, led to a balance between built-up and open space in young Rolf's environment. Designed by J. J. P. Oud, the row house itself was compact in area but generous as a dwelling, providing a plethora of amenities for 1927, including indoor plumbing, central heating, a state-of-the-art kitchen, and abundant built-in

Fig. 15.1   Rolf Fassbaender lived with his mother at 3 Pankokweg from the opening of the Weissenhof Estate in 1927 until 1939. Mr. Fassbaender's memories of the row house involve both the immediate exterior of the house, with its sunny garden and service court, and the larger neighbourhood. The interiors of the unit, such as the social space of the living room and especially the balcony off Mr. Fassbaender's bedroom (where he could sleep under the stars), also figure prominently in his narrative. © Julia Jamrozik and Coryn Kempster.

storage. Daylight poured in through large windows and through the milk-glass skylight above the stairs and bathroom. What stood out were the connections between inside and outside spaces of the dwelling, and the garden in particular. Oud took advantage of opportunities on the garden facade, using the entrance canopy as the base of a balcony and placing a concrete bench in the space in front of the living room windows. Both of these moves required extra thought; they are evidence of care and humanism in the architect's approach, an empathy and a sincere desire to provide for the inhabitants.

Fig. 15.2 Ernst Tugendhat, a retired professor of philosophy, lived in the famous house in Brno, which the family was forced to leave in 1938. Even the most idiosyncratic of the rooms in the villa did not leave a lasting impression on our interlocutor, whose memories instead revolve around the house's exterior spaces. © Julia Jamrozik and Coryn Kempster.

At eight years old, Ernst Tugendhat was the youngest of our interlocutors when he and his family left the famous Modernist home of his childhood (fig. 15.2). It is perhaps not surprising, then, that he has the fewest memories of the home's interiors and features. Given the impending invasion by Nazi forces, the circumstances of the relocation must have been deeply emotional and even traumatic, if not for him directly then for the family generally. Coincidentally or consequently, the time he spent in Brno has largely disappeared from Mr. Tugendhat's mind. In its place is not only an aversion to the house itself but also a general ambivalence towards architecture and design. The lack of emotion that the dwelling elicits in this former inhabitant is tied to his embarrassment about the opulence of the house. His indifference was striking, and one of the biggest surprises of the project for us, as designers indoctrinated through our own architectural education: that someone could grow up in one of history's most famous buildings, designed by a widely acclaimed architect, and not care about it in the slightest. Mr. Tugendhat's feelings are especially unexpected considering the affection that his parents, the clients, professed for the house even well after the family left it. Grete Tugendhat wrote that it allowed them to "feel free to an extent never experienced before";[11] in 1969, during a speech in Brno, she confirmed that she and her husband "loved the house from the very first moment."[12] The freedom the adults experienced in the house was something they anticipated would extend to their children. On 29 February 2012, when the Tugendhat House reopened after extensive renovation, Daniela Hammer-Tugendhat – the youngest daughter of the Tugendhats, an art historian, and a devoted advocate of the preservation of the house[13] – spoke to these expectations: "My father believed that the beauty and clear forms of the architecture would affect the ethos of the people living in the house and the children growing up there."[14] Fritz Tugendhat may not have guessed exactly how the dwelling would affect his children, nor could he anticipate the course that global history would take.

Fig. 15.3   Helga Zumpfe, the youngest of the Schminke children, spent her childhood in the house in Löbau. She still dreams of the house and credits the experiences she had there for informing many personal and professional aspects of her later life. Her recollections further highlight the strong and lasting friendship that developed between the architect and the family. © Julia Jamrozik and Coryn Kempster.

Helga Zumpfe's personal experience was very different, and her relationship to her childhood home, the Schminke House, stands in sharp contrast to that of Mr. Tugendhat (fig. 15.3). Even during World War II, she was able to enjoy the home that Hans Scharoun designed for her family in relative safety and comfort. Not only did she live much longer – fifteen years – in the house, she was also much older (eighteen years old) when she left it, so it follows that her memories are stronger and more vivid. While particular features and architectural details play a key role in the stories she tells about the home, it is the building's openness and spaciousness that had the most lasting impression on her, and by extension on us. She internalised these qualities to such an extent that her dreams often still take place inside the house, which, after seven decades away, is in and of itself remarkable. Further, she has tried to adapt her current living conditions – at least as much as possible, considering her more limited resources – to emulate the openness of the childhood home, privileging views and replacing doors with curtains. Last, she convinced her congregation to commission Scharoun to design a church and community space in Bochum, rekindling her relationship with the architect and bringing his architectural approach back into her life.

Fig. 15.4   Gisèle Moreau moved into Le Corbusier's Unité d'Habitation in Marseille when it opened and has resided there for the majority of her life. She has lived in several apartments in the building but now occupies the apartment in which she grew up, having inherited it from her parents. She is passionately invested in telling the story of the building that has become a significant aspect of her, and her family's, identity. © Julia Jamrozik and Coryn Kempster.

Having lived for most of her life in the Unité d'Habitation in Marseille, Gisèle Moreau is unique among our narrators (fig. 15.4). She has been a witness to the building in every era of its existence, and the mythology of the place has become a strong part of her personal story. The identity of the Unité, and by extension the identity of the architect, have over the years become intertwined with her own. She is an advocate for the building and a believer in the goals that Le Corbusier outlined for it. While her parents may have chosen to move into the building in the first place, it is explicitly by choice that Ms. Moreau has stayed there throughout her adulthood. Her emotional attachment was clear when she spoke about the apartment block and how it has changed over time. While the Unité functioned as state-run social housing only in its initial years, it does provide social infrastructures that are essential to its inhabitants, and these in turn enable a strong sense of community. The aspects of community and collective amenity that Le Corbusier embedded into the building are chief among her memories as a child and experiences as an adult.

In listening to our interlocutors' stories about these important examples of Modernism, we were most struck by how the moments of humanism in the architecture play out in the memories of those who inhabited these spaces. At the scale of a building, for example, the rooftop of the Unité – a significant social amenity – serves to this day as a place of relief and play, just as the architect intended. Organisationally, locating the playroom at the centre of the building in the Schminke House enabled and empowered the children in the home. The pass-through from the kitchen to the dining area of the Oud row house shaped family interactions, just as the playroom's wide windowsill at the Schminke House, with its conspicuously adjacent operable pane, allowed the kids direct access outside before they could even reach a door handle. It is the details, designed for utility but also beauty, that endure in inhabitants' minds: the colourful glass portholes of the Schminke House or the balcony and bench of the Oud row house.

Designers and students of architecture history must be aware of not only the utilitarian amenities adopted as standard under Modernism but also the particular generosity that was a feature of at least some of the early examples of the movement. While the lessons of Modernism's focus on efficiency have made their way into the housing canon over the last century, its humanist aspirations and social agendas, at both the individual and collective scales, have often been backgrounded. There is no doubt that specific, humane design requires inventiveness and care on the part of the architect; it often, but not always, requires an additional financial investment. Based on our conversations, we have come to believe it is precisely the moments where such thought is evident that endear buildings to people. These are significant lessons as we deepen our understanding of Modernists' audacity in questioning conventions and defying norms.

To conduct the interviews for this project, we travelled around Europe in a camper van – an *Existenzminimum* dwelling in and of itself – through a heat wave, with our child, who was just learning to stand on his own two legs. The fragility of our son's balance was a good reminder of the growing and changing child's body, while his demands for food and sleep ruled our schedule as much as the interview appointments did (fig. 15.5). Each of the conversations took place under different circumstances, and we personally learned from

Fig. 15.5   Visiting the Schminke House (left) and during our conversation with Helga Zumpfe, who grew up in the home (right). © Julia Jamrozik and Coryn Kempster.

each, even beyond the content of the stories the narrators shared about their childhood homes. We learned how to ask our questions better, how to leave more time for replies, and how not to interrupt the recording with laughter. Navigating language barriers and age differences involved deciphering body language and interpreting social customs. Perhaps having a fussy baby along for the ride helped to make the circumstances familiar or familial, disarming our narrators – or maybe it was a nuisance, though they were all too polite to say so (fig. 15.6).

Fig. 15.6   Rolf Fassbaender playing hide-and-seek with our son while showing us the port-holes that feature in the interior doors in J. J. P. Oud's Weissenhof Estate row houses. © Julia Jamrozik and Coryn Kempster.

We have often had to make the case that we are the right people to be doing this research. When we embarked on our journey of creative documentation, we were not practised interviewers, nor were we seasoned photographers. We were not experts in Modernism, nor were we historians, psychologists, or oral historians. We were, and we are, simply a couple with backgrounds in archi-tecture and visual arts and interests in spatial history and narrative. We are parents – and as these are children's stories, perhaps this is also relevant. We are designers, and we are educators. As Naomi Stead asserts, it is important to acknowledge our backgrounds:

> All scholars are influenced by the particularities of their backgrounds and education, plus the identity categories of class, race, and gender, plus the irrationalities of their emotions, but also their own bodies – we write and speak not only as disembodied floating brains, but as bodies with needs and wants of their own.[15]

Perhaps most significantly, we were curious and persistent enough to try to get in contact with these individuals and, through them, to add to our knowledge of the icons of Modernism.

We had few conscious preconceptions when we started our research. We were not sure what to expect from our interlocutors and how much or how little they would remember of their pasts in Modernist homes. We hoped their memories would be vivid – but we were aware that, because so much time had passed, this was rather unlikely. We were not sure if their recollections would be positive or negative, and the extent to which they would communicate these emotions. We found it deeply endearing that people wanted to speak with us and share their experiences. We left the interviews with genuine gratitude for the time and openness of each interlocutor, for their trust and willingness to talk to us, total strangers, about intimate details of their upbringing. We believed – and in this we were proven correct – that hearing about the history of a place from someone who grew up there would help us understand the architecture better and would make us pay attention to it in a different way.

For us, the research encompassing the Growing up Modern project has opened up various "other worlds" from the intimacy of speaking to our interlocutors to archival research to the intricacies of the publishing world, with its distinctive processes and conventions, that we were previously not acquainted with. The project has also been influential both in terms of our design practice and in teaching.

When designing domestic spaces, we are now even more sensitive to future inhabitants. We not only listen and implement the clients' desires offering pragmatic responses to stated objectives, but rather strive to further imagine opportunities for use and occupation. Through narrative projections and scenarios we thus conceive possible adaptations and changing uses over time. In our 2017 Sky House design, for example, we specifically thought about the young daughter and implemented a series of idiosyncratic spaces and elements with her in mind, imagining the memories she may possibly develop in the holiday home.

In teaching the discussion of the childhood home has further been a vehicle for eliciting more subjective conversations than are typical in architectural education. From personal memories, family histories, cultural associations, and social commentaries, the topic allows a focus on people and inhabitation. It offers a mechanism for connecting across age groups, racial, geographic, and socio-economic backgrounds. In teaching the seminar to a mix of undergraduate and graduate students at the University at Buffalo, SUNY, weekly drawing exercises of the spaces of childhood by the students became a further tool in unravelling and sharing their domestic narratives.

The topic of the childhood home becomes a link between everyday experiences and the iconic examples of architecture. While the Growing up Modern research expands our sources of knowledge through oral history to include the voices of architecture's inhabitants, more broadly, it urges us, as academics, as practitioners, and as teachers, to consider what narratives we privilege as we contribute to the writing of, making, and learning about architecture.

Acknowledgements

The Growing up Modern project and book publication was funded through the New York State Council on the Arts's Architecture + Design programme in the Independent Projects category, by Elise Jaffe and Jeffrey Brown and by the Lawrence B. Anderson Award from MIT.

Notes

1. This essay is based in large part on our book, Julia Jamrozik and Coryn Kempster, *Growing up Modern: Childhoods in Iconic Homes* (Basel: Birkhäuser, 2021).
2. The perspectives of the parents are often already recorded, especially in the cases of commissioned single-family homes. See, for example, Grete Tugendhat and Fritz Tugendhat, "The Inhabitants of the Tugendhat House Give Their Opinion," letter to the editor, *Die Form* 6, no. 11 (15 November 1931), reprinted and translated in Daniela Hammer-Tugendhat, Ivo Hammer, and Wolf Tegethoff, *Tugendhat House: Ludwig Mies van der Rohe*, new ed. (Basel: Birkhäuser, 2015), 76–77. For the role and perspective of female clients in particular, see Alice T. Friedman, *Women and the Making of the Modern House: A Social and Architectural History* (New York: Harry N. Abrams, 1998).
3. Either in the vein of quantitative post-occupancy evaluations or the more conceptual approach presented by AMO and Rem Koolhaas in their guest-edited *Domus* issue "Post-Occupancy" (2006).
4. "If a lot of architecture's meaning is made not on the drafting board but in the complex lifeworld of how it is inhabited, consumed, used, lived or neglected, that world is at once central and peculiarly under-explored." Kenny Cupers, *Use Matters: An Alternative History of Architecture* (London: Routledge, 2013), 1. See also Stephen Grabow and Kent F. Spreckelmeyer, *The Architecture of Use: Aesthetics and Function in Architectural Design* (New York: Routledge, 2015). In recent years, several significant books and exhibitions have focused on design for children, including Amy F. Ogata, *Designing the Creative Child: Playthings and Places in Midcentury America* (Minneapolis: University of Minnesota Press, 2013); Alexandra Lange, *The Design of Childhood: How the Material World Shapes Independent Kids* (New York: Bloomsbury Press, 2018); and the 2012 Museum of Modern Art exhibition *Century of the Child: Growing by Design, 1900–2000*, and its associated catalogue, Juliet Kinchin and Aidan O'Connor, *Century of the Child: Growing by Design, 1900–2000* (New York: Museum of Modern Art, 2012).
5. "Oral History, Part I: Methods and Mistakes," video recording of a seminar led by Gosseye and Stead at the Canadian Centre for Architecture, 4 July 2017, 27:57, https://www.cca.qc.ca/en/events/50476/oral-history-part-i-methods-and-mistakes.
6. Including the Archives of American Art, the British Library, the UCLA Library, and the Art Institute of Chicago, among others. See also John Peter, *The Oral History of Modern Architecture: Interviews with the Greatest Architects of the Twentieth Century* (New York: H. N. Abrams, 1994).
7. Significant exceptions are Philippe Boudon, *Lived-In Architecture: Le Corbusier's Pessac Revisited*, trans. Gerald Onn (Cambridge, MA: MIT Press, 1972); Danielle Aubert, Lana Cavar, and Natasha Chandani, eds., *Thanks for the View, Mr. Mies: Lafayette Park, Detroit* (New York: Metropolis Books, 2012), which focuses primarily on contemporary occupants of Lafayette Park but also brings forth historical information based on the stories of long-term residents; Esra Akcan, *Open Architecture: Migration, Citizenship and the*

Urban Renewal of Berlin-Kreuzberg by IBA 1984/87 (Basel: Birkhäuser, 2018); Hilde de Haan and Jolanda Keesom, *What Happened to My Buildings: Learning from 30 Years of Architecture with Marlies Rohmer* (Rotterdam: nai010, 2016); and essays in Janina Gosseye, Naomi Stead, and Deborah van der Plaat, eds., *Speaking of Buildings: Oral History in Architectural Research* (New York: Princeton Architectural Press, 2019).

8. Gosseye, Stead, and van der Plaat, *Speaking of Buildings*, 26.

9. We are not oral historians and have not been formally trained in the practice, though we have attended oral history workshops at Columbia University. We refer to significant texts on the practice of oral history in our efforts to not only record but also transcribe and represent the stories that our interlocutors narrated to us as part of this project. See Donald A. Ritchie, *Doing Oral History: A Practical Guide*, 2nd ed. (Oxford: Oxford University Press, 2003); Robert Perks and Alistair Thomson, *The Oral History Reader*, 2nd ed. (London: Routledge, 2006); and Gosseye, Stead, and van der Plaat, *Speaking of Buildings*.

10. We are careful not to attribute a child's happiness to the home where they grew up; clearly, the causality is much more complicated. While it is fair to state that Oud's design only added to Mr. Fassbaender's happy childhood, it is evident that his happiness is more in debt to the efforts of his mother – which leaves us to wonder if he would have experienced the same level of happiness in an entirely different dwelling.

11. Grete Tugendhat, "The Inhabitants of the Tugendhat House Give Their Opinion," letter to the editor, *Die Form* 6, no. 11 (15 November 1931), reprinted and translated in Daniela Hammer-Tugendhat, Ivo Hammer, and Wolf Tegethoff, *Tugendhat House: Ludwig Mies van der Rohe*, new ed. (Basel: Birkhäuser, 2015), 77.

12. Grete Tugendhat, "On the Construction of the Tugendhat House," lecture, Brno House of Arts, 17 January 1969, printed and translated in Hammer-Tugendhat et al., *Tugendhat House*, 21.

13. Daniela was born in 1946 in Caracas, Venezuela, after the family was forced to flee the house in Brno.

14. Daniela Hammer-Tugendhat, "Speech on the Occasion of the Opening of the Tugendhat House in Brno on February 29, 2012," printed in Hammer-Tugendhat et al., *Tugendhat House*, 226.

15. Naomi Stead, "Architectural Affections: On Some Modes of Conversation in Architecture, Towards a Disciplinary Theorisation of Oral History," *Fabrications: The Journal of the Society of Architectural Historians, Australia and New Zealand* 24, no. 2 (2014): 156. Quoted in Gosseye, Stead, and van der Plaat, *Speaking of Buildings*, 15.

Bibliography

Akcan, Esra. *Open Architecture: Migration, Citizenship and the Urban Renewal of Berlin-Kreuzberg by IBA 1984/87*. Basel: Birkhäuser, 2018.

Aubert, Danielle, Lana Cavar, and Natasha Chandani, eds. *Thanks for the View, Mr. Mies: Lafayette Park, Detroit*. New York: Metropolis Books, 2012.

Boudon, Philippe. *Lived-In Architecture: Le Corbusier's Pessac Revisited*, translated by Gerald Onn. Cambridge, MA: MIT Press, 1972.

Cupers, Kenny. *Use Matters: An Alternative History of Architecture*. London: Routledge, 2013.

de Haan, Hilde and Jolanda Keesom, *What Happened to My Buildings: Learning from 30 Years of Architecture with Marlies Rohmer*. Rotterdam: nai010, 2016.

Friedman, Alice T. *Women and the Making of the Modern House: A Social and Architectural History*. New York: Harry N. Abrams, 1998.

Gosseye, Janina, Naomi Stead, and Deborah van der Plaat, eds. *Speaking of Buildings: Oral History in Architectural Research*. New York: Princeton Architectural Press, 2019.

—— and Naomi Stead. "Oral History, Part I: Methods and Mistakes." Video recording of a seminar at the Canadian Centre for Architecture. 4 July 2017. https://www.cca.qc.ca/en/events/50476/oral-history-part-i-methods-and-mistakes.

Grabow, Stephen and Kent F. Spreckelmeyer. *The Architecture of Use: Aesthetics and Function in Architectural Design*. New York: Routledge, 2015.

Hammer-Tugendhat, Daniela, Ivo Hammer, and Wolf Tegethoff. *Tugendhat House: Ludwig Mies van der Rohe*. Basel: Birkhäuser, 2015.

Jamrozik, Julia and Coryn Kempster. *Growing up Modern: Childhoods in Iconic Homes*. Basel: Birkhäuser, 2021.

Kinchin, Juliet and Aidan O'Connor. *Century of the Child: Growing by Design, 1900–2000*. New York: Museum of Modern Art, 2012.

Lange, Alexandra. *The Design of Childhood: How the Material World Shapes Independent Kids*. New York: Bloomsbury Press, 2018.

Ogata, Amy F. *Designing the Creative Child: Playthings and Places in Midcentury America*. Minneapolis: University of Minnesota Press, 2013.

Perks, Robert and Alistair Thomson. *The Oral History Reader*. 2nd ed. London: Routledge, 2006.

Peter, John. *The Oral History of Modern Architecture: Interviews with the Greatest Architects of the Twentieth Century*. New York: H. N. Abrams, 1994.

Ritchie, Donald A. *Doing Oral History: A Practical Guide*, 2nd ed. Oxford: Oxford University Press, 2003.

PART 4

Stepping Back from the Object

Each of the four essays in Part 4 is involved in some way with the processes of generating and representing architectural culture through published media, including analogue books and magazines, digital blogs, and dissemination through social media. As each reveals the underlying intellectual motivations for their work and its processes, the implications for their own practice are exposed. Cathelijne Nuijsink takes a step back to interrogate Rem Koolhaas's use of writing as a design tool and the wider historical implications of this on recent architecture. This reflection on the relationships between the creative and the formal, and the intellectual and the conceptual, is brought into tangible focus through an investigation of Koolhaas's role and intentions in judging the 1992 Shinkenchiku Residential Design Competition. This detachment is continued in the essay by Joseph Bedford, who proposed the notion of a postliterate age. Through analysis of literature around recent changes in media technology, he defines a position in relation to the proliferation of images and the implications on engagement with written architectural theory that he uses to analyse the presence of a selection of architectural practices on social media. In Chapter 18, Patrick Lynch describes and analyses his role as editor of an academic journal – *Civic Architecture* – and as an architectural publisher through his company, Canalside Press, outlining how the intellectual frameworks that he has developed for these have a reciprocal relationship with his theoretical and philosophical approaches to architectural practice. Returning to his own hybrid practice as architect by training and member of an editorial collective, Carlo Menon draws from deep academic research into the role of small magazines in the field of architectural culture. He uses the concept of "ecology of practices" to develop a theoretical approach to the formative and critical that these publications play in both crossing disciplinary boundaries and forging new connections between architectural practice and theory. Their small but dispersed readerships make them an important tool for teaching, experimentation, provocation, and community formation.

CHAPTER 16

Rem Koolhaas's House with No Style: The 1992 Shinkenchiku Residential Design Competition

Cathelijne Nuijsink

If one thing became clear at the 1990 symposium How Modern is Dutch Architecture, it was architect Rem Koolhaas's unease with the issue of style.[1] Flustered by the fact that, for generations, Dutch architects had been using functionalism as a starting point for their own designs, Koolhaas stated that using the same reference for over seventy-five years was an act of despair and "a spasmodic relapse into a past heroic moment."[2] A couple of years later, his dissatisfaction with the issue of style reappeared in his book *S, M, L, X* (1995). Comparing the constant fluctuation of styles in art with those in architecture, Koolhaas asserts that this principle to facilitate comparison across time and space might work for artists to depict personal evolution. Yet, for architects that are expected to constantly respond to a changing social fabric, styles are a less fruitful tool. After the first dictionary entry in *S, M, L, X* came a second, which simply proclaimed that "the 'styles' are a lie."[3] In 1992, Koolhaas revived the two-centuries-old discussion on style within the space of the Shinkenchiku Residential Design Competition. In his role as single judge – a unique feature of this yearly housing ideas competition from Japan – Koolhaas could freely set the competition theme "House with NO Style" (fig. 16.1) and select multiple winners. Since the competition's launch in 1965, many well-known architects serving as judges have crafted an independent position for themselves in existing architectural debates with the help of this competition. Koolhaas equally used the competition as a platform to put forward his crucial observations about contemporary developments and encouraged his fellow architects to stop making references to "style."

Writing in Architecture

Thinking and theorising about architecture, independent from real building activities, has been at the core of the practice of the Office of Metropolitan Architecture (OMA) since its foundation in 1975. In his role as a journalist and scriptwriter, Koolhaas did a lot of writing before he began practising architecture, and he continued to do so even in the making of architecture. For Koolhaas, writing was a deliberate choice to position himself as another kind of architect. In his words, writing allowed him "to construct a terrain where I could eventually work as an architect."[4] In fact, OMA owes much of its early success to Koolhaas's book *Delirious New York* (1977), a five-year research project that launched his career as a "particular kind of architect."[5] Even when projects for real building started coming in the 1980s, words remained crucial to the practice of OMA. As he explained in an interview with Beatriz Colomina, each design ideally starts with a "textlike formulation of the problem," which suggests an entire architectural programme. To define a design project first in literary terms is OMA's way to "unleash the design."[6] To cover the "expansive habits of thinking and presenting," OMA needed a special foundation dedicated

Fig. 16.1 With the provocative competition theme "House with No Style," Rem Koolhaas stirred a lively cross-cultural discussion on style in the pages of *The Japan Architect* and *Shinkenchiku* magazines. Competition announcement of the 1992 Shinkenchiku Residential Design Competition. *The Japan Architect* 1992-III: 2–3 © Shinkenchiku-Sha Co Ltd.

to raising money for publications, exhibitions, and research. Spurred by former partner Donald van Dansik, the Groszstadt Foundation, founded in 1988, allowed the practice to oscillate between generating intelligence and producing actual buildings.

The privatisation of the market in the 1990s required yet another model of operating architecturally that could help OMA freely operate both as architects and intellectuals. In 1995, Koolhaas was invited as a professor at Harvard University to lead the research programme Harvard Project on the City and investigate the changing urban conditions around the world. This opened doors for a new kind of collaborative research practice. Focusing on the largely ignored territories of Lagos, Shenzhen, Singapore, and the Arab world, this academic position allowed Koolhaas to tackle a different subject each year with his students.[7] When Universal Studios asked OMA to design their new headquarters in Los Angeles (1996), Prada contacted OMA to rethink their brand (1999), and the Schiphol Group commissioned OMA to design a Schiphol airport on the sea (1998), but two of the three commissions never led anywhere, the dialectic between cultural production and professional practice swelled to a maximum.[8] In response, the independent think tank Architecture Media Office (AMO) was launched as a "critical arm" of OMA in 1999. AMO was the new intellectual apparatus that aimed to produce a fruitful dialogue between "thinking" and "doing" and helped the architectural office get the desired recognition for their knowledge production. It was established to provide strategic input to expand architecture into the realms of the virtual.[9] Acknowledging that OMA is a global office working all over the world "of which it knows fundamentally little," AMO developed an intrinsic motivation to understand how the world in which they were working worked.[10]

The Competition Forging a "Space of Ideas"

The history of the Shinkenchiku Residential Design Competition goes back to 1965, when Japanese publishing house Shinkenchiku decided to rejuvenate its long-running architecture magazine *Shinkenchiku* (New Architecture, 1925–) with an international housing ideas competition. From the outset, the Shinkenchiku Residential Design Competition (hereafter Shinkenchiku Competition) was envisioned as set of avant-garde pages inserted in what was otherwise a relatively conservative architectural magazine. What made this competition different from other contests was its international and bilingual character. Both the competition announcement as well as the winning entries were published in Japanese in *Shinkenchiku* and in English in its sister magazine *The Japan Architect*, which finally provided foreign architects an opportunity to participate in the Japanese housing debate. Besides being an exceptionally long-running competition (the competition has seen forty-nine editions since 1965), what sets this tournament of ideas apart from other such competitions is that it operates with a single-judge system. Along with Rem Koolhaas, many well-known architects have served as judges in this contest, ranging from Richard Meier (1976), Peter Cook (1977), Charles Moore (1978), Bernard Tschumi (1989), Jacques Herzog (1997), and Winny Maas (2001) to some of Japan's most respected designers – Kiyoshi Seike (1965), Kenzo Tange (1966), Kazuo Shinohara (1972), Arata Isozaki (1975), Tadao Ando (1985, 1991), Toyo Ito (1988, 2000), Kengo Kuma (2006), and Kazuyo Sejima (1996). Unlike the "mediated" briefs that result when a team of organisers or jury members must decide on one theme, the Shinkenchiku Competition allows the single judge to freely decide on a competition theme, thereby consciously and even provocatively stirring international architectural debate. When Koolhaas accepted the invitation to judge, he used the competition to prompt a new collaborative research project. Much like Harvard Project on the City, which the urban studies OMA has conducted since 1995 in collaboration with students from the Harvard Graduate School of Design, or the rebranding of Prada, the Shinkenchiku Competition operated as a fruitful intellectual experiment, and not only to the benefit of Koolhaas.

When invited to judge the 1992 Shinkenchiku Competition, Koolhaas was not new to Japan. In 1988, the Japanese journal *Architecture and Urbanism* (*A + U*) had already devoted an entire issue to OMA's paper architecture and the first realised the works of OMA. One year later, Japanese architect Arata Isozaki invited Koolhaas to participate in the innovative social housing project Nexus World in Fukuoka, which provided Koolhaas the opportunity to visit Japan on a regular basis until its completion in 1991. Koolhaas's geographical obsession with Japan stemmed from the work of the Metabolists, a mixed group of avant-garde designers from Japan who presented themselves at the 1960 World Design Conference in Tokyo. At this first international design conference held in Japan after the Second World War, and amid an international audience, the Metabolists made a profound statement about the status of modern architecture in Japan using the ninety-page document *Metabolism 1960: The Proposals for New Urbanism* as their manifesto. With large-scale visionary urban plans, the Metabolists celebrated Japan's economic recovery and growing prosperity in the 1960s. Koolhaas recognised in Japan "the first non-Western country with an architectural avant-garde." [11] This "peripheral" development of the Metabolists elucidated the shortcomings of the Euro-American canon and demonstrated that new architectural knowledge could equally be produced in other parts of the world. Koolhaas long-lasting fascination with Japan would eventually result in a written history of Metabolism, a 720-page-thick documentation-cum-oral history, produced in collaboration with a team of researchers.

Fig. 16.2 Rem Koolhaas sharing his thoughts on the 732 competition entries submitted in the final judge's remarks. *The Japan Architect* 1993-I Annual: 6–7 © Shinkenchiku-Sha Co Ltd.

This paper sets out to demonstrate that, in the Shinkenchiku Competition, the judge and contestants *collectively* produce architecture knowledge. To justify this claim, it is necessary to highlight the intrinsic logic of the contest. This logic consists of a judge setting a competition theme against the backdrop of ongoing international debates. This is followed by the submission of different competition entries that can be viewed as various cultural responses to the judge's call, illustrating diverse translations of the common design problem. These, in turn, contribute to the judge's final remarks, which offer a more nuanced understanding of the original theme. Finally, the publication of these final remarks is disseminated in different directions. In all the steps of this competition logic, local and foreign ideas regarding "house with no style" inform and mutually inspire each other.

Situating the Shinkenchiku Competition as a multidirectional portal between Koolhaas's early conceptual paper projects and individual research projects such as *Delirious New York* in the 1970s and the launch of the AMO think tank in 1999, this paper elucidates how the competition anticipated the emergence of a collaborative research practice paramount to the OMA practice even today. The contest, with all its steps of the competition logic, functions much like a research project on the key question Koolhaas posed in the competition brief: "Is it utopian to imagine a 'designer-free' zone?" The

CATHELIJNE NUIJSINK

provocative competition brief of House with No Style effectively aligned with Koolhaas's habit of undermining architectural conventions and his concept of anti-architecture, which refuses to behave the way architecture is expected to. With provocative designs shaking up established conventions, Koolhaas is known for being a controversial figure in the architecture world. His own "style" is unconcerned with conventional ideas of beauty and defies categorisation. With the same provocative stance, Koolhaas, in the 1992 Shinkenchiku Competition, also approached the contestants. In what was one of the shortest competition briefs, Koolhaas called on fellow architects to come up with methods on shedding style and stopping the automatism of simple form-making for the sake of it. A "house with no style," Koolhaas disclosed in the brief, should be a house that avoids recent clichés and nostalgia, contain a programme "purged of the frivolous and the decorative," and fit a "'designer-free' zone."

The Shinkenchiku Competition as a Collaborative Research Practice

After reviewing 732 competition entries (306 from Japan and 426 from thirty other countries), Koolhaas selected sixteen winning schemes: one first prize, one second prize, one third prize, and thirteen honourable mentions. The selection of multiple winners is emblematic of this competition, demonstrating that the competition was set up from the start as a platform of discussion rather than a search for a single right answer. In his comments (fig 16.2), Koolhaas commented on the "stupendous quantities of work, representing an enormous investment of energy, ingenuity and money."[12] The majority of the entries "represented a disease," with too many references to form, style, and aesthetics.[13] Within this massive quantity of waste production, however, Koolhaas discovered exceptionally good entries that revealed serious research on "how to shed style, how to interrupt the narcissistic automatism of form-making, and how to inject an exhausted profession with new content."[14]

The third prize went to an anonymous entry reporting from the Bosnian War (fig. 16.3). In a situation of war and destruction, the author argued that it is no longer relevant to talk about houses as the embodiment of a stylish dream. Instead, it is a matter of survival in anonymous styleless shelters built on top of the ruins. Without mentioning the quality of the project itself, its authorlessness was enough to win the third prize, as, according to the juror, it effectively demonstrated a critique of the whole system of architectural competitions.

Interested in taking a critical position in the architectural debate rather than merely accommodating popular taste as most practising architects did, Mitsugo Okagawa, with his student Yutaka Kinjo, participated in the Koolhaas edition to explore another kind of modern architecture (fig. 16.4). "Through a re-reading of Mies fan der Rohe's architecture, I tried to bend Mies fan der Rohe's 'universal space' into a 'house with no style' for AIDS patients living

in a delirious Tokyo," Okagawa explained.[15] Koolhaas lauded the courageous move of the second prize winners to introduce a disease, AIDS, into an otherwise spotless profession. "To mix architecture with AIDS forces people to think about the destiny of human beings," stated Koolhaas.[16] The first prize winner Yosuke Fujiki responded with a house catalogue containing a hundred defected houses "that help us make original lifestyles" (fig. 16.5) [17] He believed that the challenges of a house without gas pipes or waterworks or a roof would help get rid of fixed ideas about housing. Fujiki's entry exceeded all Koolhaas's expectations from the competition, indicating that the author had an even better understanding of the theme of "no style" than Koolhaas himself. Koolhaas's judge comment on him read, "A systematic suppression of elements triggers uselessness, recharges 'what we have' and, at the same time, 'destabilizes the notion of a house in an absolute anti-aesthetic way.'"[18]

The thirteen honourable mentions further enriched the discussion on what could be a designer-free house. Paulo Sanguinetti Rivas and Bane Gaiser proposed a seven-storey tower house where each floor is dedicated to one essential dwelling function. Through removing the boundaries between rooms and creating vertical relations instead, Rivas and Gaiser introduced a designer-free zone in which the occupants themselves – using moveable furniture items – decide

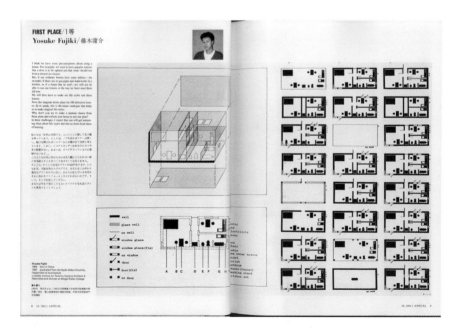

Fig. 16.5 With a diagram of one hundred "defective" houses in which residents design lifestyles themselves, Yosuke Fujiki won first prize in the 1992 Shinkenchiku Residential Design Competition. *The Japan Architect* 1993-I Annual: 8–9 © Yosuke Fujiki.

the way they want to live.[19] Akira Imafuji's designed a house for a blind person in which 1.15-metre-wide corridors provide the inhabitant freedom of movement, rather than limiting the restrictions in living. Being able to touch the walls on two sides while moving through this house, the inhabitant will feel free and comfortable.[20] Satoshi Ohashi's House with No Style is a simple squared "Pandora's box" situated in the landscape. The house operates as a "boxed infrastructure" in which functions can be switched on and off, and which is responsive and adaptive to its surrounding conditions.[21] Kevin Woods and Charlotte Sheridan, to name yet other contributors to the discussion on No Style, argued that to come up with a house with no style, the architect's mind first must be freed from any historical references or preconceptions. They reduced the design process to a mathematical formula, which resulted in a pattern of living freed from conscious and unconscious influences of style.[22] Joanne Mackenzie and Garth Davies focused on the innate responses of individuals to a personally chosen object. With a collage of bodies –from which emotionless faces are cut off the picture – holding an object, the authors evoked a universal response beyond style.[23] What the diversity of responses from these and other honourable mentions, let alone the non-winning submissions – made clear was that there exists no single correct answer to the brief, but the competition was set up as a platform for discussion to propel the discussion on style further.

Although Koolhaas, by 1992, already had access to international architectural debates, the Shinkenchiku Competition served him well as a theoretical moment at a time he was readily involved in actual building projects. The competition brief asked for alternative approaches to design, ones not focused on style, and turned, under the moderation of Koolhaas, into a lively discussion that provided clues on what could replace the formal aspect of style in the design process. The diversity of responses that were selected by Koolhaas as "winning entries" alluded that the "style" problem was much a problem of architects themselves. One possible direction that came out of this contest related to the idea of "silent authorship." The first prize, nameless entry suggested "silent authorship" as the removal of the architect as "author" of a project. Yet others explained "silent authorship" as the elimination of the architect as actor in the design process and instead giving agency to the clients to elements in the house according to their own desires or design for themselves all together. Another clue to solve architects' continuous adherence to "style" was the problem of the architect's mentality. Proposals suggested the "purification" of architects' mind from historical references or preconceptions that hindered the development of new ideas, as well as a deliberate tarnishing of architects' immaculate position. Besides instigating this cross-cultural discussion on how to shed style, the competition served Koolhaas another goal. The Shinkenchiku Competition anticipated a mode of collaborative practice that OMA continued to implement in AMO's research projects as well as in its overall office structure through removing the single architect as the heroic genius of the company and instead foreground its partners. Besides acknowledging that a collaborative practice is much more efficient in terms of gathering knowledge, it also much better reflects today's realities of global architecture practice. By now, the architectural profession has become a complex multidisciplinary practice involving count-less disciplines and stakeholders, which necessitates a mode of collaborative working. The 1992 Shinkenchiku Competition sits as a hinge in Koolhaas's decades-long career, acknowledging the benefits of a collaborative research while at the same time anticipating a mode of speculative thinking that lies at the base of think tank AMO.

Notes

1.   Koolhaas wrote on the backflap of a publication for this conference, "Hoe komt het dat in Nederland – voor alle generaties- het 'Nieuwe Bouwen' inspiratiebron or zelfs uitgangspunt blijft vormen? Is dat moed of wanhoop? Bescheidenheid of onvermogen? Hoe geloofwaardig is -uitgerekend in deze eeuw- een voedingsbodem die 75 jaar oud is? Gaat het hier om een het geduldig cultiveren van een nog steeds bewonderingswaardige traditie of het krampachtig terugvallen op een voorbij hoogtepunt?"; Bernard Leupen and Rem Koolhaas, *Hoe Modern is de Nederlandse Architectuur?* (Rotterdam: 010, 1990).

2.   Bernard Leupen and Rem Koolhaas, *Hoe Modern is de Nederlandse Architectuur?* (Rotterdam: 010, 1990).

3.   Rem Koolhaas et al., *S, M, L, XL: Small, Medium, Large, Extra-large* (New York: Monacelli Press, 1995), 1188.

4.   Rem Koolhaas, "Why I wrote Delirious New York and other textual strategies," *Architecture New York: Writing in Architecture* (May/June 1993): 42.

5.   Rem Koolhaas, "Why I wrote Delirious New York and other textual strategies," Koolhaas started formulating the idea for *Delirious New York* while at Cornell University in 1972 and continued his research at Peter Eisenman's Institute for Architecture and Urban Studies in New York between 1973 and 1977. The writing of the book itself was done in London alongside his weekly teaching at the AA School of Architecture.

6.   Rem Koolhaas, "Why I wrote Delirious New York and other textual strategies," *Architecture New York: Writing in Architecture* (May/June 1993): 42.

7.   Rem Koolhaas, "OMA*AMO: What Architecture can do?," YouTube video, 24 July 2009, http://www.youtube.com/watch?v=UViIVN6pCJo.

8.   On the how and why AMO started, see also "Reinier de Graaf in conversation with Giovanna Borasi and Mirko Zardini," YouTube video, 11 February 2016, https://www.youtube.com/watch?v=iNUoaUiUV10; and Giovanna Borasi and Canadian Centre for Architecture, *The Other Architect: Another Way of Building Architecture* (Montreal: Canadian Centre for Architecture, 2015(, 41–61.

9.   Spatial Agency. "AMO." https://www.spatialagency.net/database/amo.

10.   Rem Koolhaas, "OMA*AMO: What Architecture can do?," YouTube video, 24 July 2009, http://www.youtube.com/watch?v=UViIVN6pCJo.

11.   "the first non-Western country with an architectural avant-garde" turned into a slogan re-appears in promotional materials of the book, as well as in many interviews related to the book. Rem Koolhaas et al., *Project Japan: Metabolism Talks* (Cologne: TASCHEN, 2011).

12.   Rem Koolhaas, "About the Results," *The Japan Architect* (Spring 1993): 6.

13.   Rem Koolhaas, "About the Results," *The Japan Architect* (Spring 1993): 6.

14.   Rem Koolhaas, "About the Results," *The Japan Architect* (Spring 1993): 6.

15.   Interview between author and Mitsugo Okagawa (20 June 2019).

16.   Rem Koolhaas, "About the Results," *The Japan Architect* (Spring 1993): 7.

17.   Yosuke Fujiki, "Winners in the 1992 Shinkenchiku Residential Design Competition," *The Japan Architect* (Spring 1993): 8–11.

18.   Rem Koolhaas, "About the Results," *The Japan Architect* (Spring 1993): 7.

19.   Paulo Sanguinetti Rivas and Bane Gaiser, "Winners in the 1992 Shinkenchiku Residential Design Competition," *The Japan Architect* (Spring 1993): 20–21.

20.   Akira Imafuji, "Winners in the 1992 Shinkenchiku Residential Design Competition," *The Japan Architect* (Spring 1993): 24–25.

21.   Satoshi Ohashi, "Winners in the 1992 Shinkenchiku Residential Design Competition," *The Japan Architect* (Spring 1993): 30–31.

22. Kevin Woods and Charlotte Sheridan, "Winners in the 1992 Shinkenchiku Residential Design Competition," *The Japan Architect* (Spring 1993): 30–31.
23. Joanne Mackenzie and Garth Davies, "Winners in the 1992 Shinkenchiku Residential Design Competition," *The Japan Architect* (Spring 1993): 40–41.

Bibliography

Borasi, Giovanna and Canadian Centre for Architecture. *The Other Architect: Another Way of Building Architecture*. Montreal: Canadian Centre for Architecture, 2015.

De Graaf, Reinier, Giovanna Borasi and Mirko Zardini. "Reinier de Graaf in conversation with Giovanna Borasi and Mirko Zardini." YouTube. 2016. https://www.youtube.com/watch?v=iNUoaUiUV10.

Fujiki, Yosuke. "Winners in the 1992 Shinkenchiku Residential Design Competition." *The Japan Architect* (Spring 1993): 8–11.

Imafuji, Akira. "Winners in the 1992 Shinkenchiku Residential Design Competition." *The Japan Architect* (Spring 1993): 24–25.

Interview between author and Mitsugo Okagawa. 20 June 2020.

Interview between author and Yosuki Fujiki. 24 June 2020.

Koolhaas, Rem. "OMA*AMO: What Architecture can do?" YouTube. 2009. http://www.youtube.com/watch?v=UViIVN6pCJo.

——. "Why I wrote Delirious New York and other textual strategies." *Architecture New York, Writing in Architecture* (May/June 1993): 42

——. "About the Results." *The Japan Architect* (Spring 1993): 6–7.

——. "The Shinkenchiku Residential Design Competition 1992." *The Japan Architect* 1992-III: 2–3.

——. "Rem Koolhaas/OMA." *Architecture and Urbanism* (A+U) 1988: 10.

——, Bruce Mau, Jennifer Sigler, Hans Werlemann, and the Office for Metropolitan Architecture. *S, M, L, XL: Small, Medium, Large, Extra-large*. New York: Monacelli Press, 1995.

——, Kayoko Ōta, James Westcott, and Hans Ulrich Obrist. *Project Japan : Metabolism Talks...* Cologne: TASCHEN, 2011.

Leupen, Bernard and Rem Koolhaas. *Hoe Modern is de Nederlandse Architectuur?* Rotterdam: 010 Publishers, 1990.

Mackenzie, Joanne and Garth Davies. "Winners in the 1992 Shinkenchiku Residential Design Competition." *The Japan Architect* (Spring 1993): 40–41.

Sanguinetti Rivas, Paulo and Bane Gaiser. "Winners in the 1992 Shinkenchiku Residential Design Competition." *The Japan Architect* (Spring 1993): 20–21.

Ohashi, Satoshi. "Winners in the 1992 Shinkenchiku Residential Design Competition." *The Japan Architect* (Spring 1993): 30–31.

Woods, Kevin and Charlotte Sheridan. "Winners in the 1992 Shinkenchiku Residential Design Competition." *The Japan Architect* (Spring 1993): 30–31.

CHAPTER 17

Instagram, Indifference, and Postcritique in US Architectural Discourse

Joseph Bedford

From the 1970s through the 1990s, many architects in the United States who aspired to produce critically acclaimed or distinguished architecture found themselves reading (and writing) a lot. As the New York–based architect and professor at Princeton University Michael Meredith put it, reflecting on the 1990s, "We read almost anything related to Critical Theory. [...] whatever was published by *Zone, Semiotext(e)*, or *Verso*. And we read journals: *ANY, Assemblage, October*. We read a lot."[1] Meredith's recollections of the 1990s can be taken as exemplary of a phenomenon that has been overlooked in the history of theoretical-critical practice in architecture and the discourse of its "end" – that print-based media played a central role in facilitating the way that architects discoursed about various theoretical and critical issues, and that the particular set of journals and publishing houses helped to constitute an effective public sphere within which a theoretical discipline could critique reigning forms of power.

The idea of a theoretical-critical practice was an explicitly self-conscious construct within US architectural discourse in the years from the 1970s to the 1990s. Diana Agrest, for example, one of the principal actors within the influential Institute of Architecture and Urban Studies (IAUS) in New York titled one of her first lecture courses at Princeton "Theoretical Practice of Architecture" in 1972. And, alongside her IAUS colleagues, she described the position of its journal, *Oppositions*, as dedicated to "the importance of theory as the critical basis of significant practice."[2] In the years since the turn of the millennium, however, the United States became the epicentre of a discourse about the end of theoretical-critical practice.[3] The assumption within this discourse of "postcritique" has often been that the so-called end of critical theory in architecture was primarily the result of the *internal* conditions of the theoretical discourse, that the ideas themselves and their purported effects failed.[4]

Yet too little has been said about the evidently transforming nature of the *external* conditions underpinning such a theoretical-critical discourse as a public sphere maintained by certain media such as print. The turn of the millennia was, we should recall, a central moment in the transition of media from print to digital forms: Google was founded in 1998, "Web 2.0" became a common phrase from 1999 onwards, Facebook was founded in 2004, and Twitter in 2006. Indeed, after remarking on the degree to which he "read a lot" in the 1990s, Meredith highlighted this transition as central to the experience of young practitioners today, writing of the present situation:

> All positions have become relative; individual and institution alike are atomized into an array of indeterminate positions. [...] We all take part in the architectural potluck, consuming the very same images; all our references belong to a global market.[5]

It is this hollowing out of the public sphere over the last two decades of media-technical change that, as Frida Beckman argues, is most responsible for the discourse of postcritique.[6] The public sphere, going back to the earliest constitution of a critical literary discourse during the Enlightenment, has always had a critical relationship to the reigning forms of power.[7] Yet the most threatening forms of power today are no longer the absolutist powers of kings or churches, nor the disciplinary power of institutions that Michel Foucault once analysed. Today, and especially after half a century of neoliberal governance, globalisation and the development of networked computation, the reigning form of power is best understood in terms of what the late Gilles Deleuze described as "control" – the power to modulate and manipulate affects within free flows of movement.[8]

Today's popular discourse on the negative effects of our new media conditions developed by writers such as Shoshana Zuboff, Jaron Lanier, and Richard Seymore captures in various ways what Deleuze had in mind by "control society."[9] They have shown how the platforms of Google, Facebook, and Twitter penetrate the attentional and cognitive resources of individuals by fostering designed addiction to personal devices, and they show how these media actors engage not only in surveillance but also in behaviourist manipulation. Discipline, in the end, might turn out to have been central to the critical institutions of the public sphere, including institutions such as schools and journals, and what comes after in the form of new media and the power of "control" may be even worse.

It has also been argued by several media theorists, such as Marshall McLuhan and Walter Ong, that argument and critique was linked to literacy, and as writing gives way to the circulation of images and information in the electronic age, society also witness the re-emergence of a new "tribalism" that we might also think of as today's post-truth politics of emotion and affect.[10] Taking the work of all these writers together, we can argue that the construction of individually authored long-form writing or the creation of substantial original creative works addressed to an audience through the relatively unambiguous and rational nature of written communication have been central to the formation of a critical public sphere, and as architecture shifts from the predominant use of print publications for its discourse to the predominant use of image-based media, its role in forming a critical public sphere is undermined.

In their use of Instagram and other image-based social media like Tumblr, for example, a number of contemporary architectural practitioners can be seen to give up – somewhat uncritically – on the above formula for maintaining a critical public sphere through long-form writing. As the editors of the book *Possible Mediums* put it:

> The rapid circulation of online images has replaced the polished presentations common of earlier media forms, such as print. This creates a messy and fecund state of sharing work, facilitated by free flowing and far reaching platforms of social media. [As a result,] design starts to resemble a collective hive mind more than a traditional notion of "author."[11]

Against such a celebration of the "hive mind," Jaron Lanier offers a more critical view of the situation, arguing that it is the specific result of the new model of cultural production pioneered by Apple in 2001 with the iPod and iTunes in which cultural production is discretised, decontextualised, and algorithmically remediated. In Lanier's analysis, the result is the increasingly derivative and unoriginal forms of creative production that we see today.[12] In the larger context of behaviourist manipulation and "control," the loss of individual authorship would be precisely what a critical stance should seek to challenge.

In what follows, I will turn to four practitioners who are all more or less part of the same architectural network as Meredith: Andrew Kovacs of Office Kovacs, Jimenez Lai of Bureau Spectacular, and Atelier Fala. All of these practices might be said to operate within a "post-digital" mode, in which digital techniques have become so ubiquitous as to no longer serve as instruments of distinction for those who adopt them. All these practices might be described as post-digital for their mixture of digital and analogue forms that partly suggest a desire to critique the smooth aesthetics of high production values within mainstream digital culture. Yet, at the same time, they embrace a savvy appropriation of digital tools. Kovacs and Lai in particular are within a close circle of practices that Meredith himself has attempted to define as a group, by naming them as part of an attitude he refers to as that of "indifference," and Lai has also mapped the coherence of this same circle through their mutual participation in a set of conferences and events.[13]

Meredith and the practitioners surrounding him in his network offer a particularly useful window into the long legacy of critical theory in architecture and the turn to post-critique because, as current professors, or students of institutions like Princeton University, or as students of the theorists of the end of theory, they find themselves in the position of aspiring to produce the next body of distinctive work that in some manner inherits the lineage of the architectural neo-avant-garde of the 1970s to the 1990s, yet doing so within the changed media-technical conditions.

First, Jimenez Lai's use of image-based digital media is symptomatic of its function to blur the boundary between life and work, culture and economy. Lai is the principal architect of the young Los Angeles practice Bureau Spectacular. Of all the various architects addressed here, their use of new media is most exemplary of the casual manner in which they accept this dissolution of the work–life boundary (fig. 17.1). Their feed includes the usual mix of finished work presented in drawings, models, videos, and photographs or celebrations of public recognition in magazines, websites, and awards, but it also includes the seemingly spontaneous photographs of day-to-day activities in the office such as employees having fun building models or installing exhibitions, "Camera eats first" photos, selfies, selfies with celebrities, and cat photos. Much of this blurring is a

Fig. 17.1   Bureau Spectacular Instagram Feed © Bureau Spectacular.

common feature of many Instagram accounts, yet Bureau Spectacular go a step further in adapting the role of an "influencer": "We've been selected to become a @LIFEWTR influencer!," they write in one of their posts. Lifewtr is a new designer brand owned by Pepsi. Their branding strategy has been to associate their brand with emerging designers within the Los Angeles area who they take to be potential "influencers." Pepsi has been paying designers to incorporate their product in personalised ways within their creative output.

By accepting product placement into their feed (fig. 17.2), however, Bureau Spectacular, in Franco "Bifo" Berardi's terms, "put their soul to work." They give over their personal affectations, character, and social reputation to economic exchange.[14] For Berardi, in today's "semiocapitalism" labour is made increasingly individual and personal because today's digital labourers perform increasingly skilled and creative forms of production, which, unlike manual labour in the factory system of the ninteenth century, is not as easily exchangeable for the

Fig. 17.2   Bureau Spectacular Instagram Feed: "Lifewtr Series" © Bureau Spectacular.

labour of another. For digital labourers, according to Berardi, their labour comes from "the most essential part of their lives, the most specific and personalized."[15]

The invitation to play the role of an influencer is surely one sign of the success of an architect's use of social media – that the size and type of audience that they have fostered can be exchange for economic value. One of the reasons for any architect to reach a larger audience has long been to gain recognition that might lead to economic gains, whether in terms of commissions, invitations to lecture, or academic appointments. Architects used magazines, television, and public relations firms to this end long before Instagram. Yet never before has this relation between producer and audience been framed in such casual, everyday, personal, and intimate terms.

Second, Kovacs's use of image-based media is symptomatic of the way that it encourages its users to abandon the role of authorship. Kovacs's initial body of work was almost exclusively based on the reposting of scanned

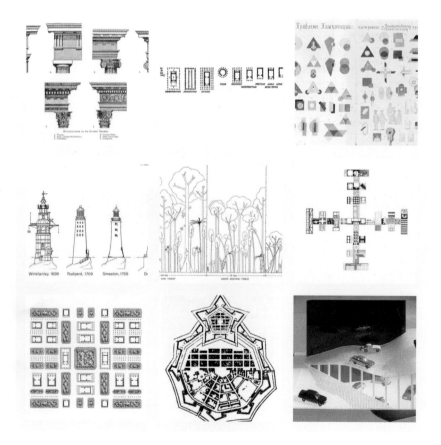

Fig. 17.3   Andrew Kovacs Instagram Feed, Collecting and Reassembling © Office Kovacs.

images of existing architectural artefacts (fig. 17.3). He built his extensive following of 230,000 on the Tumblr platform, Archive of Affinities, by digitising rare archival content, including lowbrow and kitsch artefacts. The forms of taste that facilitate Kovacs's acquisitions is highly connoisseurial, and in the tradition of Robert Venturi, the low-taste artefacts are appropriated from the perspective of high taste culture, with some measure of irony. What is unique, however, in Kovacs's acquisitions is his claim that creative work can be produced primarily through the reassemblage of the existing. Some of Kovacs's compositions, which he has increasingly come to include among his found artefacts, do involve a degree of composition that might indicate an original language, yet his most provocative pieces, upon which he gives greater emphasis in presenting his own work, are those which he himself describes as "monstrous" – the seemingly unlimited and unformed aggregations of existing things, accumulated in a way that rejects composition (fig. 17.4). These mountainous

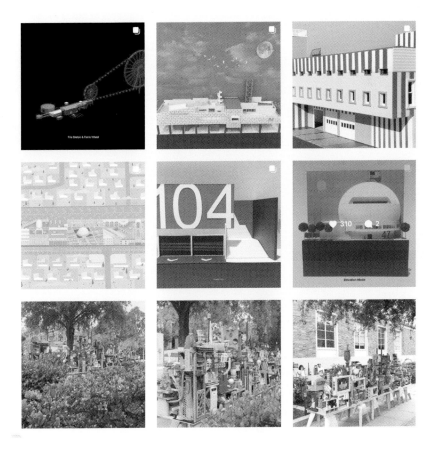

Fig. 17.4 Andrew Kovacs Instagram Feed: Constructing Architectural Monsters © Office Kovacs.

assemblages challenge the traditional role of authored architectural creativity, in which parts are organised and composed with respect to the whole in such a way as to create a language with detectable intent and meaning.

Kovacs's works instead are presented as one permutation among an infinite number. They are disembodied and given the kind of flattened equivalence that today's "content" has in general with respect to the platforms and algorithms that constantly reorganise them. Kovacs's work thus began from the practice of feeding content to followers and, in doing so, celebrating the process of discretisation and decontextualisation inherent to the medium and came in its later iterations to embrace those same processes in the way that his architectural objects themselves have been formed.

Third, Atelier Fala's use of image-based media is symptomatic of the logic of the new platforms to disaggregate the link between representations and the buildings they represent (fig. 17.5). After only 208 posts at the time of writing,

Fig. 17.5   Atelier Fala Instagram Feed © Atelier Fala.

they have acquired just short of 100,000 followers on Instagram. The work itself consists of a modest number of renovation projects. Their success, however, seems to be not simply due to the quality of their work alone, but also to the way they have mediated their work to bring out its aesthetic qualities through images that represent the same building in multiple ways.

These images, in effect, disaggregate each project into a field of moments – be it a photograph of a corner of a room with a sink and some tiles or a collage of a room made from cut-outs of paper and figures from paintings. It is difficult for their audience to relate each of those images to one another or to understand which project they come from. Fala themselves have described their work as a "network" of repeated parts.[16] All this could be said to simply reflect the mechanisms of the new media itself, yet Fala have also internalised the logic of decontextualisation and purposefully used it in other media, such as their website, to challenge the traditional manner in which architects'

Fig. 17.6 MOS Instagram Feed, including Rem's coffee cup and boring project advertisement © MOS Architects.

websites more often present correlations of plans, sections, elevations, axonometrics, and perspectives to represent a building as a complete whole. Fala detach their representations fully from this whole by randomly reshuffling the grid of images on their website according to heteroclite categories reminiscent of Foucault's famous account of Borges's "Chinese encyclopedia":[17] "mirrors," "columns," "proud patterns," "curtains," "white haven," "pretentious kitchens," "stepped surfaces," "unveiled structure," "kitchen hats," etc. Again, it is the tailoring of such images for the medium itself, which in turn comes to further inform the nature of their creative work, as they design their projects for such a mediation of networked parts.

Finally, Meredith's use of image-based media is symptomatic of the way that elite users of such media platforms thrive through the precise calculation of ambiguity. The images posted by MOS Architects on Instagram (fig. 17.6) are thus not simply publications of their works, but equally expressions of their

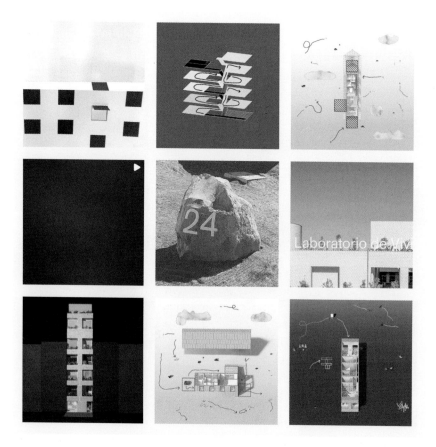

Fig. 17.7　MOS Instagram Feed, including numbered rock © MOS Architects.

overall curation of their feed. The choice to show – a finished building, sketches, publications on a desk, numbered rocks, a coffee cup said to have once been used by Rem Koolhaas, an amusing set of cabinets, job postings advertising a very "boring project" – all signal the distinctions of a particular taste culture, one trained through art historical study (fig. 17.7)

"Calculated indifference" is Meredith's own way of describing a larger attitude of which his work is a part.[18] Calculated indifference is not simply another form of postmodern irony in the manner of Venturi. It is also modelled on the purposeful hesitancy, ambiguity, and irony found in recent internet culture more generally. A growing body of literature has emerged in recent year to analyse the particular sensibility of online image culture of "Internet Ugly," the "New Aesthetic," and the political uses of gifs, memes by a younger generation of Millennials and Gen Z.[19]

Within this recent internet culture, images (and especially GIFs) play a dominant role precisely because they help individuals to avoid declarative commitments in communications and help them remain ironic and ambiguous. Images are indeed more laconic than words. When one searches for a GIF to send a friend in a chat, one is translating words with a greater degree of clear meaning and rationality into images, which carry a greater degree of affective emotional content and which remain open to interpretation depending on the context. Very often, such ambiguity is tied quite self-consciously to a resistance to make any clear political or ideological claims.

Meredith is attuned to this sensibility in "indifference, again" when he explains the attitude of the work of young architects such as Lai, Kovacs, and his own practice, MOS Architects, as an expression of some kind of "refusal" of the current social, economic, and political situation. His choice of the term "indifference" was inspired by the use of the term by the art critic Moira Roth in 1977 to indicate a "deliberately apolitical" stance.[20] Though Meredith is quick to assure his reader that, today, indifferent architects are not truly politically indifferent, but they are *performing* indifference as a means to "cool down" aesthetics, detaching it from politics.[21] Meredith describes the aesthetic he has in mind as "the ugly, the ironic, the awkward, the absurd, the cute, the humorous, the ambiguous, the banal,"[22] and he assumes that, in contrast to high-production Hollywood films, big-budget advertising, or presidential campaigns, this aesthetic will precisely be critical by its very "low-res" nature.

In responding to a critique of his position, Meredith clarified in a subsequent issue of *Log* the degree to which he hoped that such an aesthetic of indifference would nonetheless be a continuation of a kind of Enlightenment model of debate and deliberation: "I subscribe to Wölfflinian models of art history or architecture. I believe in comparison. I believe in everything being in conversation. [...] How do we look at work together? How do we discuss it?"[23]

Yet in the context of the media change from institutions such as *Zone*, *Semiotext(e)*, *October*, and *Assemblage* to that atomised and indeterminate architectural pot luck that Meredith identifies, the question would be as follows: *In what ways does that shift facilitates conversation and discussion?* Architects are still discoursing. They communicate today perhaps more than ever, and on a larger scale, reaching ever-larger or ever-more targeted audiences. Yet the new media has changed the way that that discourse operates to build a discipline, an institution, and a public sphere. As we have seen, architects are now operating within the media channels that were created to cultivate casualised production, and their creative work is being transformed in subtle ways in relation to their use of such media, blurring the boundary between life and work, celebrating the loss of authorship, or the creation of discrete works, and their replacement by a so-called "hive mind," a drip feed, a network, or the infinitely equivalent recombination of parts.

In Meredith's case, with whom we began and with whom we end, there is a hope that image-based media can still carry a form of communicative rationality through the performance of aesthetic judgement in a social and professional network. Instagram does operate in these terms, which is likely why it has been so attractive to architects. For most users of Instagram, its attraction is in the ability to curate images to communicate rapidly a kind of signature of a person's tastes to make quick judgements about whether one wants to associate with another person – indeed, to perform a kind of Turing test to decide whether what has just followed you is indeed another person. It is the same complex signature of taste that also enables those architects who operate within the legacy of neo-avant-garde theoretical architectural discourse in the United States to distinguish themselves through aesthetic production, to signal a distinctive taste, and to consider themselves to be engaged in a kind of meta discussion and conversation about subtle variants of aesthetic work.

Yet Meredith does so at the expense of no longer engaging as much in the production of long-form written arguments. Whether such an image-based discourse can constitute a public sphere in the manner once constituted by literate discourse is doubtful. Without clearly articulated argument being presented in unambiguous form, in fora that draw consistent participants together, it is not clear how architectural discourse can operate in a critical manner, and it is all too easy, as these four case studies suggest, for the medium to become the message and for the power of control to shape the very efforts of architects to build a critical public sphere through their discourse.

Notes

1.   Michael Meredith, "2,497 Words: Provincialism, Critical or Otherwise," *Log* 41
     (Fall 2017): 169.

2.   Editorial, Oppositions 2 (January 1974). Agrest's Princeton course was a weekly Tuesday
     lecture within the Arc 301 Values, Concepts and Methods course in autumn 1972.

3.   For a summary of this discourse, see W. J. T. Mitchell, "Medium Theory: Preface to the
     2003 Critical Inquiry Symposium," *Critical Inquiry* 30, no. 2 (2004): 334–335.

4.   Stan Allen, Untitled Article, *Assemblage* 41 (April 2000): 8; and Michael Speaks, "Theory
     was interesting… but now we have work: No hope no fear," *Architectural Research
     Quarterly* 6, no. 3 (September 2002): 211.

5.   Meredith, "2,497 Words," 170.

6.   Frida Beckman, "Postcritique and the Leakiness of Spheres," *Symploke* 28, no. 1 (2020):
     523–526.

7.   Jürgen Habermas, *The Structural Transformation of the Public Sphere: An Inquiry into a
     category of Bourgeois Society* (Cambridge, MA: MIT Press, 1989). Original published in
     German in 1962.

8.   Frida Beckman, *Culture Control Critique: Allegories of Reading the Present* (Lanham:
     Rowman & Littlefield, 2016). Gilles Deleuze, "Postscript on the Societies of Control,"
     October 59 (1992): 3–7.

9.   Shoshana Zuboff, *The Age of Surveillance Capitalism: The Fight for a Human Future at
     the New Frontier of* Power (New York: Public Affairs, 2017); Jaron Lanier, *Ten Arguments
     for Deleting Your Social Media Accounts Right Now* (New York: Picador, 2018); Richard
     Seymour, *The Twittering Machine* (New York: Verso, 2019).

10. Marshal McLuhan, *Understanding Media: The Extensions of* Man (New York: McGraw-
     Hill, 1964); Walter Ong, *Orality and Literacy* (London: Methuen & Co., 1982).

11. Kyle Miller et al., eds., *Possible Mediums* (New York: Actar, 2018).

12. Janor Lanier, *You Are Not a Gadget* (New York: Vintage, 2010).

13. See Michael Meredith, "Indifference, Again," *Log* 39 (Winter 2017): 79. See also Jimenez
     Lai, "Between Irony and Sincerity," *Log* 46 (Summer 2019). The events in question are:
     Firmness, Commodity, Delight Symposium at Princeton in 2014; the *Chatter: Architecture
     Talks Back* exhibition at the Art Institute in Chicago in 2015; the *Treatise Series* of books
     curated by Lai between 2013 and 2015; the first Chicago Architecture Biennale in 2017;
     the *Inscriptions* exhibition at Harvard Graduate School of Design in 2018; the Possible
     Mediums project run as a series of workshops from 2013 on; and finally published as the
     book Kyle Miller et al., eds., *Possible Mediums*, and Meredith's own exhibition, *44 Low-
     resolution Houses*, at Princeton in 2018, published as Michael Meredith, *44 Low-resolution
     Houses* (Princeton: Princeton School of Architecture, 2018).

14. Franco "Bifo" Birardi, *The Soul at Work: From Alienation to Autonomy* (Los Angeles:
     Semiotext(e), 2009).

15. Birardi, *The Soul at Work*, 76.

16. Ahmed Belkhodja in interview with the author (8 October 2020).

17. Michel Foucault, "Preface," in *The Order of Things*: An Archaeology of the Human Sciences
     (London: Routledge, 2002), i.

18. Meredith, "Indifference," 79.

19. Nick Douglas, "It's Supposed to Look Like Shit: The Internet Ugly Aesthetic," *Journal of
     Visual Culture* 13, no. 3 (2014): 314–339.

20. Meredith, "Indifference," 76.

21. Meredith, "Indifference," 79.

22. Meredith, "Indifference," 79.

23. Michael Meredith in conversation with Mark Foster Gage and Michael Young, "MMM:
     Multiple Resolutions," *Log* 46 (Summer 2019): 14, 17.

Bibliography

Allen, Stan. Untitled article. *Assemblage* 41 (April 2000): 8.

Beckman, Frida. "Postcritique and the Leakiness of Spheres." *Symploke* 28, no. 1 (2020): 523–526.

———. *Culture Control Critique: Allegories of Reading the Present.* Lanham, MD: Rowman & Littlefield, 2016.

Birardi, Franco "Bifo." *The Soul at Work: From Alienation to Autonomy.* Los Angeles: Semiotext(e), 2009.

Deleuze, Gilles. "Postscript on the Societies of Control." *October* 59 (1992): 3–7.

Douglas, Nick. "It's Supposed to Look Like Shit: The Internet Ugly Aesthetic." *Journal of Visual Culture* 13, no. 3 (2014): 314–339.

Foucault, Michel. "Preface." *The Order of Things: An Archaeology of the Human Sciences,* xvi–xxvi. London: Routledge, 2002.

Habermas, Jürgen. *The Structural Transformation of the Public Sphere: An Inquiry into a Category of Bourgeois Society.* Cambridge, MA: MIT Press, 1989.

Lai, Jimenez. "Between Irony and Sincerity." *Log* 46 (Summer 2019): 23–32.

Lanier, Jaron. *You Are Not a Gadget.* New York: Vintage, 2010.

———. *Ten Arguments for Deleting Your Social Media Accounts Right Now.* New York: Picador, 2018.

McLuhan, Marshal. *Understanding Media: The Extensions of* Man. New York: McGraw-Hill, 1964.

Meredith, Michael. "2,497 Words: Provincialism, Critical or Otherwise." *Log* 41 (Fall 2017): 169–175.

———. "Indifference, Again." *Log* 39 (Winter 2017): 75–79.

———. *44 Low-resolution Houses.* Princeton: Princeton School of Architecture, 2018.

———, Mark Foster Gage, and Michael Young, "MMM: Multiple Resolutions." *Log* 46 (Summer 2019): 9–22.

Miller, Kyle, Kelly Bair, Kristy Balliet, and Adam Fure, eds. *Possible Mediums.* New York: Actar, 2018.

Mitchell, W. J. T. "Medium Theory: Preface to the 2003 Critical Inquiry Symposium." *Critical Inquiry* 30, no. 2 (2004): 334–335.

Ong, Walter. *Orality and Literacy.* London: Methuen & Co. ltd, 1982.

Seymour, Richard. *The Twittering Machine.* New York: Verso, 2019.

Speaks, Michael. "Theory was interesting… but now we have work: No hope no fear." *Architectural Research Quarterly* 6 no. 3 (September 2002): 209–212.

Zuboff, Shoshana. *The Age of Surveillance Capitalism: The Fight for a Human Future at the New Frontier of Power.* New York: Public Affairs, 2017.

CHAPTER 18

Being-With/A Tacit Alliance: Architecture, Publishing, and the Poetic Reciprocity of Civic Culture

Patrick Lynch

Complicity with unknown people can be created only on the basis of their repeated experiences of not being disappointed [...] like-minded people who are perhaps attracted, by [...] the atmosphere or *Stimmung* of the book [...] these will be the ones [...] with whom the publisher, over time, can establish a tacit alliance.
—Roberto Calasso, The Art of the Publisher, 2015

New Phenomenology, as I have conceived and developed it, aims to make their actual lives comprehensible to humans, that is, to make accessible again spontaneous life experience in continuous contemplation after having cleared away artificial ideas pre-figured in history [...] and, in consequence, aid in finding a better way of living.
—Herman Schmitz, *New Phenomenology*, 2019

As an architect, a teacher, a publisher, and a writer, I am most interested in civic architecture. I began to realise this while preparing an exhibition called *Inhabitable Models* for the 2012 Venice Architecture Biennale, in response to David Chipperfield's curatorial theme: architectural "Common Ground." The epithet "civic" orients architecture towards city life, towards complicity, and the kinds of tacit alliances between patrons of architecture, architects, and the community more broadly, but it is also works in a wider cultural sphere. Roberto Calasso reflects on complicity as a vital aspect of the speculatively civic art of publishing, a theme that will be developed here.[1] Much contemporary architecture – High Tech architecture and its descendants – is not civic but compares instead to military architecture. Renaissance architectural treatises distinguished between and encompassed civil and military architecture. As Joseph Rykwert demonstrated, however, even a tent on a battlefield is fundamentally civic in character when it has been erected on a cardinal orientation by the Roman army, that is, created as a symbolic and actual microcosm of Rome itself each night.[2]

The name of the Venice Biennale 2012 exhibition, *Inhabitable Models*, was inspired by a phrase used by John Summerson in his essay "Heavenly Mansions: An Interpretation of Gothic," in which he reflects upon the relationship between the symbolic and the civic. His argument begins: "There is a kind of play common to nearly every child; it is that he is in a 'house' [...] It is symbolism – of a fundamental kind, expressed in terms of play. This kind of play has much to do with the aesthetics of architecture."[3] From this identification of the symbolic house, he argues that the character of Gothic architecture depends upon a combination of scales that transforms a cathedral into a symbolic microcosm of the Christian church itself, a cosmic image. This coexistence of multiple scales he defines as aedicular, noting that, "[t]he Latin word for building is aedes; the word for a little building is aedicula,"[4] where the proliferation of small houses within big ones is a vital psychological and social phenomenon. The outcome is architecture capable of situating and communicating cultural

Fig. 18.1 *Inhabitable Models* for Common Ground, Venice Architecture Biennale, 2012, Lynch Architects © Patrick Lynch.

meaning: "The aedicule unlocks door after door,"[5] transforming "the heavy prose of building into religious poetry,"[6] he suggests, "retaining and affirming its attribute of ceremoniousness"[7] and "reminding one of the innocent ceremony of the child under the table – that symbol of architecture."[8] Summerson's statement that "[t]his kind of play (aedicular house-play) has much to do with the aesthetics of architecture"[9] proposes that a fundamentally civic character emerges out of the imaginative coexistence of multiple symbolic and actual scales at once. *Inhabitable Models* was installed in the Corderie of the Arsenale, where it interjected playful civic architecture into the august and spare military setting through a series of one-third-scale models of fragments of three buildings in London, one each by Lynch Architects, Eric Parry Architects, and Haworth Thompkins. When visited by children, these objects appeared uncannily like real buildings and so embodied two scales at once.

Fig. 18.2   Books and models in the studio of Lynch Architects © Patrick Lynch.

The ethos of Canalside Press, run from within the offices of Lynch Architects, was defined in conversations held in preparation for the Venice exhibition, made possible by a web of social and intellectual connections. The biennale's assistant curator to Chipperfield was Kieran Long, who started on the project in 2011 and was simultaneously participating in Peter Carl's research seminar at London Metropolitan University. Carl's syllabus had evolved out of the MPhil in the history and philosophy of architecture that I took in 1995–1996, which he had taught alongside Joseph Rykwert and Dalibor Vesely at the University of Cambridge. I was then working on my doctoral dissertation: "Practical Poetics: Rhythmic Spatiality and the Communicative Movement Between Architecture, Sculpture and Site" This idea was explored in the exhibition catalogue *Common Ground: A Critical Reader*, most importantly in David Leatherbarrow's essay, "The Sacrifice of Space,"[10] which, combined with his belief that architecture is "oriented otherwise"[11] beyond itself, was influential in the evolution of the terms "civic ground" and "civic architecture."

Fig. 18.3   *Mimesis, Civic Ground* and *The Theatricality of the Baroque City* by Patrick Lynch © Patrick Lynch.

Fig. 18.4   Covers of the first six issues of the *JoCA* © Patrick Lynch.

Leatherbarrow's description of the portico of Andrea Palladio's Palazzo Chiericati at Vicenza situates it in the civic topography of the sixteenth-century town and suggests that its status as both grand entrance and public shortcut derives from this contingency. He describes how the location of the project on the edge of the town led to complex negotiations between the authorities and Count Girolamo Chiericati, who argued in his petition to build a colonnade beyond the limit of his property that "the 'portico' would not only offer him 'greater convenience' [greater depth for his *salone* and associated loggias] but the entire city too [the covered walk]."[12] Palladio, notes Leatherbarrow, "argued that ancient precedent provided a model for donations to the public good [...]

Porticos should be arranged around squares [...] their purpose is to enable people to escape the showers, snow, and discomfort caused by wind or sun." The inconvenience of the marginal site led to the "difficulty of assimilating Palazzo Chiericati into the typology of arcaded urban palazzi" when the base of the building meets a site that slopes and does so via a colonnade that is also open to the town. An upper logia and *salone* affords good views over a river and the countryside beyond, "the room above – an emblem of the house" gives this "greater prominence, without detaching it entirely from the running length of the colonnade. Both details bind the house to the sidewalk and therefore the public realm."[13] Palladio's projects are far from being examples of some theoretically autonomous art – as some scholar's suggest[14] – and the architect's skill lies in resolving the tension between the inhabitant's needs and the civility of their setting. Both are manifest in terms of rooms, internal and external, and reconciled and articulated by rhythmic spatial qualities that articulate a strong sense of public and domestic decorum – of what Rykwert calls the double metaphor of architecture, body, and world.[15]

Certain spatial tropes, including the growth of public spaces in particular and the porous architecture that addresses them, are obvious in the civic architecture of Renaissance cities like Verona, Venice, Mantova, Turin, and Rome. These characteristics can be described in terms of classical

Fig. 18.5 Palazzo Chiericati by Andrea Palladio © David Leatherbarrow.

architectural language.[16] Nick Temple argues in his book *Renovatio Urbi* out of these Renaissance projects of urban renovation emerges a consensus among the urban polity about what constitutes "civilitas," or urban order. Urban order is the total effect of multiple buildings together and is the result of an underlying common intellectual, political. and artistic ethos, one shared by architects and patrons equally. It is an ethos that emerges in part from Alberti's writing on the family, civic life, and then architecture, in that order.[17] Such diverse writers as Hans Baron,[18] Claire Guest,[19] Hans-Georg Gadamer,[20] and Walter Benjamin[21] have, like Summerson, emphasised the vital coexistence of symbolic, spatial, practical, and political thinking in what might be defined as the civic culture of social praxis. Civic architecture is one of the most stable and embodied modes of social praxis, which also encompasses festivals, poetic declamation, diplomatic relations, cooking, and brewing, and all manner of rhetoric and civil engineering. As Temple points out, the reason why successive popes have been known as Pontiff since Julius I is because, working alongside his architect Bramante, Julius became known as "the chief bridge builder of Rome."

"Civic ground" concerns the public nature of artistic experience, its fundamental position in our culture, and the role that architecture, sculpture, and landscape play in articulating this. "Civic" does not refer to a use type as such, but to something that orients architecture towards the shared conditions of urbanity. The term "common ground" gets close to the original meaning of *civilitas*, which more properly means "civic order."[22] The ground itself is not simply a matter of property or of one's rights to use it, nor is it just a metaphor or a philosophical construction, but it is the basis and grounds for life itself. Martin Heidegger claimed that its central orienting importance for human affairs might be best described as "motive" (what Aristotle called "mythos" or "plot" in his *Poetics*) and wrote: "Motive is a ground or human action [...] All different grounds are themselves based on the principle of ground. All that is has a ground."[23] The term "motive" fuses together the representational and practical aspects of architecture as the expression of civic ground.

This explication of a poetics of architecture as the ground of culture itself is indebted to the claim by Dalibor Vesely that "architecture contributes to the life of our culture as text does to our literacy."[24] Vesely argues that "[t] he history of architecture can be seen as a history of attempts to represent the latent order of nature and create a plausible matrix for the rest of culture,"[25] one based upon "a long process of interpretations and modifications that established an identifiable tradition." The extended field of an architectural practice can encompass the much broader project of the creation of a plausible cultural matrix including writing, teaching, and publishing.

Canalside Press, founded 2018, is based in Hackney, East London, in the offices of my practice, Lynch Architects. The principal outputs are the *Journal of Civic Architecture* and books relating to the broader cultural situation of architecture, poetry, and the visual arts.[26] The *Modern Architecture in Reflection* series seeks to create primary historical sources for further study and to reveal the depth of reflective, critical architectural practice – both writing and buildings – in the third quarter of the twentieth century. Recent and forthcoming publications include *Change is the Reality: The Work of Architect Robin Walker* (edited by Patrick Lynch and Simon Walker, 2021) and *Part of the City: The Work of Neave Brown Architect* (edited by Patrick Lynch and David Porter, 2022). In each case, the books reveal the implicit and explicit relationships between creative imaginative design work and institutions – local government, the English Crown, the Roman Catholic Church – that embody, accommodate, and often seek to articulate the civic character of their social role via policy, doctrine, and architecture. Each book seeks to reveal a relationship between theory and praxis in the work of these late modernist architect-thinkers. In uncovering the complex relationships between myth and modernity in 1960s and 1970s culture more generally, architecture is considered as just one expression of social attitudes. Thus, its civic character can be said to be not simply a matter of loggias and building types but also of architects' openness to intellectual and cultural currents that inspire (or resist) social change; civic therefore might be seen as a synonym for discourse itself.

Fig. 18.6   Launch party for issue three of the *JoCA* June 2019 © Patrick Lynch.

Another series, *Reflection in Action*, which takes a tangential view of the civic by publishing poetry and biographical prose inspired by city life and architecture, responds to a gap in mainstream architectural production today. The books in this series, for example the poetry-based *Slogans and Battlecries* by Paul Shepheard[27] are akin to curiosities like Le Corbusier's "Poem of the Right Angle" and Michelangelo's sonnets: things that can be described as the sound of the unconscious thinking. Just as architecture is a haptic, tactile, and visual experience, architecture books work well when they are pleasurable to handle, as Caroline Voet observes:

> many architects read a book from back to front, holding it in the right hand, while turning the pages with the left hand. The pace of this "reading" shows the level of accomplished complicity through images, drawings, graphic design, and oblique scan of words.[28]

Books on architecture need to work like buildings: both askance and face-on, on the surface and within, as part of a room and part of your memory chest.

The *Journal of Civic Architecture* appears twice each year – at the summer and winter equinox.[29] It is a print-only journal, available online once the print run of five hundred has sold out. Each issue of the journal is held together by philosophical and artistic themes that emerge from correspondence with contributors, who include architects, academics, photographers, novelists, and poets. These themes are not strictly typological or absolutely abstract – often they constitute a collage of resonating elements. Contributions arise through conversations. Initially, these were the continuation of discussions begun with colleagues held at various events – exhibitions, biennale, and symposia – and the social quality of this exchange is marked by the party held to celebrate each issue – a semi-extempore urban symposium. The civic becomes social in this heuristic and profoundly engaged process devised to support and encourage spontaneous dialogue and reflection. This process – both the acts of openness involved in contributions to the *Journal of Civic Architecture* and its representation via public talks – is something similar to what Herman Schmitz calls "spontaneous life experience":

> Spontaneous life experience is anything that happens to humans in a felt manner without their having intentionally constructed it. Today, human thought is so enthralled by seemingly natural assumptions of conventions and hypotheses in the service of constructions that it has become painstaking to disclose spontaneous life experience; but doing so is of great importance, because it can point the way out of dangerous limitations and entanglements of the human understanding of self and world, and, in consequence, aid in finding a better way of living.[30]

Schmitz's emphasis on spontaneity of feeling – the "felt body" – and the vitality of situations, works in concert, he claims, alongside "concept formation at a high level of abstraction," but only if we "place the other and oneself in the specifically relevant historical context [...] [an] empirical humbleness of following up on spontaneous life experience." The latter could be described as a mode of situated reflection or phenomenological hermeneutics, or "sedimentations in the understandings of self and world" emerge via critical reflection, which "expand the playing field of [...] phenomenological revision,"[31] as Schmitz puts it. Of particular interest to architects perhaps is his insistence upon "[t]he spatiality of the gripping atmosphere"[32] that characterises the public dimension of emotional experiences. His phenomenology situates reflection as a mode of civic subjectivity because humans sense "atmospheres," or common moods, shared emotional states in public, for example, "the public mood," or "the political atmosphere." Schmitz introduces the idea of "antagonist encorporation," by which he means dialogue as a mode of agonism, and the idea of "half-things," or things in flux, such as a falling stone, or an argument. He emphasises also the importance of embodied and out-of-body experience ("excorporation") to a person in a trance-like, ecstatic state – as in just after orgasm, participation in a festive music or art experience, or sport – alluding to the paradox of embodied experience as something silent, reflective, and also pre-articulate. This paradox is possible because "the silence of embodiment is always to a certain extent also

Fig. 18.7   The Silver Forest artwork on the side of Westminster City Hall
© Rut Blees-Luxemburg.

a voice of articulation," Vesely claims, and "it is only under these conditions that we can understand the language and the cultural role of architecture."[33] Understanding then – in this sense – is itself a mode of reflection spurred by certain spatial atmospheres that offer "a plausible matrix for the rest of culture."

Carl elaborates on the importance of reflection in his essay "Civic Depth," which concerns the urban and cultural conditions at play in certain modes of communicative architectural practice:

> Reflection may seem to be a fragile or even elitist concern. Aristotle was the first and is still one of the few to ask what is the ultimate purpose of a city (not simply transaction of goods and prevention of crime). He argues that a city grants the possibility of profound understanding of one's collective place in reality. The rites and ceremonies, which persisted until quite recently, accomplished the same thing, reconciling history with the cosmic conditions. Aristotle elevates this kind of insight, via tragic drama, to philosophical contemplation; but this is only the most articulate end of a spectrum that has its origins in the primordial spatiality of the civic topography.[34]

At stake in this mode of thought is the sense of a fundamental reciprocity between the embodied and articulate aspects of culture – indeed, in the necessity for reciprocity in a situated and experiential understanding of architectural praxis as a mode of being with others. Writing in issue three of the *Journal of Civic Architecture*, Temple discusses Levinas's dispute with Heidegger regarding the term *mitsein* ("being-with"), in terms of its paradigmatic importance for "Architecture as the Receptacle of Mitsein." He describes:

> a specific event that took place in Florence in the early 15th century; a poetry contest that commemorated the completion of Brunelleschi's dome for Santa Maria del Fiore – the *Certame Coronario*. A peculiar aspect of this event, which was incidentally organised by the great humanist and Renaissance architect Leon Battista Alberti, was its celebration of friendship, a theme that had resonance in the symbolism of the dome as Alberti would later describe in his preface to the Italian version of his treatise on painting, *Della Pittura*.[35]

The poetry contest resulted in the laurel being awarded, in fact, to the duomo itself, revealing that the ultimate model of civic rhetoric inherited from Cicero and Socrates – poetic-making – to be spatial situations, civic order, manifest in civic architecture. Temple is keen to emphasise continuity in architecture, and indeed culture in general, as manifestations of "being-with," even and when

[i]ncreasingly in the digital world, notions of friendship, and their associations with mutual respect, companionship and even intimacy, are constructed in such a way that no physical contact need necessarily to take place. Therefore, we are having to redefine the very meaning of friendship per se, as a relationship that can be sustained (remotely) by on-line exchange alone. Related to this specific challenge are more general concerns highlighted in Richard Sennett's seminal work *The Fall of Public Man* which explores the decline in public life and the cult of individualism in the modern age. As a consequence of this decline the very concept of "civicness," and the civic realm, are at best put into parenthesis or at worst simply denuded of any meaning or significance.[36]

In his *Journal of Civic Architecture* essay, Temple describes the São Nicolau Baths and Wash House at Porto by Paulo Providência, situating this in a trajectory of "Álvaro Siza's tidal swimming pools at Leça da Palmeira Portugal (1961–1966), and Sigurd Lewerentz's small Church of St. Peter in Klippan, Sweden (1962–1966)," as building projects that Providência identifies as examples of those "whose aurae seem to dissipate at the moment of materialization."[37] "Aurae," "atmosphere," and "being-with" are various ways of describing culture as "a tacit alliance."[38] This alliance works – like Summerson's image of the aedicular character of the imagination – at many scales and across time. It is worth reminding ourselves of architecture's deeper mission and capacity for "complicity," taking inspiration from Calasso's consideration of publishing as an art and Schmitz's task for philosophy to act as an "aid in finding a better way of living."

Notes

1. Roberto Calasso, *The Art of the Publisher* (London: Penguin, 2015), 69–70.
2. Rykwert, Joseph, *The Idea of a Town: The Anthropology of Urban Form in Rome, Italy and the Ancient World* (Cambridge, MA: MIT Press, 1988), 25–26.
3. "Heavenly Mansions: An Interpretation of Gothic" was given as a lecture at the Royal Institute of British Architects in 1946 and subsequently published in John Summerson, *Heavenly Mansions: And Other Essays* (New York: Norton, 1998), 1.
4. John Summerson, *Heavenly Mansions*, 3.
5. John Summerson, *Heavenly Mansions*, 18.
6. John Summerson, *Heavenly Mansions*, 9.
7. John Summerson, *Heavenly Mansions*, 4.
8. John Summerson, *Heavenly Mansions*, 6.
9. John Summerson, *Heavenly Mansions*, 28.
10. David Leatherbarrow, "The Sacrifice of Space," in *Common Ground: A Critical Reader*, ed. David Chipperfield, Kieran Long, Shumi Bose, and 13th International Architecture Exhibition La Biennale di Venezia (Venice: Marsilio, 2012).
11. David Leatherbarrow, *Architecture Oriented Otherwise* (Cambridge, MA: MIT Press, 2009).
12. David Leatherbarrow, "The Sacrifice of Space," 30.
13. David Leatherbarrow, "The Sacrifice of Space," 32. See also Patrick Lynch, *Civic Ground: Rhythmic Spatiality and the Communicative Movement between Architecture, Sculpture and Site* (London: Artifice Books on Architecture, 2017), 44–45.
14. See Peter Eisenman, *Palladio Virtuel* (New Haven: Yale University Press, 2016) for a discussion of what he calls "homongenous space."
15. Cf. "The metaphor with which I have been concerned with is more extended – a double one – in that it involves three terms, a body is like a building and the building in turn is like the world," Joseph Rykwert, *The Dancing Column: On Order in Architecture* (Cambridge, MA: MIT Press, 1999), 373.
16. John Summerson, *The Classical Language of Architecture* (London: Thames & Hudson, 1980).
17. The reciprocity of rhetoric and poetics in Florentine architecture is something that I explored in the essay by Patrick Lynch, "Civic Architecture," in *Mimesis: Lynch Architects* (London: Artifice Books on Architecture, 2015), 101–112.
18. Hans Baron, *In Search of Florentine Civic Humanism: Essays on the Transition from Medieval to Modern Thought*, vol. I, (New York: Princeton University Press, 1980); Lauro Martines, *Power and Imagination: City States in Renaissance Italy* (London: Pimlico, 2002), 97; see also Manfredo Tafuri, *Interpreting the Renaissance: Princes, Cities, Architects* (New Haven: Yale University Press, 2006).
19. Clare Guest, "Figural Cities," in *Rhetoric, Theatre and the Arts of Design: Essays Presented to Roy Eriksen*, ed. Clare Guest (Oslo: Novus, 2008).
20. Hans-Georg Gadamer, "The Relevance of the Beautiful: Art as Play, Symbol and Festival," in *The Relevance of the Beautiful and Other Essays* (Cambridge: Cambridge University Press, 1986).
21. Walter Benjamin and Asja Lacis, "Naples," in Walter Benjamin, *Reflections: Essays, Aphorisms, Autobiographical Writings* (New York: Random House, 1995).
22. See Nicholas Temple, "Rites of Intent: The Participatory Dimension of the City," in *Cityscapes in History: The Urban Experience*, ed. Heléna Tóth and Katrina Gulliver (Surrey: Ashgate Publishing, 2014), 155–178; and Nicholas Temple, *Renovatio Urbis: Architecture, Urbanism and Ceremony in the Rome of Julius II* (London: Routledge, 2011).
23. Martin Heidegger, *Zollikon Seminars: Protocols, Conversations, Letters*, ed. Medard Boss (Evanston: Northwestern University Press, 2001), 23.

24. Dalibor Vesely, *Architecture in the Age of Divided Representation: The Question of Creativity in the Shadow of Production* (Cambridge, MA: MIT Press, 2004), 104.

25. Dalibor Vesely, *Architecture in the Age of Divided Representation*, 103–104.

26. Recent books include Patrick Lynch, ed., *On Intricacy: The Work of John Meunier Architect* (London: Canalside Press, 2020), the first book in our *Modern Architecture in Reflection* series; and Paul Shepheard, *Slogans and Battlecries* (London: Canalside Press, 2020), the first in the *Reflection in Action* series.

27. Paul Shepheard, *Slogans and Battlecries*.

28. Comments on an Instagram post by @pad-lynch, 20 March, 2020.

29. "The term Civic Architecture occurred to me one day towards the end of my PhD research, as a perfect description of creative work that is oriented towards city life. The epiphet civic, immediately distinguishes architecture that is not civic. We live in a period of intense opinions, but arguably, of very weakly developed subjectivity. Christoper Lasch memorably described late 20th-century America as 'The Culture of Narcissism' and Saul Bellow referred to 'the moronic inferno' of modern life (Humboldt's Gift, 1975) even before the rise of the internet. The Journal of Civic Architecture is going to be a refuge from all that: a place for writing and imagery that is reflective, serious, and I hope, insightful and pleasurable." Editor's Letter, *The Journal of Civic Architecture*, Issue 1 (June 2018).

30. Herman Schmitz, *New Phenomenology: A Brief Introduction* (Milan: Mimesis International, 2019), 43.

31. Herman Schmitz, *New Phenomenology: A Brief Introduction*, 49.

32. Herman Schmitz, *New Phenomenology: A Brief Introduction*, 97.

33. Dalibor Vesely, *Architecture in the Age of Divided Representation: The Question of Creativity in the Shadow of Production* (Cambridge, MA: MIT Press, 2004), 104–106.

34. Peter Carl, "Civic Depth," in *Mimesis: Lynch Architects* (London: Artifice Books on Architecture, 2015), 121–122.

35. Nicholas Temple, "Treading Water on (Un)Common Ground: Revisiting *Mitsein*," *The Journal of Civic Architecture*, 3 (2019): 23–31. See also Nicholas Temple, "Architecture as a Receptacle of *Mitsein*," in *Intersections of Ethos and Space*, edited by Nikolaos-Ion Terzoglou, Kyriaki Tsoukala, and Charikleia Pantelidou (London: Routledge, 2015), 138–149.

36. Nicholas Temple, "Treading Water on (Un)Common Ground: Revisiting *Mitsein*," *The Journal of Civic Architecture,* 3 (2019): 23.

37. Paulo Providência, *Architectonica Percepta: Texts and Images 1985–2015* (Zurich: Park Books, 2016), 1.

38. Roberto Calasso, *The Art of the Publisher*, 69–70.

Bibliography

Baron, Hans. *In Search of Florentine Civic Humanism: Essays on the Transition from Medieval to Modern Thought*, vol. I. New York: Princeton University Press, 1980.

Benjamin, Walter and Asja Lacis. "Naples." Walter Benjamin, *Reflections: Essays, Aphorisms, Autobiographical Writing*. New York: Random House, 1995.

Calasso, Roberto. *The Art of the Publisher*. London: Penguin, 2015.

Carl, Peter. "Civic Depth." *Mimesis: Lynch Architects*. London: Artifice Books on Architecture, 2015.

"Editor's Letter." *The Journal of Civic Architecture* Issue 1 (June 2018).

Eisenman, Peter. *Palladio Virtuel*. New Haven: Yale University Press, 2016.

Gadamer, Hans-Georg. *The Relevance of the Beautiful and other essays*. Cambridge: Cambridge University Press, 1986.

Guest, Clare Lapraik. *Rhetoric, Theatre and the Arts of Design: Essays Presented to Roy Eriksen*t. Oslo: Novus, 2008.

Heidegger, Martin. *Zollikon Seminars: Protocols, Conversations, Letters*, edited by Medard Boss. Evanston: Northwestern University Press, 2001.

Leatherbarrow, David. "The Sacrifice of Space." In *Common Ground: A Critical Reader*, edited by David Chipperfield, Kieran Long, and Shumi Bose. Venice: Marsilio, 2012.

———. *Architecture Oriented Otherwise*. Cambridge, MA: MIT Press, 2009.

Lynch, Patrick, ed. *On Intricacy: The Work of John Meunier Architect*. London: Canalside Press, 2020.

———. *Civic Ground: Rhythmic Spatiality and the Communicative Movement between Architecture, Sculpture and Site*. London: Artifice Books on Architecture, 2017.

———. "Civic Architecture." *Mimesis: Lynch Architects*. London: Artifice Books on Architecture, 2015.

Martines, Lauro. *Power and Imagination: City States in Renaissance Italy*. London: Pimlico, 2002.

Providência, Paulo. *Architectonica Percepta: Texts and Images 1985–2015*. Zurich: Park Books, 2016.

Rykwert, Joseph. *The Dancing Column: On Order in Architecture*. Cambridge, MA: MIT Press, 1999.

———. *The Idea of a Town: The Anthropology of Urban Form in Rome, Italy and the Ancient World*. Cambridge, MA: MIT Press, 1988.

Schmitz, Herman. *New Phenomenology: A Brief Introduction*. Milan: Mimesis International, 2019.

Shepheard, Paul. *Slogans and Battlecries*. London: Canalside Press, 2020.

Summerson, John. *Heavenly Mansions: And Other Essays*. New York: Norton, 1998.

———. *The Classical Language of Architecture*. London: Thames and Hudson, 1980.

Tafuri, Manfredo. *Interpreting the Renaissance: Princes, Cities, Architects*. New Haven: Yale University Press, 2006.

Temple, Nicholas. "Treading Water on (Un)Common Ground: Revisiting *Mitsein*." *The Journal of Civic Architecture* 3 (2019): 23–31.

———. "Architecture as a Receptacle of *Mitsein*." In *Intersections of Ethos and Space*, edited by Nikolaos-Ion Terzoglou, Kyriaki Tsoukala, and Charikleia Pantelidou, 138–149. London: Routledge, 2015.

———. "Rites of Intent: The Participatory Dimension of the City." In *Cityscapes in History: The Urban Experience*, edited by Heléna Tóth and Katrina Gulliver. Surrey: Ashgate Publishing, 2014.

———. *Renovatio Urbis: Architecture, Urbanism and Ceremony in the Rome of Julius II*. London: Routledge, 2011.

Vesely, Dalibor. *Architecture in the Age of Divided Representation: The Question of Creativity in the Shadow of Production*. Cambridge, MA: MIT Press, 2004.

CHAPTER 19

Agency and Critical Editorial Devices in Recent Little Architecture Magazines

Carlo Menon

While there are frictions between research and design practices that need to be acknowledged, there are also forms of convergence. This paper aims to debate the recent production of little architecture magazines in this light. Hybrid modes of making architecture are increasingly common in central and northern Europe. Many architects work *across* architecture's multifaceted field, beyond the professional framework of practice. They design, build, teach, write, protest, compete, collect, research, publish, and exhibit, thus producing, de facto, hybrid kinds of architectural knowledge.[1] Researchers and designers have overlapped some of their areas of competence: academics overrun and subsume forms of knowledge, discourse, and practice outside their own field, especially within the architecture school; conversely, in the past two decades, academia has been opening up to artistic and architectural design practices, including practice-based research alternatives to the standard written dissertation.

In this ambivalent context, the production of little architecture magazines constitutes a type of architectural practice that brings together preoccupations from both inside and outside academia, and inside and outside architectural design. This in-between position represents a prolific site for the exchange of ideas in architecture, contributing to a redefinition of the practice of history, theory, and criticism in a non-prescriptive way. Little magazines use hybrid forms of inquiry and expression as well as particular modes of publication and circulation, diverting from the standards of academia. They are sites of production that are experimental, less codified, which include not only the single-authored text but also and especially a wider articulation of voices through other editorial agents such as drawings, photographs, and found images (fig. 19.1).

My research in this field focuses on two aspects of the practice of editing and producing little magazines: the method, which is theorised through the concept of critical editorial devices, and the purpose, which is analysed in terms of agency. After explaining the medium's specificities and its motives in section 1, the second section examines the agency of little magazines as "moving in the middle." Finally, in section 3, a short selection of little magazines is presented from the perspective of their different modes of articulating critical thinking and practice.

Fig. 19.1   A sample of the population of little architecture magazines that I survey in my research. Some are initiatives run by undergraduate students (*Carte Blanche*, *Carnets*), some by postgraduates (*P.E.A.R.*, *Lo–Res*), and some others are issued by a specific architectural design practices (*Map*, *AG*, *Pragma*). The others are edited by a combination of actors.
© Carlo Menon, personal collection.

1. Going Little

The term "little architecture magazines" describes self-published, non-commercial magazines produced independently from cultural, professional, or academic institutions. They are edited, published, and often designed by students or trained architects in the margins of their regular, remunerative activity. They usually appear less than three times a year, at irregular intervals. Their short distribution range and small print run means that they are of little interest to advertisers and remain niche, often flying below the radar of library subscriptions. Their financial model is minimalist, based on unpaid work, occasional sponsors and benefactors, crowdfunding and sales. Exhaustion is always around the corner: little magazines do not usually last for more than between six and ten issues – with some notable exceptions. Devoid of economic expectations, their mode of production is exclusively located in cultural terms: both internally, in the experience gained by the people involved and their devotion to a cause, and externally, in the social and cultural capital eventually acquired with visibility.[2]

While these qualities indicate that such publications are marginal and have little impact on mainstream architecture culture, the position that they hold has the prerogative of being liberated: each little magazine follows its own self-chosen set of principles, in terms of form and content, embedding sensibilities, quests, visions, and concerns of the architects involved in the making. Little magazines are not neutral and stake a position in the field of architectural discourse through their affinities with, and opposition to, other editorial projects.

In architecture, this medium has a history and a trajectory spanning the twentieth and twenty-first centuries, which can be described through three important turning points. It began around 1910, when the little magazine, as the privileged carrier of the new, or the avant-garde, contributed significantly to the spread of modernism. During the 1960s and 1970s, little magazines were used as sites of counterculture and institutional critique, exploiting the new electric environment of Xerox copying and other technologies of mechanical reproduction, above all, photography. Finally, parallel to the loss of confidence in the authority of the architectural object and to ethical stances on the role of architecture with regard to the post-bubble economy and, more recently, climate change, the digital turn of the past fifteen years has marked a major shift in the exchange of information and criticism in architecture.

Until the late 1990s, indeed, as the fastest and furthest-reaching means of communication, printed magazines monopolised architectural broadcasting, or at least held the most privileged position; but today's digital media have overpowered the press, achieving the goal of ubiquity and simultaneity between the production of architecture ideas, their dissemination, and reader feedback. Yet the current production of printed little architecture magazines remains consistent: more than a hundred titles have launched in the past fifteen years. In the post-digital age, according to observers and participants, printing is considered a "residual love from the printed matter,"[3] as well as a political act of resistance to the shallowness of which digital media are often accused.

2. Moving in the Middle

The variety of the aims, positions, intellectual affiliations and modes of organisation of little architecture magazines impedes easy classification. On a general level, they can be described as exploring and sharing ideas in architecture, and their purpose is principally intellectual, possibly political, rarely practical, and never profitable. The differences between them are located on other levels, the most important being graphic modes, editorial extroversion versus introversion, situatedness, financing, distribution and territoriality, rapport with architectural history and theory, relation to mechanisms of distinction and celebrity, and modes of criticism. The permutations of these properties are vast so that any further categorisation of little magazines would be forced: exceptions and in-betweens would be more abundant than canonical examples.

Rather than a taxonomy, then, the most fitting approach to describe this group of publications is to consider them within an "ecology of practices," as proposed – *mutatis mutandis* – by Isabelle Stengers.[4] This open, diplomatic approach to each other's specificity is not neutral; it has purpose. As an operative concept, the ecology of practice pulls the subjects in a direction. It is an action that is, literally and philosophically, *pragmatic*, as Hélène Frichot explains:

> For Stengers, because ecologies are always and necessarily open to transformation, it is less about recording a current ecology of practices, than creating connections and relations so that new practical possibilities might emerge. An ecology of practices operates in action, on the go, testing, venturing and feeling out possible sites of investigation.[5]

Moving across the field, transversally, "making each case just another case,"[6] Stengers invalidates the positivistic tendency to draw general theories out of the particular while opening up a heuristic chance for transformation. Instead of pinning down, it sets in motion.

A second concept related to that of the ecology of practice is Gilles Deleuze and Félix Guattari's notion of the "minor" and its corollary concept of "moving in the middle,"[7] which are thus resumed by art historian Mieke Bleyen writing on the photographic work of late-surrealist artist Marcel Mariën:

> I want to argue that these photographs trace a line between molar grids and molecular flows, art and pornography, the public and the private, the professional and the amateurish, which makes them particularly hard to label. By moving in the middle, they function within the logic of the "AND" which Deleuze and Parnet described as the stuttering and stammering quality of a minor literature's, its way of escaping dualisms: "AND, as something which has its place between the elements or between the sets. AND, AND, AND—stammering. And even if there are only two terms, there is an AND between the two, which is neither the one nor the other, nor the one which becomes the other, but which constitutes the multiplicity."[8]

It is easy to transfer these characteristics of moving in the middle to the little architecture magazines under scrutiny: they cross boundaries between the amateurish and the professional, between academic and design practice, between the building of a personal and professional identity through the editorial process (inwards) and the desire to take a public stance in the disciplinary debate (outwards).

These ambiguities and in-between positions – often self-chosen and assumed – tell of the little magazines' wandering and slippery positions in the field of architecture periodicals. Little magazines *move in the middle, in a minor mode*, amid a multiplicity of factors, among which can be cited intellectual probity and "the flickering flame of the avant-garde,"[9] authorial and editorial freedom, networking and emulation, polemics against the lack of criticism and experimentation in other publications. Little magazines respond to that virtue of complexity and contradiction identified by Robert Venturi in his "gentle manifesto":[10] "double-functioning," they belong to "the tradition of both-and"; they engage with history and theory, "yet" they cut ties with academic standards; they rely on mechanisms of social distinction, looking out for a public, "yet" they avoid compromise with the market, "excluding the usual suspects" and "resonating at lower resolutions."[11]

Explicitly or implicitly, this population of little architecture magazines expresses a wide range of editorial positions, attitudes, and points of interests, articulated here around two spheres: that of the motivation to start a magazine and that of the little magazine's political agency with regard to critical issues.

A Room of Our Own

Most little magazines are moved by the urge to create a space for the expression of ideas, being discontent with the established press because it limits the space available for text in general and criticism in particular, preferring the seduction of full-page photographs of famous architects' latest projects. For instance, *San Rocco* (Venice and Milan, 2010–2019) was created by four architecture studios, three photographers, and a graphic designer discontented with mainstream magazines and their lack of criticism and with academic journals and their lack of agency, as they are inaccessible to the general public in terms of language and distribution.[12] *San Rocco*, then, sought a space of "innocence," inviting architects to explore architectural design history and theory more freely.[13] With similar reasoning, but a different object of criticism, the French magazine *Criticat* (Paris, 2008–2018) sought the free space unreachable by the major titles:

> Architecture journals may display the achievements of high-profile practices and promote desirable design-related lifestyles, the landscape of their critical culture often looks as flat as the globalised world. Since these publications seem to have lost cultural significance, we thought it might be time to start a new one. The *criticat* project was founded in optimistic despair, to create a place to write, and, at least for a while, to have *a room of our own*.[14]

Other little magazines are turned inwards: they are intended as a vehicle for a self-initiated third cycle of continuing education for the editors and their guests. The three issues of *face b* (Paris, 2007–2010), subtitled "architecture from the other side," helped the editors discover their identity as practising architects. They used the little magazine "as an alibi for thinking about architecture with other people [...] a firefly, [that is,] a point of appeal and a trajectory."[15] They investigated the legacy of their predecessors, such as Denise Scott Brown and AA Bronson, and invited younger architects to discuss shared architectural concerns (fig. 19.2). Creating a room of their own allows many little magazines to explore *otherness* – themes otherwise omitted from architectural discourse. Where else, if not in a little magazine, could a young researcher publish a twelve-page article called "Adolf Loos and Masochistic Humour"?[16]

Fig. 19.2   Spread from *face b*, no. 2 (2009): 8–9. © Carlo Menon, personal collection.

Challenges in the Built Environment
Devoid of the generalist viewpoint of most established periodicals, little magazines promote a particular take on the built environment, fostering connection among a community of people, places, and projects. Civil and environmental engineer Martha Dillon founded *It's Freezing in LA!* (London, 2018–) to provide "a fresh perspective on climate change," situating the magazine in a "middle ground" between the scientific and activist publications (fig. 19.3).[17]

Fig. 19.3   Cover and back cover of *It's Freezing in L.A.!*, no. 4 (December 2019).
© Carlo Menon, personal collection.

The horizon of some magazines is planetary, whereas others are precisely situated. For instance, *GLAS paper* (Glasgow, 2001–2007) was founded by "a co-operative of architects, teachers, writers and urban activists [...] committed to fighting all manifestations of socio-spatial inequality, exploitation and deprivation."[18] It was focused on the city of Glasgow (GLAS is the acronym of Glasgow Letters on Architecture + Space) and addressed its citizens, often in combination with public events. *City as Material* (London, 2010–2012) consisted in a "series of collaborative exploratory walks and book-making events," engaging its active "readers" on a rediscovery of the urban environment in cities across England.[19] For each issue, *Flaneur* (Berlin, 2013–) squarely moves the editorial team to a specific street in a distant city where it produces the magazine's contents, all of which are linked to that street.

3. Critical Editorial Devices

The previous discussion has described some of the various motivations and positions of little architecture magazines within a vast field of cultural production. This section discusses how they operate *in practice* through an analysis of editorial work, the contents, and the graphic and publishing strategies, questioning the extent to which and in what ways these publications can be considered "critical architecture."[20]

Drawing on, and eventually moving past, the recent debate on the critical, the post-critical, and the crises of criticism,[21] the examples of "critical editorial devices" that follow refer to my wider survey of the multiple ways in which criticism can be expanded, from the typical critical essay to the full extent of the printed magazine, in particular by considering the "grey" elements of the editorial process, such as titles, leads, editors' notes, captions, and other annotations – what literary critic Gérard Genette calls *paratexts*.[22]

Genette's study concentrated on novels. Transferring his insights to the magazine format, it is clear that the play of what he calls "thresholds of interpretation" is even more important: the multiple voices of the contributors, the editors, and the graphic material collide, altering their meaning reciprocally. Accepting this perspective implies a shift of attention from the notion of authorship to that of editorship, assuming that the latter provides a more comprehensive approach to the possibilities of criticism. The critical function, then, cannot be attributed to a single person or element – the authored text – but is distributed on the page, or even performed in the process of making the magazine.

Publishing as Encounter

This critical editorial device concerns methods to maintain a spontaneous approach to the editorial work, which in turn reflects a stronger agency for the content. Like fanzines, they combine a fast process of producing contents with simple but effective means to print it.

Club Donny (Rotterdam, 2008–2013), subtitled "strictly unedited journal on the personal experience of nature in the urban environment," originated in a community of readers-contributors who shared pictures online. The project's understatement – which paradoxically provides strength to its message – consisted in the fact that professional and amateur photos were evenly selected, shuffled, printed on two sides of paper, and simply folded. As a result, readers could only see, on each spread, two halves of two different images (fig. 19.4).[23]

UP (Brussels, 2006–) is the joint project of two artists and scenographers with a keen interest in architecture. They use it almost as an alibi to visit iconic and sometimes anonymous buildings, which they reveal exclusively through photographs. *AG Architektur in Gebrauch* (Berlin, 2014–) is also published with few, simple means and was initially barely distributed outside the office of the architects who started producing it as an expansion of their built work. Like *UP*, it also publishes one building per issue, which the editors visit, research, and represent through drawings (fig. 19.5). It focuses on "architecture in use," shifting from the usual perspective of the architects' intentions to "the production of living conditions as the main discourse on built environment."[24]

Fig. 19.4 Understatement and *sprezzatura*: spread from *Club Donny*, no. 10, *Grand Finale* (2013), not paginated. © Carlo Menon, personal collection.

Fig. 19.5 A renewed encounter with architecture in use: the British Council in Bangkok, built in 1970 by architect Sumet Jumsai, featured in *AG Architektur in Gebrauch*, no. 5 (2018). © Carlo Menon, personal collection.

Creative Distribution

Some magazines creatively push the limits of distribution and the nature of their physical existence. *RROARK* (Milan, 2014–2015) was printed on the back of the menu of a kebab shop next to the school of architecture and therefore had a high print run – 25,000, the editors claim – but a very small distribution range (fig. 19.6). The magazine *Journal* (Paris, 2017–) is totally immaterial, being performed vocally by the editor-in-chief, an actor, who memorises the contributions. *Black Grout!* (London, 2013–2014), subtitled "publishing as event," took place as a meeting or round table with editors and contributors. It was also immaterial: only some audio recordings of the events were uploaded to the magazine's website.

Fig. 19.6   Creative distribution: the first "issue" of *RRoark!* (October 2014) as a menu. © Fosbury Architecture.

Parody

Parody is common among many little magazines. It is one of the qualities that make me argue – borrowing once more from Genette[25] – that most of them are conceived "in the second degree," that is, in reference to other publications (intertextuality: a claim that could easily be expanded to architectural design). The manner by which the parody is performed can open up possibilities for criticism.

San Rocco rejected some of the codes of academic journals (such as peer review), adopted others (such as the format), and invested a few with critical meaning: its call for papers is a parody that the editors overdetermine by filling in possible ideas on the next topic, to the point that one might suspect that most of their pleasure as editors comes from this speculative activity of pitching essays unlikely to be written.

Flat Out (Chicago, 2017–) attacks another common feature of magazines: the names of contributors, substituting them with fictional characters, such as The Challenger, The Genealogist, The Opinionator, The Scorekeeper, The Political Economist, to each of which corresponds a writing format (fig. 19.7). Hence, the authors of criticism become anonymous actors of a role that doesn't entirely coincide with their mode of expression as individuals. In other words, this critical editorial device allows contributors to write otherwise.

Fig. 19.7   Anonymised criticism: presentation of the contributors' fictional characters in *Flat Out*, no. 1 (2016): 77–78. © Carlo Menon, personal collection.

The picture emerging from this survey of little architecture magazines is that of a discursive practice that willingly moves in the middle across the field of architecture, in and out of its professional and educational institutions, and that uses tools borrowed from both architectural design and research. This moving in the middle possesses political significance, blurring the boundaries of what can be defined as "research," "practice," or "project." If "minor" is "little" with a political drive, with agency, then all little magazines are "minor literature" insofar as the language that they speak is not fully codified. And yet it is accepted, "read," and "spoken" by many of the actors in this field, regardless of their official position – students, teachers, designers, academics, curators. Herein lies the intrinsic agency of little architecture magazines as a medium, whatever the individual claims, critical approach or excursions in architecture culture. Content-wise, within this "ecology of practices," distinctions need to be made. Not all little magazines prove to have an agency that reaches outwards, that challenges the minds of readers and established practices. Assessing this impact could only happen through a wide sociological or ethnographic survey focused on readers, which is not my aim. My contribution, rather, seeks to present the potential of this practice in critical terms, and its current livelihood in times in which the discipline of architecture is shaken by profound societal challenges that it must face.

Notes

1.   Cf., for instance, Isabelle Doucet and Nel Janssens, eds., *Transdisciplinary Knowledge Production in Architecture and Urbanism: Towards Hybrid Modes of Inquiry* (Heidelberg: Springer, 2011).

2.   This materialistic reading of the little magazines' function is indebted to Pierre Bourdieu's analysis, in particular to his notion of *habitus*, which is strictly correlated with the idea of sacrifice and devotion. See his *Distinction. A Social Critique on the Judgement of Taste* (Cambridge, MA: Harvard University Press, 1984).

3.   Elias Redstone, ed., *Archizines* (London: Bedford Press, 2012), this is the curatorial statement of the eponymous exhibition. This statement is supported by the sixty interviews with editors as part of the exhibition.

4.   Isabelle Stengers, "Introductory Notes on an Ecology of Practices," *Cultural Studies Review* 11, no. 1 (2005): 183–196. DOI: 10.5130/csr.v11i1.3459.

5.   Hélène Frichot, *How to Make Yourself a Feminist Design Power Tool* (Bamberg: Spurbuchverlag, 2016), 21. In this book, Frichot draws Stengers's concept into design practices. See also Andrej Radman's entry, "Ecologies of Architecture," in *Posthuman Glossary*, eds. Rosi Braidotti and Maria Hlavajova (London: Bloomsbury, 2008), 117–120.

6.   Isabelle Stengers, "Introductory Notes on an Ecology of Practices," 192.

7.   Cf. Gilles Deleuze and Félix Guattari, *Kafka. Pour une littérature mineure* (Paris, Minuit, 1975), trans. Dana Polan as *Kafka: Toward a Minor Literature* (Minneapolis: University of Minnesota Press, 1986).

8.   Mieke Bleyen, "Always in the Middle: The Photographic Work of Marcel Mariën. A Minor Approach," in *Minor Photography: Connecting Deleuze and Guattari to Photography Theory*, ed. Mieke Bleyen (Leuven: Leuven University Press, 2012), 39–62. Her citations are from Gilles Deleuze and Claire Parnet, *Dialogues II* (1977), trans. H. Tomlinson and B. Habberjam (London and New York: Continuum, 2002), 26.

9.   I owe this expression to my MA thesis supervisor, Murray Fraser, when asking me about the motives of architects-editors to start a magazine.

10. Robert Venturi, *Complexity and Contradiction in Architecture* (1966; second edition New York: MoMA, 1977).

11. Both quotes are taken from the editorial statement of *Lo–Res* (Stockholm, 2015, pilot issue only). *Lo–Res*, no. 0 (November 2015): 168 [unsigned: presumably written by the editors Helen Runting, Fredrik Torisson and Erik Sigge].

12. Ludovico Centis, speaking at the Archizines Live conference in Brussels, 5 October 2012 https://youtu.be/VMpspK8VvD4 (accessed 8 May 2021)

13. *Innocence* is also the title of the pilot issue, whose editorial statement claims: "San Rocco is written by architects. As such, [it] is neither particularly intelligent nor philologically accurate. / San Rocco is serious. It takes the risk of appearing naïve." *San Rocco*, no. 0 (Spring 2010): 3 [not signed: presumably written by editor-in-chief Matteo Ghidoni in collaboration with the editorial board].

14. Françoise Fromonot, "Why Start an Architectural Journal in an Age That is Disgusted with (Most of) Them?" *OASE*, no. 81, *Constructing Criticism* (2010): 68.

15. Sébastien Martinez Barat speaking at the Archizines Live conference in Brussels.

16. Can Onaner, "Adolf Loos et l'humour masochiste," *face b*, no. 2 (2009): 72–97. The article gave its title to a PhD dissertation published in 2019, ten years after its early formulation in a little magazine.

17. Martha Dillon, editorial statement: https://www.itsfreezinginla.co.uk/about. The title is sarcastically extracted from a 2013 tweet by Donald Trump, reprinted on the back cover of each issue: "Ice storm rolls from Texas to Tennessee – I'm in Los Angeles and it's freezing. Global warming is a total, and very expensive, hoax!"

18. "Manifesto," *GLAS paper*, no. 1 (September 2001): 3.
19. Project description by the editor, Giles Lanes: http://proboscis.org.uk/projects/2011-2015/city-as-material/.
20. Jane Rendell et al., eds., *Critical Architecture* (London: Routledge, 2007); Jane Rendell, ed., *Critical Architecture*, thematic issue of *The Journal of Architecture* 10, no. 3 (2005).
21. The canonical bibliography on this US–UK debate is well known. I would add three themed issues of academic journals and magazines: Johan Lagae et al., eds., *Positions. Shared Territories in Historiography & Practice*, OASE, no. 69 (2006); Isabelle Doucet and Kenny Cupers, eds., *Agency in Architecture: Reframing Criticality in Theory and Practice*, *Footprint*, no. 4 (Spring 2009); Tom Avermaete et al., eds., *Constructing Criticism*, OASE, no. 81 (2010), which features a good review of the debate by John Macarthur and Naomi Stead, "Judge Is Not the Operator, Historiography, Criticality, and Architectural Criticism," 116–139.
22. Gérard Genette, *Seuils* (Paris: Seuil, 1987), trans. Jane E. Lewin as *Paratexts. Thresholds of Interpretation* (Cambridge: Cambridge University Press, 1997).
23. See "Club Donny," conversation between Carlo Menon and Ernst van der Hoeven, *Accattone*, no. 6 (September 2019): 33–36.
24. Editorial statement by Sandra Bartoli and Silvan Linden: http://wp.buerofuerkonstruktivismus.de/?p=96.
25. Gérard Genette, *Palimpsestes. La littérature au second degré* (Paris: Seuil, 1982), trans. Channa Newman and Claude Doubinsky as *Palimpsests: Literature in the Second Degree* (Lincoln: University of Nebraska Press, 1997).

Bibliography

Bartoli, Sandra and Silvan Linden. Editorial. http://wp.buerofuerkonstruktivismus.de/?p=96.
Bleyen, Mieke. "Always in the Middle: The Photographic Work of Marcel Mariën. A Minor Approach." *Minor Photography: Connecting Deleuze and Guattari to Photography Theory*, 39–62. Leuven: Leuven University Press, 2012.
Bourdieu, Pierre. *Distinction. A Social Critique on the Judgement of Taste*. Cambridge, MA: Harvard University Press, 1984.
Deleuze, Gilles and Félix Guattari. *Kafka. Pour une littérature mineure* (Paris, Minuit, 1975), translated by Dana Polan: *Kafka: Toward a Minor Literature*. Minneapolis: University of Minnesota Press, 1986.
Deleuze, Gilles and Claire Parnet. *Dialogues II* (1977), translated by H. Tomlinson and B. Habberjam. London and New York: Continuum, 2002.
Dillon, Martha. Editorial statement. https://www.itsfreezinginla.co.uk/about.
Doucet, Isabelle and Nel Janssens, eds. *Transdisciplinary Knowledge Production in Architecture and Urbanism: Towards Hybrid Modes of Inquiry*. Heidelberg: Springer, 2011.
Frichot, Hélène. *How to Make Yourself a Feminist Design Power Tool*. Bamberg: Spurbuchverlag, 2016.
Fromonot, Françoise. "Why Start an Architectural Journal in an Age That is Disgusted with (Most of) Them?" *OASE*, no. 81, *Constructing Criticism* (2010): 66–78.
Genette, Gérard. *Palimpsestes. La littérature au second degré* (Paris: Seuil, 1982), translated by Channa Newman and Claude Doubinsky as *Palimpsests: Literature in the Second Degree*. Lincoln: University of Nebraska Press, 1997.

———. *Seuils*. Paris: Seuil, 1987, translated by Jane E. Lewin as *Paratexts. Thresholds of interpretation*. Cambridge: Cambridge University Press, 1997.

Lagae, Johan, Marc Schoonderbeek, Tom Avermaete, and Andrew Leach, eds. *Positions. Shared Territories in Historiography & Practice*. Thematic issue of *OASE*, no. 69 (2006).

Lanes, Giles. Project description. http://proboscis.org.uk/projects/2011-2015/city-as-material/

Macarthur, John and Naomi Stead. "Judge Is Not the Operator, Historiography, Criticality, and Architectural Criticism." *Constructing Criticism*, OASE, no. 81 (2010): 116–139.

"Manifesto." *GLAS paper*, no. 1 (September 2001): 3.

Matteo Ghidoni. Editorial statement. *San Rocco*, no. 0, *Innocence* (Spring 2010).

Menon, Carlo and Ernst van der Hoeven. "Club Donny." *Accattone*, no. 6 (September 2019): 33–36.

Onaner, Can. "Adolf Loos et l'humour masochiste." *face b*, no. 2 (2009): 72–97.

Radman, Andrej. "Ecologies of Architecture." In *Posthuman Glossary*, edited by Rosi Braidotti and Maria Hlavajova, 117–120. London: Bloomsbury, 2008.

Redstone, Elias, ed., *Archizines*. London: Bedford Press, 2012.

Rendell, Jane, ed., *Critical Architecture*. Thematic issue of *The Journal of Architecture* 10, no. 3 (2005).

———, Jonathan Hill, Murray Fraser and Mark Dorrian, eds., Critical Architecture (London: Routledge, 2007). *Critical Architecture*. London: Routledge, 2007.

Runting, Helen, Fredrik Torisson, and Erik Sigge. Editorial statement. *Lo–Res*, no. 0 (November 2015).

Stengers, Isabelle. "Introductory Notes on an Ecology of Practices." *Cultural Studies Review* 11, no. 1 (2005): 183–196. DOI: 10.5130/csr.v11i1.3459

Stoner, Jill. *Toward a Minor Architecture*. Cambridge, MA: MIT Press, 2012.

Venturi, Robert. *Complexity and Contradiction in Architecture*. New York: MoMA, 1977.

PART 5

The Values of the Object

New viewpoints unfold when buildings are recognised as built testimonies to a slow and often painful design process in continuous motion, rather than perceived as a static result of an unwavering success story. Examining architecture as process creates the potential to consider construction and materialisation itself as place of cultural production, a project seen in relation to local circumstances and available sources, while revealing alternative histories and exposing hidden players. The contributions in this section bring tools and techniques from architectural practice into play within academic conventions. To start with, Wilfried Wang makes an explicit plea for a return to the object: the construction and materialisation of a project as the ultimate place of cultural production, researching the local circumstances and available sources that lead to its realisation and, in the process, producing new insights into the processes and intentions of the designs. Paulo Providência retraces the numerous sketches made by Álvaro Siza Viera's for the Porto School of Architecture. His re-enactment provides an understanding of Siza's contextual strategy as one that combines a meticulous reading of the site with continuous, subtle readjustments of the design. Luis Burriel Bielza employs examples from computer modelling, testing their value as tools for academic analysis and reflection. Burriel's drawings produce alternative insights, that nuance, and in some cases even contradict, the original architects' intentions, using the Villa dall'Ava by Rem Koolhaas as a case in point. In conclusion, Simon Henley reads his own projects in reverse, deconstructing them into discrete components. A detailed reading of the element of the wall reveals the full complexity of its construction, and the theorisation arising from this fragment suggests a way forward for operative theory.

CHAPTER 20

Understanding Architecture

Wilfried Wang

1. Introduction: Understanding and Judging Buildings

The majority of architectural media and schools of architecture work under the assumption that new buildings will continue to be the main task of architects. At the same time, architectural quality is rarely evaluated. The principle of the freedom of expression is used as an excuse in the race towards ever-more spectacular shapes and ever-more esoteric justifications for formalist design approaches. The principle of appropriateness to ecological, social, cultural, or political contexts is considered a spoilsport. Given this dominant context, it is imperative to understand built culture so that we develop the appropriate design concepts in maintaining and improving as much of the existing fabric as possible and in building better when it is necessary to do so.

As the era of rapid and conspicuous consumption comes to an end and civilisation faces the challenges of adapting its life styles to mitigate the effects of climate crisis, the opportunities for the construction of new buildings should be taken with the requisite earnestness. It is no longer acceptable to compromise the quality of building by following the conventional shortcut towards immediate gratification and ignoring the core Vitruvian tenets that a building should exhibit the qualities of *firmitas, utilitas,* and *venustas,* translated into contemporary terms as sustainability, adaptability, and aesthetic delight.

We need to understand how buildings succeed or fail to be sustainable, adaptable, and appreciated. While all buildings are superficially the same – they are all made of matter; they stand up, provide shelter, have facades, contain spaces on the inside – some buildings last longer than others, some are more flexible and adaptable than others, some are more carefully designed and assembled than others and are therefore more appreciated by users and observers.

Before buildings come into existence, it is possible to evaluate their constitutive qualities, their likely overall design quality (as defined above), and their impact on society and the environment. Some of the building's aspects can be objectively assessed (e.g. life-cycle analysis), others relatively compared, and others still subjectively gauged. The person undertaking this analysis of a design on paper needs to be practised in the reading of written and drawn documents, as well as possess a well-developed sense of spatial and material imagination to compensate for the absence of real space and form.

Once realised, buildings are incontrovertible physical evidence, leading an existence distinct from spoken or written words, drawings, or photographs. Therefore, regardless what critics, politicians, clients, architects, and others might claim about buildings, their real presence in a specific physical and cultural context can be analysed and evaluated independently from such statements. Conscientious architectural research is therefore publicly transparent, scientifically analytical, and independently verifiable, in short, *forensic*, according to the Latin origin of the word.

However, rather than investigating buildings in their pathological or criminal dimensions – some buildings indeed possess these, for example, mass housing schemes in conjunction with their occupational regimes – the goal of any research into buildings is to identify their sociocultural ambitions, their contribution to the architectural discourse, and their architectural achievements. Research should uncover a building's character of reality.[1] By that is meant the identification of the embodied intentions: How would the world be constituted and represented if only all buildings were designed and built along the same lines as the building under investigation? Every building expresses a world view, whether consciously or not.

At a basic, quotidian level, we need to understand buildings because we need to ensure that buildings reach an overall minimum design quality. In simple technical terms, most societies have planning regulations and building codes. At the most ambitious level, we should expect that buildings constitute and represent our social and cultural aspirations. We should strive for buildings to be appropriate for their tasks, that they accommodate normal needs while others should rise above this to celebrate communal values. Some buildings need only be comfortably modest; others should inspire and become symbols of a period and a society.

However, the sad reality is that few people are concerned with questions of architectural quality. Neither politicians, nor clients, not even the majority of so-called architects are interested in this. If they were, there would be better buildings in the world.

We need to understand buildings because we need to design and build better buildings. We need a differentiated understanding of buildings because we need to know when, where, and how to apply our knowledge. As diverse as society is, as varied as our needs are, and as specialised as the activities in our settlements are, we need to design buildings appropriately in response to each of these conditions. That means that not every building should be an icon. We want to learn from buildings so that we can instil in those interested in designing and building an awareness of what is appropriate, a sense of quality as well as an idea of the scope of what has been achieved and what might be possible.

Built Reality

Buildings create reality; they create facts. This reality is not only spatial as well as physical but also bears intentions and meanings. Buildings can consist of symbols, and they can also be symbols themselves.

Buildings are objects in a context; they are "figures" against a "ground." They differentiate themselves from the context and from others. The act of differentiation is spatial and physical and can be read in terms of the underlying intentions and meanings.

At the level of a building's component, a wall differentiates between two sides; further, an enclosure defines an interior and an exterior. The factual clarity of such spatial and formal divisions establishes social and cultural values. A wall between two groups of people can be used to separate these two groups. An enclosure around a group of people can both protect as well as control, even incarcerate.

The way such walls or enclosures are constructed and the way that such constructions appear – whether the walls are made of massive materials or of different layers with an outer, visibly decorative surface – can be analysed and evaluated in relation to their actual intentions and perceived meanings.

The way that a given building constitutes intentions and meanings can be compared to the way it actually represents these intentions and meanings. However, just as in any other form of human expression, what is truly intended in an expression is not necessarily what can be observed on the face of it. For example, some architects like to describe their designs with metaphors. The terms *rue corridor* or *streets in the air* were used by architects to evoke richer associations than the reality they were able to create. The phrases were coined to blur what was built rather than to precisely describe how the designed spaces really perform. A *rue corridor* inside an apartment building is not a street, since it is neither a public space nor is it connected to a network of streets. The mismatch between an intention, stated in a phrase such as *rue corridor*, when analysed, reveals the rhetorical device,[2] in this case the phrase is a hyperbolic metaphor.

The rhetorical devices themselves, by which buildings mediate between the constitution of a physical and spatial presence and the representation of a sociocultural context or value system, are subject to analysis. Any building analysis can be both exhaustive as well as subject to selective examination at junctures where indicative or characteristic revelations provide the key to the comprehensive understanding of the whole.

Buildings as Primary Evidence

In the way that buildings create facts, they offer themselves to be analysed and evaluated through their prima facie composition. Understanding buildings rests on observers looking at the physical evidence before them. Built reality supersedes spoken or written discourse. Built reality is primary evidence.

Describing and Analysing Buildings
Facts require description before they can be analysed. The methodology that is presented here in outline only was developed as part of a three-year fellowship (1981–1984) within Florian Beigel's Architecture Geometry Research Unit at the former Polytechnic of North London (currently known as the London Metropolitan University). A descriptive method for building elements led to an analytical method for the evaluation of building designs. This was subsequently integrated into a theory of architecture.

2. A Theory of Architecture

The focus of this theoretical approach is to describe and value the connections between the physical manifestation of a built edifice on the one hand and its sociocultural significance as well as its spatial and formal qualities on the other hand. Any building can therefore be described in its formal and spatial components and overall composition. In acquiring information on the building's context, both physical as well as sociocultural, it becomes possible to deduce the building's significance, its impact on the sociocultural context, and the contribution it makes to the larger architectural discourse.

In the preparation for the descriptive and analytical method, the largest impact was made by Paul Frankl's *System der Kunstwissenschaft*,[3] given its structural clarity and its comprehensive definition of art theoretical terms. The morphological variables were derived from Frankl. The concept of morphological categories was formulated independently.

Figure Against Ground
The factual basis of any phenomenon rests within the difference it establishes in contrast to a context. Its recognisability depends on the degree of differentiation from the context or background. Similarly, the joint between two objects or the abrupt change in direction on a surface permits a distinction to be made. In other words, articulations permit parts to be identified. Buildings are assemblies of parts and each articulation can be recognised for the syntactic and semantic meaning it contributes towards the overall statement.

Parts to Whole
Buildings consist of parts that are composed into wholes, which in turn can become smaller elements of larger wholes. For example, a wall could consist of blocks, and a group of walls could enclose a space. Buildings are understood by examining the material and spatial composition of parts to wholes.

Morphological Categories of Building Components
The activity of building has structured the way all societies think about its components and the resultant wholes. There are five morphological categories to the composition of buildings that are logically related by way of a hierarchical, telescopic concatenation:

1. constructional
2. tectonic
3. compartmental
4. configurational
5. contextual

Assembling elements of the constructional category renders wholes, which in turn become elements of the tectonic category, and so on.

Buildings as Ways of Making the World
On the basis of understanding buildings as primary evidence, the aim of any building analysis and evaluation is to further understand the building's implicit or explicit intentions and effective contributions to the making or shaping of the world. Which elements of a building adhere to convention, and which parts intend to reform or advance contemporary practice? How do buildings support or contradict the status quo? To what extent do the parts of a building or does the building itself change common practice, conventional patterns of use or entire lifestyles? Are the designer's claims to innovation justified, or is it simply just another bold but unsubstantiated assertion, if not a downright item of fake news?

Architecture as a Conscious Act of Building
The goal of understanding buildings is to identify their ambitions and their contributions to the discourse, their achievements as part of the culture of building. Insofar as buildings are recognisably making a conscious contribution to building culture, they can be considered pieces of architecture.

Qualities of a Building
Qualities are compared against criteria. For example, the life expectancy of a building material is known; its interplay with other elements, when properly detailed, can ensure that a building component meets that maximum life expectancy. The long endurance – *firmitas* – of a building material and a building component can be considered to be a desirable, positive quality. The durable quality of a material of component can be measured objectively; it is an *immanent* quality. The designer's choice for a specific period of endurance can be assessed by an external observer in terms of both immanent requirements as well as subjective preferences.

The different uses that a building can accommodate over its existence is limited, but could nevertheless be relatively large in range. The fitness of use – *utilitas*, the way that spaces in a building can ideally, comfortably, or merely adequately accommodate use patterns – is a *relative* quality. Further, buildings possess different degrees of flexibility based on the constructional system's adaptability and the spatial typology. A building's flexibility is a quality that is also objective, inherently defined by the building's morphological constitution as well as by designers' ability to imagine change.

Similarly, the way that people feel protected in a space to the way that a building is seen to harmonise with its context, go beyond functional fitness, and touch on psychological and atmospheric sensations. While shapes of spaces and forms, even resultant atmospheres can be described objectively, their evocation of beauty – *venustas* –is *subjective* and varies from individual to individual.

Design Quality

Given that buildings consist of different components and intentions, it is possible to evaluate the quality of each component and intention in relation to the contribution a building makes towards both the whole and to the cultural context. A building has a high level of design quality if the compositional and intentional relationships of the parts to the components and to the whole are logically coherent, mutually reinforcing and spatially and formally integrated, and if the building fulfils the designers' stated or implied intentions. Such intentions can be as abstract or theoretical as designers might like; no building is exempt from being analysed on its own as a built fact. The quality of a design, of a building, as a singular term is a synthetic judgement.

3. Exemplary Building Research

There have been few cases when buildings have been presented in a way that has made them come to another life other than their mere representation in videos, photographs, or printed words. For example, Neil Levine's brilliant lecture on Henri Labrouste's Bibliothèque St. Geneviève at the AA's symposium on neoclassicism[4] gave the audience an insight into what comprehensive research could mean. Hermann Czech's meticulous analysis in his book on Adolf Loos's Goldman & Salatsch Tailors & Outfitters provided another such experience.[5] These provided the inspiration and challenge to probe both unbuilt and realised designs, and, in the course of building research and through the acquisition of conceptual, compositional, and constructional experience, the description and analysis of buildings became more precise and permitted more immediate pinpointing of the key aspects of specific designs and their intentions. The following are a selection of such research cases.

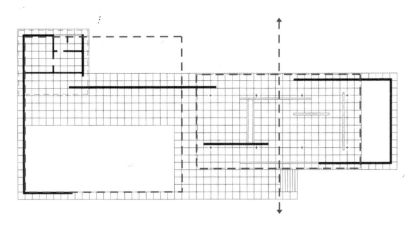

Fig. 20.1 Analytical diagram of the floor plan of the German Pavilion by Ludwig Mies van der Rohe, Barcelona (1929), showing the implied central axis of the "house" or served part and the implied square of the servant part. Diagram by the author on a plan published in Juan Pablo Bonta's book Mies van der Rohe, Barcelona 1929, Barcelona, Editorial Gustavo Gili, 1975.

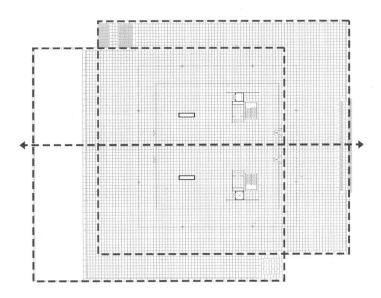

Fig. 20.2 Analytical diagram of the upper floor plan of the New National Gallery by Ludwig Mies van der Rohe, Berlin (1968), showing the two interlocking rectangles. Diagram: Wilfried Wang.

Ludwig Mies van der Rohe

Early topics of analysis continued from research carried out by others, for example, in 1979, I carried on from Wolfram Hoepfner and Fritz Neumeyer's study of Peter Behrens's Wiegand Haus, built in 1911 in Berlin.[6] The research was published in the magazine *9H*. Ludwig Mies van der Rohe's direct involvement in this domestic project, his evident fascination with the typology and proportional systems of the Wiegand Haus, led to his development of abstracted versions of the underlying served to serviced typology in houses of the same period as well as to his later interwar brick houses in Krefeld. The ultimate instance of this relationship can be found in the New National Gallery in Berlin.

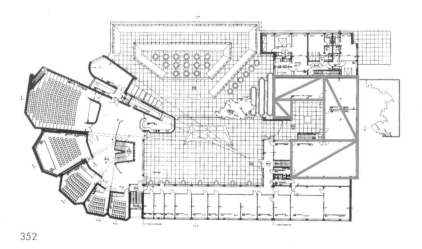

352

Fig. 20.3 Analytical diagram of the upper floor of the Cultural Centre by Alvar Aalto, Wolfsburg (1962), showing the idea of geometric growth. Diagram: Wilfried Wang.

Alvar Aalto

This interest in tracing typologies and proportional systems has continued throughout my research activities; for instance, it was the basis for looking at Alvar Aalto's predilection for U-shaped configurations with emphasised high points. It became clear that Aalto had pursued this idea of encapsulating humanity's progress from primary forms of life to the utmost manifestation of the human spirit as expressed through the fine arts from the Villa Mairea to the Cultural Centre in Wolfsburg.[7]

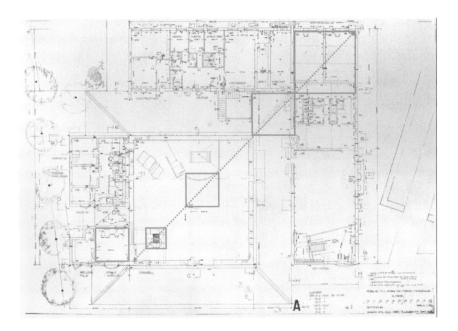

Fig. 20.4 Analytical diagram of the ground floor plan of St. Petri Church by Sigurd Lewerentz, Klippan (1966), showing the idea of the central sacraments all aligned on a diagonal axis. Diagram: Wilfried Wang.

Sigurd Lewerentz

On a related note, studying Sigurd Lewerentz's St. Petri Church in Klippan revealed a similar programmatic inscription in the underlying spatial thrust of the building complex as can be found in Aalto's Cultural Centre.[8] Besides the reflexive ontology expressed in the church's architectural language,[9] the five central ceremonies or marriage, baptism, communion, mass, and confirmation are aligned along the diagonal of the nave and the parish offices. Lewerentz returns to a topic that he had integrated in his first crematorium project for Helsingborg in 1914.

Heinrich Tessenow

What appears to be conservative, a temple-fronted festival hall, as in Tessenow's auditorium for Hellerau, was in fact a collective work of art. The pioneer of rhythmic dance Émile Jacques-Dalcroze, the innovator of abstract stage design Adolphe Appia, the experimenting artist Alexander von Salzmann, and Heinrich Tessenow were the beneficiaries of Wolf Dohrn, the Maecenas of Hellerau's Educational Institute for Rhythmic Gymnastics Jaques-Dalcroze. This was an early twentieth-century successor to the nearby festival town of Bayreuth, Richard Wagner's chosen site for his operatic version of the *Gesamtkunstwerk*.[10]

Tessenow's interpretation of modern abstraction was indeed an attempt at conserving archetypes, but they were highly refined humane attempts, contrary to the assertive brutality of the resuscitated neoclassicism of one of his students: Albert Speer.

Hans Scharoun

For many architectural critics and teachers, Scharoun's work remains an enigma. The Philharmonie remains an unrivalled sociopolitical manifestation of absolute architectural clarity. The concert hall declares the possibility of the lightness of the newly established democracy, as an antithesis to Albert Speer's megalomaniacal capital of the world. The auditorium's inclined blocks of seats celebrate the strength of the group in balance with the orchestra, as opposed to the indistinguishable fanaticised mass that the Nazi regime envisaged.[11]

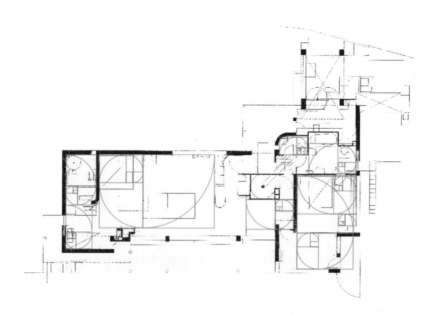

Fig. 20.5   Analytical diagram of the upper floor plan of E.1027 by Eileen Gray, Roquebrune (1929), showing the pervasive application of the Golden Section in the composition of elements. Diagram: Wilfried Wang.

Eileen Gray

The extended and comprehensive study of Eileen Gray's E.1027 in Roquebrune has provided a true understanding of what building research means. There is not an equivalent total work of art undertaken by one person of the early twentieth century. As casual as it looks, as poorly constructed as it was – in the bric-à-brac manner that persists to this day in this part of the world – its intentions were universal and its inventiveness astonishing. As her first piece of landscape architecture, architecture, interior, and furniture design, Gray managed to make the entire composition look relaxed, open, unspecific, and undogmatic. And yet, a few clues left to the archive of the Victoria and Albert Museum such as the drawings of the Golden Section and the Golden Rectangle provided the key to unlocking the underlying compositional rigour that underlies this design.[12] The four years of research were crowned by a full-scale installation of the master bedroom at four venues.[13]

Álvaro Siza

The interest in the work of Álvaro Siza has endured since the 1980s. The Boa Nova Tea House is as fresh as it was in its year of completion in 1963. Siza's projects for Berlin remain potent exchanges with the city's complex history. His school of architecture in Porto is specific to its site, city, and cultural context, yet it is also generally relevant as an enlightened educational institution. The Church for St. Jacques-de-la-Lande in Rennes is proof that it is possible to circle a square. In contrast to many of his colleagues of a similar age, Siza's work has remained meaningful, architecturally innovative, and of the highest cultural ambition.

Fig. 20.6   Escuela Nueva Esperanza, Puerto Cabuyal, Manabí, Ecuador (2009). Architects Al Borde, Quito.

Al Borde

Directly answering needs, the young practice of Al Borde of Quito, Ecuador, pursues a contemporary form of bottom-up architecture. The accumulated academic design knowledge is filtered through the daily realities of communities without financial means but with basic needs such as a primary school for a fishing village on the Pacific coast. Given that the "clients" only had $50 for the school building, Al Borde nevertheless agreed to undertake this task by engaging the villagers themselves for the construction as well as local material. Al Borde is one of a number of pioneering architects working outside the starchitecture circle, addressing energies to real needs.

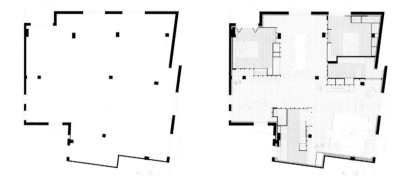

Fig 20.7   Can Gabriel, apartment conversion before (a) and after (b) plans, Mallorca (2012). Architects TEd'Arquitectes, Palma de Mallorca.

TEd'A arquitectes

Behind the cryptic name of TEd'A arquitectes stand Irene Perez and Jaume Mayol. The practice is refreshing in its direct use of local crafts without resorting to any regionalist kitsch, its inventive detailing, its spatial and formal precision, and its synthesis of the great architectural themes with everyday tasks – in other words, their sensitivity for knowing when to say what in a dignified way.[14]

4. Conclusion

The analysis of individual buildings has permitted reflection on more general architectural topics such as the abiding relevance of the sublime and the picturesque or the differences between minimal and minimalist, or modern and modernist, architecture.

In the context of climate change, the 2003 essay "Sustainability is a Cultural Problem"[15] makes the case that measures against climate change will need to begin with redefining cultural ideals and that the reliance on innovative technology will lead to failure. Subsequently, the 2020 essay on "Site-Specificity, Skilled Labour, and Culture: Architectural Principles in the Age of Climate Change"[16] argues that, for architecture to become sustainable, it needs to embrace principles that ensure an immediate connectedness between regional resources and craft construction techniques to contribute to a lasting and stable regional culture. It is a summary reckoning with the failures of technocratic modernism and a plea for an architecture in the coming age of climate change that acknowledges the unique qualities of place, the creative role of skilled labour, and the need for the presenting of physically constructed culture – as opposed to placeless virtuality – as the matrix for our existence:

> designing architectures in the age of climate change could give rise to the creation of authentic identities that are based primarily on specific responses to the sites in their climatic, physical, and socio-cultural dimensions. Skilled labor with knowledge of and experience with regenerative or recyclable materials is needed to translate sustainable designs into credible and legible tectonics and construction details. [...] Culture in the age of climate change should mark the beginning of the reversal of the process of autonomy to a process of synergy between nature and humankind. In this necessary transformation, existing buildings and settlements play the main role; new buildings and new settlements should be the exceptions.

Future generations of architects need to be nurtured in the culture of care, in the knowledge and skill of looking after the built fabric. The future hierarchy of importance should be

> maintenance and renovation first, before adaptation, addition and replacement. It means recognizing the built environment as a large part of civilization's heritage. [...] It means facing the reality of professional life that a large component of building activity in industrialized countries has to do with the maintenance and renovation of the built fabric. [...] It means elevating the task of the small intervention, the self-effacing renovation and adaptation to a cultural goal. [...] It means transferring knowledge and aesthetic sensibilities from the specialist to the people.[17]

Notes

1. Dagobert Frey, "Zur Wissenschaftliche Lage der Kunstgeschichte," in *Kunstwissen-schaftliche Grundfragen: Prolegomena zu einer Kunstphilosophie* (Vienna: R.M. Rohrer, 1946), 96–101.
2. Rhetorical figures of composition and of conception.
3. Paul Frankl, *Das System der Kunstwissenschaft* (Brno and Leipzig: Rudolf Rohrer, 1938).
4. Neil Levine, "The Book and the Building: Hugo's Theory of Architecture and Labrouste's Bibliothèque Ste- Geneviève," in *The Beaux-Arts in 19th Century French Architecture*, ed. Robin Middleton (Cambridge, MA: MIT Press, 1982).
5. Hermann Czech and Wolfgang Mistelbauer, *Das Looshaus* (Vienna: Löcker, 1976).
6. Wilfried Wang, "The Influence of the Wiegand Haus on Mies van der Rohe," *9H*, no. 2 (1980): 44–46.
7. Wilfried Wang, *Stadt werden – Mensch sein: Alvar Aaltos Kulturhaus und Hans Scharouns Theater in Wolfsburg als Leitbilder der heutigen Architektur* (Wolfsburg: Institut für Museen und Stadtgeschichte, 2000).
8. Wilfried Wang, "The Transcendence of Architecture," in *O'NFM_2: St. Petri,* ed. Wilfried Wang (Berlin: Wasmuth, 2009), 14–22.
9. Wilfried Wang, "Architecture as an Extension of Life," in *Architect Sigurd Lewerentz: Vol. 1*, ed. Claes Dymling (Stockholm: Byggförlaget, 1997), 40.
10. Wilfried Wang, "Elusive Ideals: Manu-Facture and Small Towns," in *Modulus 22: Crafts and Architecture*, The Architectural Review of the University of Virginia, ed. Mason Hollier (Charlottesville: Disosway, 1998), 40–53.
11. Wilfried Wang, "The Lightness of Democracy," in *O'NFM_5: Philharmonie*, ed. Wilfried Wang (Berlin: Wasmuth, 2013), 13–22.
12. Wilfried Wang, *O'NFM_7: E.1027* (Berlin: Wasmuth, 2017).
13. The full-scale installation of the Master Bedroom from Eileen Gray's E.1027 was exhibited at the School of Architecture, the University of Texas at Austin (autumn 2017), subsequently at the Akademie der Künste in Berlin (summer 2019), the Faculty of Architecture, University of Porto (autumn 2019), and at the Basque Institute of Architecture (summer 2021).
14. Wilfried Wang, "Transformations and Paradigms: On the Built Works of TEd'A arquitect-es," in *El Croquis*, vol. 196, edited by Cecilia Fernando Márquez (2018): 184–205.
15. Wilfried Wang, "Sustainability is a Cultural Problem," *Harvard Design Magazine*, no. 18 (Spring/Summer 2003): 1–3.
16. Wilfried Wang, "Site-Specificity, Skilled Labor, and Culture: Architectural Principles in the Age of Climate Change," in *Modern Architecture and the Lifeworld: Essays in Honor of Kenneth Frampton*, ed. Karla Cavarra Briton and Robert McCarter (London: Thames & Hudson, 2020), 53–63.
17. Wilfried Wang, "The Education of an Architect," *Domus*, no. 1018 (November 2017): 6–11.

Bibliography

Czech, Hermann and Wolfgang Mistelbauer. *Das Looshaus*. Vienna: Löcker Verlag, 1976.
Frankl, Paul. *Das System der Kunstwissenschaft*. Brno and Leipzig: Rudolf M. Rohrer Verlag, 1938.
Frey, Dagobert. *Kunstwissenschaftliche Grundlagen: Prolegomena zu einer Kunstphilosophie*, Vienna: Rudolf M. Rohrer Verlag, 1946.

Levine, Neil. "The Book and the Building: Hugo's Theory of Architecture and Labrouste's Bibliothèque Ste-Geneviève." In *The Beaux-Arts in 19th Century French Architecture*, edited by Robin Middleton. Cambridge, MA: MIT Press, 1982.

Wang, Wilfried. "Site-Specificity, Skilled Labor, and Culture: Architectural Principles in the Age of Climate Change." In *Modern Architecture and the Lifeworld: Essays in Honor of Kenneth Frampton*," edited by Karla Cavarra Briton and Robert McCarter, 53–63. London: Thames & Hudson, 2020.

———. "Transformations and Paradigms: On the Built Works of TEd'A arquitectes." *El Croquis*, vol. 196, edited by Cecilia Fernando Márquez Cecilia, 184–205. Barcelona: El Croquis, 2018.

———. *O'NFM_7: E.1027*. Berlin: Wasmuth Verlag, 2017.

———. "The Education of an Architect." *Domus*, no. 1018 (November 2017): 6–11.

———. "The Lightness of Democracy." In *O'NFM_5: Philharmonie*, edited by Wilfried Wang, 13–22. Berlin: Wasmuth Verlag, 2013.

———. "Sustainability is a Cultural Problem." *Harvard Design Magazine*, no. 18 (Spring/Summer 2003): 1–3.

———. *Stadt werden – Mensch sein: Alvar Aaltos Kulturhaus und Hans Scharouns Theater in Wolfsburg als Leitbilder der heutigen Architektur*. Wolfsburg: Institut für Museen und Stadtgeschichte, 2000.

———. "Elusive Ideals: Manu-Facture and Small Towns." In *Modulus 22: Crafts and Architecture*, The Architectural Review of the University of Virginia, edited by Mason Hollier, 40–53. Charlottesville: Disosway, 1998.

———. "Architecture as an Extension of Life." In *Architect Sigurd Lewerentz: Vol. 1*, edited by Claes Dymling. Stockholm: Byggförlaget, 1997.

———. "The Influence of the Wiegand Haus on Mies van der Rohe," *9H*, no. 2 (1980): 44–46.

CHAPTER 21

Tracing Álvaro Siza's Traces: To Fabricate A Construction of Time

Paulo Providência

Consider a place: presence of outlines, sketches, fictions, apparitions, X-rays of thoughts. Meditations on the meaning of erasures. To fabricate a construction of time.
—John Hejduk, 1986

The Catalan architect Carlos Martí once wrote that formwork is to the arch what theory is to architectural practice: an auxiliary construction that is no longer necessary when the arch is completed; as a final form, only the arch has the right to appear, not the formwork that allowed its construction.[1] Architectural tracings are like the formwork of architectural design: they exist as supporting elements for design construction – but when the architectural work is finished, the tracings that ruled the architectural design are no longer needed.

However, there is a fallacy in this reasoning: the formwork for construing the arch is something that we previously know – we know precisely the radius of the arch that we want to build, and we know the arch's form in advance – but thinking about tracings, it is quite the opposite. Through tracings, we assert the site's geometric modulations, we discover new relationships between parts and whole in the project, and we draw lines that construct the architectural form – tracings are constructions in time revealed by inscriptions on tracing papers, overlapping other traces. Therefore, as an architectural generative tool, why should we hide the traces that allowed the form to appear? Should architecture not aim to construct a theory of practice, a theory coming from architectural tracings, instead of a theory previous to the practice?

The following lines search for the role of tracings in crafting the design process of Álvaro Siza in the 1980s, how tracings are produced, and what tracings produce in Siza's design process through time.[2] Deeply related to projective geometry[3] and fundamental in architectural design practice since at least the sixteenth century, tracing drawings have a specific role in that process, in parallel with hand-drawn sketches, perspective drawings, detailed and constructional drawings, projective design, and annotations about design motivations.

Writing, Sketching, Tracing, Drawing

Architectural layout is the set of lines that configure the rules of a given design drawing or architectural representation. The Portuguese word *traçado* is ambiguous in that it refers to the past participle of the verb *to trace* or to a noun that refers to the geometric qualities of a drawing or representation. Conversely, the word *tracing* in English means a process of drawing and overlapping lines that configures certain graphic information; in that language, the word also has a meaning of *trace, mark, follow-up,* or *copy*, which is not unreasonable considering the design process as a dynamic event, subject to the pursuit of *clues* or *marks*; in the case of the French language, we have two words, *tracé* as outline (like in Portuguese) and épure, a word that designates what we call *tracing*, meaning the clearance of drawing in the design process, *cleaning up.*

In the past, when *tracing paper* was still in use, making pencil traces on paper allowed its progressive correction, or transformation, by repeating the gesture on translucent paper over the previous drawings. The design layers were physically constituted by the overlapping sheets of tracing paper, with the upper sheets showing the purified versions of the traces buried on the lower levels.

Among many other architectural representations, tracing drawings have a specific role in the design process, as they incorporate the characteristics attributed by Bruno Latour to architectural drawings, being "immutable, presentable, readable, combinable and mobile."[4] More than perspectives, which do not allow dimensions or architectural sketches to be read, and which present specific aspects of the architectural object, architectural tracings give precise geometric information that would allow us to construct the building, and vice versa: through the survey of a specific building, we can get back architectural representations and deduce the tracings as explicit geometric rules.[5] Therefore, the objectivity of tracings can be translated as "form information," "readable order," "rules to be respected," "instructions about how to build," or as "drawing discipline." [6] Order seems the main subject of drawing tracings on a blank sheet of paper. In a time of many possible orders – fractal and non-Euclidian geometries – what can we learn from the construction of tracings in Siza's projects?

Álvaro Siza's work is known, among other things, for incorporating tracings as contextual elements in the design project; in fact, he "starts a project when he visits a site,"[7] meaning that the site visit is the necessary impulse to start the drawing process. This "trace" of his architectural composition is deeply related to construing the project through line drawings – abstract lines compose the form of the building, articulating the urban context with the programme or architectural aim, tectonic readings and topological relations. "Siza's line as geometry, contour, and profile thus merges the tectonic and the topological," says Peter Testa or, in Siza's own words: "ideas come to me without materiality, lines on a sheet of paper."[8]

The geometric orthographic projection drawings have a dialectical relationship with the sketches drawn in the sketchbook, as if each complement and tests the other. "Order is the approach of the opposites,"[9] would be valid also in the case of complementary systems of representation. And this "double" approach would be a way of overcoming the division between subjective and objective, sensation and communication, expression and rule, subject and object. According to Peter Testa, Siza's *cadernos* (sketchbooks) are spaces for multiplicity in perception, through multiple views, turning things into objects: "An attitude toward latent multiplicity in perception is evident as multiple views of either the same object or multiple objects occupy the same page. He turns things into objects through repeated drawing, positioning, and scaling."[10]

Architectural drawings, in the design process of Siza, are the abstract lines shared with his collaborators in order to construct the project, as he "wouldn't like to execute (the project) with his own hands. Nor even to design alone, because it would become sterile. The body-hand and mind and everything – doesn't fit the body of each one. And there's no autonomous part."[11] However, those drawings are subjected to scrutiny. The architectural sketches, produced by Siza in sketchbooks, are a way to scrutinise the table tracing drawings.

June 1985 / The Walled Garden of Quinta Da Póvoa: Bringing Context to the Drawing Table

When Siza initiated the project for the Porto Faculty of Architecture, the crossings of fast-traffic road accesses with urban streets, a panoramic road, and rural paths generated a particularly complex situation, due to their diversity of scale, purpose, or time of construction. In addition, the fragmentation caused by the *percements* operated by the access roads to the bridge gave rise to clues to difficulty of access or that they conflicted with each other. But, as Álvaro Siza says, "the essential problem is to be able to connect different things because the city today is a set of very different fragments."[12] The first "fragment" for the installation of the University of Porto Faculty of Architecture in the early 1980s consisted of the lot of walled land at Quinta da Póvoa, which included a house, a garden, and some stables.

The difficulties with starting a design proposal, with drawing the first traces over a blank sheet of paper, as Siza used to say, is maybe a reason to begin a project through reading the historical charts of a given place. A photograph of Siza leaning over a big chart in his office when he was starting the design proposals for a project in Berlin in the 1980s, is the best image of this initial process of site reading (fig. 21.1). Reading and interpreting historical charts give clues about the rhythms of the cadastre and land parcelling, the peculiarities of a topographic situation, the overlapping of historically diverse urban fabrics, the inflexion of the tracing of a street or boulevard, and the physical history of a

Fig. 21.1 Álvaro Siza working in his office in July 1983, when he was participating in Berlin Kulturforum Competition. Photograph: Brigitte Fleck.

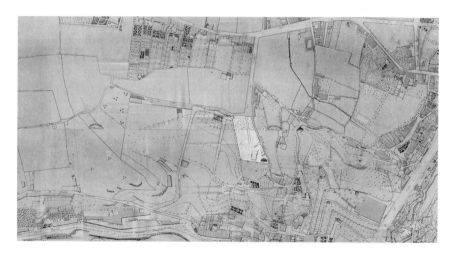

Fig. 21.2 Extract of the Topography Chart of the City of Porto by Telles Ferreira, 1892.

place (fig. 21.2).[13] The annotations, drawings, and sketches were later translated into architectural drawings and tracings, and those marks became "measurable, editable, comparable" plan drawings. Tracings fix spatial relationships of the site through topographic peculiarities; the analogue drawing produced on the desk should be as rigorous as possible and communicate with certainty the spatial and geometric relationships of the site. Marks and traces chosen among a diversity of topographic signs are the foundations for the design because "in difficult terrain we know to choose the place where to put our feet."[14]

Particular attention to the set of elements that make up houses and annexes in Quinta da Póvoa (stables, greenhouse) are revealed in the careful rehabilitation and extended to the arrangement of the gardens. The urgent need to build a new pavilion was to be a determining element in the design of the complex future expansion. Its placement at the north end of the lot, pressed against the boundary wall, allows the remaining garden to be freed and the internal area between the house and pavilion to be polarised (fig. 21.3). The tracings of the two volumes of the Carlos Ramos Pavilion converge in two corners of the main house, accentuating the house–pavilion polarisation. On the west wall, there is a large window opening over the grounds of Quinta da Esperança – at that time not yet assigned to the Faculty of Architecture. To the north side, the building has a small balcony, looking over the wall, with a view of the highway coming from Arrábida Bridge.

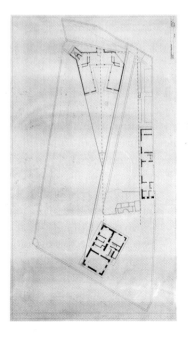

Fig. 21.3 Tracings of the Carlos Ramos Pavilion. Archive Arqt⁰ Álvaro Siza. Col. Fundação de Serralves – Museu de Arte Contemporânea, Porto. Donation 2015.

The north-east access provided for the project was to be carried out through a mediation space, reusing a small castellated evocative construction, which would constitute a polarisation with the belvedere at the south-west end of the plot, over the landscape of the mouth of the Douro River.

September 1986–January 1987 / Protocols of Communication: Sketching and Tracing the Quinta Da Esperança

Soon after the completion of the Carlos Ramos Pavilion at Quinta da Póvoa, Siza started developing the project for the new Faculty of Architecture on the grounds of Quinta da Esperança. The contract for the project was signed in September 1986, with the development of the project scheduled in four phases: programme, base project, execution project, and exterior spaces project. The architect in charge at his office was Peter Testa, who developed the designed programme, and during a full year, a hectic process took place.[15] Most probably all the initial drafts are drawn by Testa, as the project protocols followed the project of Malagueira. A blank A4 sketchbook served as a diary for Siza, in which he drew all the ideas and annotations concerning the project, like sections, spatial, and topographic relationship of volumes, measures and sizes, spatial modulation, openings and facades. "The *cadernos* document inquiry into the form of things,"[16] as Testa says. These sketches were then passed on to the architect in charge, in order to test the design through rigorous drafts or models. Regular orthographic projections were then produced, searching the design translations of the sketched drawings, and introducing the necessary spatial modulations and tracings. The process is reciprocal: sketched volumes and drawings proceed the necessary rigorous representations and vice versa, those drawings triggering the impulse to new sketches, perspectives, and volume articulations.

Sets of layout drawings, organised by floor (first, second, third, and fourth floor) and incorporating the main south facade and a section, seem to punctuate the free expression drawings, exploring the disposition, internal functional organisation, and partitions of the volumes. Four series of complete versions (the four floors, sections, facades) were then produced.[17] The translucency of the tracing paper allows the drawings to be superimposed, showing the vertical continuity (stair columns, structure) and expression of the volumes.

The first sketches produced by Siza translated into elemental orthographic drawings, focusing on the construction of a cloistered volume at the northern limit of the terrain, a reference to the bishop's palace built over the cathedral's cliffs. A set of volumes appears at the southern limit on the panoramic road, and the boundary wall of the Quinta da Póvoa plot consistently appears as a fundamental reference in the construction of the project (fig. 21.4). In addition, the volume of the Quinta da Póvoa House is taken as an ordering element for the volumes of the new programme.

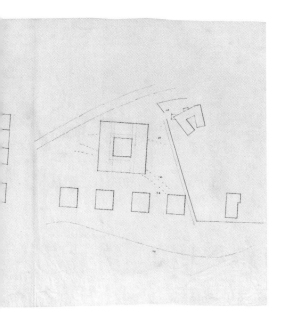
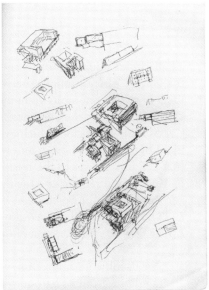

Fig. 21.4   First Studies for the FAUP Building, 1986 – 1987. Archive Arqtº Álvaro Siza. Col. Fundação de Serralves – Museu de Arte Contemporânea, Porto. Donation 2015 and CCA.

The various designs consider the fragmentation of the volumes to the south side and certain forms of continuity, construing a wall or barrier to the north side. An "iterative practice of drawing renders familiar objects as abstract."[18] The volumetric opposition corresponds to a programmatic one: the southern volumes would include the design studio and lecture rooms, and the north side would include the collective programmes, such as the auditoria, library, museum, the school offices, and the cafeteria. The difficulty in linking to the northern volume convincingly led to the design of a patella, linking the two directions of the north wall and causing a deviation in the volume of the library, allowing the west facade of Carlos Ramos Pavilion to be seen. Thus, the geometry of the layout of the faculty, in its various design versions, starts from the two elements that constitute the polarities of Quinta da Póvoa: the Carlos Ramos Pavilion and the house of Quinta da Póvoa. The alignments of the two paths converge at the west limit of the Quinta da Esperança lot, close to the viaduct of the highway. "Arguably, the author [Siza] cares less about the objects themselves than about their relations; their compositional structure is what matters."[19]

June 1987 / Iterations: Sense-making, Tuning Geometric Tracings

After approving the design programme, the second design moment, the base project, started, fine-tuning the proportions and connections of the January drawing (fig. 21.5). The autonomous volumes at the south side become rectangular instead of square, due to interior arrangements; the patella becomes a half-circle building (the museum building), joining the auditoria galleries to the library. Three fundamental strokes appear in the composition: the alignment of the autonomous volumes to the south by the volume of the house of Quinta da Póvoa; the alignment, originating in the south-east corner of the Carlos Ramos Pavilion, which extends perpendicular to the west wall containment of Quinta da Póvoa, and which affirms this alignment in the volumes that delimits the set to the north; and the outline of the coordinating hinge between that direction and the direction of the library volume, delimiting the central space to the north.

The opposition between the continuity of the north and south volumes can be seen as an expression of various cultural references, according to Testa:

> The Faculty of Architecture posits a coexistence of typologically unrelated buildings, from its baroque enchainment of institutional spaces that form a boundary to the north to its neoclassical and modernist studio pavilions overlooking the Douro River. In the *cadernos*, it is not each thing separately but all things separately that form a whole understanding of individual yet not isolated types.[20]

A geometric drawing produced on the drawing table resumes the main tracings that the project should respect. We don't know when it was produced, but as *pavilion* was written by hand in English, we suspect that it was drawn by Peter Testa. Due to its abstract nature, an interpretation is needed. Three lines define

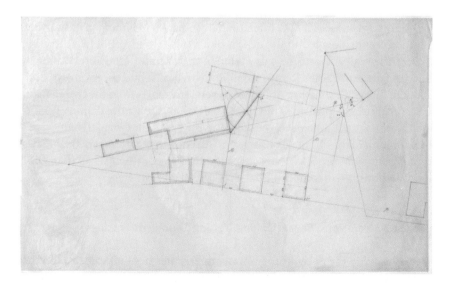

Fig. 21.5   Study of the FAUP Building, June 1987. Archive Arqtº Álvaro Siza. Col. Fundação de Serralves – Museu de Arte Contemporânea, Porto. Donation 2015.

a direction, with inscription of the word *muro* (wall); a circle is inscribed in those three lines, and a fourth line crosses the centre of the circle; this line has the word *casa* (house). A fifth line, with a diverse direction, and with the word *pavilion*, refers to the direction of the main west wall of the Carlos Ramos Pavilion; the line includes a small triangle, which in fact is the entrance of the pavilion. This line gives a clue to the purpose of the drawing: to join the west wall of the pavilion with the tracings of the west wall of the house of Quinta da Póvoa and the west wall that defines the limit of Quinta da Esperança. In addition to the lines, two dashed lines included in the central circle report the two earth terraces of Quinta da Esperança, which would be incorporated in the central square of the project. This drawing resumes the main directions of the Faculty of Architecture tracings (fig. 21.6).

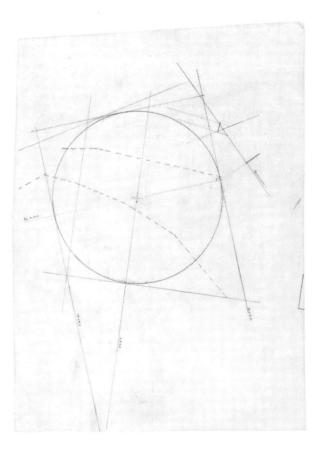

Fig. 21.6   Main directions in the FAUP Building. Archive Arqtº Álvaro Siza. Col. Fundação de Serralves – Museu de Arte Contemporânea, Porto. Donation 2015.

October 1987 / Tracings as Instructions for Building – Sending Back Tracings

After setting the detailed tracings between the north and south volumes, the project of the exterior spaces was produced. The exterior spaces, including the connections between the various elements (walled garden of Quinta da Póvoa, western access close to the highway bridge, links with the panoramic route and public walk), were then subjected to a detailed construction project that explored the expression of granite masonry retaining walls, pavements, and the paths that conduct the overall structure. A new layout of the Panoramic Road, completed in October 1987 and negotiated with the author of the general plan, was designed, allowing the expansion of the platform necessary for the implantation of the southern volumes.

A *folie*, close to the Panoramic Road viaduct, respecting the pedestrian access layout of the general plan in the west, was designed. This *folie*, inserted in the system of pedestrian spaces, replicates the north-east entrance of Quinta da Póvoa, showing some similarities with the Quinta da Conceição reception yard, a project by Fernando Távora from the 1960s. A set of platforms starting from the *folie* and progressing to Quinta da Póvoa were incorporated into the project, taking the west wall of the Quitan da Póvoa lot into account. The central platform in particular is placed at an accurate level in relation to the sidewalk, making its entire length visible from the entrance.

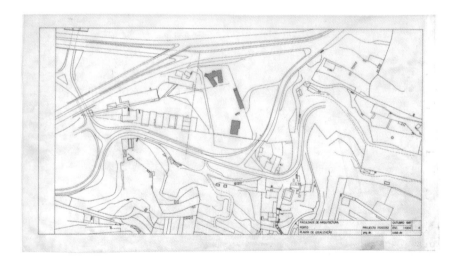

Fig. 21.7   Study of the FAUP Building in the context, October 1987. Archive Arqtº Álvaro Siza. Col. Fundação de Serralves – Museu de Arte Contemporânea, Porto. Donation 2015.

The tracings of exterior spaces are resumed to the most elemental, bringing basic instructions to the implementation of the volumes on-site. They include perpendicular lines, convergent lines in a node or a point, rebatement, but also rotation, translation, transfer, symmetry. The operations implied in the geometric projections are set as rules for drawing construction (fig. 21.7).

The variable dimensions of the tracing paper caused by humidity implies strategies of drawing based on a set of geometric rules that can, by analogy, be transposed to the implantation of volumes and platforms in a specific place. The circle of bringing the lot, terrain, or topography onto the drawing table is now sent back from the drawing table to the lot, terrain, or topography.

Concluding Remarks

Architectural traces appear in Álvaro Siza's projects as a particular moment of linking architectural and urban form to the social, cultural, and physical context. As a territorial inscription, the layout emerges as (1) an incorporation of the paths of the inhabitants of the urban space (features), (2) a technique for rescuing the past by affirming settlement archaeologies (readings of the territorial palimpsest), (3) a recording of tensions and negotiations of the project with the territorial management institutions or promoters (the plan-project conflict), (4) a mnemonic for local architectural references, and (5) an element of linkage of the landscape to the memory of physical places (orography, topography, among others).

In the design process, outlines are a form of self-knowledge, a dialogue with oneself, an affirmation that is privately tested before being publicly declared. And in the design studio, the most obvious way to test the layout is to transmit it: to the collaborators who will follow it as a design rule in the production of drawings and models or a geometric norm that surpass and direct the myriad of options and decisions; to the specialist engineer, who needs it to calculate his infrastructure; to the foreman who cannot do without it, through a set of lines, to replicate the designed alignments; to the executors or workers, who see in it the geometric rule needed to perform their task. Traces are elements of mediation between the project and work, but they are also elements of mediation between the various actors in the processes of planning, design, and execution, and this mediation implies the sharing of codes of spatial representation, codes of geometric construction, a set of design instruments only accessible within the design process.

Notes

1. Carlos Martí Arís, *La Cimbra y el Arco* (Madrid: Fund. Caja Arquitectos, 2008).
2. The essay is based on a detailed study of the sketchbooks at the Álvaro Siza Fund at Canadian Centre for Architecture AP178.S2.248 (May 1987), AP178.S2.256 (August 1987), AP178.S2.257 (August 1987), AP178.S2. 260 (September 1987), and the drawing folders of the Álvaro Siza Fund at the Serralves Museum: PT-FS-ASV-16 PT-FS-ASV-18, PT-FS-ASV-19, PT-FS-ASV-19(2).
3. Robin Evans, *The Projective Cast: Architecture and Its Three Geometries* (Cambridge, MA: MIT Press, 2000), 107–121.
4. Bruno Latour, *"Les 'vues' de l'esprit." Une introduction à l'anthropologie des sciences et techniques*, quoted by Stalder infra. See online: http://www.bruno-latour.fr/node/296.html.
5. Robin Evans, "Translations from Drawing to Building," in *Translations from Drawing to Building and Other Essays*; Evans, *The Projective Cast: Architecture and Its Three Geometries*; Mario Carpo, *The Alphabet and the Algorithm*; more recently, Laurent Stalder and Andreas Kalpakci, "A Drawing Is Not a Plan," in *Architectural Ethnography*, edited by Momoyo Kaijima, Laurent Stalder, and Yu Iseki (Tokyo: Toto, 2018), 15–17.
6. Lorraine Daston and Peter Galison, *Objectivity* (New York: Zone Books, 2010).
7. Álvaro Siza, *Textos*, vol. I, Oito Pontos (Lisbon: Parceria A M Pereira, 2019), 22: "começo um porjeto quando visito um sítio."
8. Álvaro Siza, *Textos*, vol. I, Materiais, 36: "as ideias vêm-me imateriais, linhas sobre um papel."
9. Álvaro Siza, *Textos*, vol. I, Oito Pontos, 22: "a ordem é a aproximação dos opostos."
10. Peter Testa was invited to the programme *Find and Tell*, at the Canadian Centre for Architecture in November 2018, where the selected several sketchbooks by Siza. Please see "On Line: Álvaro Siza's Cadernos Pretos" – Peter Testa on the Álvaro Siza Fonds Sketchbooks/cadernos, at Canadian Centre for Architecture.
11. Álvaro Siza, *Textos*, vol. I, Oito Pontos, 23.
12. Álvaro Siza, quoted in Pierluigi Nicolin, *Álvaro Siza Professione Poetica/Poetic Profession* (Quaderni di Lotus #6. Milan: Electa, 1986).
13. In another context, when Siza was starting the plan for the expansion of the city of Évora, the site drawings in his sketchbooks (*cadernos*), photographed by Roberto Collová, also testify to the same interest in reading the main topographical signs, the undulations of the terrain, the territorial traces, the lines of force of the plan composition, made of paths, walks, and routes. In this case, we still have the drawings produced in the sketchbook, which were later brought to the office in Porto to start the design process. Those *cadernos* are now at Niall Hobhouse's "Drawing Matter" archive. In fact, Siza started to draw in *cadernos* from the Évora project on. He used to spend two days travelling from Porto to Évora every week and used to bring annotations on small pieces of paper, until one of his collaborators gave him a notebook and asked him to draw in that notebook. That is how the famous *cadernos* started.
14. Álvaro Siza, "Piscina de Leça da Palmeira," *Textos*, vol. I, 20.
15. See *A+U Álvaro Siza 1954–1988*, June 1989, extra edition; and *El Croquis, Álvaro Siza 1958–1994*, #68/69, 1994. Peter Testa was in charge of the basis and the concrete project, Adalberto Dias the detailed construction project, and Chiara Porcu the exterior spaces project.
16. Peter Testa, "Find and Tell: Peter Testa on Álvaro Siza," YouTube video, 30 November 2018, Canadian Centre for Architecture , https://www.youtube.com/watch?v=cInwou7BnR8.
17. The correspondence between sets of sketches in *cadernos*, and desk drawings, is not easy because finally both types of drawings were set in different archives. The project or desk

drawings were archived in Serralves Museum in Porto, and the sketches or *cadernos* were archived at the Canadian Centre for Architecture , so it is now difficult to compare them. At Canadian Centre for Architecture, related with the Faculdade de Arquitectura da Universidade do Porto buildings are the following sketchbooks: 197, 203, 204, 205, 207, 208, 209, 213, 220, 225, 226, 229, 238, 240, 243, 244, 246, 248, 251, 252, 256, 257, 258, 259, 292, 294, 301, 317, 318, 324, 325, covering a time period from February 1985 to January 1992.

18. Peter Testa, "Find and Tell: Peter Testa on Álvaro Siza," YouTube video, 30 November 2018, Canadian Centre for Architecture , https://www.youtube.com/watch?v=cInwou7BnR8.

19. Peter Testa, "Find and Tell."

20. Peter Testa, "Find and Tell.".

Bibliography

Angelillo, Antonio. *Álvaro Siza: Scritti di architettura.* Milan: Skira Editore, 1997.

Alves Costa, Alexandre. *Arquitectura Álvaro Siza.* Exhibition catalogue. Madrid: Ministerio de Obras Públicas y Urbanismo de España (MOPU), 1990.

Carpo, Mario. *The Alphabet and the Algorithm.* Cambridge, MA: MIT Press, 2011.

Daston, Lorraine and Peter Galison. *Objectivity.* New York: Zone Books, 2010.

Evans, Robin. *The Projective Cast: Architecture and Its Three Geometries.* Cambridge, MA: MIT Press, 2000.

Evans, Robin. "Translations from Drawing to Building." *Translations from Drawing to Building and Other Essays.* London: Architectural Association, 2003.

Lucas, Ray. "The Discipline of Tracing in Architectural Drawing." In *The Materiality of Writing: A Trace Making Perspective,* edited by C. Johannessen and T. Van Leeuwen, 116–137. London: Routledge, 2017.

Martí Arís, Carlos. *La Cimbra y el Arco.* Madrid: Fund. Caja Arquitectos, 2008.

Nicolin, Pierluigi, ed. *Álvaro Siza Professione Poetica/Poetic Profession.* Quaderni di Lotus #6. Milan: Electa, 1986.

——. "Il método di Siza." *Lotus International* #32 (1981).

Ramos, Sílvia. "Campo Alegre Cidade: da sua longa metamorfose." PhD diss., Faculdade de Arquitectura da Universidade do Porto, 2017.

Stalder, Laurent and Andreas Kalpakci. "A Drawing Is Not a Plan." In *Architectural Ethnography* edited by Momoyo Kaijima, Laurent Stalder, and Yu, 15–17. Tokyo: Toto, 2018.

Siza, Álvaro. *Imaginar a evidência.* Porto: Figueirinhas, 2004.

——. *Textos 01, 02, 03.* Lisbon: Parceria A M Pereira, 2019.

Testa, Peter. *The Architecture of Álvaro Siza.* Master of Science in Architecture Studies thesis, MIT, 1984.

——. *The Architecture of Álvaro Siza.* Porto: Faculdade de Arquitectura da Universidade do Porto, 1988.

——. *Find and Tell: Peter Testa on Álvaro Siza.* 30 November 2018. Canadian Centre for Architecture. https://www.youtube.com/watch?v=cInwou7BnR8..

Wang, Wilfried, ed. *Álvaro Siza: Figures and Configurations, Buildings and Projects 1986–1988.* New York: Rizzoli and Harvard University Graduate School of Design, 1988.

CHAPTER 22

Drawing as a Research Tool: The Case Of Villa Dall'Ava

Luis Burriel-Bielza

On 15 February 2018, the French Minister of Culture, Higher Education, Research and Innovation published a decree[1] introducing the special status of the "teacher-researcher" that was automatically granted to every lecturer and professor working within the National System of Architecture Schools. In an effort to narrow the gap between these institutions[2] and the universities, a certain number of changes were brought into play, the one mentioned above being crucial. As a consequence, any practising architect involved in design studios became a "researcher" and therefore needs now to comply with goals, criteria, and standards equally applied to, for example, historians. However, the architect's understanding of history is quite different. Carles Martí is well aware of this specificity when he reflects on the work of Enric Miralles:

> For the architect, the history of architecture is a history of questions and interests shared with those who have come before us. [...] While the writer engages this conversation with the authors and the texts that have preceded him through words, the practicing architect does so through drawing and construction.[3]

This new status points out questions, which nonetheless were already part of the pedagogical debate: How can practitioners actively contribute to research? Are there any research methods, means, or tools specifically related to their skills? Since the early stages of my career, I have developed my professional activity around three poles: teaching, practising, and researching. Besides selecting research subjects specifically linked to our field of expertise, it is my belief that exploring new research methodologies and tools would be a much more valuable contribution, because in the long term, these tools might be appropriated by others, transferred, and then applied to a wide variety of subjects.

Within the framework of the present publication, I would like to focus on one of the most powerful tools available to practitioners: drawing. I have chosen to refer to it as a verb, an "action," and I shall not only consider the final product in terms of format, medium, and technique but also the process as a method with specific implications. I will be talking about a particular kind of drawings, not those produced during the design process, but those generated in the analytical process, travelling from real space, where the building exists and has been given a dimension, onto a thinking space. The opening page of *Les cahiers Forces Vives* collection published by Jean Petit, trusted editor of Le Corbusier, starts off with this statement: "we always need to say what we see, but above all, the most difficult thing, we always need to see what we see."[4]. This quote belongs to Charles Peguy and first appears in an issue of the 1953 *L'Art Sacré* journal, which Corbusier kept in his personal library.[5] The sentence brings to light the main goal behind any research drawing: it allows us to understand what is already in front of our eyes. Whereas a written discourse also serves this purpose, as practising architects, we use the tools that are at the heart of our discipline. The kind of drawing that I am looking for should have the same capacity as, for example, the "photographic rifle" developed by Etienne Jules Marey that made time visible, to which Bruno Latour and Albena Yaneva refer in their article "Give me a gun and I will make all buildings move: an ant's view of Architecture." In the text, they also cynically state that architectural theory can be considered as "a rather parasitical endeavor that adds historical, philosophical, stylistic, and semiotic 'dimensions' to a conception of buildings that has not moved an inch."[6]

Methodology

As a hybrid practitioner, I conceive history more as a playground, as a field of forces, as a toolbox. From this position, analysing a project means to decipher and reveal its rules, its logic, its components, the pertinence of a specific solution within the design process, but mostly, the possibility of transferring any of these aspects into teaching or practising, not as a ready-made object, but as a collection of questions and spatial devices triggering new solutions, as an operational tool. A specific case study will allow me to delve deeper into the subject: Villa Dall'Ava, a single-family house by OMA in the outskirts of Paris (1984–1991). Even though the villa figures in an extensive number of publications, not a single critical study has ever been conducted based on archival research.[7] Not only does this material help us to understand the creative process but also the final proposal and its pertinence in relation to the original intentions of the author.

Plans, sections, and elevations, either existing or made for the purpose, are the most common graphic tools when designing a building. They are so universal that they are sometimes identified with the space itself. However, we should be aware that they are, in fact, an abstraction, a highly codified reduction of reality, interrelated with social, political, economic, and even geographical conditions. Olivier Meystre's work on Japanese representation methods[8] illustrates the perfect alliance between drawing and spatial perception. This observation pertains to the design process, but it can equally be applied when reading or analysing a given architectural project. There is a change when you move from the three-dimensional real world to the thinking space provided by a drawing, a two-dimensional support, for at that point, certain data need to be removed. If we include time in those parameters, we will agree that any kind of drawing is a biased form of perception. To bypass the typical analytical approach, I have pursued a different path, structured in two stages, and depending on a particular transfer: from real space onto virtual space, and then from the latter onto what I would call "space-montage" or "space-palimpsest." Mediating between them, computer drawing software has been deployed as a key player. Even though architectural offices have fully embraced it in the design process, in scientific research it has barely been taken it into account. As practitioners, 3D modelling is one of our tools, so it can be naturally integrated in this analytical process, allowing for a deeper understanding than orthogonal projections afford. Of course, the latter constitutes the basis to fully reconstruct the Villa, but we must not forget a crucial gap, because actions performed on a particular software are based on a different logic than those taking place in the real world. Virtual matter is extruded, intersected, joined, subtracted, trimmed. or split, whereas real matter is subject to operations such as digging, pouring, cutting, screwing, or welding. Yet, building experience and mastering technical details are essential knowledge that enable this transition. This first stage fully recreates the real construction process, from concrete foundations to finishing touches, including furniture, and it is based on archival execution documents and on-site visits. Each component is now perfectly identified, far from the abstraction of the orthogonal plan, which reduces every item to lines. This is not to underestimate the power of plans, since it is precisely this abstraction that leaves space for multiple interpretations during the design process. Furthermore, the virtual model gives us the opportunity to integrate options, solutions, or devices eventually discarded during the design process, offering a final version more faithful to the original intentions of the architect and thus better fulfilling its role regarding its contribution to the discipline.

Now, while this virtual model is not a cast object, but instead an assemblage of different pieces, there is still too much information, and of course, no meaningful drawings have yet been produced. Many other reading levels are embedded in this realistic 3D model, but they can only be properly identified through the careful study of the design process, based on archival documentation. Only when the crucial design questions are pointed out, when a hypothesis is established, we might have a hint of how to dissect the model again and then, selectively, how to erase unwanted or irrelevant information. We are now fully immerged into the second stage, travelling from "virtual space" onto this "space-montage." The final drawings produced in this research are

2D axonometric projections or perspectives, while omitting the orthographic projections, which have been rarely employed as a tool for understanding. Each selected point of view is not directly rendered by the software but exported as distinct 2D line graphics. All elements are first separated in independent layers, then reassembled with a different visual hierarchy in a final 2D Autocad drawing.

The choices of elements selected during this phase depend on the question we are dealing with, which is not just spatial but also intellectual. The composite drawing is not the product of an automated process, it is performed "through" but not "by" digital software.[9] The drawing transfers a myriad of elements that are, however, subjected to the laws of perspective. Not by chance, "to render," also means "to translate" from one place to another, but in this voyage, new meanings, logics, and reading levels emerge. Robins Evans points out a parallel between drawing and language, pointing out that "the substratum across which the sense of words is translated from language to language does not appear to have the requisite evenness and continuity; things can get bent, broken or lost on the way."[10] This gap is crucial, because it is precisely the distance from the real world that allows the researcher to test hypothesis. The software does not know what to select, where to cut, how to disassemble, or what to leave translucent. In this second stage, we have hijacked the software's rendering inner logic. It no longer travels to the real world, but in another direction, performing new functions related to the research goals already pointed out at the beginning of the paper. The realistic model was nearly as disorienting as the empty ocean chart in *The Hunting of the Snark* by Lewis Carroll.[11] These drawings, however, define a specific playground, a new cartography, which will formulate the question as well as the answer: What does the drawing reveal that the building cannot?

Limits

For most architects, the site plan simply locates the building in its immediate surroundings. However, in the early work of Miralles&Pinós,[12] it was redrawn at every stage of the design process, challenging and retracing legal plot boundaries by juxtaposing other urban elements to actively integrate them in a fruitful dialogue. These new limits were questioned and redefined depending on the issue at hand. The compositional structure and laws behind these drawings remind us of David Hockney's experiments on photography published in *Camera Works*,[13] which the architects had seen in New York. At Villa Dall'Ava, when we stand beside the bookcase of the wooden "equipped wall"[14] running through the ground floor (fig. 22.1), five domestic landscapes or "inner horizons" can be captured. They connect different parts of the house, including landings of the stairs and the ramp going up and down from the apartment, the hall, and the garage, but also specific parts of the garden. They set up the real limits of the Villa, as Rem Koolhaas points out:

the site was surrounded by walls; it was already a kind of interior. The small rectangle of the glass house represents the minimal footprint. It is only a preliminary enclosure; the real house ends at the walls, where the "others" begin.[15]

This drawing traces a map whose limits are defined and adjusted at a certain moment in space and time. Mapping and drawing both imply identifying different layers embedded in the real world and transferring them onto a flat surface, might it be a piece of paper or a fixed computer screen.[16] The scale is the outcome of an equation, relating the question we are addressing to the necessary amount of information and the dimensions of this flat physical medium. In computer drawings, we can zoom in or out as much as needed: they lack the scale that is necessary not only for the readability, but most important as an architect, for laying the relation to the dimensions of our body.

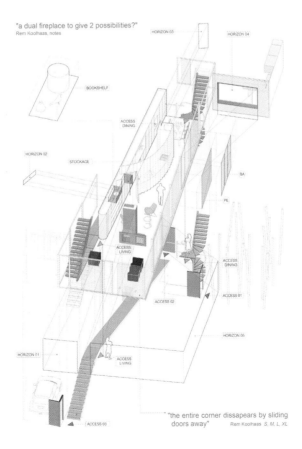

Fig. 22.1   Inner horizons from reading room. © Luis Burriel-Bielza.

Syntax

Most of the drawings used in this research use axonometric and conic projections. Historically, each one has been given a specific role. Alberto Pérez-Gómez and Louise Pelletier note: "Writers on modern architecture have overemphasized a polarity between perspective and axonometry, stating that while perspective is about the subject (a specific observer), axonometry is about the object."[17] In this way, the first one would be related with perception, and the second one with syntax. In linguistics, syntax deals with the assemblage of words to form a sentence. In our discipline, this term applies to identifying "devices": an assemblage of basic architectural elements, structured and arranged to comply to a specific intention (e.g. functional, symbolic, programmatic). We need to first dissect and pinpoint those elements, then determine the way in which they relate to each other and, most importantly, to understand their influence on domestic rituals. Besides their offering of a particular solution, we can test their real value by tracing their presence in other projects. Do they conform to a pattern? Can they be, therefore, framed, appropriated, transferred, and reproduced in other contexts with a different formal expression? When going up to the owner's apartment, either in Villa Dall'Ava or in Villa Lemoine (fig. 22.2), we will realise that they share the same intertwined basic elements: the stairs, with its overhanging steps; the beam, with a different geometry or material;

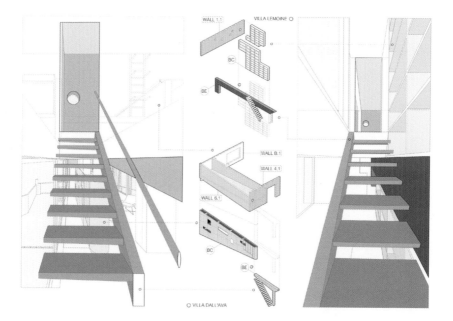

Fig. 22.2 View going up to master bedrooms Villa Dall'Ava and Villa Lemoine.
© Luis Burriel-Bielza.

the bookcase, slightly pushed to the back but always parallel to the ascending motion; and, most surprisingly, the bullseye window placed exactly at the top of the stairs. In the case of Villa Dall'Ava, it sneaks into the swimming pool blue waterscape; at Villa Lemoine, it offers a glance at the blue skyscape. This continuity helps to understand key issues that are basic to OMA's research on single-family houses, establishing a sort of a lineage. The pattern runs through several works where a specific assemblage of elements is not considered an isolated solution but a theme that can be varied upon. Syntax allows to determine a context, which in this case applies to the elements comprised in this particular device, as well as to its possible transformation throughout Rem Koolhaas's other work.

Perception

A next drawing (fig. 22.3) invites us to discover the effect of the fully mirrored surfaces of the main bathroom when lying inside the tub of Villa Dall'Ava. Its rather small size suddenly explodes, but mostly, a whole new set of relations is disclosed, laying multiple connections with other parts of the house. Koolhaas deploys the same strategy in the bathrooms of each single-family house built

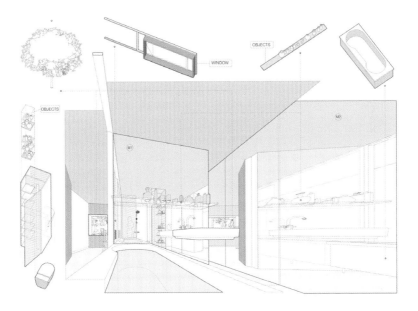

Fig. 22.3   View from the bathtub in the main bathroom. © Luis Burriel-Bielza.

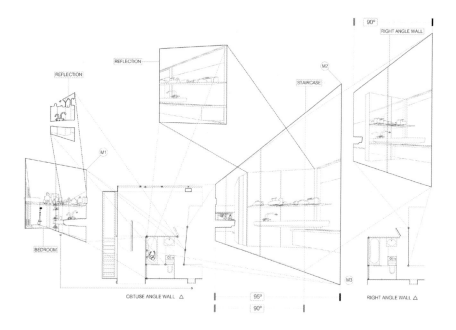

Fig. 22.4 Mirrored surfaces © Luis Burriel-Bielza.

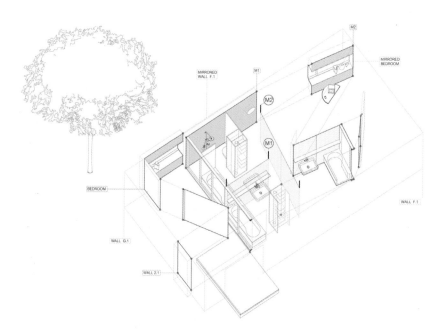

Fig. 22.5 Enlarged context created to re-enact the mirrored surfaces seen in fig. 22.4. © Luis Burriel-Bielza.

between 1984 and 1998,[18] this continuity adding value to this mirror experiment. Perspectives usually follow geometrical rules set up back in the Renaissance. However, certain manipulations can be integrated, as Le Corbusier had done in the past, for example, in one of his drawings for the Villa Meyer.[19] Researcher Victor Hugo Velásquez[20] revealed that it was built using three points of view aligned on the same axis but moving in depth, resulting in three distinct vertical segments, which are then reassembled, bringing us closer to a perception in movement. Throughout my work on Villa Dall'Ava, I chose not to stay within the thirty-five-degree angle related to human vision, instead trying to overcome the limits attached to our head's static position in order to enlarge our field of vision. However, we must be aware that the inner logic of the computer drawing software imposes a certain way of making and thinking. In the case of this particular perspective, the software alone was not able to render the effect of the reflecting surfaces (fig. 22.4). It needed to be combined with a plug-in, and the resulting image could not be exported as a 2D Autocad line drawing. Still, being trained in geometry, I could manually reproduce the effect of these mirrored surfaces by mirroring existing volumes symmetrically from these same surfaces. The resulting composite axonometric view (fig. 22.5) offers the virtual space necessary to recreate the mirror effect as seen in the perspective, thus showing this new unfolded context and learning how mirror surfaces works.

Time

These two drawings (figs. 22.6–22.7) deal with the relation between the inhabitant and the first pillar of the colonnade supporting the swimming pool. In the construction stage, the logic of the structure was fully readable. Loads travel from top to bottom through a collage of structural elements first studied as isolated solutions and then reassembled like a *cadavre exquis,* achieving new equilibrium. Once the house is finished, built-in furniture, namely the wooden wall, breaks up the continuity of the columns. The concrete structure is reduced to a minimum, without disappearing, subjected to an atomised, fragmented perception, present but visually devoid of its supporting condition. Its surface organises circulation, frames perspectives, regulates rituals, and imbues atmospheres, like any other non-supporting architectural element. The first column is veiled by the wooden wall rising up to the first floor. Only two fragments remain visible at two key moments that are separated in time: first, when we enter the house and then, when ascending the ramp. In this research, both perspectives and axonometric views undergo analogue manipulations, whereby the chosen angle forces some of the existing elements to be superimposed, preventing a correct reading. Rotation, erasure, fragmentation, displacement, detachment, or translucency offer options that the draughtsperson (who is simultaneously the researcher) must carefully discriminate in order to respect the original goal.

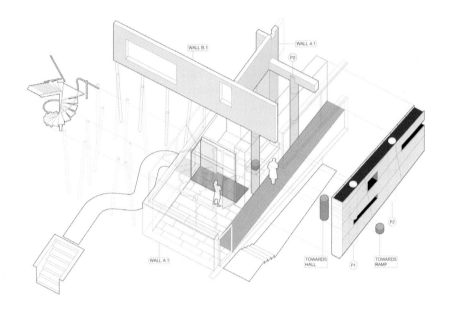

Fig. 22.6 Axonometric view of the entrance hall with the first column. © Luis Burriel-Bielza.

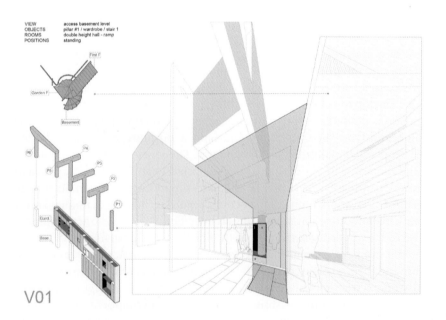

Fig. 22.7 View from the main entrance. © Luis Burriel-Bielza.

Two-dimensional Autocad line graphic elements have been identified, exported in separate layers, and superimposed later on in a new way so as to control the integration, readability, and hierarchy. Some of the layers were assigned a translucent condition, giving these drawings the power to enhance real perception. Ubiquity is now possible. Real space has been subjected to a form of temporal, perceptual, and conceptual compression that makes these composite drawings denser in terms of information and embedded meanings, and thus more efficient. As stated before, perspectives seem to convey real perception, but they are in fact building up a mental space, allowing reflection and understanding, a sort of space-palimpsest or space-montage constructed by different fragments assigned to different layers. This principle of superposition is exclusive to the drawing, enhancing its value, since text cannot handle it.

Conclusions

The drawings constructed for this research cannot be made automatically. They are not the result of a purely spatial question, but of an intellectual one. If we compare them with the space rendered automatically by the software (fig. 22.8), differences clearly arise. These alterations that I have proposed were necessary

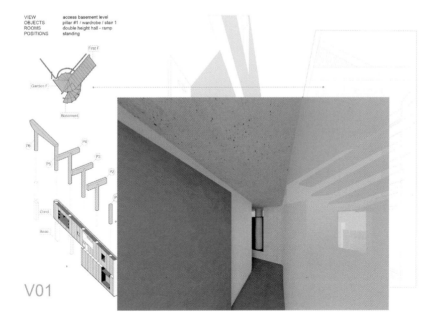

Fig. 22.8 Software automatically rendered view superimposed over the analytical drawing. © Luis Burriel-Bielza.

to understand certain relations or associations between all the elements. The drawings here strive to be readable by themselves, avoiding multiple interpretations. They do not represent anything, there is no symbolic meaning attached, they do not express something, and they reveal it. They allow to discover and define limits, to determine syntax, to enrich perception, and to introduce the measure of time. These are just a few examples of a much larger research project[21] that aims to test Rem Koolhaas's statement: "the house is not an object." At the end of this work, the drawings allowed me to further develop this assertion, but also to understand that the project is in fact the result of three different strategies where motion, furniture, views, and structure are correlated. These documents have unveiled the richness and the complexities attached to the built proposal. They have revealed the different layers embedded in the Villa, as well as identifying a whole range of architectural devices integrated within. Only through an analytical, drawing-based process were they made explicit, appearing as individual entities with specific dimensions. Even more, what we have learned from this research can certainly be transferred to teaching or to practice. First, the drawings are the outcome of a research methodology that can be re-enacted and applied to other case studies. Second, the devices and logics discovered in this building could function as a starting point for a design process applied elsewhere, where it can trigger new questions, offer new solutions, and stimulate new approaches.

Notes

1. Decree JORF n°0040 du 17 février 2018 - texte n° 22.
2. It is important to be aware that French architecture schools were born out of the May 1968 protests, detaching themselves from the Académie des beaux-arts. Therefore, they are organised according to principles and methods that differ from those of other higher education institutions.
3. Carles Martí, "Enric Miralles: la conversación como forma de conocimiento," in *Conversaciones con Enric Miralles*, ed. Carles Muro (Barcelona: Gustavo Gili, 2017), 87. Translation by the author.
4. Le Corbusier, *Le livre de Ronchamp. Le Corbusier* (Paris: Éditions Minuit, 1961). Translation by the author.
5. *L'Art Sacré*, "De quel esprit serez-vous ?," n° 1–2, September–October 1953.
6. Reto Geiser, *Explorations in Architecture: Teaching Design Research* (Basel: Birkhaüser, 2008), 88.
7. I would like to express my deepest gratitude to Talitha van Dijk, Head of the OMA Archive Department, who gave me full access to Villa Dall'Ava files.
8. Olivier Meystre, *Pictures of the Floating Microcosm: New Representations of Japanese Architecture* (Zurich: Park Books, 2017).
9. Architectural Association's Diploma Unit 15 has been exploring drawing as the main tool in their pedagogy for years. It is not surprising to learn that it declares itself as a "render-free zone." See Francesca Hughes, *Drawings that Count* (London: Architectural Association, 2013), 68.
10. Robins Evans, "Translations from Drawing to Building," in *Translations from Drawing to Building and Other Essays* (London: AA Documents, 1986), 154.
11. Lewis Carroll, *The Hunting of the Snark* (London: Macmillan, 1876).
12. See, for example, site plan for the new pedestrian bridge in Lérida, 1986, Benedetta Tagliabue, *Enric Miralles, Obras y Proyectos* (Milan: Electa, 1996), 81.
13. Lawrence Weschler, *David Hockney: Camera Works* (London: Thames & Hudson, 1984).
14. This term refers to the experiences carried on by Le Corbusier within the frame of his theory "the 4th wall": a partition frequently used in facades, thick enough to offer storage space (for clothes and books, for example). In the case of Villa Dall'Ava, it also integrates domestic appliances (such as kitchen appliances) and technical equipment.
15. Rem Koolhaas, *S, M, L, XL* (London: TASCHEN, 1995), 134.
16. In José Luis Borges's short story "On Rigor and Science," maps for the empire were made in a 1:1 scale to provide cartographers with the utmost precision. Cumbersome for later generations, they were abandoned, bound to disappear under the wind and the sun. The story is based on a concept found in Lewis Carroll, *Sylvie and Bruno* (London: Macmillan, 1889).
17. Albert Pérez-Gómez and Louise Pelletier, *Architectural Representation and the Perspective Hinge* (Boston: MIT Press, 1997), 317.
18. Villa Linthorst (1984–1988), Villa Dall'Ava (1984–1991), Villa Lemoine (1994–1998).
19. Le Corbusier, *Œuvre complete 1910–1929* (Zurich: Girsberger, 1937), 89.
20. Victor Hugo Velásquez, "Un dibujo de la Villa Meyer," *Massilia 2002, Anuario de estudios lecorbuserianos* (Barcelona: Associació d'Idées, 2002), 71–83.
21. Habilitation à Diriger des Recherches (Accreditation to Supervise Research), under the title "Voir comme choses les intervalles entre les choses," currently developed at the Université Paris-Diderot, CERILAC Research Laboratory.

Bibliography

Carroll, Lewis. *The Hunting of the Snark*. London: Macmillan Publishers, 1876.

Carroll, Lewis. *Sylvie and Bruno*. London: Macmillan Publishers, 1889.

Borasi, Giovana. *Besides History: Go Hasegawa, Kersten Geers, David van Severen*. Montreal: Canadian Centre for Architecture, 2018.

Eisenman, Peter. *Giuseppe Terragni. Transformations. Decompositions. Critiques*. New York: Monacelli, 2003.

Evans, Robin. "Translations from Drawing to Building." *Translations from Drawing to Building and Other Essays*. London: AA Documents, 1986.

Geiser, Reto. *Explorations in Architecture: Teaching Design Research*. Basel: Birkhäuser, 2008.

Goldsmith, Kenneth. *Displacement is the New Translation*. Paris: Jean Boîte Éditions, 2016.

Hughes, Francesca. *Drawings that Count*. London: Architectural Association, 2013.

Koolhaas, Rem. *S, M, L, XL*. London: TASCHEN, 1995.

Le Corbusier. *Le livre de Ronchamp*. Paris: Éditions Minuit, 1961.

Le Corbusier. *Œuvre complete 1910–1929*. Zurich: Girsberger, 1937.

Luscombre, Desley. *Architecture through Drawing*. London: Lund Humphries, 2019.

Martí, Carles. "Enric Miralles: la conversación como forma de conocimiento." In *Conversaciones con Enric Miralles*, edited by Carles Muro. Barcelona: Gustavo Gili, 2017.

Meystre, Olivier. *Pictures of the Floating Microcosm: New Representations of Japanese Architecture*. Zurich: Park Books, 2017.

Pérez-Gómez, Albert and Louise Pelletier. *Architectural Representation and the Perspective Hinge*. Boston: MIT Press, 1997.

Tagliabue, Benedetta. *Enric Miralles, Obras y Proyectos*. Milan: Electa 1996.

Velásquez, Victor Hugo. "Un dibujo de la Villa Meyer." *Massilia 2002. Anuario de estudios lecorbuserianos*. Barcelona: Associació d'Idées, 2002.

Weschler, Lawrence. *David Hockney: Camera Works*. London: Thames and Hudson, 1984.

CHAPTER 23

Facade Studies

Simon Henley

The nature of the wall or envelope has changed radically in the last fifty years. In the past, the construction of buildings had been vernacular, by which I mean governed or at least influenced by available materials, be that stone, clay, earth, or timber. The plan forms of buildings were dictated by both the availability of those materials and by their capacity to bear load and to span, and therefore shape and define space for shelter, storage, exchange and congregation. Furthermore, that causality was transposed to the face of the building, wherein ideas of shelter were perceptible. Despite changes in technology, a similar causality remained evident for much of the nineteenth and twentieth centuries, and the type of building and type of facade, in many ways, remained connected.

One aspect of technological culture has been to focus on the environment[1] or, at least, on the fabric and componentry used in response to it. Of course, buildings have always provided shelter from their environment to those who dwell in them. The ways used to devise shelter resulted in perceptible character: mass offering the possibility of stable temperatures in warm or cold climates, carefully sized and distributed windows,[2] and large eaves and canopies affording protection from the sun and the rain.

Modern technologies, fabrics, and systems evolved intermittently throughout the nineteenth and twentieth centuries, moving away from the handmade and substantial towards the technological and the lamina. This progression arguably reached its conceptual apotheosis in Buckminster Fuller's proposal for a geodesic dome over midtown Manhattan (1968), which reduced the construction of wall and roof to a single membrane. Graphically and geometrically, the architect's goal had hypothesised that there need only be a line separating inside and out. The High-Tech architects sought to promulgate this dubious correlation of ethic and aesthetic. Physically and conceptually, the building had evolved from one of substance (typically, walls) to an envelope. Not surprisingly, these glasshouses and membrane-clad buildings did not perform well and relied heavily on energy-intensive conditioning systems to create habitable interiors. Nevertheless, the damage was done; a technological conclusion of sorts had been reached, which revealed the facade not to be a cultural proposition, which had to do with history, but simply a technological device.

Recent intensification of concern for the environment, and more specifically and prosaically for performance, has led to assemblies that only appear like walls. The *wall* in this new guise is a complex configuration consisting of a number of layers or elements, some serving its performance and others its character, the latter potentially reduced to an arbitrary appearance. Inside, the envelope is divided into abstract and imperceptible technical systems: not matter, but a series of lines that perform discrete technological roles. Importantly, the reasoning that underpins these abstract elements has been separated from the sensible and discernible aspects of building.

The current technological concern for performance has displaced the art (*techne*) of construction. The absolute and abstract requirements of building physics translate into physical things – the various elements – that now constitute what is commonly called the building envelope. The cause and effect of this technology – that the skin performs as an environmental device on the building's perimeter – prevents materials from being used appropriately. In so doing, forms of construction – physical phenomena – to which we had become accustomed and which had been observed to work, have been lost. In other words, the perceptible (material), which had previously served an approximate (technical) role, has been lost. It seems the architect is deprived of reason.

"They are, above all, *built*"

A conscious study of the facade is a study of how architects bring meaning to material, as the below examination of projects, both by my practice Henley Halebrown and by others, will illustrate.

Chadwick Hall (2012–2016) for the University of Roehampton, comprising three student residences, developed into conscious research exploring the nature of the wall. The design involves the interplay of masterplan – which took pre-existing landscape features and used these to compose associations between buildings and their inhabitants – and wall. Both plan types and construction take their cue from the dual histories of the nearby eighteenth-century villas and the mid-twentieth-century blocks on the London County Council's Alton West Estate – the wall from the former and the frame from the latter.

The design encases conventional concrete structures inside load-bearing walls of brick piers and concrete beams.[3] Interiors are wrapped in heavy *ruins* that orient each student to the landscape, mediating between the private realm of the room and the common ground of the garden. The facade plays down the performative aspects of the enclosure by heightening the primitive and perceptual dimension of human experience, the *wall* becoming two walls, one technical, the other perceptible. The former encased by the latter. The brick piers, with their arrowhead plan, transvert and spatialise the wall. The construction realises a third condition, between interior and garden, which in effect becomes another building that frames another space. By contrast to congregation space and the collective experience that affords, this construction offers those who dwell in these rooms common experience – an isolated experience, but one that is repeated in the construction of the perimeter walls and spaces, which are common to all. Construction gives rise to forms of inhabitation, perception and social experience.

Not long after building Chadwick Hall, I visited Årsta Church (2006–2011) with its architect Johan Celsing. In it, I discovered another building that addresses the performative and cultural aspects of construction. The church is an extension to an existing building. The cube-like structure is founded directly on a rock outcrop and constructed from diaphragm walls of load-bearing brickwork. The interior of the church is a square room. The part of the wall that one can reach and touch is glazed brickwork, which thickens further at the base to form a bench. Above this terrestrial realm, the celestial: roughly mortared brickwork walls are coated with limewash and punctuated by substantial openings. In this space, there is just one window at eye level. The glass is set on the outside face of the wall revealing the metre-deep construction. This amplifies

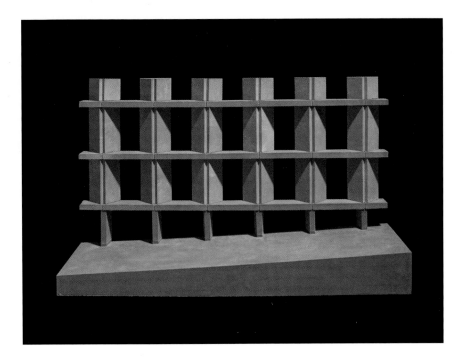

Fig. 23.1   Chadwick Hall, 2016, Henley Halebrown © Ståle Eriksen.

the depth of space and the amount of air within the wall construction required for structural stability and thermal insulation. Celsing managed to construct the building in such a way that it performs but also communicates approximately what it means to shelter the inhabitant using structural brickwork and a cavity of air at that latitude. Standing in the space, we spoke about the ethical dimension of the work – its appropriateness – and what Celsing called a "kindness"[4] for those who use his buildings.

What unites Årsta and Chadwick Hall is an ambition to make sense of the imperceptible aspects of construction and, in response, to build with load-bearing walls. "They are, above all, *built*."[5] But the way in which they are configured as a type of explicitly constructed liminal space serves two further equally important ambitions: the first, designed to orient its inhabitant to the natural world, to an awareness of our environment and notions of shelter; the other, to the idea of common experience and the social dimension of the facade. The plans for Chadwick Hall cluster students in flats and houses, and in so doing, provide a modicum of social structure for – by contrast to civic buildings, schools, and places of work – housing does not involve substantive congregation space and the collective experience that it affords. Could the facade offer an alternative? It is these three themes – *building*, nature and shelter, and social infrastructure – and their generative potential that characterise our thinking, our work, and this paper.

Fig. 23.2   Chadwick Hall, 2016, Henley Halebrown © Nick Kane.

Nature and Shelter

While Chadwick Hall marked a shift in emphasis from the plan type to the generative potential of the facade, this concern can be traced to two early adaptations made to existing buildings. The first, Shepherdess Walk (1997–1999), was originally built for industrial use, occupying a whole urban block surrounded by narrow streets. It was to be redeveloped as loft apartments to exploit the scale of industrial space in which the interior fulfils the role of synthetic exterior, so creating its context. Here, however, we made the addition of a pavilion on the roof of each apartment on the top floor. These offered an analogous architecture – a suburban house and garden – superimposed on the interiors below. Each was a simple oblong with three blank facades and an active one oriented south, east, or west. The facade consisted of an elementary system of modular parts – fixed panes of glass to see through and transmit light, a door to walk through, and a shutter for the passage of air – all of which could be rearranged in response to the eventual layout and inhabitation of apartment and garden.

The pavilion's linear plan orients internal space towards a primary aspect. Each facade is a constructed threshold mediating between the absolute conditions of interior and exterior. The connection to the natural world was made explicit – an approach that developed (unknowingly) the thinking of Ted Cullinan, whose Camden Mews (1963) orients the house away from the mews towards the afternoon sun, turning its back on the cold north-east winds.[6] While it remains in the city, the house has been abstracted from its urban situation. Instead, it is intimately associated with the elements and, more immediately, its garden. For Ted Cullinan, in the first few years, to build was simply to draw a line between inside and outside, so as to draw our attention to nature through the architecture.

Barry Gasson, John Meunier and Brit Andresen's building for the Burrell Collection (1983) does something similar to Cullinan's houses. They invite us to inhabit the edge of their building, and in so doing, to inhabit the woods outside. The facade screen is the architecture. It adopts the space outside, inside, and conceives of the inside itself as a canopy, much like the woods outside. The phenomenon stems from an experience that Meunier recounts from an early encounter with a Burrell artwork. Meunier realised that "the less we can put between the observer and the object, and also the more we were able to see the object in daylight, and in a natural setting, the better." This is what the Burrell does: illuminated by natural light, the artefacts are poised on the threshold with the natural world, and the visitor too; mind and body are exposed to the artworks and their architectural setting, unguarded and vulnerable, and as a result, more receptive to each artefact. With the Burrell Collection, the fabric of the woodland becomes the substance of the architecture, and the morphologies of landscape complement the intricacies of its interiors.

With the offices for Talkback (1999–2001) – like Cullinan and Gasson, Meunier and Andresen – we sought to draw attention to nature, but also to make sense of the social dimension of work. Whereas a new building offers a multitude of possibilities, adaptation asks of the architect: 'What might be different?' The project for the television production company concerned itself with the meta-functional configuration of a plan and how it relates to an institution and, more broadly, society. The process of making television programmes involves a small team researching ideas, some of which are translated into programmes by a larger cohort. The cloistered plan form was made in response to a collegiate approach to work and as a multistorey structure devised to unify the original buildings. This created an intimate place of work removed from the disturbances of the city. Windows that had previously only let in light and air but created a barrier between inside and out, were replaced by doors opening onto galleries that frame the garden. The office and the idea of work is associated not with the interior but with the captured landscape in which liminal space – the depth of the original wall and that of the gallery – is the prime generator of experience. The facade is inhabited and sociable and orients the inhabitant to the natural world due to their association, perception, and encounters with the garden and the weather.

Fig. 23.3   Talkback, 2001,
Henley Halebrown
© Nick Kane.

Over the next decade, we continued to adapt and design buildings, directing our thinking towards plan types and type forms in response to the idea of the institution. We also continued to explore the potential of the building perimeter, developing the idea of a *brim* (much like that of a hat), first for our unbuilt Letchworth Town Hall (2002–2003) competition scheme and subsequently the Junction Arts and Civic Centre in Goole (2005–2010). Letchworth Town Hall envisaged the adaptation of an existing building and the construction of two new ones. For each, the brim affords those outside the committee rooms and council chamber both shelter and proximity to the democratic process. The adaptations we made to these buildings worked through the adjustment of walls. With the cloister and the brim – both repeating archetypes for the practice – we extended the facade to encompass its immediate surroundings, to spatialise and inhabit it, and to temper the interior. In each of these projects, the facade directs us to the natural world, as opposed to simply demarcating synthetic spaces set apart from it.

Social Infrastructure – "The Wall as Living Place"[7]

More recently, we have designed a number of apartment buildings. In London, there are strict space standards not only for the interior of the dwelling but also for private outside space. In this situation, the configuration of the common parts – hallways, corridors, and staircases – does much to inform the type of building. Where possible, we remove the "common parts" from the interior and replace them with external circulation to generate a critical mass of outside space for social and sensible experience. The technological consequences of this decision in turn does much to characterise the architecture.

Two buildings on the Frampton Park Estate (2013–2021) follow this logic. The first, Taylor and Chatto Courts, proposes three villas, two of which are conjoined. The design brings together two architectural traditions, one that uses the wall to shape rooms, the other a frame to make platforms. The two offer parity (even in the UK climate) between a life lived indoors and one lived outside. The frames are oriented to fragments of lawn, binding the inhabitants to the unlikely parkland that separates the archipelago of buildings on the estate, with the buildings also negotiating between this landscape and the contrasting urban condition of the Victorian street. There is a playfulness in the way the design uses a balcony to create an entrance canopy and bridges to connect dwellings in one villa to the stairs and lift in another.

By contrast to the villas, Wilmott Court may be a palazzo. The frames that wrap around the surface of this building vary in depth in response to orientation, and quiet and busy thoroughfares moderate the presence of street life on the interior. The frame has a more fluid relationship to the mass of the palazzo, appearing as loggias on two facades and as pronounced stringcourses on the third.

At three to four storeys, the height of the buildings at Chadwick Hall permitted the relatively small differences in the thermal movement of the "warm"
concrete frame inside and the cold brick and precast concrete structure outside,
allowing for the construction of load-bearing walls. With the taller Taylor &
Chatto and Wilmott Courts, this would not be possible, so if we were again to
explore the construction of facades, they would need to be different. As before,
the masonry conceals an in situ frame but this time with all the paraphernal-
lia required to support brickwork, except where concrete frame and masonry
facade meet. Here, the concealed and visible frames are coupled together by
the loggia floor, and, as a consequence, the performative and perceptible layers
of the wall are divided between one frame and the other: the *warm* layers
of the wall supported by the concealed frame, the *cold* masonry supported
by the visible frame. Precast figures contrast with monolithic bodies of wild
bond brickwork. The facades and liminal space immediately adjacent to them
establish a dialectic between two types of space and two forms of construction.

Fig. 23.4   Wilmott Court,
Frampton Park Estate, 2021,
Henley Halebrown © David
Grandorge.

While the liminal structures at Frampton Park are precast, those for the Kings Crescent II (2017–) estate will be in situ. This more economical approach creates absolute parity between the frame within the building and the visible one outside. In this case, the external frame consists of two lines of columns and takes the form of a loggia moulded to the horseshoe shape of the courtyard, one cast adjacent to the other. Where there would once have been a single load-bearing wall, it is here to be constructed in two non-structural halves, one on the internal frame, the other on the external frame, on either side of the thermal line. The internal linings and performative layers of the facade are aligned with the internal frame whereas the brickwork that we associate with a wall bears on the concrete floor of the loggia and external frame, not the building per se.[8] The plan form, and the dependency of the facade on the loggia, is intended to emphasise the urban ensemble uniting new and existing buildings within the estate, orienting residents of the new building to one another, and attuning them to their southern aspect and the path of the sun.

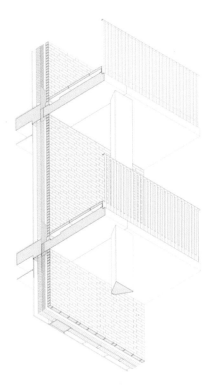

Fig. 23.5 Taylor & Chatto Courts, Frampton Park Estate, 2021, Henley Halebrown © Henley Halebrown.

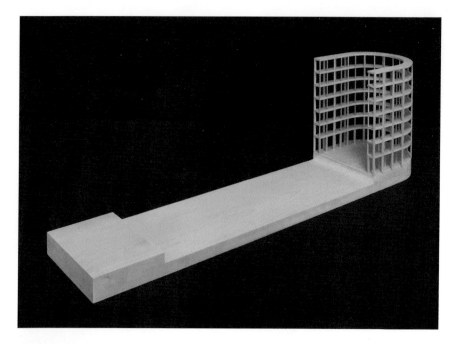

Fig. 23.6 Kings Crescent II, 2017–2023, Henley Halebrown © David Grandorge.

Fig. 23.7 Hackney New Primary School & 333 Kingsland Road, 2020, Henley Halebrown © Henley Halebrown.

So far in this paper, the social dimension of the facade has primarily been developed by coupling a structure to the building, and so inviting proximity and inhabitation. As shown in the last of these studies, Hackney New Primary School, the street elevation is constructed with a plinth as a bench. Much like the unfurled perimeter of a chapter house, this south-facing wall serves the casual encounters of parents at each end of the school day. Inside, the school's courtyard walls are sheltered by canopies. Beneath, there are various apertures and seats cut into the inside and outside of the 80 cm thick wall. The seats in the courtyard and bench on the street embed social patterns into the architecture of walls and thresholds. As the sociologist Eric Klinenberg writes, "Schools are organisations but they're also social infrastructures."[9] As he goes on to say, this has to do with how they are planned and built, which we might perhaps interpret as how thick the walls are. As Francesco Cacciatore writes, there is a history of "thickness"[10] dating back to the Egyptians and Romans, reinvented in the last century by Louis Kahn as an architecture of "hollow stones."[11]

The Useless Facade

In the 2019–2020 academic year, we directed our MArch studio[12] at the Kingston School of Art to the facade. What we termed *the useless facade* invited students to explore the generative potential of the facade. Their research led to some healthy confusion about the nature of a facade. For example, Gehry's House depends on the dialogue between the carcass of the original house, the carapace of the 1970s one, and the spaces between. Kahn's Salk Institute, Gillespie, Kidd and Coia's St Bride's Church, Stirling's Florey, and Piano+Rogers's Pompidou all disaggregate the facade and spatialise its properties. And Lacaton & Vassal's use of the proprietary greenhouse results in an architecture of interstices. Of all their precedent studies, Jørn Utzon's windowless windows facilitated by loggias at Can Lis and Can Feliz most successfully bind inside and outside, culture and nature.

The facade studies in our practice stemmed first from the adaptation of buildings, where the world outside was arguably of more interest than that inside. This led us to rethink the thresholds of buildings. The technique would superimpose a plausible typological reading that was dependent on the reciprocal connection between building and landscape. But any typological rereading was only possible with adjustments to the wall and the liminal space within and immediately beyond the wall. With the renovation project Talkback, the outside space could only be understood to be a cloister due to changes to the facade, and what followed was to continue to explore the reciprocity between facade and type.

The buildings, and the way in which they are constructed, can once again seek to be perceptible, appropriate and approximate instead of only performative, technocratic and laminate. Thickness does play a part, either in the wall itself (Chadwick Hall and Hackney New Primary School) or in the depth of the liminal structure (brim, cloister, loggia). The facades can be classified in three types: the load-bearing wall (a *ruin*), a wall bearing on a *cold* frame coupled to the inner frame, and a wall bearing on an independent *cold* frame. In each case, the work demonstrates that it is possible for a wall or facade to convey meaning through its composition and construction and so to be understood, not to stupefy. We comprehend it due to its construction, its potential for inhabitation, its capacity to orient the inhabitant to the outside world and to the elements, and so to demystify the environment. The facade's capacity to expose each of us to natural phenomena – consciousness breeds conscience – is in complete opposition to the prevailing technocratic response to the environment and the amoral citizen-consumer of buildings and space. Finally, the liminal properties of a wall may translate the facade into a form of social infrastructure.

Practice is by its very nature contingent. The sequence – practice, research and teaching – is one of design, reflection and discussion, and does, to a certain extent, reflect a shift from intuition to logic and reason. The wall will continue to be a conundrum but to focus on the facade, its liminality and generative potential in the design of buildings – type, construction, inhabitation, orientation to the natural world and role as social infrastructure – reactivates the ethics of both wall and building.

> I only wish that the first really worthwhile discovery of science would be that it recognised that the unmeasurable is what they're really fighting to understand, and that the measurable is only the servant of the unmeasurable; that everything that man makes must be fundamentally unmeasurable.[13]
> —Louis Kahn, 1969

Notes

1. Kate Nesbitt, in her introduction to an excerpt from Karsten Harries's book *The Ethical Function of Architecture*, restates his argument "that the 'objectivity' characteristic of modernity has contributed two unfortunate ideas," one of which is, "that architecture is part of a technological culture that demands (Corbusian) 'machines for living,' instead of (Heideggerian) dwellings." Karsten Harries, "The Ethical Function of Architecture," in *Theorizing a New Agenda for Architecture: An Anthology of Architectural Theory 1965–1995*, ed. Kate Nesbitt (New York: Princeton University Press, 1995), 392.
2. Andrea Palladio, *I Quattro libri dell'architectura*, trans. Isaac Ware, taken from Dean Hawkes, *The Environmental Imagination* (Abingdon: Taylor and Francis, 2008).
3. Conventionally, shelf angles bear the weight of a brick skin. The shelf angles and masonry in turn place a cantilever effect on the concrete frame, increasing the quantities of concrete and steel reinforcement. So the cost of loadbearing brickwork proved to be interchangeable with that of additional concrete and steel.
4. Johan Celsing, conversation with author during visit to building, 19 June 2018.
5. Vincent Scully, "Introduction," in David B. Brownlee and David G. De Long, *Louis Kahn: In the Realm of Architecture* (New York: Rizzoli, 1991), 12.
6. Camden Mews develops the plan type of his earlier Horder House in Hampshire and the Marvin House in California, both designed in 1959 and constructed in open landscape.
7. Francesco Cacciatore, *The Wall as Living Place* (Syracuse: Lettera Ventidue Edizioni Sri, 2008).
8. The outer frame reduces the load on the inner frame, and Schock Isokorb connectors (elements that minimise the thermal bridge between the internal and external structures) are all but eliminated, once again reducing the cost of hidden construction in favour of perceptible ones.
9. Eric Klinenberg, *Palaces for the People, How to Build a More Equal & United Society* (London: Penguin Random House, 2018).
10. Francesco Cacciatore, *The Wall as Living Place*.
11. Louis I. Kahn, "The Relation of Light to Form," lecture at the School of Design of North Carolina State College, 23 January 1953; also in *Proposed City Hall Building*. The conference text includes this passage: "We know that in Gothic days they built in solid stones. Now we can build with hollow stones."
12. My teaching partner during the academic year 2019–2020 was Matthew Blunderfield.
13. Louis I. Kahn, "Silence and Light," lecture at ETH Zurich, 1969.

Bibliography

Cacciatore, Francesco. *The Wall as Living Place*. Syracuse: Lettera Ventidue Edizioni Sri, 2008.

Harries, Karsten. "The Ethical Function of Architecture." In *Theorizing a New Agenda for Architecture: An Anthology of Architectural Theory 1965–1995*, edited by Kate Nesbitt, 392–397. New York: Princeton University Press, 1995.

Hawkes, Dean. *The Environmental Imagination*. Abingdon: Taylor and Francis, 2008.

Henley, Simon. *Redefining Brutalism*. London: RIBA Publications, 2017.

Kahn, Louis I. "The Relation of Light to Form." Lecture at the School of Design of North Carolina State College, 23 January 1953.

———. "Silence and Light." Lecture at ETH Zurich, 1969.

Klinenberg, Eric. *Palaces for the People, How to Build a More Equal & United Society.* London: Penguin Random House, 2018.

Lynch, Patrick, John Meunier, and Simon Henley. *On Intricacy: The Work of John Meunier Architect.* London: Canalside Press, 2020.

Palladio, Andrea. *I Quattro libri dell'architectura* (1570), translated by Isaac Ware as *The Four Books of Architecture* (1738). Reprint, *Andrea Palladio: The Four Books of Architecture,* Introduction by A. K. Placzek. Mineola, NY: Dover Publications, 1965.

Scully, Vincent. "Introduction." In David B. Brownlee and David G. De Long, *Louis Kahn: In the Realm of Architecture.* New York: Rizzoli International Publications, 1991.

About the Authors

Joseph Bedford

Joseph Bedford is an assistant professor of history and theory at Virginia Tech. He holds a PhD in history, theory, and criticism of architecture from Princeton University and was the recipient of the 2008–2009 Rome Prize at the British School in Rome. He has taught at Princeton University and Columbia University and is the founding director of the *Architecture Exchange*, a platform for theoretical exchange between architecture and other fields, which houses an audio journal, books, workshops, oral history projects, and curricula projects. He has published numerous book chapters as well as articles in journals such as *AA Files*, *OASE*, and *Log*.

Luis Burriel Bielza

Researcher, practising architect, and associate professor, Luis Burriel Bielza completed his PhD from the Polytechnic University of Madrid in 2010. His main research subjects are Le Corbusier's thinking process and the dialogue between structure and architecture as a creative tool. In 2013, he curated an exhibition on Le Corbusier's postcard collection at the CIVA Museum. As a practising architect, he is co-founder of SOMOS Arquitectos, with a specific focus on domesticity and collective housing. As an associate professor, he has been working between Spain and France, currently teaching design studio at the École nationale supérieure d'architecture de Paris-Belleville.

Elke Couchez

In her work, Elke Couchez explores the intersections between intellectual history of architecture and urban design, visual studies, and pedagogy. In 2018 and 2019, she worked as a postdoctoral fellow on the project Is Architecture Art? at the University of Queensland's Centre for Architecture, Theory, Criticism and History. As a postdoctoral researcher at UHasselt, she teaches art and architecture history and is currently working on a research project entitled Pedagogical Tools and Design Strategies for Urban Regeneration. International Laboratory for Architecture & Urban Design (1976–2015).

Thomas Coward

Tom Coward co-founded AOC Architecture Ltd. In 2005, he gained recognition for inventive inquiry, participatory practice, and characterful designs for high-quality public buildings, cultural institutions, and residential projects in sensitive contexts. Tom studied at the University of Nottingham and the Royal College of Art. He was Louis I. Kahn Visiting Professor at Yale University in 2011. He is currently year leader of the MArch course at Kingston University, where he is also undertaking a PhD by practice. Tom sits on the GLA Architecture & Urbanism Panel, he is a RIBA Client Advisor, and a member of the Southwark and Croydon Design Review Panels.

Philip Christou

Philip Christou lives in London and has worked with Florian Beigel Architects and the Architecture Research Unit since 1985. He studied at McGill University, Montreal, the University of Lethbridge, and the Nova Scotia College of Art and Design in Halifax, Canada, before studying architecture at the Architectural Association in London. He is professor emeritus at the London Metropolitan University, where he taught architectural design with Florian Beigel from 1985 to 2017. He has lectured in numerous schools of architecture internationally, and the work of Florian Beigel Architects and Architecture Research Unit is widely published.

Jana Culek

Jana Culek is a Croatian architect and urbanist living in the Netherlands. She is the founder of Studio Fabula, a Delft-based architecture and urban planning office that focuses on narrative-based design methods. Since 2018, she is a PhD researcher with the Chair of Methods of Analysis and Imagination at the Faculty of Architecture in TU Delft, where she also teaches. Her research focuses on utopias as a critical method in architecture and literature.

Rosamund Diamond

Rosamund Diamond teaches at the University of Nottingham where she is a BArch design studio unit head. She founded Diamond Architects after studying architecture at the Bartlett School, University College London. She has taught at the Architectural Association and the Bartlett Graduate School. Her research areas include work on Eileen Gray. She is the author of various architectural essays, published, for example, in *9H*, and has edited several books, including *From City to Detail: Diener & Diener* (1992). She is the London correspondent of *werk bauen + wohnen*.

Irina Davidovici

Irina Davidovici is senior lecturer and researcher at ETH Zurich, where she directs the doctoral programme in the history and theory of architecture. Her writings include the monograph *Forms of Practice: German-Swiss Architecture 1980–2000* (2012, second expanded edition 2018) and articles in *AA Files, The Journal of Architecture, Architectural Theory Review, ARCH+, Casabella, OASE, Joehlo, Project Journal, werk, bauen + wohnen*, and *Archithese*. Two more books, *Common Grounds: A Comparative History of European Housing Estates, 1850–1934* (Triest Verlag) and *Tendenzen: The Autonomy of Theory* (gta Verlag) are planned for publication in 2022.

Christoph Grafe

Christoph Grafe is an architect and writer as well as a professor of architectural history and theory at the University of Wuppertal and vice dean of research at the Faculty of Architecture and Building Engineering. He served as director of the Flanders Architecture Institute in Antwerp from 2011 to 2017 and as interim Antwerp city architect (with bOb van Reeth) in 2015. He has held visiting professorships at Hasselt (Belgium) and Milan. His book *People's Palaces – Architecture, Culture and Democracy in Post-War Western Europe* was published in 2014, and *Umbaukultur* (with Tim Rieniets) in 2020. He is an editor of *OASE* and publisher and editor of *Eselsohren*. Since 2020, he has been involved in the project C-Straßen, an initiative of local politician, activists, and architects aiming to transform the inner city of Bremen by creating opportunities for creative and cultural producers, and he collaborates with students at the University of Wuppertal on the exhibition *KlimaWandelStadt*.

Birgitte Louise Hansen

D Arch Birgitte Louise Hansen has her own office in Rotterdam. She is a Danish architect, independent researcher, teacher in architecture analysis and research, writer and curator of exhibitions. She was the editor of the publication *Beyond Clinical Buildings* (2008), has written for different publications and magazines, and has spoken at diverse conferences and symposia. In 2018, she defended her PhD "Architectural Thinking in Practice" at TU Delft. As a designer, she has worked with, among others, exhibition design, site-specific performance art, landscape, and interiors. She is currently developing exhibition projects on architectural practice.

Simon Henley

Simon Henley combines his practice Henley Halebrown with teaching, writing, and research. He is a postgraduate unit master at the Kingston School of Art. In 2018, Quart Verlag published a monograph on the practice in their *De Aedibus International* series. In the same year, Henley Halebrown was shortlisted for the RIBA Stirling Prize. Simon is an external examiner at the University of Moratuwa in Sri Lanka and Brother of the Art Workers' Guild. Recent publications include *Redefining Brutalism* (2017) and "At the Edge of the Forest and a Field," in *On Intricacy: The Work of John Meunier Architec* (2020).

Julia Jamrozik

Julia Jamrozik is an assistant professor in the Department of Architecture at the University at Buffalo, SUNY. Formerly, Julia was an architect at Herzog & de Meuron and taught architectural design studios at the ETH in Zurich as part of the Gastdozentur of Manuel Herz. She collaborates with Coryn Kempster on projects in different media and at a variety of scales, from temporary installations to permanent public artworks and architectural projects, including the book *Growing up Modern: Childhoods in Iconic Homes* (2021). Their multidisciplinary practice was recognised in 2018 with the League Prize by the Architectural League of New York.

Sepideh Karami

Sepideh Karami is a writer, architect, teacher, and researcher and currently a Lecturer in Architecture at the University of Edinburgh, School of Architecture and Landscape Architecture (ESALA). She holds a PhD in architecture and critical studies from the KTH School of Architecture, where she also held a lecturer position until 2020. She developed her thesis *Interruption: Writing a Dissident Architecture*, through writing practices and critical fiction as political practices of making architectural spaces. She completed her architecture education at Iran University of Science and Technology (MA, 2002) and Chalmers University (MSc, 2010). She has been committed to teaching, research, and practice in different international contexts and has developed her work through artistic research and interdisciplinary approaches at the intersection of architecture, performing arts, literature and geology, with the ethos of decolonisation, minor politics and criticality from within. She has presented, performed and exhibited her work at international conferences and platforms, and she is published in peer-reviewed journals.

Pauline Lefebvre

Pauline Lefebvre is Chargée de recherches FNRS at Faculté d'Architecture de l'ULB. Her PhD was about the recent encounters between architecture and the pragmatist tradition in philosophy. Her current research aims to understand architects' engagements in the course of the design process, by conducting immersive fieldwork within architecture firms. She focuses on the forms of practice that emerge when architects engage more directly in fabrication and construction.

Patrick Lynch

Patrick Lynch holds an MPhil in the history and philosophy of architecture from the University of Cambridge (1995–1996), where he was supervised by Dalibor Vesely, and a PhD from London Metropolitan University (2015), where he was supervised by Peter Carl, Helen Mallinson, and Joseph Rykwert. He represented Ireland at the Venice Biennale in 2008. Lynch Architects exhibited at Venice again in 2012, and at the Milan Triennale in 2016. Recent books include *The Theatricality of the Baroque City* (2011) and *Mimesis* (2015). *Civic Ground*, a version of his PhD, was published in 2017. Besides being the founding director of Lynch Architects, Patrick has taught at the Architectural Association, the London Met, University College Dublin, Kingston University, and most recently at Cambridge University. He is currently an honorary professor at the University of Liverpool School of Architecture and teaches as part of the MA Landscape Architecture programme at the Bartlett, UCL.

Sereh Mandias

Sereh Mandias is a lecturer and researcher at the Chair of Interiors Buildings Cities at TU Delft. She also works as a visiting lecturer at the Rotterdam Academy of Architecture and as editor at platform for city culture *De Dépendance*. She was a co-editor of the thirteenth *Architectural Review Flanders* and of the publication *The New Craft School*. She is a member of the editorial board of *OASE* and co-founder of the architecture podcast *Windoog*.

Louis Mayes

Louis Mayes is an architect and researcher based in London. Louis founded Studio MAY with an equal focus on design and research – through an approach of writing, teaching, and practice. Having studied the history of architecture at the University of Reading before completing his architectural education at London Metropolitan University and the University of Cambridge, the confluence between practice and theory continues to be present in the studio's work. Studio MAY's research arm, River Walks, runs walks and talks that ask people to question the role of the changing city today. Alongside writing for *Blueprint Magazine* and *Architecture Today*, recent projects include starting a series of conversations with designers about the importance of the sketch in practice.

Carlo Menon

Carlo Menon is an architect and researcher in history and theory, with degrees from La Cambre, Brussels (2006) and the Bartlett, London (2013). His collaborative practice, mostly with partner Sophie Dars, interweaves architectural thinking with publications, exhibitions, and education. In particular, he has developed writing and editorial skills, whose outputs mostly appear in the magazine *Accattone*. He is completing a PhD in history and theory at the Bartlett School of Architecture under the supervision of Jane Rendell (primary) and Penelope Haralambidou, funded by a full scholarship by the London Arts and Humanities Partnership (2014–2018).

Marjan Michels

Marjan Michels graduated as an architect at the Henry van de Velde Institute, Antwerp, Belgium. As a practising architect, she won the Meesterproef 2005. Since 2020, she is assistant professor at the Faculty of Design Sciences, University of Antwerp. She completed a PhD, entitled "A Sentiment for Architecture. Educating Embodied Architectural Knowledge in the Design Studio." Michels is co-author of *Morphology of Interiors. Fragments of Space Examined* (2019) and has published in academic journals such as *Interiors: Design, Architecture, Culture* and *TvHO*. Her current research focuses on design studio education and the practice of evidence-based informed design approaches.

Cathelijne Nuijsink

Cathelijne Nuijsink is a lecturer and postdoctoral researcher at the Institute for the History and Theory of Architecture at ETH Zurich. She obtained a master's degrees in architecture from TU Delft and the University of Tokyo before earning a PhD in East Asian languages and civilizations from the University of Pennsylvania. Her current research focuses on cross-cultural, interdisciplinary knowledge exchange and aims to contribute to a more dynamic and inclusive history of architectural modernism. Nuijsink is writing the book *Another Historiography: The Shinkenchiku Residential Design Competition, 1965–2020* (Jap Sam Books, 2022), which is the outcome of her postdoctoral research project "Architecture as a Cross-Cultural Exchange: The Shinkenchiku Residential Design Competition, 1965–2017," funded by the European Union's Horizon 2020 research and innovation programme under the Marie Sklodowska-Curie grant agreement no. 797002.

Paulo Providência

Paulo Providência is an architect and researcher at the Centre of Social Studies at the University of Coimbra. He graduated in architecture at the Faculty of Architecture of the University of Porto in 1989, and he teaches at the Department of Architecture, Faculty of Sciences and Technology, University of Coimbra. He completed his PhD on architecture at the University of Coimbra in 2007. He has been researching and publishing on architectural practice and teaching. He is author of *Architectonica Percepta* (2016), and he co-edited *Bartolomeu Costa Cabral 18 obras* (2016), *Leprosaria Nacional* (2013), and *Teaching Through Design*, a special issue of the journal *Joelho* (2014). *Leprosaria Nacional* was a finalist for the FAD Pensamento y Crítica prize in 2014.

Sophia Psarra

Professor Sophia Psarra is author of *The Venice Variations* (2018), which explores cities and buildings as multi-authored processes of formation alongside authored projects of individual design intention. Her book *Architecture and Narrative* (2009) explores the relationship between design conceptualisation, narrative, and human cognition. Her edited book *The Production Sites of Architecture* (2019) addresses the production of knowledge in architecture. Sophia is the director of the History and Theory PhD programme at the Bartlett School of Architecture, and she has taught undergraduate and graduate studios and seminars at the Bartlett, the University of Michigan (2005–2011), Cardiff University (1997–2004), and the University of Greenwich (1992–1997).

Steven Schenk

Steven Schenk studied at the University College of Antwerp in Belgium (MSc. Architecture with highest honours) and the Accademia di Architettura in Mendrisio in Switzerland. He is currently involved in teaching as a design-related researcher at the KU Leuven, Faculty of Architecture, Campus St-Lucas Ghent and Brussels. Connected to the studio work and his practice, he is conducting PhD research on the thematic of perception and imagination, which is supervised by H. Fallon, C. Voet, J. Van Den Berghe, J. Sergison, and M. Steinmann. In 2014, he co-founded the office Schenk Hattori Architecture Atelier, mainly active in Europe and Japan, whose work investigates the understanding of presence and its possibilities for making architecture as a result of modernity. Their current projects include both public and private commissions, as well as research and competitions.

Eireen Schreurs

Eireen Schreurs is a Dutch architect and academic. She combines a PhD position at the KU Leuven/University of Antwerp with a teaching and research position at the TU Delft. Trained as an architect at the TU Delft, she founded the practice SUBoffice architects in Rotterdam with Like Bijlsma. Their co-housing project Hooidrift won the Rotterdam Architecture prize 2017. Her position between practice and academia shows in her contribution to various books and magazines; she has co-edited, among others, the fourteenth *Architectural Review Flanders* (2020) and the publication *The New Craft School* (2018). Her doctorate is called "Material Dialogues".

Eva Storgaard

Eva Storgaard graduated as an architect from the Royal Danish Academy of Fine Arts, Copenhagen, Denmark. She completed a PhD in architecture at University of Antwerp: "The Architecture of Danish Modern. Empiricism. Craft. Organicism" (2019). She is a doctoral assistant at the Faculty of Design Sciences at the University of Antwerp where she is teaching and researching evidence-based informed design approaches. Storgaard is co-author of *Morphology of Interiors. Fragments of Space Examined* (2019). She has published in various academic books and journals. Recently, she curated *Invisible Present*, an exhibition about the interior architects Bataille & ibens for the Flanders Architecture Institute.

Helen Thomas

Helen Thomas is an architect, writer, and editor with a PhD from the University of Essex in art history and theory. Having worked as an editor and senior lecturer at institutions such as the Victoria & Albert Museum, Phaidon Press, Drawing Matter, the Architectural Association, and London Metropolitan University, she now writes and creates books and other text-based productions. Her most recent publications include *Extracts: Women Writing Architecture* (2021), *Architecture Through Drawing* (2019), *Drawing Architecture* (2018), *morethanone(fragile)thingattime* (with muf architecture/art, 2016), and, with Adam Caruso at ETH Zurich, both *Hopkins in the City* (2019) and *Rudolf Schwarz and the Monumental Order of Things* (2016). Among her other projects is an annotated bibliography, which can be found at www.womenwritingarchitecture.org.

Caroline Voet

Dr. Caroline Voet, architect PhD is a practising architect and professor at KU Leuven, Faculty of Architecture. She holds degrees in architecture and arts from the Architectural Association in London and the Henry van de Velde Institute in Antwerp. Her research and teaching focus on young architectural heritage (Pioneering Practices), spatial systematics, and design history (e.g. www.domhansvanderlaan.nl) and has been published in, for example, *Architectural Research Quarterly* and *Interiors Routledge*. She has written for the *Architectural Yearbook Flanders* and, in 2016, she was co-editor of the book *Autonomous Architecture in Flanders*. She recently published *Dom Hans van der Laan. Tomelilla* (2016) and *Dom Hans van der Laan. A House for the Mind* (DAM Architecture Book of the Year Award 2018). After working in the offices of Zaha Hadid and Christian Kieckens, she started her own practice, Voet architectuur (www.voetarchitectuur.be), in Antwerp, Belgium. They focus on heritage, conversions, and the design of public interiors and scenography.

Wilfried Wang

Wilfried Wang, together with Barbara Hoidn, is founder of Hoidn Wang Partner in Berlin. Born in Hamburg, he studied architecture in London and became a partner with John Southall in SW Architects. Founding co-editor with Nadir Tharani of *9H Magazine,* he was a co-director with Ricky Burdett of the 9H Gallery and director of the German Architecture Museum. Wang has taught at the Polytechnic of North London, University College London, ETH Zurich, Städelschule, Harvard University, the University of Texas at

Austin, and the Universidad de Navarra. He is author and editor of various architectural mono- and topographs. Wang is a foreign member of Kungliga Akademien för de fria konsterna in Stockholm; member of the Akademie der Künster in Berlin, recipient of an honorary doctorate from Kungliga Tekniska Högskolan in Stockholm, and an honorary member of the Ordem dos Arquitectos of Portugal.